KT-526-167

# Contents at a Glance

WITHDRAWN

# Table of Contents

# Computer Security Fundamentals

## Third Edition

Chuck Easttom

PEARSON

800 East 96th Street, Indianapolis, Indiana 46240 USA

# Computer Security Fundamentals, Third Edition

Copyright © 2016 by Pearson Education, Inc.

ISBN-13: 978-0-7897-5746-3
ISBN-10: 0-7897-5746-X

Library of Congress control number: 2016940227

Printed in the United States of America

1          16

## Trademarks

All terms mentioned in this book that are known to be trademarks or service marks have been appropriately capitalized. Pearson IT Certification cannot attest to the accuracy of this information. Use of a term in this book should not be regarded as affecting the validity of any trademark or service mark.

## Warning and Disclaimer

Every effort has been made to make this book as complete and as accurate as possible, but no warranty or fitness is implied. The information provided is on an "as is" basis. The author and the publisher shall have neither liability nor responsibility to any person or entity with respect to any loss or damages arising from the information contained in this book.

## Special Sales

For information about buying this title in bulk quantities, or for special sales opportunities (which may include electronic versions; custom cover designs; and content particular to your business, training goals, marketing focus, or branding interests), please contact our corporate sales department at corpsales@pearsoned.com or (800) 382-3419.

For government sales inquiries, please contact governmentsales@pearsoned.com.

For questions about sales outside the U.S., please contact intlcs@pearson.com.

**Executive Editor**
Brett Bartow

**Acquisitions Editor**
Betsy Brown

**Development Editor**
Christopher Cleveland

**Managing Editor**
Sandra Schroeder

**Senior Project Editor**
Tonya Simpson

**Copy Editor**
Gill Editorial Services

**Indexer**
Brad Herriman

**Proofreader**
Paula Lowell

**Technical Editor**
Dr. Louay Karadsheh

**Publishing Coordinator**
Vanessa Evans

**Cover Designer**
Chuti Prasertsith

**Compositor**
Mary Sudul

# About the Author

**Chuck Easttom** is a computer security and forensics expert. He has authored 20 books, including several on computer security, forensics, and cryptography. He holds 6 patents and 40 computer certifications, including many security and forensics certifications. He has conducted training for law enforcement, federal agencies, and friendly foreign governments. He frequently works as an expert witness in computer-related cases. He is also a frequent speaker on computer security topics at a variety of security-related conferences. You can visit his website at www.chuckeasttom.com.

## About the Technical Reviewer

**Dr. Louay Karadsheh** has a Doctorate of Management in information technology from Lawrence Technological University, Southfield, Michigan. His research interest includes cloud computing, information assurance, knowledge management, and risk management. Dr. Karadsheh has published 11 articles in refereed journals and international conference proceedings and has extensive knowledge in operating system, networking, and security. Dr. Karadsheh has provided technical edits/reviews for several major publishing companies, including Pearson and Cengage Learning. He holds CISSP, CEH, CASP, CCSK, CCE, Security+, VCA-C, VCA-DCV, SCNP, Network+, and Mobility+ certifications.

# Dedication

*This book is dedicated to my wife, Teresa,*
*who has helped me become who I am.*

# Acknowledgments

The creation of a book is not a simple process and requires the talents and dedication from many people to make it happen. With this in mind, I would like to thank the folks at Pearson for their commitment to this project.

Specifically, I would like to say thanks to Betsy Brown for overseeing the project and keeping things moving.

# We Want to Hear from You!

As the reader of this book, *you* are our most important critic and commentator. We value your opinion and want to know what we're doing right, what we could do better, what areas you'd like to see us publish in, and any other words of wisdom you're willing to pass our way.

We welcome your comments. You can email or write to let us know what you did or didn't like about this book—as well as what we can do to make our books better.

*Please note that we cannot help you with technical problems related to the topic of this book.*

When you write, please be sure to include this book's title and author as well as your name and email address. We will carefully review your comments and share them with the author and editors who worked on the book.

Email:      feedback@pearsonitcertification.com

Mail:       Pearson IT Certification
            ATTN: Reader Feedback
            800 East 96th Street
            Indianapolis, IN 46240 USA

# Reader Services

Register your copy of *Computer Security Fundamentals* at www.pearsonitcertification.com for convenient access to downloads, updates, and corrections as they become available. To start the registration process, go to www.pearsonitcertification.com/register and log in or create an account*. Enter the product ISBN 9780789757463 and click Submit. When the process is complete, you will find any available bonus content under Registered Products.

*Be sure to check the box that you would like to hear from us to receive exclusive discounts on future editions of this product.

# Introduction

It has been more than 10 years since the publication of the original edition of this book. A great deal has happened in the world of computer security since that time. This edition is updated to include newer information, updated issues, and revised content.

The real question is: Who is this book for? This book is a guide for any computer-savvy person. That means system administrators who are not security experts or anyone who has a working knowledge of computers and wishes to know more about cyber crime and terrorism could find this book useful. However, the core audience will be students who wish to take a first course in security but may not have a thorough background in computer networks. The book is in textbook format, making it ideal for introductory computer security courses that have no specific prerequisites. That lack of prerequisites means that people outside the normal computer science and computer information systems departments could also avail themselves of a course based on this book. This might be of particular interest to law enforcement officers, criminal justice majors, and even business majors with an interest in computer security.

As was previously mentioned, this book is intended as an introductory computer security book. In addition to the numerous end notes, the appendixes will guide you to a plethora of additional resources. There are also review questions and practice exercises with every chapter. Appendix C contains the answers to the multiple choice questions for your review. Exercises and projects don't have a single answer. They are intended to encourage the reader to explore, so answers will vary.

This book is not a cookbook for hackers. You will see exactly how hackers target a system and get information about it. You will also see step-by-step instructions on how to use some password-cracking utilities and some network-scanning utilities. You will also be given a reasonably in-depth explanation of various hacking attacks. However, you won't see a specific step-by-step recipe for executing an attack.

This book assumes that you are a competent computer user. That means you have used a computer at work and at home, are comfortable with email and web browsers, and know what words like RAM and USB mean. For instructors considering this as a textbook, that means students will have had some basic understanding of PCs but need not have had formal computer courses. For this reason, there is a chapter on basic networking concepts to get you up to speed. For readers with more knowledge, such as system administrators, you will find some chapters of more use to you than others. Feel free to simply skim any chapter that you feel is too elementary for you.

Chapter | **1**

# Introduction to Computer Security

## Chapter Objectives

**After reading this chapter and completing the exercises, you will be able to do the following:**

- Identify the top threats to a network: security breaches, denial of service attacks, and malware
- Assess the likelihood of an attack on your network
- Define key terms such as *cracker*, *penetration tester*, *firewall*, and *authentication*
- Compare and contrast perimeter and layered approaches to network security
- Use online resources to secure your network

## Introduction

Since the first edition of this book, the prevalence of online transactions has increased dramatically. In 2004 we had e-commerce via websites; in 2016 we have smart phone apps, the Internet of Things, as well as an expanded use of e-commerce websites. Internet traffic is far more than just humorous YouTube videos or Facebook updates about our vacations. Now it is the heart and soul of commerce, both domestic and international. Internet communication even plays a central role in military operations and diplomatic relations. In addition to smart phones, we now have smart watches and even vehicles that have Wi-Fi hotspots and smart technology. Our lives are inextricably intertwined with the online world. We file our taxes online, shop for a home online, book our next vacation online, and even look for a date online.

Because so much of our business is transacted online, a great deal of personal information is stored in computers. Medical records, tax records, school records, and more are all stored in computer databases. This leads to some very important questions:

1. How is information safeguarded?

2. What are the vulnerabilities to these systems?

3. What steps are taken to ensure that these systems and data are safe?

4. Who can access my information?

---

**FYI: Where Is the Internet Going?**

Obviously the Internet has expanded, as previously mentioned. We now have smart phones, smart watches, even smart cars. We have the Internet of things (IoT) which involves devices communicating on the Internet. What do you think the next 10 years will bring?

---

Unfortunately, not only has technology and Internet access expanded since the original publication of this book, but so have the dangers. How serious is the problem? According to a 2014 article in *SC Magazine*,[1] "Cyber-crime and economic espionage cost the global economy more than $445 billion annually, which a report from the Center for Strategic and International Studies, says puts cyber-crime on par with the economic impact of global drug trafficking."

Another study[2] looked at specific companies and the cost of cybercrime in 2013. That study reported, "We found that the average annualized cost of cyber-crime for 60 organizations in our study is $11.6 million per year, with a range of $1.3 million to $58 million. In 2012, the average annualized cost was $8.9 million. This represents an increase in cost of 26 percent or $2.6 million from the results of our cyber cost study published last year."

The situation is not improving, either. According to a Pricewaterhouse Coopers study, in 2015 38% more security incidents were detected than in 2014. The same study showed a 56% increase in theft of intellectual property.

In spite of daily horror stories, however, many people (including some law enforcement professionals and trained computer professionals) lack an adequate understanding about the reality of these threats. Clearly the media will focus attention on the most dramatic computer security breaches, not necessarily giving an accurate picture of the most plausible threat scenarios. It is not uncommon to encounter the occasional system administrator whose knowledge of computer security is inadequate.

This chapter outlines current dangers, describes the most common types of attacks on your personal computer and network, teaches you how to speak the lingo of both hackers and security professionals, and outlines the broad strokes of what it takes to secure your computer and your network.

In this book, you will learn how to secure both individual computers and entire networks. You will also find out how to secure data transmission, and you will complete an exercise to find out about your region's laws regarding computer security. Perhaps the most crucial discussion in this chapter is what

---

1. http://www.scmagazine.com/cyber-crime-costs-445-billion-globally-gdps-take-hit/article/354844/
2. http://media.scmagazine.com/documents/54/2013_us_ccc_report_final_6-1_13455.pdf

attacks are commonly attempted and how they are perpetrated. In this first chapter we set the stage for the rest of the book by outlining what exactly the dangers are and introducing you to the terminology used by both network security professionals and hackers. All of these topics are explored more fully in subsequent chapters.

# How Seriously Should You Take Threats to Network Security?

The first step in understanding computer and network security is to formulate a realistic assessment of the threats to those systems. You will need a clear picture of the dangers in order to adequately prepare a defense. There seem to be two extreme attitudes regarding computer security. The first group assumes there is no real threat. Subscribers to this belief feel that there is little real danger to computer systems and that much of the negative news is simply unwarranted panic. They often believe taking only minimal security precautions should ensure the safety of their systems. The prevailing sentiment is, if our organization has not been attacked so far, we must be secure. If decision makers subscribe to this point of view, they tend to push a reactive approach to security. They will wait to address security issues until an incident occurs—the proverbial "closing the barn door after the horse has already gotten out." If you are fortunate, the incident will have only minor impact on your organization and will serve as a much-needed wakeup call. If you are unfortunate, then your organization may face serious and possible catastrophic consequences. One major goal of this book is to encourage a proactive approach to security.

People who subscribe to the opposite viewpoint overestimate the dangers. They tend to assume that talented, numerous hackers are an imminent threat to their system. They may believe that any teenager with a laptop can traverse highly secure systems at will. Such a worldview makes excellent movie plots, but it is simply unrealistic. The reality is that many people who call themselves hackers are less knowledgeable than they think they are. These people have a low probability of being able to compromise any system that has implemented even moderate security precautions.

This does not mean that skillful hackers do not exist, of course. However, they must balance the costs (financial, time) against the rewards (ideological, monetary). "Good" hackers tend to target systems that yield the highest rewards. If a hacker doesn't perceive your system as beneficial to these goals, he is less likely to expend the resources to compromise your system. It is also important to understand that real intrusions into a network take time and effort. Hacking is not the dramatic process you see in movies. I often teach courses in hacking and penetration testing, and students are usually surprised to find that the process is actually a bit tedious and requires patience.

Both extremes of attitudes regarding the dangers to computer systems are inaccurate. It is certainly true that there are people who have the understanding of computer systems and the skills to compromise the security of many, if not most, systems. A number of people who call themselves hackers, though, are not as skilled as they claim to be. They have ascertained a few buzzwords from the Internet and may be convinced of their own digital supremacy, but they are not able to effect any real compromises to even a moderately secure system.

The truly talented hacker is no more common than the truly talented concert pianist. Consider how many people take piano lessons at some point in their lives. Now consider how many of those ever truly become virtuosos. The same is true of computer hackers. Keep in mind that even those who do possess the requisite skills need to be motivated to expend the time and effort to compromise your system.

A better way to assess the threat level to your system is to weigh the attractiveness of your system to potential intruders against the security measures in place.

Keep in mind, too, that the greatest external threat to any system is not hackers, but malware and denial of service (DoS) attacks. Malware includes viruses, worms, Trojan horses, and logic bombs. And beyond the external attacks, there is the issue of internal problems due to malfeasance or simple ignorance.

Security audits always begin with a risk assessment, and that is what we are describing here. First you need to identify your assets. Clearly, the actual computers, routers, switches and other devices that make up your network are assets. But it is more likely that your most important assets lie in the information on your network. Identifying assets begins with evaluating the information your network stores and its value. Does your network contain personal information for bank accounts? Perhaps medical information, health care records? In other cases your network might contain intellectual property, trade secrets, or even classified data.

Once you have identified the assets, you need to take inventory of the threats to your assets. Certainly any threat is possible, but some are more likely than others. This is very much like what one does when selecting home insurance. If you live in a flood plain, then flood insurance is critical. If you live at a high altitude in a desert, it may be less critical. We do the same thing with our data. If you are working for a defense contractor, then foreign state-sponsored hackers are a significant threat. However, if you are the network administrator for a school district, then your greatest threat involves juveniles attempting to breach the network. It is always important to realize what the threats are for your network.

Now that you have identified your assets and inventoried the threats, you need to find out what vulnerabilities your system has. Every system has vulnerabilities. Identifying your network's specific vulnerabilities is a major part of risk assessment.

The knowledge of your assets, threats, and vulnerabilities will give you the information needed to decide what security measures are appropriate for your network. You will always have budget constraints, so you will need to make wise decisions on selecting security controls. Using good risk assessment is how you make wise security decisions.

> **Note**
>
> There are a number of industry certifications that emphasize risk assessment. The Certified Information System's Security Professional (CISSP) puts significant emphasis on this issue. The Certified Information Systems Auditor (CISA) places even more focus on risk assessment. One or more appropriate industry certifications can enhance your skillset and make you more marketable as a security professional. There are many other certifications including the CompTIA Certified Advanced Security Practitioner (CASP) and Security+ certifications.

# Identifying Types of Threats

As was discussed in the last section, identifying your threats is a key part of risk assessment. Some threats are common to all networks; others are more likely with specific types of networks. Various sources have divided threats into different categories based on specific criteria. In this section we will examine threats that have been divided into categories based on the nature of the attack. Since the last edition of this book I have separated out one of the security breach subcategories into its own category: insider threats. Most attacks can be categorized as one of seven broad classes:

- **Malware:** This is a generic term for software that has a malicious purpose. It includes virus attacks, worms, adware, Trojan horses, and spyware. This is the most prevalent danger to your system.

- **Security breaches:** This group of attacks includes any attempt to gain unauthorized access to your system. This includes cracking passwords, elevating privileges, breaking into a server…all the things you probably associate with the term *hacking*.

- **DoS attacks:** These are designed to prevent legitimate access to your system. And, as you will see in later chapters, this includes distributed denial of service (DDoS).

- **Web attacks:** This is any attack that attempts to breach your website. Two of the most common such attacks are SQL injection and cross-site scripting.

- **Session hijacking:** These attacks are rather advanced and involve an attacker attempting to take over a session.

- **Insider threats:** These are breaches based on someone who has access to your network misusing his access to steal data or compromise security.

- **DNS poisoning:** This type of attack seeks to compromise a DNS server so that users can be redirected to malicious websites, including phishing websites.

There are other attacks, such as social engineering. The forgoing list is just an attempt to provide a broad categorization of attack types. This section offers a broad description of each type of attack. Later chapters go into greater detail with each specific attack, how it is accomplished, and how to avoid it.

## Malware

*Malware* is a generic term for software that has a malicious purpose. This section discusses four types of malware: viruses, Trojan horses, spyware, and logic bombs. Trojan horses and viruses are the most widely encountered. One could also include rootkits, but these usually spread as viruses and are regarded as simply a specific type of virus.

According to Symantec (makers of Norton antivirus and other software products), a *virus* is "a small program that replicates and hides itself inside other programs, usually without your knowledge"

(Symantec, 2003). While this definition is a bit old, it still applies. The key characteristic of a computer virus is that it self-replicates. A computer virus is similar to a biological virus; both are designed to replicate and spread. The most common method for spreading a virus is using the victim's email account to spread the virus to everyone in his address book. Some viruses don't actually harm the system itself, but *all* of them cause network slowdowns due to the heavy network traffic caused by the virus replication.

The *Trojan horse* gets its name from an ancient tale. The city of Troy was besieged for an extended period of time. The attackers could not gain entrance, so they constructed a huge wooden horse and one night left it in front of the gates of Troy. The next morning the residents of Troy saw the horse and assumed it to be a gift, so they rolled the wooden horse into the city. Unbeknownst to them, several soldiers where hidden inside the horse. That evening the soldiers left the horse, opened the city gates, and let their fellow attackers into the city. An electronic Trojan horse works the same way, appearing to be benign software but secretly downloading a virus or some other type of malware onto your computer from within.

Another category of malware currently on the rise is *spyware*. Spyware is simply software that literally spies on what you do on your computer. Spyware can be as simple as a *cookie*—a text file that your browser creates and stores on your hard drive—that a website you have visited downloads to your machine and uses to recognize you when you return to the site. However, that flat file can then be read by the website or by other websites. Any data that the file saves can be retrieved by any website, so your entire Internet browsing history can be tracked. Spyware may also consist of software that takes periodic screenshots of the activity on your computer and sends those to the attacker.

Another form of spyware, called a *key logger*, records all of your keystrokes. Some key loggers also take periodic screenshots of your computer. Data is then either stored for later retrieval by the person who installed the key logger or is sent immediately back via email. We will discuss specific types of key loggers later in this book.

A *logic bomb* is software that lays dormant until some specific condition is met. That condition is usually a date and time. When the condition is met, the software does some malicious act such as delete files, alter system configuration, or perhaps release a virus. In Chapter 5, "Malware," we will examine logic bombs and other types of malware in detail.

## Compromising System Security

Next we will look at attacks that breach your system's security. This activity is what is commonly referred to as *hacking*, though that is not the term hackers themselves use. We will delve into appropriate terminology in just a few pages; however, it should be noted at this point that *cracking* is the appropriate word for intruding into a system without permission, usually with malevolent intent. Any attack that is designed to breach your security, either via some operating system flaw or any other means, can be classified as cracking.

Essentially any technique to bypass security, crack passwords, breach Wi-Fi, or in any way actually gain access to the target network fits into this category. That makes this a very broad category indeed.

However, not all breaches involve technical exploits. In fact, some of the most successful breaches are entirely nontechnical. *Social engineering* is a technique for breaching a system's security by exploiting human nature rather than technology. This was the path that the famous hacker Kevin Mitnick most often used. Social engineering uses standard con techniques to get users to give up the information needed to gain access to a target system. The way this method works is rather simple: The perpetrator gets preliminary information about a target organization and leverages it to obtain additional information from the system's users.

Following is an example of social engineering in action. Armed with the name of a system administrator, you might call someone in the business's accounting department and claim to be one of the company's technical support personnel. Mentioning the system administrator's name would help validate that claim, allowing you to ask questions in an attempt to ascertain more details about the system's specifications. A savvy intruder might even get the accounting person to say a username and password. As you can see, this method is based on how well the prospective intruder can manipulate people and actually has little to do with computer skills.

The growing popularity of wireless networks gave rise to new kinds of attacks. One such activity is *war-driving*. This type of attack is an offshoot of *war-dialing*. With war-dialing, a hacker sets up a computer to call phone numbers in sequence until another computer answers to try to gain entry to its system. War-driving is much the same concept, applied to locating vulnerable wireless networks. In this scenario, the hacker simply drives around trying to locate wireless networks. Many people forget that their wireless network signal often extends as much as 100 feet (thus, past walls). At the 2004 DefCon convention for hackers, there was a war-driving contest where contestants drove around the city trying to locate as many vulnerable wireless networks as they could (BlackBeetle, 2004). These sorts of contests are now common at various hacking conventions.

Recent technological innovations have introduced new variations of war driving/dialing. Now we have war flying. The attacker uses a small private drone equipped with Wi-Fi sniffing and cracking software, flies the drone in the area of interest, and attempts to gain access to wireless networks.

Of course, Wi-Fi hacking is only one sort of breach. Password cracking tools are now commonly available on the Internet. We will examine some of these later in this book. There are also exploits of software vulnerabilities that allow one to gain access to the target computer.

## DoS Attacks

In a DoS, the attacker does not actually access the system. Rather, this person simply blocks access from legitimate users (CERT, 2003). One common way to prevent legitimate service is to flood the targeted system with so many false connection requests that the system cannot respond to legitimate requests. DoS is a very common attack because it is so easy.

In recent years there has been a proliferation of DoS tools available on the Internet. One of the most common such tools is the Low Orbit Ion Cannon (LOIC). Because these tools can be downloaded for free from the Internet, anyone can execute a DoS attack, even without technical skill.

We also have variations, such as the DDoS attack. This uses multiple machines to attack the target. Given that many modern websites are hosted in network clusters or even in clouds, it is very difficult for a single attacking machine to generate enough traffic to take down a web server. But a network of hundreds or even thousands of computers certainly can. We will explore DoS and DDoS attacks in more detail in Chapter 4, "Denial of Service Attacks."

## Web Attacks

By their nature, web servers have to allow communications. Oftentimes, websites allow users to interact with the website. Any part of a website that allows for user interaction is also a potential point for attempting a web-based attack. SQL injections involve entering SQL (Structured Query Language) commands into login forms (username and password text fields) in an attempt to trick the server into executing those commands. The most common purpose is to force the server to log the attacker on, even though the attacker does not have a legitimate username and password. While SQL injection is just one type of web attack, it is the most common.

### SQL Injection

SQL injection is still quite common, though it has been known for many years. Unfortunately, not enough web developers take the appropriate steps to remediate the vulnerabilities that make this attack possible. Given the prevalence of this attack, it warrants a bit more detailed description.

Consider one of the simplest forms of SQL injection, used to bypass login screens. The website was developed in some web programming language, such as PHP or ASP.NET. The database is most likely a basic relational database such as Oracle, SQL Server, MySQL, or PostGres. SQL is used to communicate with the database, so we need to put SQL statements into the web page that was written into some programming language. That will allow us to query the database and see if the username and password are valid.

SQL is relatively easy to understand; in fact, it looks a lot like English. There are commands like SELECT to get data, INSERT to put data in, and UPDATE to change data. In order to log in to a website, the web page has to query a database table to see if that username and password are correct. The general structure of SQL is like this:

```
select column1, column2 from tablename
```

or

```
select * from tablename;
Conditions:
select columns from tablename where condition;
```

For example:

```
SELECT * FROM tblUsers WHERE USERNAME = 'jsmith'
```

This statement retrieves all the columns or fields from a table named `tblUsers` where the username is `jsmith`.

The problem arises when we try to put SQL statements into our web page. Recall that the web page was written in some web language such as PHP or ASP.net. If you just place SQL statements directly in the web page code, an error will be generated. The SQL statements in the programming code for the website have to use quotation marks to separate the SQL code from the programming code. A typical SQL statement might look something like this:

```
"SELECT * FROM tblUsers WHERE USERNAME = '" + txtUsername.Text +' AND PASSWORD = '" +
txtPassword.Text +"'" .
```

If you enter username `'jdoe'` and the password `'password'`, this code produces this SQL command:

```
SELECT * FROM tblUsers WHERE USERNAME = 'jdoe' AND PASSWORD = 'password'
```

This is fairly easy to understand even for nonprogrammers. And it is effective. If there is a match in the database, that means the username and password match. If no records are returned from the database, that means there was no match, and this is not a valid login.

The most basic form of SQL injection seeks to subvert this process. The idea is to create a statement that will always be true. For example, instead of putting an actual username and password into the appropriate text fields, the attacker will enter `' or '1' = '1` into the username and password boxes. This will cause the program to create this query:

```
SELECT * FROM tblUsers WHERE USERNAME = '' or '1' = '1' AND PASSWORD = '' or '1' = '1'.
```

So you are telling the database and application to return all records where username and password are blank or if 1 = 1. It is highly unlikely that the username and password are blank. But I am certain that 1 =1 always. Any true statement can be substituted. Examples are a = a and bob = bob.

The tragedy of this attack is that it is so easy to prevent. If the web programmer would simply filter all input prior to processing it, then this type of SQL injection would be impossible. That means that before any user input is processed, the web page programming code looks through that code for common SQL injection symbols, scripting symbols, and similar items. It is true that each year fewer and fewer websites are susceptible to this. However, while writing this chapter there was a report that the Joomla Content Management System, used by many web developers, was susceptible to SQL injection.[3]

## Cross-Site Scripting

This attack is closely related to SQL injection. It involves entering data other than what was intended, and it depends on the web programmer not filtering input. The perpetrator finds some area of a website that allows users to type in text that other users will see and then instead injects client-side script into those fields.

---

3. https://blog.perimeterx.com/joomla-cve-2015-7297/

> **Note**
>
> Before I describe this particular crime, I would point out that the major online retailers such as eBay and Amazon.com are not susceptible to this attack; they do filter user input.

To better understand this process, let's look at a hypothetical scenario. Let's assume that ABC online book sales has a website. In addition to shopping, users can have accounts with credit cards stored, post reviews, and more. The attacker first sets up an alternate web page that looks as close to the real one as possible. Then the attacker goes to the real ABC online book sales website and finds a rather popular book. He goes to the review section, but instead of typing in a review he types in this:

```
<script> window.location = "http://www.fakesite.com"; </script>
```

Now when users go to that book, this script will redirect them to the fake site, which looks a great deal like the real one. The attacker then can have the website tell the user that his session has timed out and to please log in again. That would allow the attacker to gather a lot of accounts and passwords. That is only one scenario, but it illustrates the attack.

## Session Hijacking

Session hijacking can be rather complex to perform. For that reason, it is not a very common form of attack. Simply put, the attacker monitors an authenticated session between the client machine and the server and takes that session over. We will explore specific methods of how this is done later in this book.

A 1985 paper written by Robert T. Morris titled "A Weakness in the 4.2BSD Unix TCP/IP Software" defined the original session hijacking.

By predicting the initial sequence number, Morris was able to spoof the identity of a trusted client to a server. This is much harder to do today.

In addition to flags (syn, ack, syn-ack), the packet header will contain the sequence number that is intended to be used by the client to reconstitute the data sent over the stream in the correct order. If you are unfamiliar with network packet flags, we will be exploring that topic in Chapter 2, "Networks and the Internet."

The Morris attack and several other session hijacking attacks require the attacker to be connected to the network and to simultaneously knock the legitimate user offline and then pretend to be that user. As you can probably imagine, it is a complex attack.

## Insider Threats

Insider threats are a type of security breach. However, they present such a significant issue that we will deal with them separately. An insider threat is simply when someone inside your organization either misuses his access to data or accesses data he is not authorized to access.

The most obvious case is that of Edward Snowden. For our purposes we can ignore the political issues connected with his case and instead focus solely on the issue of insiders accessing information and using it in a way other than what was authorized.

In 2009 Edward Snowden was working as a contractor for Dell, which manages computer systems for several U.S. government agencies. In March 2012 he was assigned to an NSA location in Hawaii. While there he convinced several people at that location to provide him with their login and password, under the pretense of performing network administrative duties. Some sources dispute whether or not this is the specific method he used, but it is the one most widely reported. Whatever method he used, he accessed and downloaded thousands of documents that he was not authorized to access.

Again, ignoring the political issues and the content of the documents, our focus is on the security issues. Clearly there were inadequate security controls in place to detect Edward Snowden's activities and to prevent him from disclosing confidential documents. While your organization may not have the high profile that the NSA has, any organization is susceptible to insider threats. Theft of trade secrets by insiders is a common business concern and has been the focus of many lawsuits against former employees. In both Chapter 7, "Industrial Espionage in Cyberspace," and Chapter 9, "Computer Security Technology," we will see some countermeasures to mitigate this threat.

While Edward Snowden is an obvious example of insider threats, that is only one example. A common scenario is when someone who has legitimate access to some particular source of data chooses either to access data he is not authorized to access or to use the data in a manner other than how he has been authorized. Here are a few examples:

- A hospital employee who accesses patient records to use the data to steal a patient's identity, or someone with no access at all who accesses records.

- A salesperson who takes the list of contacts with him before leaving the company.

This is actually a much greater problem than many people appreciate. Within an organization, information security is often more lax than it should be. Most people are more concerned with external security than internal security, so it is often rather easy to access data within an organization. In my career as a security consultant, I have seen networks where sensitive data is simply placed on a shared drive with no limiting of access to it. That means anyone on the network can access that data. In a case such as this, no crime has been committed. However, in other cases, employees purposefully circumvent security measures to access data they are not authorized to. The most common method is to simply log in with someone else's password. That enables the perpetrator to access whatever resources and data to which that other person has been granted access. Unfortunately, many people use weak passwords or, worse, they write their password somewhere on their desk. Some users even share passwords. For example, suppose a sales manager is out sick but wants to check to see if a client has emailed her. So she calls her assistant and gives him her login so he can check her email. This sort of behavior should be strictly prohibited by company security policies, but it still occurs. The problem is that now two people have the sales manager's login. Either one could use it or reveal it to someone else (accidentally or on purpose). So there is a greater chance of someone using that manager's login to access data he has not been authorized to access.

## DNS Poisoning

Most of your communication on the Internet will involve DNS, or Domain Name Service. DNS is what translates the domain names you and I understand (like www.ChuckEasttom.com) into IP addresses that computers and routers understand. DNS poisoning uses one of several techniques to compromise that process and redirect traffic to an illicit site, often for the purpose of stealing personal information.

Here is one scenario whereby an attacker might execute a DNS poisoning attack:

First the attacker creates a phishing website. It spoofs a bank that we will call ABC Bank. The attacker wants to lure users there so he can steal their passwords and use those on the real bank website. Since many users are too smart to click on links, he will use DNS poisoning to trick them.

The attacker creates his own DNS server. (Actually, this part is relatively easy.) Then he puts two records in that DNS server. The first is for the ABC Bank website, pointing to his fake site rather than the real bank site. The second entry is for a domain that does not exist. The attacker can search domain registries until he finds one that does not exist. For illustration purposes, we will refer to this as XYZ domain.

Then the attacker sends a request to a DNS server on the target network. That request purports to be from any IP address within the target network and is requesting the DNS server resolve the XYZ domain.

Obviously the DNS server does not have an entry for the XYZ domain since it does not exist. So it begins to propagate the request up its chain of command eventually to its service provider DNS server. At any point in that process the attacker sends a flood of spoofed responses claiming to be from a DNS server that the target server is trying to request records from but are actually coming from his DNS server and offering the IP address for XYZ domain. At that point the hacker's DNS server offers to do a zone transfer, exchanging all information with the target server. That information includes the spoofed address for ABC Bank. Now the target DNS server has an entry for ABC Bank that points to the hacker's website rather than the real ABC Bank website. Should users on that network type in the URL for ABC Bank, their own DNS server will direct them to the hacker's site.

This attack, like so many, depends on vulnerabilities in the target system. A properly configured DNS server should never perform a zone transfer with any DNS server that is not already authenticated in the domain. However, the unfortunate fact is that there are plenty of DNS servers that are not properly configured.

## New Attacks

Many of the threats discussed in the first two editions of this book are still plaguing network security. Malware, DoS, and other such attacks are just as common today as they were 5 years ago or even 10 years ago.

One new phenomenon is doxing, which is the process of finding personal information about an individual and broadcasting it, often via the Internet. This can be any personal information about any person. However, it is most often used against public figures. While writing this book, the director of the CIA was the target of doxing.[4]

---

4. http://gawker.com/wikileaks-just-doxxed-the-head-of-the-cia-1737871619

Hacking of medical devices is also a new attack. Hacker Barnaby Jack first revealed a vulnerability in an insulin pump that could allow an attacker to take control of the pump and cause it to dispense the entire reservoir of insulin in a single does, thus killing the patient.[5] To date there are no confirmed incidents of this having actually been done, but it is disturbing nonetheless. Similar security flaws have been found in pacemakers.

In July 2015 it was revealed that Jeep vehicles could be hacked and shut down during normal operation.[6] This means that a hacker could cause the Jeep to stop in the middle of heavy, high-speed traffic. This has the potential to cause a serious automobile accident.

All of these attacks show a common theme. As our lives become more interconnected with technology, there are new vulnerabilities. Some of these vulnerabilities are not merely endangering data and computer systems, but potentially endangering lives.

# Assessing the Likelihood of an Attack on Your Network

How likely are these attacks? What are the real dangers facing you as an individual or your organization? What are the most likely attacks, and what are your vulnerabilities? Let's take a look at what threats are out there and which ones are the most likely to cause you or your organization problems.

At one time, the most likely threat to individuals and large organizations was the computer virus. And it is still true that in any given month, several new virus outbreaks will be documented. This situation means that new viruses are being created all the time and old ones are still out there. However, there are other very common attacks, such as spyware. Spyware is fast becoming as big a problem, even bigger than viruses.

After viruses, the most common attack is unauthorized usage of computer systems. Unauthorized usage includes everything from DoS attacks to outright intrusion of your system. It also includes internal employees misusing system resources. The first edition of this book referenced a survey by the Computer Security Institute of 223 computer professionals showing over $445 million in losses due to computer security breaches. In 75% of the cases, an Internet connection was the point of attack, while 33% of the professionals cited the location as their internal systems. A rather astonishing 78% of those surveyed detected employee abuse of systems/Internet (Computer Security Institute, 2002). This statistic means that in any organization, one of the chief dangers might be its own employees. A 2007 study by Jeffery Johnson and Zolt Ugray, of Utah State University, showed similar problems. And in 2015/2016 similar threats still exist with only slight changes in the percentages.

The 2014 Data Breach Investigation Report from Verizon surveyed 63,437 security incidents with 1,367 confirmed breaches in 95 countries. This survey still showed significant employee abuse of the

---

5. http://go.bloomberg.com/tech-blog/2012-02-29-hacker-shows-off-lethal-attack-by-controlling-wireless-medical-device/

6. http://www.wired.com/2015/07/hackers-remotely-kill-jeep-highway/

network as well as many of the familiar attacks we have already discussed in this chapter. The 2015 Data Breach Investigation Report did not show significant improvement.

# Basic Security Terminology

Before you embark on the rest of this chapter and this book, it is important to know some basic terminology. The security and hacking terms in this section are merely an introduction to computer security terminology, but they are an excellent starting point to help you prepare for learning more about computer security. Additional terms will be introduced throughout the text and listed in the Glossary at the end of this book.

The world of computer security takes its vocabulary from both the professional security community and the hacker community.

## Hacker Slang

You probably have heard the term *hacker* used in movies and in news broadcasts. Most people use it to describe any person who breaks into a computer system. In the hacking community, however, a hacker is an expert on a particular system or systems, a person who simply wants to learn more about the system. Hackers feel that looking at a system's flaws is the best way to learn about that system. For example, someone well versed in the Linux operating system who works to understand that system by learning its weaknesses and flaws would be a hacker.

This process does often mean seeing if a flaw can be exploited to gain access to a system. This "exploiting" part of the process is where hackers differentiate themselves into three groups:

- A white hat hacker, upon finding some flaw in a system, will report the flaw to the vendor of that system. For example, if a white hat hacker were to discover some flaw in Red Hat Linux, he would then email the Red Hat company (probably anonymously) and explain exactly what the flaw is and how it was exploited. White hat hackers are often hired specifically by companies to do penetration tests. The EC Council even has a certification test for white hat hackers: the Certified Ethical Hacker test.

- A black hat hacker is the person normally depicted in the media. Once she gains access to a system, her goal is to cause some type of harm. She might steal data, erase files, or deface websites. Black hat hackers are sometimes referred to as crackers.

- A gray hat hacker is normally a law-abiding citizen, but in some cases will venture into illegal activities.

Regardless of how hackers view themselves, intruding on any system is illegal. This means that technically speaking all hackers, regardless of the color of the metaphorical hat they may wear, are in violation of the law. However, many people feel that white hat hackers actually perform a service by finding flaws and informing vendors before those flaws are exploited by less ethically inclined individuals.

## Script Kiddies

A hacker is an expert in a given system. As with any profession, it includes its share of frauds. So what is the term for someone who calls himself a hacker but lacks the expertise? The most common term for this sort of person is *script kiddy* (Raymond, 1993). Yes, that is an older resource, but the term still means the same thing. The name comes from the fact that the Internet is full of utilities and scripts that one can download to perform some hacking tasks. Many of these tools have an easy-to-use graphical user interface that allows someone with very little if any skill to operate the tool. A classic example is the Low Earth Orbit Ion Cannon tool for executing a DoS attack. Someone who downloads such a tool without really understanding the target system is considered a script kiddy. A significant number of the people you are likely to encounter who call themselves hackers are, in reality, mere script kiddies.

## Ethical Hacking: Penetration Testers

When and why would someone give permission to another party to hack his system? The most common answer is in order to assess system vulnerabilities. This used to be called a *sneaker*, but now the term *penetration tester* is far more widely used. Whatever the term, the person legally breaks into a system in order to assess security deficiencies, such as portrayed in the 1992 film *Sneakers*, starring Robert Redford, Dan Aykroyd, and Sidney Poitier. More and more companies are soliciting the services of such individuals or firms to assess their vulnerabilities.

Anyone hired to assess the vulnerabilities of a system should be both technically proficient and ethical. Run a criminal background check, and avoid those people with problem pasts. There are plenty of legitimate security professionals available who know and understand hacker skills but have never committed security crimes. If you take the argument that hiring convicted hackers means hiring talented people to its logical conclusion, you could surmise that obviously those in question are not as good at hacking as they would like to think because they were caught.

Most importantly, giving a person with a criminal background access to your systems is on par with hiring a person with multiple DWI convictions to be your driver. In both cases, you are inviting problems and perhaps assuming significant civil liabilities.

Also, some review of their qualifications is clearly in order. Just as there are people who claim to be highly skilled hackers yet are not, there are those who will claim to be skilled penetration testers yet lack the skills truly needed. You would not want to inadvertently hire a script kiddy who thinks she is a penetration tester. Such a person might then pronounce your system quite sound when, in fact, it was simply a lack of skills that prevented the script kiddy from successfully breaching your security. Later in this book, in Chapter 11, "Network Scanning and Vulnerability Scanning," we discuss the basics of assessing a target system. In Chapter 11 we also discuss the qualifications you should seek in any consultant you might hire for this purpose.

## Phreaking

One specialty type of hacking involves breaking into telephone systems. This subspecialty of hacking is referred to as *phreaking*. The *New Hacker's Dictionary* actually defines phreaking as "the action of using mischievous and mostly illegal ways in order to not pay for some sort of telecommunications bill, order, transfer, or other service" (Raymond, 2003). Phreaking requires a rather significant knowledge of telecommunications, and many phreakers have some professional experience working for a phone company or other telecommunications business. Often this type of activity is dependent upon specific technology required to compromise phone systems more than simply knowing certain techniques.

## Professional Terms

Most hacker terminology, as you may have noticed, is concerned with the activity (phreaking) or the person performing the activity (penetration tester). In contrast, security professional terminology describes defensive barrier devices, procedures, and policies. This is quite logical because hacking is an offensive activity centered on attackers and attack methodologies, whereas security is a defensive activity concerning itself with defensive barriers and procedures.

### Security Devices

The most basic security device is the *firewall*. A firewall is a barrier between a network and the outside world. Sometimes a firewall takes the form of a standalone server, sometimes a router, and sometimes software running on a machine. Whatever its physical form, a firewall filters traffic entering and exiting the network. A *proxy server* is often used with a firewall to hide the internal network's IP address and present a single IP address (its own) to the outside world.

Firewalls and proxy servers guard the perimeter by analyzing traffic (at least inbound and in many cases outbound as well) and blocking traffic that has been disallowed by the administrator. These two safeguards are often augmented by an *intrusion detection system* (IDS). An IDS simply monitors traffic, looking for suspicious activity that might indicate an attempted intrusion. We will examine these technologies, and others, in Chapter 9.

### Security Activities

In addition to devices, we have activities. *Authentication* is the most basic security activity. It is merely the process of determining if the credentials given by a user or another system (such as a username and password) are authorized to access the network resource in question. When you log in with your username and password, the system will attempt to authenticate that username and password. If it is authenticated, you will be granted access.

Another crucial safeguard is *auditing*, which is the process of reviewing logs, records, and procedures to determine if these items meet standards. This activity will be mentioned in many places throughout this book and will be a definite focus in a few chapters.

The security and hacking terms that we have just covered are only an introduction to computer security terminology, but they provide an excellent starting point that will help you prepare for learning more about computer security. Additional terms will be introduced throughout the text as needed and compiled in the Glossary at the end of the book.

# Concepts and Approaches

The approach you take toward security influences all subsequent security decisions and sets the tone for the entire organization's network security infrastructure. Before we delve into various network security paradigms, let us take a moment to examine a few concepts that should permeate your entire thinking about security.

The first concept is the *CIA triangle*. This does not refer to clandestine operating involving the Central Intelligence Agency; rather, it is a reference to the three pillars of security: confidentiality, integrity, and availability. When you are thinking about security, your thought processes should always be guided by these three principles. First and foremost, are you keeping the data confidential? Does your approach help guarantee the integrity of data? And does your approach still make the data readily available to authorized users?

Another important concept to keep in mind is *least privileges*. This means that each user or service running on your network should have the least number of privileges/access required to do her job. No one should be granted access to anything unless it is absolutely required for the job. In military and intelligence circles this is referred to as "need to know."

Network security paradigms can be classified by either the scope of security measures taken (perimeter, layered) or how proactive the system is.

In a *perimeter security approach*, the bulk of security efforts are focused on the perimeter of the network. This focus might include firewalls, proxy servers, password policies, or any technology or procedure to make unauthorized access of the network less likely. Little or no effort is put into securing the systems within the network. In this approach the perimeter is secured, but the various systems within that perimeter are often vulnerable.

There are additional issues regarding perimeter security that include physical security. That can include fences, closed-circuit TV, guards, locks, and so on, depending on the security needs of your organization.

The perimeter approach is clearly flawed, so why do some companies use it? Small organizations might use the perimeter approach if they have budget constraints or inexperienced network administrators. A perimeter method might be adequate for small organizations that do not store sensitive data, but it rarely works in a larger corporate setting.

A *layered security approach* is one in which not only is the perimeter secured, but individual systems within the network are also secured. All servers, workstations, routers, and hubs within the network are secure. One way to accomplish this is to divide the network into segments and secure each segment as if it were a separate network, so if the perimeter security is compromised, not all the internal systems are affected. This is the preferred method whenever possible.

You should also measure your security approach by how proactive/reactive it is. This is done by gauging how much of the system's security infrastructure and policies are dedicated to preventive measures and how much of the security system is designed to respond to attack. A passive security approach takes few or no steps to prevent an attack. A dynamic or proactive defense is one in which steps are taken to prevent attacks before they occur.

One example of this defense is the use of IDSs, which work to detect attempts to circumvent security measures. These systems can tell a system administrator that an attempt to breach security has been made, even if that attempt is not successful. IDSs can also be used to detect various techniques intruders use to assess a target system, thus alerting a network administrator to the potential for an attempted breach before the attempt is even initiated.

In the real world, network security is usually not completely in one paradigm or another; it is usually a hybrid approach. Networks generally include elements of both security paradigms. The two categories also combine. One can have a network that is predominantly passive but layered, or one that is primarily perimeter but proactive. It can be helpful to consider approaches to computer security along a Cartesian coordinate system, as illustrated in Figure 1.1, with the $x$ axis representing the level of passive-active approaches and the $y$ axis depicting the range from perimeter to layered defense.

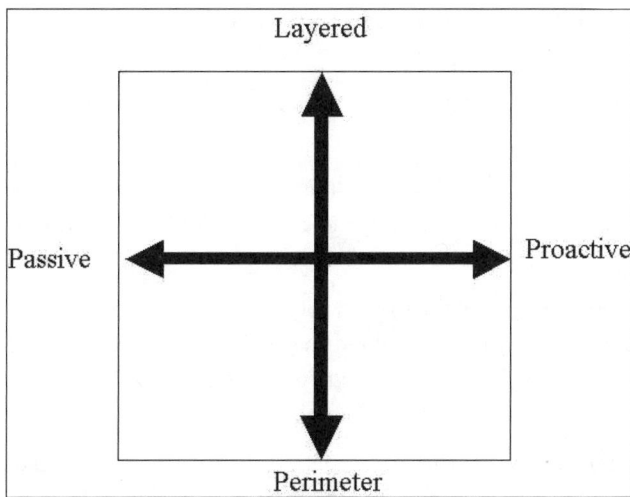

**FIGURE 1.1**   The security approach guide.

The most desirable hybrid approach is a layered paradigm that is dynamic, which is the upper-right quadrant of the figure.

## How Do Legal Issues Impact Network Security?

An increasing number of legal issues affect how one approaches computer security. If your organization is a publicly traded company, a government agency, or does business with either one, there may be legal constraints regarding your network security. Even if your network is not legally bound to these security guidelines, it's useful to understand the various laws impacting computer security. You may choose to apply them to your own security standards.

One of the oldest pieces of legislation in the United States that affects computer security is the Computer Security Act of 1987 (100th Congress, 1987). It requires government agencies to identify sensitive systems, conduct computer security training, and develop computer security plans. This law was a vague mandate ordering federal agencies in the United States to establish security measures, but it did not specify standards.

This legislation established a legal mandate to enact specific standards, paving the way for future guidelines and regulations. It also helped define terms, such as what information is considered "sensitive." This quote is found in the legislation itself:

> The term 'sensitive information' means any information, the loss, misuse, or unauthorized access to or modification of which could adversely affect the national interest or the conduct of Federal programs, or the privacy to which individuals are entitled under section 552a of title 5, United States Code (the Privacy Act), but which has not been specifically authorized under criteria established by an Executive order or an Act of Congress to be kept secret in the interest of national defense or foreign policy. (100th Congress, 1987)

This definition of the word *sensitive* should be kept in mind because it is not just social security information or medical history that must be secured.

When considering what information needs to be secure, simply ask this question: Would the unauthorized access or modification of this information adversely affect your organization? If the answer is yes, then you must consider that information sensitive and in need of security precautions.

Another more specific federal law that applied to mandated security for government systems was OMB Circular A-130 (specifically, Appendix III). This document required that federal agencies establish security programs containing specified elements. It also described requirements for developing standards for computer systems and for records held by government agencies.

Most states have specific laws regarding computer security, such as legislation like the Computer Crimes Act of Florida, the Computer Crime Act of Alabama, and the Computer Crimes Act of Oklahoma. If you're responsible for network security, you might find yourself part of a criminal investigation. This could be an investigation into a hacking incident or employee misuse of computer resources. A list of computer crime laws (organized by state) can be found at http://criminal.findlaw.com/criminal-charges/cyber-crimes.html.

---

### Caution

### Privacy Laws

It is critical to keep in mind that any law that governs privacy (such as the Health Insurance Portability and Accountability Act of 1996, HIPAA) also has a direct impact on computer security. If your system is compromised, and thus data that is covered under any privacy statute is compromised, you may need to prove that you exercised due diligence in protecting that data. If it can be shown that you did not take proper precautions, you might be found civilly liable.

# Online Security Resources

As you read this book, and when you move out into the professional world, you will have frequent need for additional security resources. Appendix B, "Resources," includes a more complete list of resources, but this section highlights a few of the most important ones you may find useful now.

## CERT

The *Computer Emergency Response Team* (CERT, www.cert.org) is sponsored by Carnegie-Mellon University. CERT was the first computer incident-response team, and it is still one of the most respected in the industry. Anyone interested in network security should visit the site routinely. On the website you will find a wealth of documentation, including guidelines for security policies, cutting-edge security research, and more.

## Microsoft Security Advisor

Because so many computers today run Microsoft operating systems, another good resource is the Microsoft Security Advisor website: https://technet.microsoft.com/en-us/library/security/dn631936.aspx. This site is a portal to all Microsoft security information, tools, and updates. If you use any Microsoft software, then it is advised that you visit this website regularly.

## F-Secure

The F-Secure corporation maintains a website at www.f-secure.com. This site is, among other things, a repository for detailed information on virus outbreaks. Here you will find not only notifications about a particular virus but detailed information about the virus. This information includes how the virus spreads, ways to recognize the virus, and frequently, specific tools for cleaning an infected system of a particular virus.

## SANS Institute

The SANS Institute website (www.sans.org) is a vast repository of security-related documentation. On this site you will find detailed documentation on virtually every aspect of computer security you can imagine. The SANS Institute also sponsors a number of security research projects and publishes information about those projects on its website.

# Summary

Network security is a complex and constantly evolving field. Practitioners must stay on top of new threats and solutions and be proactive in assessing risk and protecting their networks. The first step to understanding network security is to become acquainted with the actual threats posed to a network. Without a realistic idea of what threats might affect your systems, you will be unable to effectively protect them. It is also critical that you acquire a basic understanding of the terminology used by both security professionals and those who would seek to compromise your security.

## Test Your Skills

### MULTIPLE CHOICE QUESTIONS

1. One extreme viewpoint about computer security is what?

    A. The federal government will handle security.

    B. Microsoft will handle security.

    C. There are no imminent dangers to your system.

    D. There is no danger if you use Linux.

2. Before you can formulate a defense for a network you need what?

    A. Appropriate security certifications

    B. A clear picture of the dangers to be defended against

    C. To finish this textbook

    D. The help of an outside consultant

3. Which of the following is not one of the three major classes of threats?

    A. Attempts to intrude on the system

    B. Online auction fraud

    C. Denial of service attacks

    D. A computer virus

4. What is a computer virus?

    A. Any program that is downloaded to your system without your permission

    B. Any program that self-replicates

    C. Any program that causes harm to your system

    D. Any program that can change your Windows Registry

5. What is spyware?

   **A.** Any software that monitors your system

   **B.** Only software that logs keystrokes

   **C.** Any software used to gather intelligence

   **D.** Only software that monitors what websites you visit

6. What is a penetration tester?

   **A.** A person who hacks a system without being caught

   **B.** A person who hacks a system by faking a legitimate password

   **C.** A person who hacks a system to test its vulnerabilities

   **D.** A person who is an amateur hacker

7. What is the term for hacking a phone system?

   **A.** Telco-hacking

   **B.** Hacking

   **C.** Cracking

   **D.** Phreaking

8. What is malware?

   **A.** Software that has some malicious purpose

   **B.** Software that is not functioning properly

   **C.** Software that damages your system

   **D.** Software that is not properly configured for your system

9. What is war-driving?

   **A.** Driving and seeking a computer job

   **B.** Driving while using a wireless connection to hack

   **C.** Driving looking for wireless networks to hack

   **D.** Driving and seeking rival hackers

10. When a hacking technique uses persuasion and deception to get a person to provide information to help compromise security, this is referred to as what?

   **A.** Social engineering

   **B.** Conning

   **C.** Human intel

   **D.** Soft hacking

**11.** What is the most common threat on the Internet?

    **A.** Auction fraud

    **B.** Hackers

    **C.** Computer viruses

    **D.** Illegal software

**12.** What are the three approaches to security?

    **A.** Perimeter, layered, hybrid

    **B.** High security, medium security, low security

    **C.** Internal, external, and hybrid

    **D.** Perimeter, complete, none

**13.** An intrusion detection system is an example of which of the following?

    **A.** Proactive security

    **B.** Perimeter security

    **C.** Hybrid security

    **D.** Good security practices

**14.** Which of the following is the most basic security activity?

    **A.** Authentication

    **B.** Firewalls

    **C.** Password protection

    **D.** Auditing

**15.** The most desirable approach to security is one that is which of the following?

    **A.** Perimeter and dynamic

    **B.** Layered and dynamic

    **C.** Perimeter and static

    **D.** Layered and static

**16.** According to a recent survey of 223 computer professionals prepared by the Computer Security Institute, which of the following was cited as an issue by more of the respondents?

    **A.** Internal systems

    **B.** Employee abuse

    **C.** Routers

    **D.** Internet connection

17. Which of the following types of privacy law affects computer security?

    A. Any state privacy law

    B. Any privacy law applicable to your organization

    C. Any privacy law

    D. Any federal privacy law

18. The first computer incident-response team is affiliated with what university?

    A. Massachusetts Institute of Technology

    B. Carnegie-Mellon University

    C. Harvard University

    D. California Technical University

19. Which of the following is the best definition of the term *sensitive information*?

    A. Any information that has impact on national security

    B. Any information that is worth more than $1,000

    C. Any information that if accessed by unauthorized personnel could damage your organization in any way

    D. Any information that is protected by privacy laws

20. Which of the following is a major resource for detailed information on a computer virus?

    A. The MIT Virus Library

    B. The Microsoft Virus Library

    C. The F-Secure Virus Library

    D. The National Virus Repository

## EXERCISES

### EXERCISE 1.1: How Many Virus Attacks Have Occurred This Month?

1. Using some website resource, such as www.f-secure.com, look up recent computer virus outbreaks.

2. How many virus outbreaks have occurred in the past 7 days?

3. Write down how many outbreaks there have been in the past 30 days, 90 days, and 1 year.

4. Are virus attacks increasing in frequency?

## EXERCISE 1.2: Learning About Cookies as Spyware

1. Get an idea of what kind of information cookies store. You might find the following websites helpful:

    www.allaboutcookies.org/
    www.howstuffworks.com/cookie1.htm

2. Write a brief essay explaining in what way cookies can invade privacy.

## EXERCISE 1.3: Hacker Terminology

1. Use the *Hacker's Dictionary* at http://www.outpost9.com/reference/jargon/jargon_toc.html.

    Hacker terms:

    A. Alpha geek
    B. Grok
    C. Red Book
    D. Wank

## EXERCISE 1.4: Using Security Resources

1. Using one of the preferred web resources listed in this chapter, find three policy or procedure documents from that resource.

2. List the documents you selected.

3. Write a brief essay explaining why those particular documents are important to your organization's security.

## EXERCISE 1.5: Learning About the Law

1. Using the Web, journals, books, or other resources, find out if your state or territory has any laws specific to computer security. You might find the following websites helpful:

    www.pbs.org/wgbh/pages/frontline/shows/hackers/blame/crimelaws.html
    www.cybercrime.gov/

2. List three laws that you find, with a brief description of each. The list can be a simple one, noting the pertinent laws in your region. Describe each one with one or two sentences.

## PROJECTS

### PROJECT 1.1: Learning About a Virus

1. Using web resources from Appendix B and sites such as www.f-secure.com, find a virus that has been released in the past 6 months.

2. Research how the virus spread and what damage it caused.

3. Write a brief (half to one page) paper on this virus. Explain how the virus worked, how it spread, and any other essential information you can find.

### PROJECT 1.2: Considering the Law (a Group Project)

Write a description of a computer law that you would like to have passed, along with specifications as to its implementation, enforcement, and justification.

### PROJECT 1.3: Recommending Security

1. Using the Web, journals, or books, locate security recommendations from any reputable source, such as the SANS Institute. Any of the sites mentioned in the "Online Security Resources" section of this chapter would be a good choice.

2. List five of those recommendations.

3. Explain why you agree or disagree with each one.

---

### Case Study

In this case study we will consider a network administrator for a small, family-oriented video store. The store is not part of a chain of stores and has a very limited security budget. It has five machines for employees to use to check out movies and one server on which to keep centralized records. That server is in the manager's office. The administrator takes the following security precautions:

1. Each machine is upgraded to Windows XP, with the personal firewall turned on.

2. Antivirus software was installed on all machines.

3. A tape backup is added to the server, and tapes are kept in a file cabinet in the manager's office.

4. Internet access to employee machines is removed.

Now consider these questions:

1. What did these actions accomplish?

2. What additional actions might you recommend?

# Chapter 2

# Networks and the Internet

## Chapter Objectives

**After reading this chapter and completing the exercises, you will be able to do the following:**

- Identify each of the major protocols used in network communication (for example, FTP and Telnet), and what use you can make of each
- Understand the various connection methods and speeds used on networks
- Compare and contrast a hub and switch
- Identify what a router is and what it's used for
- Understand how data is transmitted over a network
- Explain how the Internet works and the use of IP addresses and URLs
- Recount a brief history of the Internet
- Use network utilities such as these: `ping`, `IPConfig`, and `tracert`
- Describe the OSI model of network communication and the use of MAC addresses

## Introduction

To be able to manage network security, you will need knowledge about how computer networks operate. Those readers who already have a strong working knowledge of network operations may choose to skim this chapter or perhaps give it a quick read as a review. For other readers new to computer networking, studying this chapter will give you a basic introduction to how networks and the Internet work, including a history of the Internet. This understanding of networks and the Internet will be crucial to your comprehension of later topics presented in this book.

We will begin by examining the basic technologies, protocols, and methods used for networks and the Internet to communicate. Then we will take a look at the history of the Internet. This information forms the background knowledge you will need to understand various cyber attacks and how they are defended against. In the exercises at the end of the chapter, you will be able to practice using some protective methods, such as `IPConfig`, `tracert`, and `ping`.

# Network Basics

Getting two or more computers to communicate and transmit data is a process that is simple in concept but complex in application. Consider all the factors involved. First you will need to physically connect the computers. This connection usually requires either a cable that plugs into your computer or wireless connection. The cable then is plugged either directly to another computer or into a device that will, in turn, connect to several other computers.

Of course, wireless communication is being used with more frequency, and wireless connecting, obviously, doesn't require a cable. However, even wireless communication relies on a physical device to transmit the data. There is a card in most modern computers called a *network interface card*, or NIC. If the connection is through a cable, the part of the NIC that is external to the computer has a connection slot that looks like a telephone jack, only slightly bigger. Wireless networks also use a NIC; but rather than having a slot for a cable to connect to, the wireless network simply uses radio signals to transmit to a nearby wireless router or hub. Wireless routers, hubs, and NICs must have an antenna to transmit and receive signals. These devices are connective devices that will be explained in detail later in this chapter.

## The Physical Connection: Local Networks

As mentioned, cables are one of the ways that computers are connected to each other. The cable connection used with traditional NICs (meaning not wireless) is an RJ-45 connection. (*RJ* is short for Registered Jack, which is an international industry standard.) In contrast to the computer's RJ-45 jacks, standard telephone lines use RJ-11 jacks. The biggest difference between jacks involves the number of wires in the connector, also called the *terminator*. Phone lines have four wires (though some have six wires), whereas RJ-45 connectors have eight wires.

If you look on the back of most computers or the connection area of a laptop, you will probably find two ports that, at first glance, look like phone jacks. One of the two ports is probably for a traditional modem and accepts a standard RJ-11 jack. The other port is larger and accepts an RJ-45 jack. It would be extremely rare to find a modern computer that did not have a NIC.

This standard connector jack must be on the end of the cable. The cable used in most networks today is a Category 5 or 6 cable abbreviated as Cat 5 cable or Cat 6 cable. Table 2.1 summarizes the various categories of cable and their uses.

**TABLE 2.1**  Cable Types and Uses

| Category | Specifications | Uses |
|---|---|---|
| 1 | Low-speed analog (less than 1MHz) | Telephone, doorbell |
| 2 | Analog line (less than 10MHz) | Telephone |
| 3 | Up to 16MHz or 100Mbps (megabits per second) | Voice transmissions |
| 4 | Up to 20MHz/100Mbps | Data lines, Ethernet networks |
| 5 | 100MHz/100Mbps | Most common a few years ago, still widely used |
| 6 | 1000Mbps (some get 10Gbps) | Most common type of network cable |
| 6a | 10Gbps | High-speed networks |
| 7 | 10Gbps | Very high-speed networks |
| 8 | 40Gbps | Not yet commonly found |

The type of cable used in connecting computers is also often referred to as unshielded twisted-pair (UTP) cable. In UTP, the wires in the cable are in pairs, twisted together without additional shielding. As you can see in Table 2.1, each subsequent category of cable is somewhat faster and more robust than the last. It should be noted that although Cat 4 can be used for networks, it almost never is used for that purpose, as it is simply slower, less reliable, and an older technology. You will usually see Cat 5 cable and, increasingly, Cat 6. You should note that we are focusing on UTP because that is what is found most often. There are other types of cable such as shielded twisted-pair (STP), but they are not nearly as common as UTP.

---

**FYI: Cable Speed**

Category 6 cable is for the new Gigabit Ethernet. Cat 5 cable works at speeds of up to 100Mbps, whereas Cat 6 works at 1000Mbps. Cat 6 is widely available and has been for several years. However, for Cat 6 to truly function properly, you need hubs/switches and NICs that also transmit at gigabit speeds; thus, the spread of gigabit Ethernet has been much slower than many analysts expected. We will discuss hubs, switches, NICs, and other hardware in more detail later in this chapter.

---

As shown in Table 2.1, a key specification is speed, measured in Mbps, or megabits per second (though more and more gigabits per second or Gbps is common). You are probably already aware that ultimately everything in the computer is stored in a binary format—namely, in the form of a 1 or a 0. These units are called bits. It takes 8 bits, which equals 1 byte, to represent a single character such as a letter, number, or carriage return. Remember that the data specification for each cable is the maximum that the cable can handle. A Cat 5 cable can transmit up to 100 mega (million) bits per second. This is known as the *bandwidth* of the cable. If multiple users are on a network, all sending data, that traffic uses up bandwidth rather quickly. Any pictures transmitted also use a lot of bandwidth. Simple scanned-in photos can easily reach 2 megabytes (2 million bytes, or 16 million bits) or much more. And streaming media, such as video, is perhaps the most demanding on bandwidth.

If you simply want to connect two computers, you can have the cable go directly from one computer to the other. You would have to use a crossover cable, but you could connect two computers directly. But what do you do if you wish to connect more than two computers? What if you have 100 computers that you need to connect on a network? There are three devices that can help you to accomplish this task: the hub, the switch, and the router. These each use Cat 5 or Cat 6 cable with RJ-45 connectors and are explained in the following sections.

## The Hub

The simplest connection device is the *hub*. A hub is a small box-shaped electronic device into which you can plug network cables. It will have four or more (commonly up to 24) RJ-45 jacks, each called a *port*. A hub can connect as many computers as it has ports. (For example, an 8-port hub can connect eight computers.) You can also connect one hub to another; this strategy is referred to as "stacking" hubs. Hubs are quite inexpensive and simple to set up; just plug in the cable. However, hubs have a downside. If you send a packet (a unit of data transmission) from one computer to another, a copy of that packet is actually sent out from every port on the hub. All these copies leads to a lot of unnecessary network traffic. This occurs because the hub, being a very simple device, has no way of knowing where a packet is supposed to go. Therefore, it simply sends copies of the packet out all of its ports. While you may go to your favorite electronic store and buy something called a "hub," true hubs no longer exist. What you are really getting is a switch, which we will discuss later in this section.

## Repeater

A *repeater* is a device used to boost signal. Basically if your cable needs to go further than the maximum length (which is 100 meters for UTP), then you need a repeater. There are two types of repeaters: amplifier and signal. Amplifier repeaters simply boost the entire signal they receive, including any noise. Signal repeaters regenerate the signal, and thus don't rebroadcast noise.

## The Switch

The next connection device option is the *switch*. A switch is basically an intelligent hub; it works and looks exactly like a hub, with one significant difference. When a switch receives a packet, it will send that packet only out the port for the computer to which it needs to go. A switch is essentially a hub that is able to determine where a packet is being sent. How this determination is made is explained in the "Data Transmission" section.

## The Router

Finally, if you wish to connect two or more networks, you use a *router*. A router is similar in concept to a hub or switch, as it does relay packets; but it is far more sophisticated. You can program most routers and control how they relay packets. Most routers have interfaces allowing you to configure them. The more robust routers also offer more programming possibilities. The specifics of how you program the router are different from vendor to vendor, and there are entire books written specifically on just programming routers. It is not possible to cover specific router programming techniques in this book; however, you should be aware that most routers are programmable, allowing you to change how they route traffic. Also, unlike using a hub or switch, the two networks connected by a router are still separate networks.

## Faster Connection Speeds

The previous explanation covers the connections between computers on a local network, but surely there are faster connection methods. Well, there are; in fact, your Internet service provider or the company for which you work probably has a much faster connection to the Internet. Table 2.2 summarizes the most common high-speed connection types and their speeds.

**TABLE 2.2**   Internet Connection Types

| Connection Type | Speed | Details |
|---|---|---|
| DS0 | 64Kbps | Standard phone line. |
| ISDN | 128Kbps | Two DS0 lines working together to provide a high-speed data connection. |
| T1 | 1.54Mbps | Twenty-four DS0 lines working as one. Twenty-three carry data, and one carries information about the other lines. This type of connection has become common for schools and businesses. |
| T3 | 43.2Mbps | 672 DS0 lines working together. This method is the equivalent of 28 T1 lines. |
| OC3 | 155Mbps | All OC lines are optical and do not use traditional phone lines. OC3 lines are quite fast and very expensive. They are often found at telecommunications companies. |
| OC12 | 622Mbps | The equivalent of 336 T1 lines, or 8,064 phone lines. |
| OC48 | 2.5Gbps | The equivalent of four OC12 lines. |

It is common to find T1 connection lines in many locations. A cable modem can sometimes achieve speeds comparable to a T1 line. Note that cable modems were not listed on the chart simply because their actual speeds vary greatly depending on a variety of circumstances including how many people in your immediate vicinity are using the same cable modem provider. You are not likely to encounter the OC lines unless you work in telecommunications.

## Data Transmission

We've seen, briefly, the physical connection methods; but how is data actually transmitted? To transmit data, a packet is sent. The basic purpose of a cable is to transmit packets from one machine to another. It does not matter whether that packet is part of a document, a video, an image, or just some internal signal from the computer. So what, exactly, is a packet? As we discussed earlier, everything in a computer is ultimately stored as 1s and 0s, called *bits*, which are grouped into sets of eight, called a *byte*. A packet is a certain number of bytes divided into a header and a body. The header is 20 bytes at the beginning of the packet that tells you where the packet is coming from, where it is going, and more. The body contains the actual data, in binary format, that you wish to send. The aforementioned routers and switches work by reading the header portion of any packets that come to them. This process is how they determine where the packet should be sent.

## Protocols

There are different types of network communications for different purposes. The different types of network communications are called protocols. A *protocol* is, essentially, an agreed-upon method of communication. In fact, this definition is exactly how the word protocol is used in standard, noncomputer usage, too. Each protocol has a specific purpose and normally operates on a certain port. (Ports are discussed in more detail later.) Some of the most important, and most commonly used, protocols are listed in Table 2.3.

**TABLE 2.3**  TCP/IP Protocols

| Protocol | Purpose | Port |
| --- | --- | --- |
| FTP (File Transfer Protocol) | For transferring files between computers. | 20 and 21 |
| TFTP (Trivial File Transfer Protocol) | A quicker but less reliable form of FTP. | 69 |
| Telnet | Used to remotely log on to a system. You can then use a command prompt or shell to execute commands on that system. Popular with network administrators. | 23 |
| SMTP (Simple Mail Transfer Protocol) | Sends email. | 25 |
| WhoIS | A command that queries a target IP address for information. | 43 |
| DNS (Domain Name Service) | Translates URLs into web addresses. | 53 |
| HTTP (Hypertext Transfer Protocol) | Displays web pages. | 80 |
| POP3 (Post Office Protocol version 3) | Retrieves email. | 110 |
| NNTP (Network News Transfer Protocol) | Used for network newsgroups (Usenet newsgroups). You can access these groups over the Web via www.google.com by selecting the Groups tab. | 119 |
| NetBIOS | An older Microsoft protocol that is for naming systems on a local network. | 137, 138, 139 |
| IRC (Internet Relay Chat) | Used for chat rooms. | 194 |
| ICMP (Internet Control Message Protocol) | Packets that contain error messages, informational messages, and control messages. | No specific port |
| HTTPS | Encrypted HTTP; used for secure websites | 443 |

Each of these protocols will be explained in more detail, as needed, in later chapters of this book. You should also note that this list is not complete, as there are dozens of other protocols; but these are the basic protocols we will be discussing in this book. All of these protocols are part of a suite of protocols referred to as *TCP/IP* (Transmission Control Protocol/Internet Protocol). But no matter the particular protocol being used, all communication on networks takes place via packets, and those packets are transmitted according to certain protocols, depending on the type of communication that is occurring.

### Ports

You may be wondering what a port is, especially since we've already talked about the ports that are the connection locations on the back of your computer, such as a serial port, a parallel port, or RJ-45 and RJ-11 ports. A *port*, in networking terms, is a handle, or a connection point. It is a numeric designation for a particular pathway of communications. You can think of a port like a channel number on your television. You may have one cable coming into your TV, but you can tune to a variety of channels. The combination of your computer's IP address and port number is referred to as a *socket*. All network communication, regardless of the port used, comes into your computer via the connection on your NIC.

So, the picture we've drawn of networks, to this point, is one of machines connected to each other via cables, and perhaps to hubs, switches, or routers. These networks transmit binary information in packets using certain protocols and ports.

# How the Internet Works

Now that you have a basic idea of how computers communicate with each other over a network, it is time to discuss how the Internet works. The Internet is essentially a large number of networks that are connected to each other. Therefore, the Internet works exactly the same way as your local network. It sends the same sort of data packets, using the same protocols. These various networks are simply connected into main transmission lines called *backbones*. The points where the backbones connect to each other are called *network access points (NAPs)*. When you log on to the Internet, you probably use an *Internet service provider (ISP)*. That ISP has a connection either to the Internet backbone or to yet another provider that has a backbone. So, logging on to the Internet is a process of connecting your computer to your ISP's network, which is, in turn, connected to one of the backbones on the Internet.

## IP Addresses

With tens of thousands of networks and millions of individual computers communicating and sending data, a predictable problem arises. That problem is ensuring that the data packets go to the correct computer. This task is accomplished in much the same way as traditional "snail" letter mail is delivered to the right person: via an address. With network communications, this address is a special one, referred to as an "IP" address. An IP address can be IP version 4 or version 6.

**IPv4**

An *IP address* is a series of four values, separated by periods. (An example would be 107.22.98.198.) Each of the three-digit numbers must be between 0 and 255; thus, an address of 107.22.98.466 would not be a valid one. These addresses are actually four binary numbers; you just see them in decimal format. Since each of these numbers is really just a decimal representation of 8 bits, they are often referred to as octets. So there are four octets in an IP v4 address. Recall that a byte is 8 bits (1s and 0s), and an 8-bit binary number converted to decimal format will be between 0 and 255. So you don't have to do the math yourself, I will tell you that this rule means there are a total of over 4.2 billion possible IP addresses. You should not be concerned, however, that we will run out of new IP addresses soon. There are methods already in place (which are discussed later) to extend the use of addresses.

---

**FYI: Converting Binary Numbers**

For those readers not familiar with converting decimal to binary, there are several methods, one of which is shown here. You should be aware that the computer will do this for you in the case of IP addresses, but here's one way—and perhaps the simplest—this is done:

Divide repeatedly by 2, using "remainders" rather than decimal places, until you get down to 1. For example, convert decimal 31 to binary:

31/2 = 15 Remainder 1

15/2 = 7 Remainder 1

7/2 = 3 Remainder 1

3/2 = 1 Remainder 1

1/2 = 0 Remainder 1

Now read the remainders from bottom to top: The binary equivalent is 11111.

---

The IP addresses come in two groups: public and private. The public IP addresses are for computers connected to the Internet. No two public IP addresses can be the same. However, a private IP address, such as one on a private company network, only has to be unique in that network. It does not matter if other computers in the world have the same IP address because this computer is never connected to those other worldwide computers. Often network administrators use private IP addresses that begin with a 10, such as 10.102.230.17.

It should also be pointed out that often an ISP will buy a pool of public IP addresses and assign them to you when you log on. An ISP might own 1,000 public IP address and have 10,000 customers. Because all 10,000 customers will not be online at the same time, the ISP simply assigns an IP address to a customer when he logs on, and the ISP unassigns the IP address when the customer logs off.

The address of a computer tells you a lot about that computer. The first byte (or the first decimal number) in an address tells you to what class of network that machine belongs. Table 2.4 summarizes the five network classes.

**TABLE 2.4**   Network Classes

| Class | IP Range for the First Byte | Use |
|-------|----------------------------|-----|
| A | 0–126 | Extremely large networks. No Class A network IP addresses are left. All have been used. |
| B | 128–191 | Large corporate and government networks. All Class B IP addresses have been used. |
| C | 192–223 | The most common group of IP addresses. Your ISP probably has a Class C address. |
| D | 224–247 | These are reserved for multicasting (transmitting different data on the same channel). |
| E | 248–255 | Reserved for experimental use. |

These five classes of networks will become more important later in this book (or should you decide to study networking on a deeper level). Observe Table 2.4 carefully, and you probably will discover that the IP range of 127 was not listed. This omission is because that range is reserved for testing. The IP address of 127.0.0.1 designates the machine you are on, regardless of that machine's assigned IP address. This address is often referred to as the *loopback address*. That address will be used often in testing your machine and your NIC. We will examine its use a bit later in this chapter in the section on network utilities.

These particular classes are important as they tell you what part of the address represents the network and what part represents the node. For example, in a Class A address, the first octet represents the network, and the remaining three represent the node. In a Class B address, the first two octets represent the network, and the second two represent the node. And finally, in a Class C address, the first three octets represent the network, and the last represents the node.

There are also some very specific IP addresses and IP address ranges you should be aware of. The first, as previously mentioned, is 127.0.0.1, or the loopback address. It is another way of referring to the network interface card of the machine you are on.

Private IP addresses are another issue to be aware of. Certain ranges of IP addresses have been designated for use within networks. These cannot be used as public IP addresses but can be used for internal workstations and servers. Those IP addresses are

- 10.0.0.10 to 10.255.255.255
- 172.16.0.0 to 172.31.255.255
- 192.168.0.0 to 192.168.255.255

Sometimes people new to networking have some trouble understanding public and private IP addresses. A good analogy is an office building. Within a single office building, each office number must be unique. You can only have one 305. And within that building, if you discuss office 305 it is immediately clear what you are talking about. But there are other office buildings, many of which have their own office 305. You can think of private IP addresses as office numbers. They must be unique within their network, but there may be other networks with the same private IP.

Public IP addresses are more like traditional mailing addresses. Those must be unique worldwide. When communicating from office to office you can use the office number, but to get a letter to another building you have to use the complete mailing address. It is much the same with networking. You can communicate within your network using private IP addresses, but to communicate with any computer outside your network, you have to use public IP addresses.

One of the roles of a gateway router is to perform what is called network address translation (NAT). That takes the private IP address on outgoing packets and replaces it with the public IP address of the gateway router so that the packet can be routed through the Internet.

## Subnetting and CIDR

We have already discussed IP version 4 network addresses; now let's turn our attention to subnetting. If you are already familiar with this topic, feel free to skip this section. For some reason this topic tends to give networking students a great deal of trouble. So we will begin with a conceptual understanding. *Subnetting* is simply chopping up a network into smaller portions. For example, if you have a network using the IP address 192.168.1.X (x being whatever the address is for the specific computer), then you have allocated 255 possible IP addresses. What if you want to divide that into two separate subnetworks? Subnetting is how you do that.

More technically, the subnet mask is a 32-bit number that is assigned to each host to divide the 32-bit binary IP address into network and node portions. You also cannot just put in any number you want. The first value of a subnet mask must be 255; the remaining three values can be 255, 254, 252, 248, 240, or 224. Your computer will take your network IP address and the subnet mask and use a binary AND operation to combine them.

It may surprise you to know that you already have a subnet mask even if you have not been subnetting. If you have a Class C IP address, then your network subnet mask is 255.255.255.0. If you have a Class B IP address, then your subnet mask is 255.255.0.0. And finally, if it is Class A, your subnet mask is 255.0.0.0.

Now think about these numbers in relationship to binary numbers. The decimal value 255 converts to 11111111 in binary. So you are literally "masking" the portion of the network address that is used to define the network, and the remaining portion is used to define individual nodes. Now if you want fewer than 255 nodes in your subnet, then you need something like 255.255.255.240 for your subnet. If you convert 240 to binary, it is 11110000. That means the first three octets and the first 4 bits of the last octet define the network. The last 4 bits of the last octet define the node. That means you could have as many as 1111 (in binary) or 15 (in decimal) nodes on this subnetwork. This is the basic essence of subnetting.

## CIDR

Subnetting only allows you to use certain, limited subnets. Another approach is CIDR, or classless interdomain routing. Rather than define a subnet mask, you have the IP address followed by a slash and a number. That number can be any number between 0 and 32, which results in IP addresses like these:

192.168.1.10/24 (basically a Class C IP address)

192.168.1.10/31 (much like a Class C IP address with a subnet mask)

When you use this, rather than having classes with subnets, you have variable-length subnet masking (VLSM) that provides classless IP address. This is the most common way to define network IP addresses today.

## IPv6

You have probably heard talk of IP version 6, or IPv6, as an extension of IPv4. Essentially, IP version 4 is limited to 4.2 billion IP addresses. Even with the use of private IP addresses, we will run out of available IP addresses. Think of all the computers, printers, routers, servers, smart phones, tablets, and so on connected to the Internet. IP version 6 was designed to alleviate this problem. And if you looked around in the network settings described in the last section, you probably saw the option to enable IPv6. IPv6 utilizes a 128-bit address (instead of 32), so there is no chance of running out of IP addresses in the foreseeable future. IPv6 also utilizes a hex numbering method in order to avoid long addresses such as 132.64.34.26.64.156.143.57.1.3.7.44.122.111.201.5. The hex address format will appear in the form of 3FFE:B00:800:2::C, for example.

There is no subnetting in IPv6. Instead, it only uses CIDR. The network portion is indicated by a slash followed by the number of bits in the address that are assigned to the network portion, such as

/48

/64

There is a loopback address for IPv6, and it can be written as ::/128. Other differences between IPv4 and IPv6 are described here:

- Link/machine-local.

  IPv6 version of IPv4's APIPA or Automatic Private IP Addressing. So if the machine is configured for dynamically assigned addresses and cannot communicate with a DHCP server, it assigns itself a generic IP address. DHCP, or Dynamic Host Configuration Protocol, is used to dynamically assign IP addresses within a network.

  IPV6 link/machine-local IP addresses all start with fe80::. So if your computer has this address, that means it could not get to a DHCP server and therefore made up its own generic IP address.

- Site/network-local.

  IPv6 version of IPv4 private address. In other words, these are real IP addresses, but they only work on this local network. They are not routable on the Internet.

  All site/network-local IP addresses begin with FE and have C to F for the third hexadecimal digit: FEC, FED, FEE, or FEF.

- DHCPv6 uses the Managed Address Configuration Flag (M flag).

  When set to 1, the device should use DHCPV6 to obtain a stateful IPv6 address.

- Other stateful configuration flag (O flag).

   When set to 1, the device should use DHCPv6 to obtain other TCP/IP configuration settings. In other words, it should use the DHCP server to set things like the IP address of the gateway and DNS servers.

- M flag

   This indicates that the machine should use DHCPv6 to retrieve an IP address.

This is the essence of IPv6. You still have all the same utilities you used with IPv4. However, there is a number 6 after the `ping` or `traceroute`, so if your computer has IPv6 enabled, you can use the following:

```
ping6 www.yahoo.com
```

We will be discussing `ping`, `traceroute`, and other commands later in this chapter.

## Uniform Resource Locators

After you connect to your ISP, you will, of course, want to visit some websites. You probably type names, rather than IP addresses, into your browser's address bar. For example, you might type in www.chuckeasttom.com to go to my website. Your computer, or your ISP, must translate the name you typed in (called a *uniform resource locator [URL]*) into an IP address. The DNS protocol, mentioned in Table 2.3, handles this translation process. So you are typing in a name that makes sense to humans, but your computer is using a corresponding IP address to connect. If that address is found, your browser sends a packet (using the HTTP protocol) to port 80. If that target computer has software that listens and responds to such requests (like web server software such as Apache or Microsoft Internet Information Server), then the target computer will respond to your browser's request and communication will be established. This method is how web pages are viewed.

If you have ever received an Error 404: File Not Found, what you are seeing is that your browser received back a packet (from the web server) with error code 404, denoting that the page you requested could not be found. There are a series of error messages that the web server can send back to your web browser, indicating different situations. Many of these problems the browser handles itself, and you never see the error message. All error messages in the 400 series are *client errors*. This term means something is wrong on your side, not the web server. Messages in the 500 series are *server errors*, which means there is a problem on the web server. The 100 series messages are simply informational; 200 series messages indicate success (you usually do not see these, the browser simply processes them); and 300 series messages are redirectional, meaning the page you are seeking has moved and your browser is then directed to the new location.

Email works the same way as visiting websites. Your email client will seek out the address of your email server. Then your email client will use either the POP3 protocol to retrieve your incoming email or the SMTP protocol to send your outgoing email. Your email server (probably at your ISP or your company) will then try to resolve the address you are sending to. If you send something to chuck@chuckeasttom.com, your email server will translate that email address into an IP address for the email server at yahoo.com, and your server will send your email there. Note that there are newer email protocols available, but POP3 is still the most commonly used.

Many readers are probably familiar with chat rooms. A chat room, like the other methods of communication we have discussed, works with packets. You first find the address of the chat room; then you connect. The difference here is that your computer's chat software is constantly sending packets back and forth, unlike email, which only sends and receives when you tell it to (or on a predetermined time interval).

Remember that a packet has a header section and that header section contains your IP address and the destination IP address that you are going to (as well as other information). This packet structure will become important as we proceed through this book.

## What Is a Packet?

We have mentioned network packets and how they are routed through a network and through the Internet. What we have not discussed is exactly what a packet is. You probably know that network traffic is really a lot of 1s and 0s that are in turn transmitted as voltages (over UTP), light wave (over optic cable), or radio frequencies (over Wi-Fi). The data is divided into small chunks called *packets*.

Packets are divided into three sections. Those are header (actually there are at least three headers, but we will get to that in just a moment), data, and footer. The header will contain information about how to address the packet, what kind of packet it is, and related data. The data portion is obviously the information you want to send. The footer serves both to show where the packet ends and to provide error detection.

As we mentioned, there are usually at least three headers. In normal communications there is usually an Ethernet header, a TCP header, and an IP header. Each contains different information. Combined they have several pieces of information that will be interesting for forensic investigations.

Let's begin with the TCP header. It contains information related to the transport layer of the OSI model. (We will be discussing the OSI model later in this chapter.) It will contain the source and destination port for communications. It will also have the packet number, such as packet 10 of 21.

There is also an IP header. The most obvious useful information are source and destination addresses. The IP header has the source IP address, the destination IP address and the protocol. The IP header also has version number, showing if this is a version 4.0 or 6.0 IP packet. The size variable describes how large the data segment is. There is also information regarding the protocol this packet represents.

The Ethernet header contains information regarding the source MAC address and destination MAC address. When a packet gets to the last network segment in its journey, it is the MAC address that is used to find the NIC that the packet is being sent to.

## Basic Communications

The packet headers described in the last section also contain some signal bits. These are single bit flags that are turned on to indicate some type of communication. A normal network conversation starts with one side sending a packet with the SYN (SYNchronize) bit turned on. The target responds with both SYN and ACK (ACKnowledge) bits turned on. Then the sender responds with just the ACK bit turned on, and communication commences. After a time, the original sender terminates the communication by sending a packet with the FIN (FINish) bit turned on.

There are some attacks that depend on sending malformed packets. For example, the common denial of service (DoS) attack, the SYN flood is based on flooding the target with SYN packets but never responding to the SYN/ACK that is sent back. Some session hijacking attacks use the RST command to help hijack communications.

# History of the Internet

At this point, you should have a basic understanding of how networks and the Internet work, as well as some familiarity with IP addresses, protocols, and packets. It is also helpful to know the history of the Internet, as many find that this overview helps put all of the material learned thus far into historical perspective.

The Internet traces its roots to the Cold War. One positive thing that can be said about the Cold War is that it was a time of significant investment in science and technology. In 1957, after the Soviet Union launched the Sputnik satellite, the U.S. government formed the Advanced Research Projects Agency (ARPA) within the Defense Department. ARPA's sole purpose was to fund and facilitate research into technology. Obviously, this aim would include weapons technology, but the total focus would also include communications technology.

In 1962, a study by the Rand Corporation proposed devising a communication method wherein data was sent in packets between locations. If a packet was lost, the originator of the message would automatically resend the message. This idea was a precursor to the Internet communication methodologies that would eventually arise.

In 1968, ARPA commissioned the construction of ARPANET, a simple Internet web of four points (called *nodes*): UCLA, Stanford, UC Berkley, and the University of Utah. Although no one knew it at the time, this small web was the birth of what would become the Internet. At this point, ARPANET had only these four nodes connected.

The year 1972 was a milestone for the development of the Internet, in more than one sense. That year ARPA was renamed DARPA, the Defense Advanced Research Projects Agency. Also that year, Ray Tomlinson invented the first email program. At this point, four years after the birth of ARPANET, there were 23 hosts on the network. (A *host* is a machine with data on it, to which you can connect; for example, a web server is a host.)

The following year, 1973, would mark the birth of the TCP/IP protocol, which allowed the various computers to communicate in a uniform fashion, regardless of their hardware or operating system.

In 1974, Vince Cerf published a paper on the TCP protocol, and for the first time in computer history used the term *Internet*. In 1976, Ethernet cable was developed (the same cabling we use today), and DARPA began to require the use of TCP/IP protocol on its network. This year also marked the beginning of widespread distribution of the UNIX operating system. The development of UNIX and the Internet would go hand in hand for many years to come. By this time, 8 years after the birth of ARPANET, there were 111 hosts on the network.

In 1979, a major development occurred: the birth of Usenet newsgroups. These groups are essentially bulletin boards open to the entire world. (Today you can access these groups via newsgroup reader software or via the Web by navigating to www.google.com and selecting Groups. There are thousands of newsgroups devoted to every topic imaginable.) Just 2 years later, the National Science Foundation (NSF) created CSNET for universities and research centers that were not part of ARPANET. That same year, Cerf proposed connecting CSNET and ARPANET. By 1981, the University of Wisconsin had created DNS (Domain Name Service) so that people could find nodes on the network via a name rather than the actual IP address. At this point (1981), there were 562 hosts on the network.

The early 1980s saw enormous growth in the early Internet. DARPA divided its ARPANET into military and nonmilitary segments, thus allowing more people to use the nonmilitary segment. And the NSF introduced the T1 line (a very fast connection). In 1986, the Internet Engineering Task Force (IETF) was formed to oversee the creation of standards for the Internet and Internet protocols. By this time, the Internet consisted of 2,308 hosts.

A pivotal year for Internet development turned out to be 1990. That year, Tim Berners-Lee, working at CERN laboratories in Europe, developed the *Hypertext Transfer Protocol (HTTP)* and gave the world its very first web pages. Via the HTTP protocol and the *Hypertext Markup Language (HTML)*, people could publish ideas on the Internet for anyone (with a connection) to view. By 1990, there were over 300,000 hosts on the Internet. (Fast-forward to 2004; Tim Berners-Lee receives the first Millennium Prize for contributions to technology. He is widely regarded as the father of the *World Wide Web [WWW]*.)

Internet growth and activity exploded in the 1990s. In 1992, CERN released the invention of web pages to the world at large. In 1993, the first graphical web browser, named Mosaic, was invented. By 1994, Pizza Hut began taking orders via web pages. The Internet has continued to grow; today, there are millions of websites around the world. Every organization has a site, from university departments, government agencies, corporations, schools, and religions to nearly any group you can imagine. Many individuals have personal websites as well. Lots of you will use the Web for banking, shopping, information, and entertainment. Additionally, you likely use email on a daily basis. (By the way, I primarily use email for communication, so that is the best way to contact me if you wish: chuck@chuckeasttom.com.) The Internet has become a virtual "living level" of interaction in our society. What company does not have a website? What movie release does not have a website? What political candidate does not have a website? In just over three decades, the Internet has become an integral part of our society.

# Basic Network Utilities

Later in this book, you will use information and techniques that are based, in part, on certain techniques anyone can perform on her own machine. There are network utilities that you can execute from a command prompt (Windows) or from a shell (UNIX/Linux). Many readers are already familiar with

Windows, so the text's discussion will execute the commands and discuss them from the Windows command prompt perspective. However, it must be stressed that these utilities are available in all operating systems. In this section, you will read about IPConfig, ping, and tracert utilities.

## IPConfig

The first step in studying networks is to get information about your own system. To accomplish this fact-finding mission, you will need to get to a command prompt. In Windows XP, go to the Start menu, select All Programs (in Windows Vista or 7), and then choose Accessories. You will then see an option called Command Prompt. (For Windows 2000 users, the process is identical, except the first option is simply called Programs rather than All Programs.) Next, type in ipconfig. (You could input the same command in UNIX or Linux by typing in ifconfig once inside the shell.) After typing ipconfig and pressing the Enter key, you should see something much like what is shown in Figure 2.1.

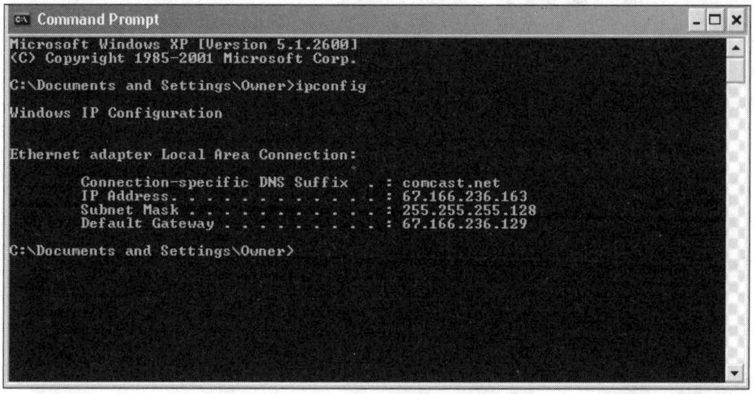

```
Command Prompt                                          _ □ x
Microsoft Windows XP [Version 5.1.2600]
(C) Copyright 1985-2001 Microsoft Corp.

C:\Documents and Settings\Owner>ipconfig

Windows IP Configuration

Ethernet adapter Local Area Connection:

        Connection-specific DNS Suffix  . : comcast.net
        IP Address. . . . . . . . . . . . : 67.166.236.163
        Subnet Mask . . . . . . . . . . . : 255.255.255.128
        Default Gateway . . . . . . . . . : 67.166.236.129

C:\Documents and Settings\Owner>
```

**FIGURE 2.1**   IPConfig.

This command gives you some information about your connection to a network (or to the Internet). Most importantly, you find out your own IP address. The command also has the IP address for your default gateway, which is your connection to the outside world. Running the IPConfig command is a first step in determining your system's network configuration. Most commands that this book will mention, including IPConfig, have a number of parameters, or flags, that can be passed to the commands to make the computer behave in a certain way. You can find out what these commands are by typing in the command, followed by a space, and then typing in hyphen question mark, -?. Figure 2.2 shows the results of this method for the IPConfig command.

As you can see in Figure 2.2, there a number of options you might use to find out different details about your computer's configuration. The most commonly used method would probably be the IPConfig/all, shown in Figure 2.3. You can see that this option gives you much more information. For example, IPConfig/all gives the name of your computer, when your computer obtained its IP address, and more.

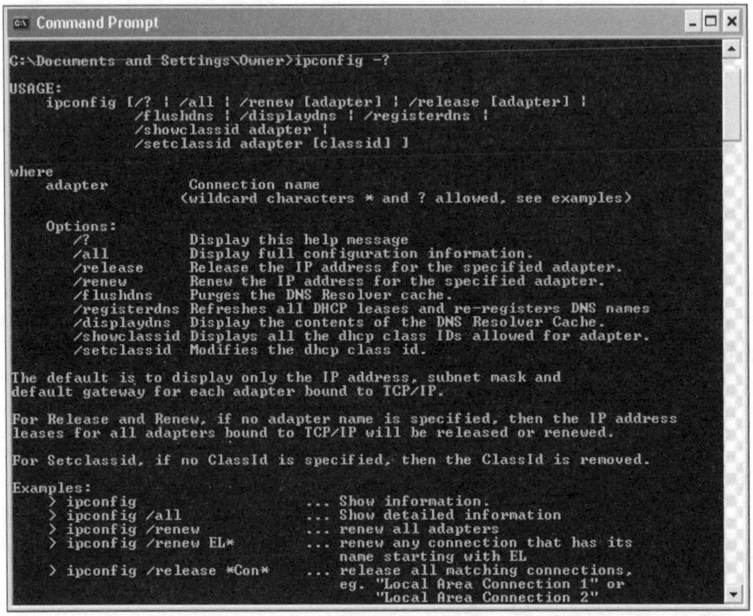

FIGURE 2.2   IPConfig help.

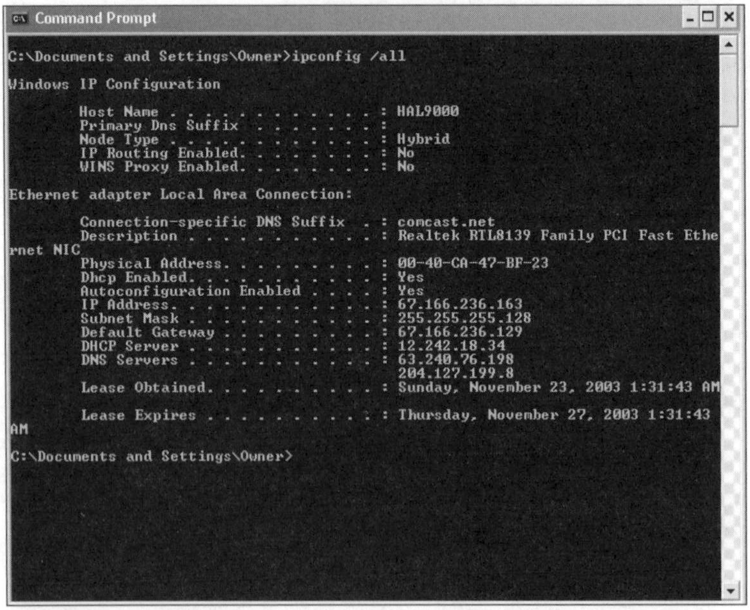

FIGURE 2.3   IPConfig/all.

## Ping

Another commonly used command is `ping`. `ping` is used to send a test packet, or echo packet, to a machine to find out if the machine is reachable and how long the packet takes to reach the machine. This useful diagnostic tool can be employed in elementary hacking techniques. In Figure 2.4 you see a `ping` command executed on www.yahoo.com.

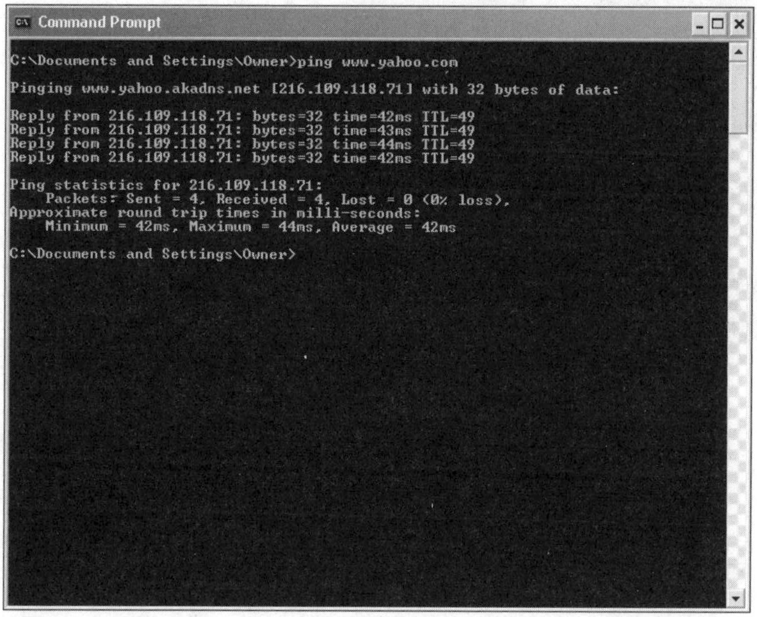

```
Command Prompt                                              _ □ ×

C:\Documents and Settings\Owner>ping www.yahoo.com

Pinging www.yahoo.akadns.net [216.109.118.71] with 32 bytes of data:

Reply from 216.109.118.71: bytes=32 time=42ms ITL=49
Reply from 216.109.118.71: bytes=32 time=43ms ITL=49
Reply from 216.109.118.71: bytes=32 time=44ms ITL=49
Reply from 216.109.118.71: bytes=32 time=42ms ITL=49

Ping statistics for 216.109.118.71:
    Packets: Sent = 4, Received = 4, Lost = 0 (0% loss),
Approximate round trip times in milli-seconds:
    Minimum = 42ms, Maximum = 44ms, Average = 42ms

C:\Documents and Settings\Owner>
```

FIGURE 2.4  Ping.

This figure tells you that a 32-byte echo packet was sent to the destination and returned. The TTL (Time To Live) item shows how many intermediary steps, or hops, the packet should take to the destination before giving up. Remember that the Internet is a vast conglomerate of interconnected networks. Your packet probably won't go straight to its destination; it will take several hops to get there. As with `IPConfig`, you can type in `ping -?` to find out various ways you can refine your ping.

## Tracert

The final command we will examine in this chapter is the `tracert` command. This command is a more or less "ping deluxe." `tracert` not only tells you if the packet got to its destination and how long it took, but also tells you all the intermediate hops it took to get there. This utility will prove very useful to you later in this book. Figure 2.5 illustrates a `tracert` to www.yahoo.com. (This same command can be executed in Linux or UNIX, but there it is called `traceroute` rather than `tracert`.)

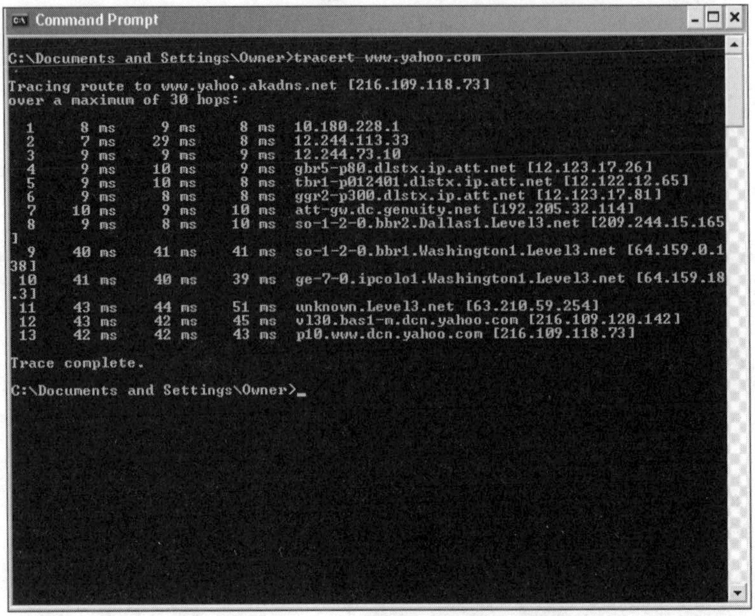

```
Command Prompt                                                    _ □ ×

C:\Documents and Settings\Owner>tracert www.yahoo.com

Tracing route to www.yahoo.akadns.net [216.109.118.73]
over a maximum of 30 hops:

  1     8 ms     9 ms     8 ms   10.180.228.1
  2     7 ms    29 ms     8 ms   12.244.113.33
  3     9 ms     9 ms     9 ms   12.244.73.10
  4     9 ms    10 ms     9 ms   gbr5-p80.dlstx.ip.att.net [12.123.17.26]
  5     9 ms    10 ms     8 ms   tbr1-p012401.dlstx.ip.att.net [12.122.12.65]
  6     9 ms     8 ms     8 ms   ggr2-p300.dlstx.ip.att.net [12.123.17.81]
  7    10 ms     9 ms    10 ms   att-gw.dc.genuity.net [192.205.32.114]
  8     9 ms     8 ms    10 ms   so-1-2-0.bbr2.Dallas1.Level3.net [209.244.15.165
]
  9    40 ms    41 ms    41 ms   so-1-2-0.bbr1.Washington1.Level3.net [64.159.0.1
38]
 10    41 ms    40 ms    39 ms   ge-7-0.ipcolo1.Washington1.Level3.net [64.159.18
.3]
 11    43 ms    44 ms    51 ms   unknown.Level3.net [63.210.59.254]
 12    43 ms    42 ms    45 ms   v130.bas1-m.dcn.yahoo.com [216.109.120.142]
 13    42 ms    42 ms    43 ms   p10.www.dcn.yahoo.com [216.109.118.73]

Trace complete.

C:\Documents and Settings\Owner>_
```

**FIGURE 2.5**    Tracert.

With `tracert`, you can see (in milliseconds) the IP addresses of each intermediate step listed and how long it took to get to that step. Knowing the steps required to reach a destination can be very important, as you will find later in this book.

Certainly there are other utilities that can be of use to you when working with network communications. However, the three we just examined are the core utilities. These three (`IPConfig`, `ping`, and `tracert`) are absolutely essential to any network administrator, and you should commit them to memory.

## Netstat

`Netstat` is another interesting command. It is an abbreviation for Network Status. Essentially this command tells you what connections your computer currently has. Don't panic if you see several connections; that does not mean a hacker is in your computer. You will see many private IP addresses. This means your network has internal communication going on. You can see this in Figure 2.6.

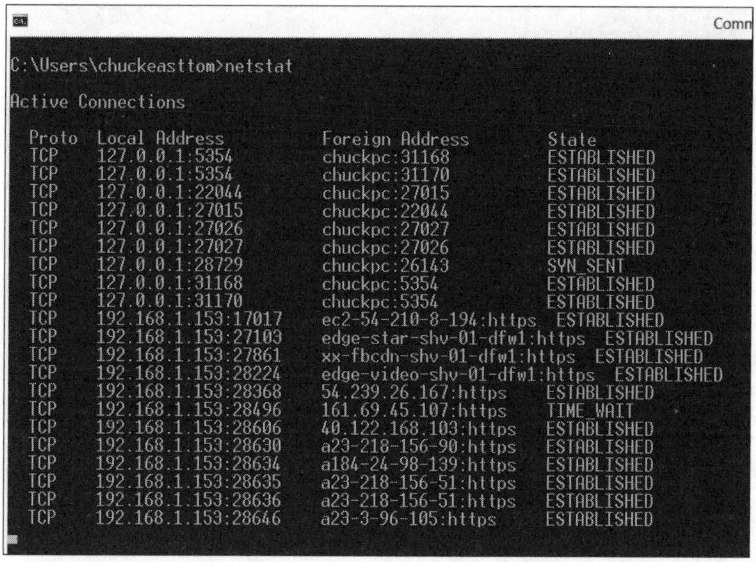

```
C:\Users\chuckeasttom>netstat

Active Connections

  Proto  Local Address          Foreign Address        State
  TCP    127.0.0.1:5354         chuckpc:31168          ESTABLISHED
  TCP    127.0.0.1:5354         chuckpc:31170          ESTABLISHED
  TCP    127.0.0.1:22044        chuckpc:27015          ESTABLISHED
  TCP    127.0.0.1:27015        chuckpc:22044          ESTABLISHED
  TCP    127.0.0.1:27026        chuckpc:27027          ESTABLISHED
  TCP    127.0.0.1:27027        chuckpc:27026          ESTABLISHED
  TCP    127.0.0.1:28729        chuckpc:26143          SYN_SENT
  TCP    127.0.0.1:31168        chuckpc:5354           ESTABLISHED
  TCP    127.0.0.1:31170        chuckpc:5354           ESTABLISHED
  TCP    192.168.1.153:17017    ec2-54-210-8-194:https  ESTABLISHED
  TCP    192.168.1.153:27103    edge-star-shv-01-dfw1:https  ESTABLISHED
  TCP    192.168.1.153:27861    xx-fbcdn-shv-01-dfw1:https   ESTABLISHED
  TCP    192.168.1.153:28224    edge-video-shv-01-dfw1:https ESTABLISHED
  TCP    192.168.1.153:28368    54.239.26.167:https    ESTABLISHED
  TCP    192.168.1.153:28496    161.69.45.107:https    TIME_WAIT
  TCP    192.168.1.153:28606    40.122.168.103:https   ESTABLISHED
  TCP    192.168.1.153:28630    a23-218-156-90:https   ESTABLISHED
  TCP    192.168.1.153:28634    a184-24-98-139:https   ESTABLISHED
  TCP    192.168.1.153:28635    a23-218-156-51:https   ESTABLISHED
  TCP    192.168.1.153:28636    a23-218-156-51:https   ESTABLISHED
  TCP    192.168.1.153:28646    a23-3-96-105:https     ESTABLISHED
```

FIGURE 2.6   Netstat.

## NSLookup

This command is an abbreviation for Name Server lookup. It is used to connect with your network's DNS server. Often it can be used just to verify the DNS server is running. It can also be used to execute commands. Recall from Chapter 1, "Introduction to Computer Security," that we discussed DNS poisoning. One of the first steps in DNS poisoning is to see if the target DNS server will perform a zone transfer. (It should not do so with any machine other than another DNS server that is authenticated in the domain.) That can be attempted with nslookup, as shown here:

```
run: nslookup
type: ls -d domain_name <enter>
```

You can see the basic nslookup command in Figure 2.7.

```
C:\Users\chuckeasttom>nslookup
Default Server:  FIOS_Quantum_Gateway.fios-router.home
Address:  192.168.1.1
>
```

FIGURE 2.7   nslookup.

# Other Network Devices

There are other devices involved in networking that work to protect your computer from the outside world, some of which were briefly mentioned in Chapter 1. Now we will review a couple of them in a bit more detail. The two most common are the firewall and the proxy server. A *firewall* is essentially a barrier between your network and the rest of the Internet. A personal computer (PC) can be used as a firewall; in many cases, a special router can function as a firewall. Firewalls use different techniques to protect your network, but the most common strategy is packet filtering. In a packet-filtering firewall, each incoming packet is examined. Only those packets that match the criteria you set are allowed through. (Commonly, only packets using certain types of protocols are allowed through.) Many operating systems, such as Windows (all versions since XP) and many Linux distributions, include basic packet-filtering software.

The second very common type of defensive device is a *proxy server*. A proxy server will almost always be another computer. You might see the same machine used as both a proxy server and a firewall. A proxy server's purpose is quite simple: It hides your entire network from the outside world. People trying to investigate your network from the outside will see only the proxy server. They will not see the actual machines on your network. When packets go out of your network, their headers are changed so that the packets have the return address of the proxy server. Conversely, the only way you can access the outside world is via the proxy server. A proxy server combined with a firewall is basic network security. It would frankly be negligent to ever run a network that did not have a firewall and proxy server. We examine firewalls in more detail in Chapter 9.

# Advanced Network Communications Topics

These subjects are not absolutely required for you to understand this book, but they will give you a broader understanding of networks in general. If you have any intention of delving into network security on a professional level, then you will need this information—and much more.

## The OSI Model

Let's begin with the *OSI model*, or Open Systems Interconnection model. This model is a description of how networks communicate. It describes the various protocols and activities, and it tells how the protocols and activities relate to each other. This model is divided into seven layers, as shown in Table 2.5, and was originally developed by the International Standards Organization (ISO) in the 1980s.

**TABLE 2.5**  The OSI Model

| Layer Number | Layer | Description | Protocols |
|---|---|---|---|
| 7 | Application | This layer interfaces directly to the application and performs common application services for the application processes. | POP, SMTP, DNS, FTP, and so on |
| 6 | Presentation | The presentation layer relieves the application layer of concern regarding syntactical differences in data representation within the end-user systems. | |
| 5 | Session | The session layer provides the mechanism for managing the dialogue between end-user application processes. | NetBIOS |
| 4 | Transport | This layer provides end-to-end communication control. | TCP, UDP |
| 3 | Network | This layer routes the information in the network. | IP, Address Resolution Protocol, Internet Control Message Protocol |
| 2 | Data Link | This layer describes the logical organization of data bits transmitted on a particular medium. Data link is divided into two sublayers: the Media Access Control layer (MAC) and the Logical Link Control layer (LLC). | Serial Line Internet Protocol, Point-to-Point Protocol |
| 1 | Physical | This layer describes the physical properties of the various communications media, as well as the electrical properties and interpretation of the exchanged signals. In other words, the physical layer is the actual NIC, Ethernet cable, and so forth. This layer is where bits are translated into voltages, and vice versa. | None |

Many networking students memorize this model. It's good to at least memorize the names of the seven layers and to understand basically what they each do. From a security perspective, the more you understand about network communications, the more sophisticated your defense can be. The most important thing for you to understand is that this model describes a hierarchy of communication. One layer will only communicate with the layer directly above it or below it.

## Media Access Control (MAC) Addresses

*MAC addresses* are unique addresses for a NIC. (MAC is also a sublayer of the data link layer of the OSI model.) Every NIC in the world has a unique address that is represented by a 6-byte hexadecimal number, and an Address Resolution Protocol (ARP) is used to convert IP addresses to MAC addresses.

When you type in a web address, the DNS protocol is used to translate that into an IP address; then the ARP protocol will translate that IP address into a specific MAC address of an individual NIC.

This brings us to how DNS is accomplished; or rather, how does a URL get translated into an IP address? How does the computer know what IP goes with what URL? There are servers known as DNS servers that are set up just to do this task. If you are on a corporate network, you probably have a DNS server on your network. If you are not, then your ISP has one. These servers maintain a table of IP-to-URL entries. From time to time there are transfers of DNS data, called *zone transfers*, that allow one DNS server to send its changes to another. Across the Internet, there are root DNS servers that are maintained with centralized data for all registered URL/IP addresses.

# Summary

This chapter cannot make you a networking expert. However, you should now have a basic under-standing of how networks and the Internet work. Before you move on to subsequent chapters, you should make certain you completely understand basic hardware like switches, NICs, routers, and hubs. You should also be familiar with the basic protocols presented in this chapter. It is important that you be comfortable with the utilities presented. It is strongly suggested that you experiment with these utilities extensively. It is also important that you be comfortable with the basics of the OSI model. Many students struggle with it at first, but at least make sure you have a general understanding of it before you move on to Chapter 3, "Cyber Stalking, Fraud, and Abuse."

This material will be critical in later chapters. If you are new to this material, you should thoroughly study this chapter before continuing. In the exercises at the end of this chapter, you will be able to practice using IPConfig, tracert, and ping.

## Test Your Skills

## MULTIPLE CHOICE QUESTIONS

1. What type of cable do most networks use?

   A. Net cable

   B. Category 3 cable

   C. Phone cable

   D. Category 5 cable

2. The connector used with network cables is called what?

   A. RJ-11

   B. RJ-85

   C. RJ-12

   D. RJ-45

3. The cable used in networks is also referred to as what?

   A. Unshielded twisted-pair

   B. Shielded twisted-pair

   C. Unshielded untwisted-pair

   D. Shielded untwisted-pair

4. The simplest device for connecting computers is called what?

    **A.** NIC

    **B.** Interface

    **C.** Hub

    **D.** Router

5. What is a NIC?

    **A.** Network interface card

    **B.** Network interaction card

    **C.** Network interface connector

    **D.** Network interaction connector

6. A device used to connect two or more networks is a what?

    **A.** Switch

    **B.** Router

    **C.** Hub

    **D.** NIC

7. A T1 line sends data at what speed?

    **A.** 100Mbps

    **B.** 1.54Mbps

    **C.** 155Mbps

    **D.** 56.6Kbps

8. How big is a TCP packet header?

    **A.** The size is dependent on the data being sent.

    **B.** The size is always 20 bytes.

    **C.** The size is dependent on the protocol being used.

    **D.** The size is always 40 bytes.

9. A protocol that translates web addresses into IP addresses is called what?

    **A.** DNS

    **B.** TFTP

    **C.** DHCP

    **D.** SMTP

**10.** What protocol is used to send email, and on what port does it work?

    **A.** SMTP, port 110

    **B.** POP3, port 25

    **C.** SMTP, port 25

    **D.** POP3, port 110

**11.** What protocol is used for remotely logging on to a computer?

    **A.** Telnet

    **B.** HTTP

    **C.** DNS

    **D.** SMTP

**12.** What protocol is used for web pages, and what port does it work on?

    **A.** HTTP, port 21

    **B.** HTTP, port 80

    **C.** DHCP, port 80

    **D.** DHCP, port 21

**13.** The point where the backbones of the Internet connect is called what?

    **A.** Connectors

    **B.** Routers

    **C.** Network access points

    **D.** Switches

**14.** Which of the following is not a valid IP address?

    **A.** 127.0.0.1

    **B.** 295.253.254.01

    **C.** 127.256.5.2

    **D.** 245.200.11.1

**15.** What class would the IP address of 193.44.34.12 be?

    **A.** A

    **B.** B

    **C.** C

    **D.** D

16. The IP address of 127.0.0.1 always refers to your what?

    A. Nearest router

    B. ISP

    C. Self

    D. Nearest NAP

17. Internet addresses of the form www.chuckeasttom.com are called what?

    A. User-friendly web addresses

    B. Uniform resource locators

    C. User-accessible web addresses

    D. Uniform address identifiers

18. Which U.S. government agency created the distributed network that formed the basis for the Internet?

    A. Advanced Research Projects Agency

    B. Central Intelligence Agency

    C. NASA

    D. Department of Energy

19. Which of the following was one of the three universities involved in the original distributed network setup by a government agency?

    A. Berkeley

    B. Harvard

    C. MIT

    D. Princeton

20. Vince Cerf invented what?

    A. The World Wide Web

    B. Email

    C. TCP

    D. The first computer virus

21. Tim Berners-Lee invented what?

    A. The World Wide Web

    B. Email

    C. TCP

    D. The first computer virus

22. Which utility gives you information about your machine's network configuration?

 A. Ping

 B. IPConfig

 C. Tracert

 D. MyConfig

23. The TCP protocol operates at what layer of the OSI model?

 A. Transport

 B. Application

 C. Network

 D. Data link

24. Which layer of the OSI model is divided into two sublayers?

 A. Data link

 B. Network

 C. Presentation

 D. Session

25. A unique hexadecimal number that identifies your network card is called what?

 A. A NIC address

 B. A MAC address

 C. A NIC ID

 D. A MAC ID

## EXERCISES

### EXERCISE 2.1: Using IPConfig

1. Open your command prompt or DOS prompt. (Go to Start > All Programs > Accessories > Command Prompt [DOS prompt in Windows 98].)

2. Type in `ipconfig`.

3. Use the `IPConfig` command to find out information about your computer.

4. Write down your computer's IP address, default gateway, and subnet mask.

## EXERCISE 2.2: **Using Tracert**

1.  Open your command prompt or DOS prompt.

2.  Type in `tracert www.chuckeasttom.com`.

3.  Note what hops your computer takes to get to www.chuckeasttom.com.

4.  Then try the same process with `www.whitehouse.gov` and `http://home.pearsonhighered.com/`.

5.  Notice that the first few hops are the same. Write down what hops are taken to reach each destination and what hops are the same. Then briefly describe why you think some of the intermediate steps are the same for different destinations.

## EXERCISE 2.3: **NSLOOKUP**

The command `NSLOOKUP` is not mentioned in this chapter. But if you are comfortable with `ping`, `tracert`, and `IPConfig`, this command will be easy to learn.

1.  Go to the command prompt

2.  Type `nslookup www.chuckeasttom.com`.

3.  Note that this command gives you the actual name of the server, as per the hosting company's naming conventions; its IP address; and any aliases under which that server operates.

## EXERCISE 2.4: **More About IPConfig**

1.  Open your command prompt or DOS prompt.

2.  Use the `-?` flag on the `IPConfig` command to find out what other options you have with these commands. You should notice a number of options, including `/all`, `/renew`, and others.

3.  Now try `ipconfig /all`. What do you see now that you didn't see when you simply used `ipconfig` in Exercise 1?

## EXERCISE 2.5: **More About Ping**

1.  Open your command prompt or DOS prompt.

2.  Use the `-?` flag on the `ping` command and find out what other options you have with these commands. You should notice several additional options, such as `-w`, `-t`, `-n`, and `-i`.

3.  Try a simple ping of `www.chuckeasttom.com`.

4.  Try the option `ping -n 2 www.chuckeasttom.com`. Then try `ping -n 7 www.chuckeasttom.com`. What differences do you notice?

## PROJECTS

### PROJECT 2.1: **Learning About DNS**

1. Using web resources, look up the DNS protocol. You may find the following website to be of help:

   www.freesoft.org/CIE/Topics/75.htm

2. Look up these facts: Who invented this protocol? What is its purpose? How is it used?

3. Write a brief paper describing what the protocol does. Mention a bit about who invented it, when, and how it works.

### PROJECT 2.2: **Learning About Your System**

1. Find out if your organization (for example, your school or business) uses switches, hubs, or both. Why does your group use these? You can find out by simply asking the network administrator or the help desk. Make sure you tell them that you are seeking this information for a class project.

2. Write a brief paper explaining your findings and any changes you would make if you could. For example, if your organization uses only hubs, would you change that method? If so, why?

### PROJECT 2.3: **Learning About NetStat**

1. At the command prompt, type `netstat`. Notice the information it provides you. You should be seeing any IP addresses or server names that are currently connected to your computer. If you are using a home computer, you will need to log on to your Internet service provider to see anything.

---

**CAUTION**

### Stopping NetStat

Note that with many versions of Windows, for the next steps you will need to use the Ctrl-Break key combination to stop `netstat` before starting it again with a new option.

---

- Now type in `netstat -?` to see options with this command. You should see –a, –e, and others.

- Now type in `netstat -a` and note the information you see.

- Finally, try `netstat -e`. What do you see now?

## Chapter 3

# Cyber Stalking, Fraud, and Abuse

## *Chapter Objectives*

**After reading this chapter and completing the exercises, you will be able to do the following:**

- Know the various types of Internet investment scams and auction frauds
- Know specific steps one can take to avoid fraud on the Internet
- Have an understanding of what identity theft is and how it is done
- Know specific steps that can be taken to avoid identity theft
- Understand what cyber stalking is, and be familiar with relevant laws
- Know how to configure a web browser's privacy settings
- Know what laws apply to these computer crimes

## Introduction

In every new frontier, a criminal element is bound to emerge. In times past, the high seas gave rise to pirates, and America's wild west produced gangs of outlaws. The Internet is no different than any other frontier; it has its share of outlaws. Besides hacking and virus creation, both mentioned in Chapter 1, "Introduction to Computer Security," there are other dangers. Fraud is one of the most common dangers of the Internet. As more people utilize the Internet as a conduit for commerce, there arises a greater opportunity for fraud. Fraud has been a part of life for as long as civilization has existed; in past centuries "snake oil" salesmen roamed the country selling face cures and elixirs. The Internet makes such fraud even easier. In fact, many experts would consider fraud to be the most prevalent danger on the Internet. There are multiple reasons for the popularity of Internet fraud among con artists. First, committing an Internet fraud does not require the technical expertise that hacking and virus creation require. Second, there are a great number of people engaging in various forms of online commerce, and this large amount of business creates a great many opportunities for fraud.

There are many avenues for fraud on the Internet. In this chapter, we will explore what the various major types of fraud are, what the law says, and what you can do to protect yourself. Fortunately for some readers, this particular chapter is not particularly technical because most Internet fraud does not rely on in-depth technological expertise. Internet fraud merely uses the computer as a venue for many of the same fraud schemes that have been perpetrated throughout history.

# How Internet Fraud Works

There are a variety of ways that a fraud can be perpetrated via the Internet. The Securities and Exchange Commission lists several types of Internet fraud on their website;[1] we will briefly discuss each of those and others, but it is not possible for us to cover every variation of each fraud scheme that has been used on the Internet. Such an undertaking would fill not only an entire book, but also possibly several volumes. What we can do is to cover the more common scams and try to extrapolate some general principles that you can apply to any potential fraud. If you use these specific cases to extrapolate some general principles, then you should be prepared to avoid most fraud schemes.

## Investment Offers

Investment offers are nothing new. Even some legitimate stockbrokers make their living by cold calling, the process of simply calling people (perhaps from the phone book) and trying to get them to invest in a specific stock. This practice is employed by some legitimate firms, but it is also a favorite con game for perpetrators of fraud. The Internet has allowed investment offers—both genuine and fraudulent—to be more easily disseminated to the general public. Most readers are probably familiar with investment offers flooding their inbox on a daily basis. Some of these email notifications entice you to become directly involved with a particular investment plan; other emails offer seemingly unbiased information from investors, free of charge. (Unfortunately, much of this advice is not as unbiased as it might appear to be.) While legitimate online newsletters can help investors gather valuable information, keep in mind that some online newsletters are fraudulent.

### Common Schemes

One of the more common schemes involves sending out an email that suggests that you can make an outrageous sum of money with a very minimal investment. Perhaps the most famous of these schemes has been the Nigerian fraud. In this scenario, an email is sent to a number of random email addresses. Each one contains a message purporting to be from a relative of some deceased Nigerian doctor or government official. The deceased person will be someone you would associate with significant social standing, thus increasing the likelihood that you would view the offer more favorably. The offer goes like this: A person has a sum of money he wishes to transfer out of his country, and for security reasons, he cannot use normal channels. He wishes to use your bank account to "park" the funds

---

1. The U.S. Securities and Exchange Commission. "Internet Fraud: How to Avoid Internet Investment Scams." Washington, D.C.: Author, November 15, 2001. Accessed April 2011: www.sec.gov/investor/pubs/cyberfraud.htm

temporarily. If you will allow him access to your account, you will receive a hefty fee. If you do agree to this arrangement, you will receive, via normal mail, a variety of very official-looking documents, enough to convince most casual observers that the arrangement is legitimate. You will then be asked to advance some money to cover items such as taxes and wire fees. Should you actually send any money, you will have lost the money you advanced and you will never hear from these individuals again. The U.S. Secret Service has a bulletin issued detailing this particular fraud scheme.[2]

Now consider this investment scam, and variations of it, from a logical point of view. If you had large sums of money you needed to transfer, would you send it to a person in a foreign country, someone you had never met? Wouldn't you be worried that the recipient would cash out her account and take the next plane to Rio? If a person needs to transfer money internationally, why doesn't he just transfer the money to an account in the Bahamas? Or cash out the account and send it via Federal Express or United Parcel Service to a storage facility in the United States? The point is that there are many ways a person could get money out of a country without trusting some stranger he has never seen before. That fact alone should indicate to you that this offer is simply not legitimate. This concept is the first general principle you should derive concerning fraud. In any offer, consider the point of view of the person offering it. Does it sound as if he is taking an inordinately large risk? Does the deal seem oddly biased in your favor? Put yourself in his position. Would you engage in the deal if you were in his position? If not, then this factor is a sign that the deal might not be what it seems.

## Investment Advice

Such blatant fraud schemes are not the only investment pitfall on the Internet. Some companies pay the people who write online newsletters to recommend their stocks. While this activity isn't actually illegal, U.S. federal securities laws do require the newsletters to disclose that they were paid to proffer this advice. Such laws are in place because when the writers are recommending any product, their opinion might be swayed by the fact that compensation is being provided to them for that opinion. Many online investment newsletters do not disclose that they are actually being paid to recommend certain stocks. This situation means that the "unbiased" stock advice you are getting could actually be quite biased. Rather than getting the advice of an unbiased expert, you may be getting a paid advertisement. This pitfall is one of the most common traps of online investment advice, more common than the blatant frauds.

Sometimes these online stock bulletins can be part of a wider scheme, often called a *pump and dump*. A classic pump and dump is rather simple. The con artist takes a stock that is virtually worthless and purchases large amounts of it. The con artist then artificially inflates the value in several ways. One common method is to begin circulating rumors on various Internet bulletin boards and chat rooms that the stock is about to go up significantly. Often it is suggested by the trickster that the company has some new innovative product due to come out in the next few weeks. Another method is to simply push the stock on as many people as possible. The more people vying to buy a stock, the higher its price will rise. If both methods are combined, it is possible to take a worthless stock and temporarily double or

---

2. The U.S. Secret Service. "Public Awareness Advisory Regarding '4-1-9' or 'Advance Fee Fraud' Schemes." Washington, D.C.: Author, 2002. Accessed April 2011: www.lbl.gov/IT/CIS/CITG/email/419-Fraud.html

triple its value. The perpetrator of the fraud has already purchased volumes of the stock, at a very low price, before executing this scheme. When the stock goes as high as she thinks it can, she then dumps her stock and takes the money. In a short time, and certainly by the time the company's next quarterly earnings report is released, the stock returns to its real value. This sort of scheme has been very popular in the past several decades; thus, you should always be wary of such "insider" information. If a person is aware that Company X is about to release an innovative new product that will drive her stock value up, why would she share that information with total strangers?

The U.S. Securities and Exchange Commission lists several tips for avoiding such scams:[3]

- Consider the source. Especially if you are not well versed in the market, make sure you accept advice only from well-known and reputable stock analysts.

- Independently verify claims. Do not simply accept someone else's word about anything.

- Research. Read up on the company, the claims about the company, its stock history, and so forth.

- Beware of high-pressure tactics. Legitimate stock traders do not pressure customers into buying. They help customers pick stocks that customers want. If you are being pressured, that is an indication of potential problems.

- Be skeptical. A healthy dose of skepticism can save you a lot of money. Or, as the saying goes, "If it sounds too good to be true, it probably is"

- Make sure you thoroughly research any investment opportunity.

The truth is that these types of fraud depend on the greed of the victim. It is not my intent to blame victims of fraud, but it is important to realize that if you allow avarice to do your thinking for you, you are a prime candidate to be a victim of fraud. Your 401K or IRA may not earn you exorbitant wealth overnight, but it is steady and relatively safe. (No investment is completely safe.) If you are seeking ways to make large sums of money with minimal time and effort, then you are an ideal target for perpetrators of fraud.

### In Practice

Practically speaking, the recommended way to handle online investments is to only participate in them if you initiated the discussion with a reputable broker. This would mean you would never respond to or participate in any investment offer that was sent to you via email, online ads, and so on. You would only participate in investments that you initiated with well-known brokers. Usually such brokers are traditional investment firms with long-standing reputations that now simply offer their services online. It is also important to check out any broker with the Securities and Exchange Commission (SEC).

---

3. The U.S. Securities and Exchange Commission "Pump+Dump.con: Avoiding Stock Scams on the Internet." Washington, D.C.: Author, September 8, 2000. April 2011: www.sec.gov/investor/pubs/pump.htm

## Auction Frauds

Online auctions, such as eBay, can be a wonderful way to find merchandise at very good prices. I routinely use such auctions to purchase goods. However, any auction site can be fraught with peril. Will you actually get the merchandise you ordered? Will it be "as advertised"? Most online auctions are legitimate, and most auction websites take precautions to limit fraud on their website. But problems still occur. In fact, the U.S. Federal Trade Commission[4] (FTC) lists the following four categories of online auction fraud:

- Failure to send the merchandise
- Sending something of lesser value than advertised
- Failure to deliver in a timely manner
- Failure to disclose all relevant information about a product or terms of the sale

The first category, failure to deliver the merchandise, is the most clear-cut case of fraud and is fairly simple. Once you have paid for an item, no item arrives. The seller simply keeps your money. In organized fraud, the seller will simultaneously advertise several items for sale, collect money on all the auctions, and then disappear. If he has planned this well, the entire process was done with a fake identification, using a rented mailbox and anonymous email service. The person then walks away with the proceeds of the scam.

The second category of fraud, delivering an item of lesser value than the one advertised, can become a gray area. In some cases, it is outright fraud. The seller advertises something about the product that simply is not true. For example, the seller might advertise a signed copy of the first printing of a famous author's book but then instead ship you a fourth printing with either no autograph or one that is unverified. However, in other cases of this type of problem, it can simply be that the seller is over-zealous, or frankly mistaken. The seller might claim his baseball was signed by a famous athlete but not be aware himself that the autograph is a fraud.

The second category is closely related to the fourth item on the FTC list: failure to disclose all relevant facts about the item. For example, a book might be an authentic first printing and autographed but be in such poor physical condition as to render it worthless. This fact may or may not be mentioned in advance by the seller. Failure to be forthcoming with all the relevant facts about a particular item might be the result of outright fraud or simply of the seller's ignorance. The FTC also lists failure to deliver the product on time as a form of fraud. It is unclear whether or not that is fraud in many cases or merely woefully inadequate customer service.

### The FTC and Auction Fraud

The FTC also lists three other areas of bidding fraud that are growing in popularity on the Internet. From the FTC website:[4]

- *Shill bidding,* when fraudulent sellers (or their "shills") bid on the seller's items to drive up the price.

4. The U.S. Federal Trade Commission, Accessed April 2011: https://www.onguardonline.gov/articles/0020-shopping-online

- *Bid shielding,* when fraudulent buyers submit very high bids to discourage other bidders from competing for the same item. The fake buyers then retract their bids so that people they know can get the item at a lower price.

- *Bid siphoning,* when con artists lure bidders off legitimate auction sites by offering to sell the "same" item at a lower price. Their intent is to trick consumers into sending money without proffering the item. By going off-site, buyers lose any protections the original site may provide, such as insurance, feedback forms, or guarantees.

### Shill Bidding

Shill bidding has been probably the most common of these three auction frauds. It is not very complex. If the perpetrator is selling an item at an auction site, she will also create several fake identities. She will use these fake identities to bid on the item and thus drive the price up. It is very difficult to detect if such a scheme is in operation. However, a simple rule of thumb on auctions is to decide, before you start bidding, what your maximum price is. And then, under no circumstances, do you exceed that price by even one penny.

### Bid Shielding

While shill bidding may be difficult to combat, bid shielding can be addressed fairly easily by the proprietors of the auction site. Many of the major auction sites, such as eBay, have taken steps to prevent bid shielding. The most obvious is to revoke bidding privileges for bidders who back out after they have won an auction. So if a person puts in a very high bid to keep others away, then at the last moment retracts his bid, he might lose his ability to be on that auction site.

### Bid Siphoning

Bid siphoning is a less common practice. In this scheme, the perpetrator places a legitimate item up for bid on an auction site. But then, in the ad for that item, she provides links to sites that are not part of the auction site. The unwary buyer who follows those links might find himself on an alternative site that is a "setup" to perpetrate some sort of fraud.

All of these tactics have a common aim: to subvert the normal auction process. The normal auction process is an ideal blend of capitalism and democracy. Everyone has an equal chance to obtain the product in question if she is willing to outbid the other shoppers. The buyers themselves set the price of the product, based on the value they perceive the product to have. In my opinion, auctions are an excellent vehicle for commerce. However, unscrupulous individuals will always attempt to subvert a process for their own goals.

# Identity Theft

Identity theft is a growing problem and a very troubling one. The concept is rather simple, though the process can be complex, and the consequences for the victim can be quite severe. The idea is simply for one person to take on the identity of another. This is usually attempted to make purchases; but identity theft can be done for other reasons, such as obtaining credit cards in the victim's name, or even driver's licenses. If the perpetrator obtains a credit card in someone else's name, then he can purchase products, and the victim of this fraud is left with debts she was not aware of and did not authorize.

In the case of getting a driver's license in the victim's name, this fraud might be attempted to shield the perpetrator from the consequences of her own poor driving record. For example, a person might get your driving information to create a license with her own picture. Perhaps the criminal in this case has a very bad driving record and even warrants out for immediate arrest. Should the person be stopped by law enforcement officers, she can then show the fake license. When the police officer checks the license, it is legitimate and has no outstanding warrants. However, the ticket the criminal receives will be going on your driving record because it is your information on the driver's license. It is also unlikely that the perpetrator of that fraud will actually pay the ticket, so at some point you—whose identity was stolen— will receive notification that your license has been revoked for failure to pay a ticket. Unless you can then prove, with witnesses, that you were not at the location the ticket was given at the time it was given, you may have no recourse but to pay the ticket, in order to reestablish your driving privileges.

The U.S. Department of Justice defines identity theft in this manner:[5]

> "*Identity theft* and *identity fraud* are terms used to refer to all types of crime in which someone wrongfully obtains and uses another person's personal data in some way that involves fraud or deception, typically for economic gain."

The advent of the Internet has made the process of stealing a person's identity even easier than it used to be. Many states now have court records and motor vehicle records online. In some states, a person's social security number is used for the driver's license number. So if a criminal gets a person's social security number, he can look up that person's driving record, perhaps get a duplicate of the person's license, find out about any court records concerning that person, and on some websites, even run the person's credit history. Later in this book, we will examine using the Internet as an investigative tool. Like any tool, it can be used for benign or malevolent purposes. The same tools you can use to do a background check on a prospective employee can be used to find out enough information to forge someone else's identity.

---

### FYI: Alternate Means of Identity Theft

There are other means for a perpetrator to conduct identity theft that do not involve the Internet. A ring of criminals in the Dallas-Fort Worth metroplex were working with waiters in restaurants. When the waiter took your credit card or debit card to pay for the meal, he would also use a small handheld device (kept hidden in a pocket) to scan in your credit card information. He would then give this information to the identity theft ring, who could either make online purchases or use that information to produce fake credit cards with your name and account data. The only way to avoid this sort of danger is to never use your credit or debit card unless it is going to be processed right there in front of you. Do not let someone take your card out of your site to process it.

---

5. The U.S. Department of Justice Identity Theft web page, Accessed April 2011: https://www.justice.gov/criminal-fraud/identity-theft/identity-theft-and-identity-fraud

## Phishing

One of the more common ways to accomplish identity theft is via a technique called *phishing*, which is the process of trying to induce the target to provide you with personal information. For example, the attacker might send out an email purporting to be from a bank and telling recipients that there is a problem with their bank account. The email then directs them to click on a link to the bank website where they can log in and verify their account. However, the link really goes to a fake website set up by the attacker. When the target goes to that website and enters his information, he will have just given his username and password to the attacker.

Many end users today are aware of these sorts of tactics and avoid clicking on email links. But unfortunately, not everyone is so prudent, and this attack still is effective. It is also the case that the attackers have come up with new ways of phishing. One of these methods is called cross-site scripting. If a website allows users to post content that other users can see (such as a product review), the attacker then posts, but instead of posting a review or other legitimate content, the attacker posts a script (JavaScript or something similar). Now when other users visit that web page, instead of loading a review or comment, it will load the attacker's script. That script may do any number of things, but it is common for the script to redirect the end user to a phishing website. If the attacker is clever, the phishing website looks identical to the real one, and end users are not aware they have been redirected. Cross-site scripting can be prevented by web developers filtering all user input.

# Cyber Stalking

Stalking in general has received a great deal of attention in the past few years. The primary reason is that stalking has often been a prelude to violent acts, including sexual assault and homicide. For this reason, many states have passed a variety of antistalking laws. However, stalking has expanded into cyberspace. What is cyber stalking? It is using the Internet to harass another person; or, as the U.S. Department of Justice[6] puts it:

> "Although there is no universally accepted definition of *cyber stalking*, the term is used in this report to refer to the use of the Internet, e-mail, or other electronic communications devices to stalk another person. Stalking generally involves harassing or threatening behavior that an individual engages in repeatedly, such as following a person, appearing at a person's home or place of business, making harassing phone calls, leaving written messages or objects, or vandalizing a person's property. Most stalking laws require that the perpetrator make a credible threat of violence against the victim; others include threats against the victim's immediate family; and still others require only that the alleged stalker's course of conduct constitute an implied threat. While some conduct involving annoying or menacing behavior might fall short of illegal stalking, such behavior may be a prelude to stalking and violence and should be treated seriously."

---

6. The U.S. Department of Justice Cyber Stalking page. Accessed April 2011: https://www.justice.gov/criminal/cybercrime/cyberstalking.htm

If someone uses the Internet to harass, threaten, or intimidate another person, then the perpetrator is guilty of cyber stalking. The most obvious example is sending threatening email. The guidelines on what is considered "threatening" can vary a great deal from jurisdiction to jurisdiction. But a good rule of thumb is that if the email's content would be considered threatening in normal speech, then it will probably be considered a threat if sent electronically. Other examples of cyber stalking are less clear. If you request that someone quit emailing you, yet she continues to do so, is that a crime? Unfortunately, there is no clear answer on that issue. The truth is that it may or may not be considered a crime, depending on such factors as the content of the emails, the frequency, the prior relationship between you and the sender, as well as your jurisdiction.

## Real Cyber Stalking Cases

The following cases, also from the Department of Justice website, illustrate cases of cyber stalking. Examining the facts in these cases might help you to get an idea of what legally constitutes cyber stalking.

- In the first successful prosecution under California's new cyber stalking law, prosecutors in the Los Angeles District Attorney's Office obtained a guilty plea from a 50-year-old former security guard who used the Internet to solicit the rape of a woman who rejected his romantic advances. The defendant terrorized his 28-year-old victim by impersonating her in various Internet chat rooms and online bulletin boards, where he posted, along with her telephone number and address, messages that she fantasized being raped. On at least six occasions, sometimes in the middle of the night, men knocked on the woman's door saying they wanted to rape her. The former security guard pleaded guilty in April 1999 to one count of stalking and three counts of solicitation of sexual assault. He faces up to six years in prison.

- A local prosecutor's office in Massachusetts charged a man who, using anonymous re-mailers, allegedly engaged in a systematic pattern of harassment of a co-worker, which culminated in an attempt to extort sexual favors from the victim under threat of disclosing past sexual activities to the victim's new husband.

- An honors graduate from the University of San Diego terrorized five female university students over the Internet for more than a year. The victims received hundreds of violent and threatening emails, sometimes receiving four or five messages a day. The graduate student, who has entered a guilty plea and faces up to six years in prison, told police he committed the crimes because he thought the women were laughing at him and causing others to ridicule him. In fact, the victims had never met him.

- A man in South Carolina allegedly fixated on news anchors at the WRAL TV station. He sent a large number of emails to the news anchors. Those emails contained sexually explicit material as well as references to cross burnings. The case was investigated by the South Carolina Bureau of Investigation.

- Robert James Murphy was the first person charged under federal law for cyber stalking. He was accused of violating Title 47 of U.S. Code 223, which prohibits the use of telecommunications to annoy, abuse, threaten, or harass anyone. Mr. Murphy was accused of sending sexually explicit messages and photographs to his ex-girlfriend. This activity continued for a period of years. He was charged and eventually pled guilty to two counts of cyber stalking.

- James Allen was convicted in 2015 of both child pornography and cyber stalking. He was accused of having harassed 18 New York girls online. He used the harassment to extort illicit pictures from the girls.

Clearly, using the Internet to harass people is just as serious a crime as harassing them in person. And it can lead to real-world crimes. This problem has even extended to workplace issues. For example, court cases have upheld that unwanted email pornography can be construed as sexual harassment. If an employee complains about unwanted email, the employer has a duty to at least attempt to ameliorate the situation. This attempt can be as simple as installing a very inexpensive spam blocker (software that tries to limit or eradicate unwanted email). However, if the employer takes no steps whatsoever to correct the problem, that reticence may be seen by a court as contributing to a hostile work environment. As previously stated, if the stalking act would constitute as harassment in person, then it would be considered harassment in cyberspace. *Black's Law Dictionary*[7] defines *harassment* as follows:

> "A course of conduct directed at a specific person that causes substantial emotional distress in such person and serves no legitimate purpose."

> "Words, gestures, and actions that tend to annoy, alarm, and abuse (verbally) another person."

Usually law enforcement officials will need some credible threat of harm in order to pursue harassment complaints. In simple terms, this situation means that if you are in an anonymous chat room and someone utters some obscenity, that act probably will not be considered harassment. However, if you receive specific threats via email, those threats would probably be considered harassment.

Many states specifically prohibit cyber stalking; and in general, existing anti-stalking laws can be applied to the Internet. In 2001, in California a man was convicted of cyber stalking under existing antistalking statutes.[8] Other countries also have existing antistalking laws that can be applied to cyber stalking as well. Canada has had a comprehensive antistalking law since 1993. Unfortunately, there are many similar cases. Just a few include the following:

- From 2010, there is the case of Joseph Medico (70 years old), who met a 16-year-old girl at his church. Mr. Medico followed the girl to her car and tried to talk her into going to dinner with him and then back to his home. When she rejected his advances, he began calling and texting her several times a day. His activities escalated until the girl reported the activities and Mr. Medico was arrested for stalking.

- In 2008 Shawn Michael Hutchinson, 20, posted threats and nude pictures of a former girlfriend. His threats included statements such as "'I told you that if I saw you with David that would be the end of you. That's not a threat, it's a promise."

---

7. Blacks Law Dictionary, 1999, West Publishing Company, 7th Edition.
8. The Identity Theft and Deterrence Act of 1998, USC 1028

One reason law enforcement agencies are taking a much closer look at cyber crimes is the frequency with which they become real-world crimes with real consequences in the physical world. We have already mentioned cyber stalking that has, in some cases, escalated to real-world assaults and even homicides. Let's examine a few other ways that the cyber world can be connected to physical crimes. These crimes were selected over the period of 2006 to 2015.

- In 2006, Arizona resident Heather Kane was arrested for using MySpace to attempt to solicit a hit man to kill a woman whose picture had appeared on Ms. Kane's boyfriend's MySpace page. After finding a person she thought was a hit man, she met with him and gave him a $400 down payment. The individual was in fact an undercover police officer.

- In February 2009 in the United Kingdom, Edward Richardson stabbed his wife to death because she had changed her marital status on her Facebook page from married to single.

- In July 2008, Scott Knight of Aurora, Oregon, was arrested on charges that he raped a 13-year-old girl he had met through MySpace.[9] A similar case occurred in 2009, when William Cox of Kentucky was charged with raping a 13-year-old girl that he, too, met on MySpace.

- In 2012, in the town of McKinney, Texas—which just happens to be very close to my own home—a man used Craigslist apartment ads to lure women to a location so he could rape them. He was captured, convicted, and sentenced to 20 years in prison.

- Also in 2012, U.S. Forest Rangers in Utah were trying to find who was responsible for setting up medieval booby traps along hiking trails in Utah. The police were tipped off that two men, Benjamin Rutkowsky and Kai Christenson, had been chatting about setting the traps on Facebook.

- 2015 brought a new twist on cyber stalking. David Matusiewicz, his sister Amy Gonzalez, and his mother Lenore Matusiewicz are the first defendants in the United States charged with cyber stalking resulting in death. The three were found guilty of conspiracy and cyber stalking that led to the death of Mr. Matusiewicz's ex-wife. The victim was killed by Mr. Matusiewicz's father after a long pattern of cyber stalking by the defendants in this case. The shooter took his own life after shooting the victim and the victim's friend as they showed up at a Delaware courthouse for a child support hearing.

One could fill several volumes with similar cases. The common element of all but the last of these is that a computer was used as either an agent or a catalyst for a real-world violent crime. These cases should make clear to the reader that computer crime is not just about hacking, fraud, and property crimes. It is becoming more common for law-enforcement officers to find a computer/Internet element in traditional crimes. And I am sure most readers have heard about Craigslist's "erotic services" ads, which are in reality advertisements for prostitution. The last case shows that although a computer might not always be a part of the crime, it could lead to evidence of the crime. There are numerous other cases of criminals posting Facebook messages, tweets, and YouTube videos that contain incriminating evidence and, in some cases, full confessions.

---

9. The Minneapolis-St.Paul Star Tribune, Accessed August 23, 2001: www.startribune.com/

# How to Evaluate Cyber Stalking

Unfortunately, it is not always clear if a given communication rises to the level of cyber stalking or not. One obvious example of cyber stalking is the sending of threatening email messages. But even the definitions of *harass*, *threaten*, and *intimidate* are somewhat vague. Obviously, if a person sends an email to another person threatening to kill that person and provides photos of the recipient to demonstrate that the sender is familiar with the target's appearance and address, that would clearly be cyber stalking. But what about a situation in which a person is upset with a product and emails a harshly worded message to an executive at the product's manufacturer? If the email has a vague threat, such as "You will get what you deserve," is that cyber stalking? This is not an easy question to answer, and no single answer applies to all jurisdictions and all situations. What constitutes threatening, harassing, or intimidating can vary a great deal from jurisdiction to jurisdiction. But a general guideline is that that if the email's (or instant message's, newsgroup posting's, and so on's) content would be considered threatening in normal speech, then it would probably be considered a threat if sent electronically.

The other element of a threat is viability. Is the threat credible? On the Internet, people are frequently more vocal and often more hostile than they are in other venues. That means a law enforcement officer must to some extent differentiate between someone simply spouting off or venting versus someone making a real, serious threat. The question becomes, how do you determine whether to take a threat seriously? The key is to look for four factors:

- **Credibility:** For a threat to be credible, there must be some reasonable expectation that it could be carried out. For example, suppose a woman in Nebraska is on an Internet discussion board and receives a general threat from another user living in Bangkok in the course of a heated debate. In this scenario, the sender very likely has no idea where the recipient lives. Indeed, because many people use screen names on the Internet, the sender may not even know the recipient's real name, gender, age, or appearance. That means this threat has a very low level of credibility. If, however, the woman in Nebraska receives a threat from the user in Bangkok accompanied with personal information such as her address, her place of work, or a photo of her, that is a very credible threat.

- **Frequency:** Unfortunately, people often make ill-advised comments on the Internet. Often, however, a single hostile comment is just a person reacting too emotionally and too quickly online. For this reason, this type of comment is less of a concern than a pattern of threats over a period of time. Frequently, stalkers escalate their comments and threats over time, gradually building up to a point where they act violently. While there certainly may be cases in which a single threat warrants investigation, as a general rule, isolated threats are of less concern than a pattern of harassment and threats.

- **Specificity:** Specificity refers to how specific the perpetrator is regarding the nature of the threat, the target of the threat, and the means of executing the threat. Of course, it is very important for law enforcement officers to realize that real threats can sometimes be vague. Put another way, real threats aren't always specific. But specific threats are usually real. As an example, someone receiving an email saying, "You will pay for that" is less of a concern than an email containing a specific threat of a very specific type of violence, such as, "I will wait for you after work and shoot you in the head with my 9mm" along with a photo of the recipient leaving work. (The photo also makes it very credible.) This threat is specific and should be of much greater concern to law enforcement.

- **Intensity:** This refers to the general tone of the communications, the nature of the language, and the intensity of the threat. Graphic and particularly violent threats should always be taken very seriously by law enforcement. Often, when someone is simply venting or reacting emotionally, he may make statements that could be considered threatening. In these cases, however, most people make low-intensity statements, such as threatening to beat someone up. Threats such as these are of less concern than, say, a threat to dismember someone. This is because normal, nonviolent people can lose their temper and want to punch someone in the nose. But normal, nonviolent people don't usually lose their temper and want to cut someone into pieces with a chainsaw. Anytime a threat is raised to a level that is beyond what a reasonable person might say, even in a hostile situation, that threat becomes of greater concern.

All four of these criteria need not be met for a cyber threat to be considered viable. Law enforcement officers must always rely on their own judgment and should err on the side of caution. A particular officer may feel a given threat is very serious even if several of these criteria are not met. That officer should then treat the threat as a serious concern. And if one or more of these criteria *are* present, the officer should always treat the matter seriously, regardless of her personal inclinations. A credible, frequent, specific, and intense threat is very often a prelude to real-world violence.

## Crimes Against Children

Of even more concern are cases in which the cyber stalking involves minors. Pedophiles now use the Internet extensively to interact with minors and, in many cases, arrange in-person meetings with children. This must be a significant concern for all parents, law enforcement officials, and computer security professionals. Often, pedophiles use chat rooms, online discussion boards, and various other Internet media to meet with children. The discussions often turn more sexually explicit and eventually lead to an attempt to meet in person. Fortunately, this sort of activity is relatively easy to investigate. The pedophile normally wishes to continue communication with the victim and to escalate communication. The process is referred to as *grooming*. The pedophile is cultivating a relationship with the victim. This often includes gifts sent to the victim. A common gift would be a cell phone, allowing the pedophile and the victim to communicate through a channel the victim's parents are not even aware exists. While variations exist, the common process is as follows:

1. The initial conversation the predator initiates with a minor will probably be about an innocuous topic that is of interest to a minor. During this initial phase the predator is often looking for key signs that this child might be a likely target. For example, children that feel like they don't belong, are not getting enough attention from parents, or are going through some major life issue such as parental divorce are likely targets.

2. Once the predator has identified a potential target, he will then begin trying to extend the conversations outside the chat room or social page, into private chats or emails. He will also

likely be very sympathetic to whatever the child's problem is. Predators often use flattery with their intended victims. Children who feel like they don't belong or who have low self-esteem are very susceptible to these sorts of tactics.

3. The next step is to begin easing sexual content into the conversation. Their intent is to gradually get the child comfortable discussing sexual topics. Usually they are careful to take this phase carefully so as not to cause the targeted child to panic. If this process proceeds to a point the predator feels comfortable, he will then suggest a face-to-face meeting. In some cases the face-to-face meeting is expressly for the purpose of sex; in others, the predator will lure the child to a location with the promise of some seemingly benign activity such as video games or a movie.

4. Of course, there are sometimes deviations from this pattern. Some predators move much quicker to meet with the child face to face. They may also avoid sexual conversations at all and simply try to lure the child out of her house with the intent of forcibly molesting the child. Whether the predator chooses to lure the child and then force a sex act or attempts to seduce the child depends on how the predator views the act. It may surprise some readers to discover that some pedophiles actually view themselves not as child molesters, but rather as being in a relationship with the child. They actually think their behavior is acceptable and it is simply society that fails to understand them. This sort of pedophile is much more likely to use a method of gradually increasing the sexual content and explicitness of the online conversation. Their intent is to seduce the child.

There have been a number of well-publicized sting operations with the purpose of catching online predators. In these operations, adults (sometimes law enforcement officers, sometimes not) pose as minors online and wait for a pedophile to approach them and attempt to engage in sexually explicit conversations. These attempts have been quite controversial. Given the nature of the activities, however, it seems unlikely that a nonpedophile adult could accidentally or mistakenly become involved in explicit sexual discussions with a minor. It is even less likely that a nonpedophile adult would attempt to meet in the physical world with a person she believed to be a minor. It would certainly seem that these programs, if conducted properly, can be an invaluable tool in combating online predators.

It should be noted that many states have an online sex offender database. This allows you to look up anyone who might be on the sex offender list. In many cases such databases provide a photo and a birthdate to help prevent misidentifications due to similar names. The following list are a few such directories:

- **Texas:** https://records.txdps.state.tx.us/sexoffender/

- **U.S. Department of Justice:** https://www.nsopw.gov/?AspxAutoDetectCookieSupport=1

- **Alabama:** https://app.alea.gov/Community/wfSexOffenderSearch.aspx

- **New York:** http://www.criminaljustice.ny.gov/SomsSUBDirectory/search_index.jsp

## Laws About Internet Fraud

Over the past several years, various legislatures (in the United States and in other countries) have passed laws defining *Internet fraud* and stating the proscribed punishments. In many cases, existing laws against fraud and harassment are applicable to the Internet as well; however, some legislators have felt that cyber crime warranted its own distinct legislation.

Identity theft has been the subject of various state and federal laws. Most states now have laws against identity theft. This crime is also covered by federal law. In 1998, the federal government passed 18 U.S.C. 1028, also known as the Identity Theft and Assumption Deterrence Act of 1998. This law made identity theft a federal crime. Throughout the United States, federal law now covers identity theft. In many states identity theft is also covered by state law.

One nation that has decided to crack down hard on cyber criminals is Romania. Some experts have described Romanian cyber crime law as the strictest in the world. However, what is most interesting about Romanian law is how specific it is. The crafters of this legislation went to some effort to very specifically define all the terms used in the legislation. This specificity is very important in order to avoid defendants finding loopholes in laws. Unfortunately, the Romanian government only took such measures after media sources around the world identified their country as a "Citadel for Cyber Crime." The country's reactive approach to cyber crime is probably not the best solution.

The University of Dayton School of Law has an entire website devoted to cyber crime. The school has some rather extensive links on cyber crime, cyber stalking, and other Internet-based crimes. As we move forward in the twenty-first century, one can expect to see more law schools with courses dedicated to cyber crime.

An interesting phenomenon has begun in the past few years: the emergence of attorneys who specialize in cyber crime cases. The fact that there are lawyers who specialize in this area of law is a strong indicator that Internet crime is a growing problem in modern society.

# Protecting Yourself Against Cyber Crime

Now that you know about the various frauds that are prevalent on the Internet and have looked at the relevant laws, you might be wondering what you can do to protect yourself. There are several specific steps you can take to minimize the chances of being the victim of Internet crime. There are also some clear guidelines on how you should handle the situation, should you become a victim.

## Protecting Against Investment Fraud

To protect yourself against investment fraud, follow these guidelines:

1. Only invest with well-known, reputable brokers.

2. If it sounds too good to be true, then avoid it.

3. Ask yourself why this person is informing you of this great investment deal. Why would a complete stranger decide to share some incredible investment opportunity with you?

4. Remember that even legitimate investment involves risk, so never invest money that you cannot afford to lose.

## Protecting Against Identity Theft

When the issue is identity theft, your steps are clear:

1. Do not provide your personal information to anyone if it is not absolutely necessary. This rule means that when communicating on the Internet with anyone you do not personally know, do not reveal anything about yourself—not your age, occupation, real name, anything.

2. Destroy documents that have personal information on them. If you simply throw away bank statements and credit card bills, then someone rummaging through your trash can get a great deal of personal data. You can obtain a paper shredder from an office supply store or many retail department stores for less than $20. Shred these documents before disposing of them. This rule may not seem like it is related to computer security, but information gathered through nontechnical means can be used in conjunction with the Internet to perpetrate identity theft.

3. Check your credit frequently. Many websites, including www.consumerinfo.com, allow you to check your credit and even get your beacon score for a nominal fee. I check my credit twice per year. If you see any items you did not authorize, that is a clear indication that you might be a victim of identity theft.

4. If your state has online driving records, then check yours once per year. If you see driving infractions that you did not commit, this evidence is a clear sign that your identity is being used by someone else. In an upcoming chapter on cyber detective work, we will explore in detail how to obtain such records online, often for less than $5.

To summarize, the first step in preventing identity theft is restricting the amount of personal information you make available. The next step is simply monitoring your credit and driving records so that you will be aware if someone attempts to use your identity.

Another part of protecting your identity is protecting your privacy in general. That task means preventing others from gaining information about you that you don't explicitly provide them. That preventive method includes keeping websites from gathering information about you without your knowledge. Many websites store information about you and your visit to their site in small files called *cookies*. These cookie files are stored on your machine. The problem with cookies is that any website can read any cookie on your machine—even ones that the website you are currently visiting did not create. So if you visit one website and it stores items like your name, the site you visited, and the time you were there, then another website could potentially read that cookie and know where you have been on the Internet. One of the best ways to stop cookies you don't want is anti-spyware software. We will discuss such software in more detail in a later chapter. Right now, let's see how to change your Internet settings to help reduce exposures to your privacy.

## Secure Browser Settings

If you are using Microsoft Internet Explorer, you can go to Tools and use the drop-down menu; then select Options. After that you will see a screen much like the one shown in Figure 3.1. You can then select the third tab, labeled Privacy.

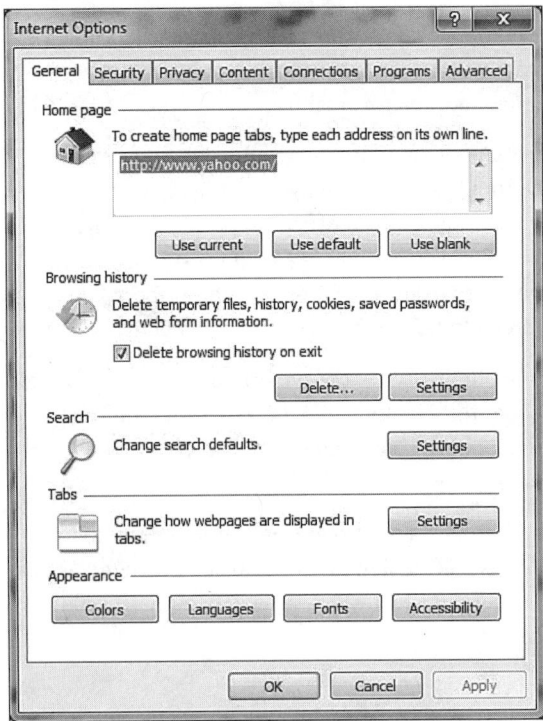

**FIGURE 3.1**    Internet Explorer options.

When you select that Privacy tab, you will see the screen shown in Figure 3.2. Notice the sliding bar on the left that lets you select various levels of general protection against cookies. It is recommended that you select Medium High as your level.

Note the Advanced button at the bottom of the screen. This button allows you to block or allow individual websites from creating cookies on your computer's hard drive. Altering cookie settings on your machine is just one part of protecting your privacy, but it is an important part.

You probably also want to ensure that you have selected the InPrivate Browsing option, shown in Figure 3.2.

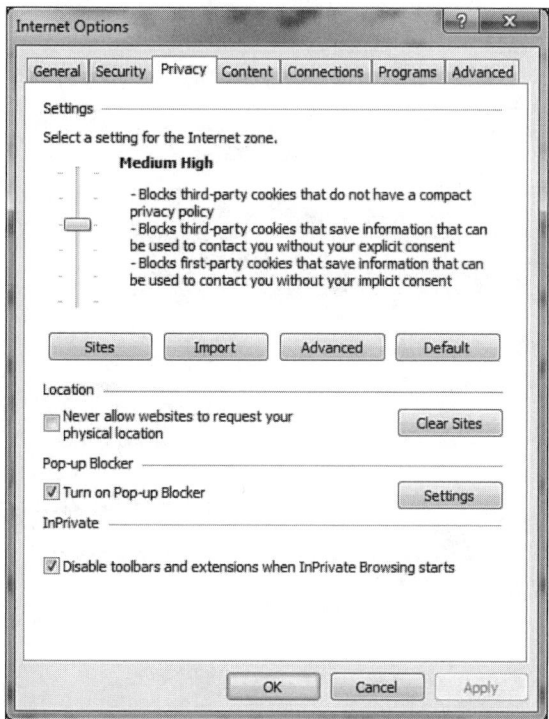

**FIGURE 3.2**    Internet Explorer privacy options.

If you are working with Firefox, the process is similar. You select Tools from the drop-down menu and then select Options. You will see the screen shown in Figure 3.3.

FIGURE 3.3 Firefox options.

Notice the Privacy option, and you will see a screen much like the one shown in Figure 3.4.

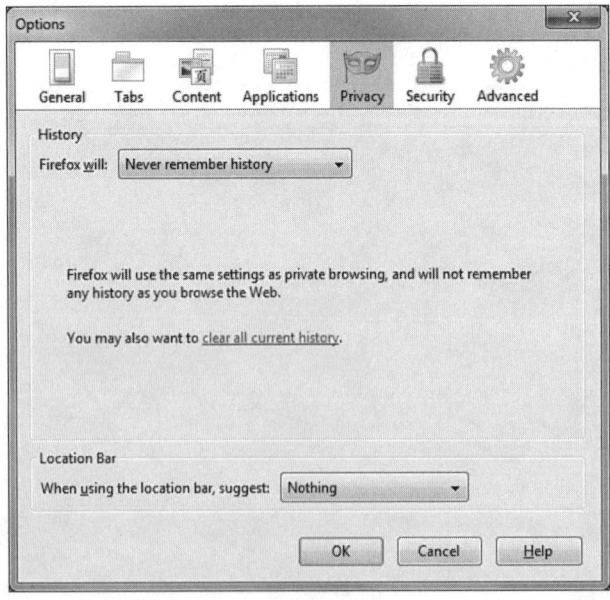

FIGURE 3.4 Firefox privacy.

As you can see from Figure 3.4, there are a number of privacy settings for you to select, and they are self-explanatory. You can also select the Security tab and see the screen in Figure 3.5.

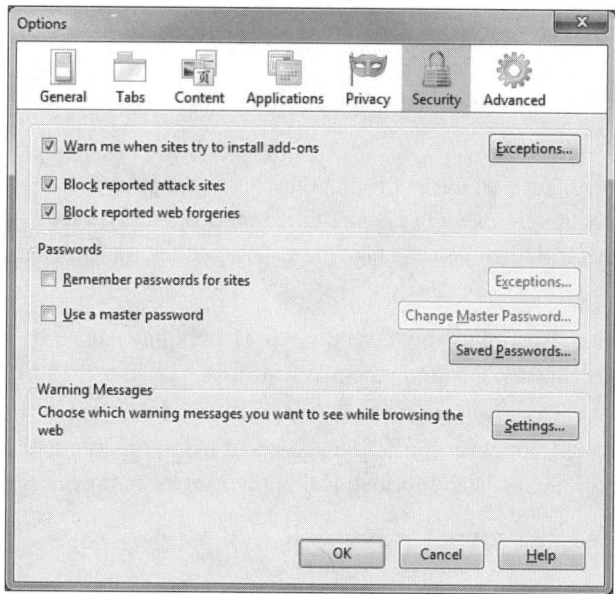

**FIGURE 3.5** Firefox security.

I recommend selecting High Security. Also, I would only allow first-party cookies. Third-party cookies are notorious for behaving in ways that violate user privacy. We will discuss cookies and spyware in much more detail in a later chapter, but the simple steps just examined can go a long way toward helping to secure your privacy.

Dealing with auction fraud involves a different set of precautions; here are four good ideas.

1. Only use reputable auction sites. The most well-known site is eBay, but any widely known, reputable site will be a safer gamble. Such auction sites tend to take precautions to prevent fraud and abuse.

2. If it sounds too good to be true, don't bid.

3. Some sites actually allow you to read feedback other buyers have provided on a given seller. Read the feedback, and only work with reputable sellers.

4. When possible use a separate credit card, one with a low limit, for online auctions. That way, should your credit card be compromised, your liability is limited. Using your debit card is simply inviting trouble.

Online auctions can be a very good way to get valuable merchandise at low prices. However, one must exercise some degree of caution when using these services.

Protecting yourself from online harassment also has its own guidelines:

1. If you use chat rooms, discussion boards, and so forth, do not use your real name. Set up a separate email account with an anonymous service, such as Yahoo!, Gmail, or Hotmail. Then use that account and a fake name online. This makes it very hard for an online stalker to trace back to you personally.

2. If you are the victim of online harassment, keep all the emails in both digital and printed format. Use some of the investigative techniques we will explore later in this book to try to identify the perpetrator. If you are successful, then you can take the emails and the information on the perpetrator to law enforcement officials.

3. Do not, in any case, ignore cyber stalking. According to the Working to Halt Online Abuse website, 19% of cyber stalking cases escalate to stalking in the real world.

It is not the intent of this chapter or of this book to make you frightened about using the Internet. I routinely use the Internet for entertainment, commerce, and informational purposes. One simply needs to exercise some caution when using the Internet.

# Summary

Clearly, fraud and identity theft are very real and growing problems. In this modern age of instant access to information and online purchasing, it is critical that you take steps to protect yourself against this issue. You must work to protect your privacy using steps outlined in this chapter. It is also imperative for law enforcement officers to obtain the skills needed to investigate and solve these sorts of cyber crimes.

Cyber stalking is one area that is often new to both civilians and law enforcement. It is very important that both groups have a clear understanding of what is, and is not, cyber stalking. Unfortunately, cyber stalking cases can escalate into real-world violence.

## Test Your Skills

### MULTIPLE CHOICE QUESTIONS

1. The most common Internet investment fraud is known as what?

    A. The Nigerian fraud

    B. The Manhattan fraud

    C. The pump and dump

    D. The bait and switch

2. What is the most likely problem with unsolicited investment advice?

    A. You might not earn as much as claimed.

    B. The advice might not be truly unbiased.

    C. The advice might not be from a legitimate firm.

    D. You might lose money.

3. Artificially inflating a stock in order to sell it at a higher value is referred to as what?

    A. Bait and switch

    B. The Nigerian fraud

    C. Pump and dump

    D. The Wall Street fraud

4. What is the top rule for avoiding Internet fraud?

    A. If it seems too good to be true, it probably is.

    B. Never use your bank account numbers.

    C. Only work with people who have verifiable email addresses.

    D. Don't invest in foreign deals.

5. Which of the following is not one of the Security and Exchange Commission's tips for avoiding investment fraud?

    A. Don't invest online.

    B. Consider the source of the offer.

    C. Always be skeptical.

    D. Always research the investment.

6. What are the four categories of auction fraud?

    A. Failure to send, failure to disclose, sending to wrong address, failure to deliver

    B. Failure to send, failure to disclose, sending something of lesser value, failure to deliver

    C. Failure to disclose, sending something to wrong address, failure to send, failure to deliver

    D. Failure to disclose, sending something of lesser value, failure to send, sending something of greater value

7. A seller bidding on her own item to drive up the price is referred to as what?

    A. Bid siphoning

    B. Bid shielding

    C. Shill bidding

    D. Ghost bidding

8. Submitting a fake but very high bid to deter other bidders is referred to as what?

    A. Bid siphoning

    B. Bid shielding

    C. Shill bidding

    D. Ghost bidding

9. Identity theft is most often attempted in order to accomplish what goal?

    A. To make illicit purchases

    B. To discredit the victim

    C. To avoid criminal prosecution

    D. To invade privacy

10. According to the U.S. Department of Justice, identity theft is generally motivated by what?

    A. Malicious intent

    B. Personal hostility toward the victim

    C. Economic gain

    D. Thrill seeking

11. Why is cyber stalking a serious crime?

   A. It is frightening to the victim.

   B. It can be a prelude to violent crime.

   C. It is using interstate communication.

   D. It can be a prelude to identity theft.

12. What is cyber stalking?

   A. Any use of the Internet to send or post threats

   B. Any use of electronic communications to stalk a person

   C. Only use of email to send threats

   D. Only the use of email to stalk a person

13. What will law enforcement officials usually require of the victim in order to pursue harassment allegations?

   A. A verifiable threat of death or serious injury

   B. A credible threat of death or serious injury

   C. A verifiable threat of harm

   D. A credible threat of harm

14. If you are posting anonymously in a chat room and another anonymous poster threatens you with assault or even death, is this person's post harassment?

   A. Yes; any threat of violence is harassment.

   B. Probably not because both parties are anonymous, so the threat is not credible.

   C. Yes; chat room threats are no different from threats in person.

   D. Probably not because making a chat room threat is not the same as making a threat in person.

15. What must exist for cyber stalking to be illegal in a state or territory?

   A. Specific laws against cyber stalking in that state or territory.

   B. Specific laws against cyber stalking in that nation.

   C. Nothing; existing stalking laws can apply.

   D. Nothing; existing international cyber stalking laws apply.

16. What is the first step in protecting yourself from identity theft?

   A. Never provide personal data about yourself unless absolutely necessary.

   B. Routinely check your records for signs of identity theft.

   C. Never use your real name on the Internet.

   D. Routinely check for spyware on your computer.

17. What can you do on your local computer to protect your privacy?

    A. Install a virus scanner.

    B. Install a firewall.

    C. Set your browser's security settings.

    D. Set your computer's filter settings.

18. What is a cookie?

    A. A piece of data that web servers gather about you

    B. A small file made that contains data and then is stored on your computer

    C. A piece of data that your web browser gathers about you

    D. A small file made that contains data and then is stored on the web server

19. Which of the following is not an efficient method of protecting yourself from auction fraud?

    A. Only use auctions for inexpensive items.

    B. Only use reputable auction sites.

    C. Only work with well-rated sellers.

    D. Only bid on items that seem realistic.

20. The top rule for chat room safety is what?

    A. Make certain you have antivirus software installed.

    B. Never use your real name or any real personally identifying characteristics.

    C. Only use chat rooms that encrypt transmissions.

    D. Use chat rooms that are sponsored by well-known websites or companies.

21. Why is it useful to have a separate credit card dedicated to online purchases?

    A. If the credit card number is used illegally, you will limit your financial liability.

    B. You can keep better track of your auction activities.

    C. If you are defrauded, you can possibly get the credit card company to handle the problem.

    D. You can easily cancel that single card, if you need to do so.

22. What percentage of cyber stalking cases escalate to real-world violence?

    A. Less than 1%

    B. 25%

    C. 90% or more

    D. About 19%

**23.** If you are a victim of cyber stalking, what should you do to assist the police?

    **A.** Nothing; it is their job and you should stay out of it.

    **B.** Attempt to lure the stalker into a public place.

    **C.** Keep electronic and hard copies of all harassing communications.

    **D.** Try to provoke the stalker into revealing personal information about himself.

**24.** What is the top way to protect yourself from cyber stalking?

    **A.** Do not use your real identity online.

    **B.** Always use a firewall.

    **C.** Always use a virus scanner.

    **D.** Do not give out email addresses.

## EXERCISES

### EXERCISE 3.1: Setting Web Browser Privacy in Internet Explorer

**1.** This process was described in detail with images in the chapter, but we will walk through the process here:

- Select Tools from the drop-down menu at the top of Internet Explorer, and then choose Internet Options.

- Select the third tab, which is labeled Privacy.

- Click the Advanced button.

- Set your browser to accept first-party cookies, prompt for third-party cookies, and accept session cookies.

### EXERCISE 3.2: Using Alternative Web Browsers

**1.** Download the Firefox browser from www.mozilla.org.

**2.** Set privacy and security settings.

# PROJECTS

## PROJECT 3.1: Finding Out About Cyber Stalking and the Law

1. Using the Web or other resources, find out what your state, country, or province's laws are regarding cyber stalking.

2. Write a brief paper describing those laws and what they mean. You may select to do a quick summary of several laws or a more in-depth examination of one law. If you choose the former, then simply list the laws and write a brief paragraph explaining what they cover. If you choose the latter option, then discuss the law's authors, why it was written, and possible ramifications of the law.

## PROJECT 3.2: Looking for Auction Fraud

Go to any auction site and try to identify if there are any sellers you feel might be fraudulent. Write a brief paper explaining what about that seller indicated that he may not be dealing honestly.

## PROJECT 3.3: Examining Cyber Stalking Case Studies

1. Using the Web, find a case of cyber stalking not mentioned in this chapter. You may find some of the following websites helpful:

   - www.safetyed.org/help/stalking/

   - www.cyber-stalking.net/

   - www.technomom.com/harassed/index.shtml

2. Write a brief paper discussing this case, with particular attention to steps you think might have helped avoid or ameliorate the situation.

### Case Study

Consider the case of an intrepid identity thief. The perpetrator, Jane, encounters the victim, John, online in a chat room. John is using his real first name but only his last initial. However, over a series of online conversations between Jane and John, he does reveal personal details about his life (marital status, children, occupation, region he lives in, and so forth). Eventually, Jane offers John some piece of information, such as perhaps an investment tip, as a trick to get John's email address from him. Once she gets his email address, an email exchange begins outside of the chat room, wherein Jane purports to give John her real name, thus encouraging John to do the same. Of course, the perpetrator's name is fictitious, such as "Mary." But Jane now has John's real name, city, marital status, occupation, and so on.

Jane has a number of options she can try, but we will choose a simple one. She begins by using the phone book or the Web to get John's home address and phone number. She can then use this information to get John's social security number in a variety of ways. The most straight-forward would be to go through John's trash while he is at work. However, if John works in a large company, Jane can just call (or enlist someone to call), claiming to be John's wife or another close relative, wanting to verify personnel data. If Jane is clever enough, she may come away with John's social security number. Then it is a trivial matter (as we will see in Chapter 13, "Cyber Detective") to get John's credit report and to get credit cards in his name.

From this scenario, consider the following questions:

1. What reasonable steps could John have taken to protect his identity in the chat room?

2. What steps should any employer take to prevent being unwittingly complicit in identity theft?

# Chapter | **4**

# Denial of Service Attacks

## Chapter Objectives

**After reading this chapter and completing the exercises, you will be able to do the following:**

- Understand how denial of service attacks are accomplished
- Know how certain denial of service attacks work, such as SYN flood, Smurf, and distributed denial of service
- Take specific measures to protect against denial of service attacks
- Know how to defend against specific denial of service attacks

## Introduction

By now you are aware, in a general way, of the dangers of the Internet, and you have explored a few basic rules for protection on the Internet. In Chapter 3, "Cyber Stalking, Fraud, and Abuse," you were introduced to some fraud, stalking, and related crimes. It is now time to become more specific about how attacks on systems are conducted. In this chapter, we will examine one category of attack that might be used to cause harm to a target computer system. This chapter will describe for you, in depth, the workings of the *denial of service (DoS)* attack. This threat is one of the most common attacks on the Internet, so it is prudent for you to understand how it works and how to defend yourself against it. Further, in the exercises at the end of the book, you will practice stopping a DoS attack. In information security, the old adage that "knowledge is power" is not only good advice, but also an axiom upon which to build your entire security outlook.

# DoS

As was said in the Introduction, one of the most common and simplest forms of attack on a system is a DoS. This attack does not even attempt to intrude on your system or to obtain sensitive information; it simply aims to prevent legitimate users from accessing the system. This type of attack is fairly easy to execute. The basic concept requires a minimum of technical skill. It is based on the fact that any device has operational limits. For example, a truck can only carry a finite load or travel a finite distance. Computers are no different than any other machine; they, too, have limits. Any computer system, web server, or network can only handle a finite load. A workload for a computer system may be defined by the number of simultaneous users, the size of files, the speed of data transmission, or the amount of data stored. If you exceed any of those limits, the excess load will stop the system from responding. For example, if you can flood a web server with more requests than it can process, it will be overloaded and will no longer be able to respond to further requests (Webopedia, 2004). That is just as true today as it was in 2004. Every technology has limits; if you can exceed those limits, then you can take the system offline. This reality underlies the DoS attack. Simply overload the system with requests, and it will no longer be able to respond to legitimate users attempting to access the web server.

# Illustrating an Attack

One simple way to illustrate this attack, especially in a classroom setting, involves the use of the `ping` command discussed in Chapter 2, "Networks and the Internet":

1. Start a web server service running on one machine. (You can use Apache, IIS, or any web server.)

2. Ask several people to open their browsers and key the IP address of that machine in the address bar. They should then be viewing the default website for that web server.

Now you can do a rather primitive denial of service attack on the system. Recall from Chapter 2 that typing in `ping /?` will show you all the options for the `ping` command. The `-l` option changes the size of the packet you can send. Remember that a TCP packet can be only of a finite size. Thus, you are going to set these packets to be almost as large as you can send. The `-w` option determines how many milliseconds the `ping` utility will wait for a response from the target. You are going to use `-0` so that the `ping` utility does not wait at all. Then the `-t` instructs the ping utility to keep sending packets until explicitly told to stop.

1. Open the command prompt in Windows 7/8/8.1/10. (That is the shell in UNIX/Linux.)

2. Type in `ping <address of target machine goes here>-l 65000 -w 0 -t`. You will then see something very much like what is shown in Figure 4.1. Note that, in the figure, I am pinging the loop-back address for my own machine. You will want to substitute the address of the machine on which you are running the web server.

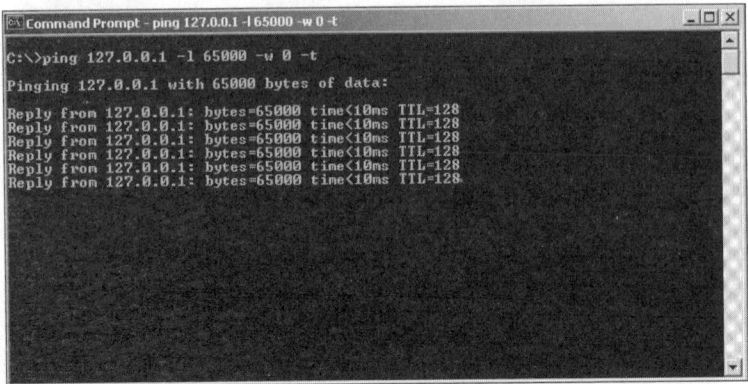

**FIGURE 4.1** Ping from the command prompt.

What is happening at this point is that this single machine is continually pinging away at the target machine. Of course, just one machine in your classroom or lab that is simply pinging on your web server is not going to adversely affect the web server. However, you can now, one by one, get other machines in the classroom pinging the server in the same way. After each batch of three or four machines you add, try to go to the web server's default web page. After a certain threshold (certain number of machines pinging the server), it will stop responding to requests, and you will no longer be able to see the web page.

How many machines it will take to deny service depends on the web server you are using. In order to see this denial happen with as few machines involved as possible, you could use a very low-capacity PC as your web server. For example, running an Apache web server on a simple laptop running Windows 7 Home Edition, it can take about 15 machines each running about 10 different command windows simultaneously pinging to cause a web server to stop responding to legitimate requests. This strategy is, of course, counter to what you would normally select for a web server—no real web server would be running on a simple laptop with Windows 7 Home Edition (or even Windows 10). Likewise, actual DoS attacks use much more sophisticated methods. This simple exercise, however, should demonstrate for you the basic principle behind the DoS attack: Simply flood the target machine with so many packets that it can no longer respond to legitimate requests. It is important to be aware that this is just an illustration. With modern servers, and many servers actually being hosted in clusters or server farms, this exact illustration would not work against a modern target.

Generally, the methods used for DoS attacks are significantly more sophisticated than the illustration. For example, a hacker might develop a small virus whose sole purpose is to infect as many computers as possible and then get each of the infected computers to initiate a DoS attack on the target. Once the virus has spread, the various machines that are infected with that virus then begin their flood of the target system. This sort of DoS is easy to do, and it can be hard to stop. A DoS that is launched from several different machines is called a distributed denial of service (DDoS).

Regardless of the methods or the tools (many of which we will describe in this chapter), DoS and DDoS attacks are becoming even more prevalent. According to Akamai research, "DDoS attacks grew seven percent since the last quarter and a staggering 132 percent compared to this time last year. In the quarter there were also 12 attacks that were categorized as "mega attacks," peaking at more than 1,000 gigabits per second (Gbps) and 50 million packets per second (Mpps)."[1]

## Common Tools Used for DoS

As with any of the security issues discussed in this book, you will find that hackers have at their disposal a vast array of tools with which to work. The DoS arena is no different. While it is certainly well beyond the scope of this book to begin to categorize or discuss all of these tools, a brief introduction to just a few of them will prove useful. The two tools discussed here, TFN and Stacheldraht, are typical of the types of tools that someone wishing to perform a DoS attack would utilize.

### Low Orbit Ion Cannon

This is one of the most widely known DoS tools available. It has a very easy to use graphical user interface, shown in Figure 4.2.

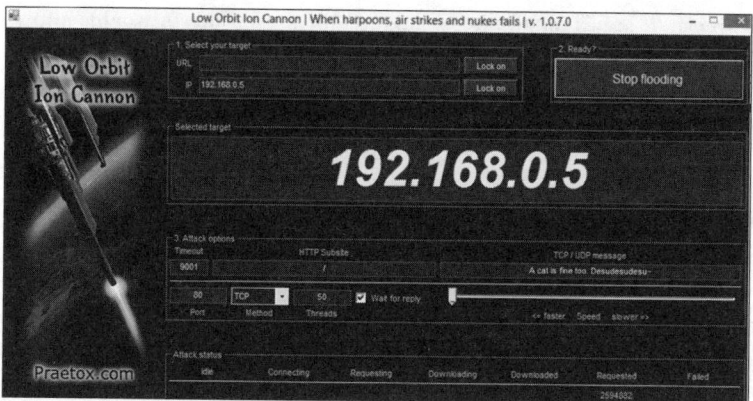

**FIGURE 4.2**   LOIC.

This tool is very easy to use. As you can see in Figure 4.2, it simply requires the user to put in the target URL or IP address and then begin the attack. Fortunately, this tool also does nothing to hide the attacker's address and thus makes it relatively easy to trace the attack back to its source.

### XOIC

This tool is similar to LOIC. It has three modes. You can send a message, execute a brief test, or start a DoS attack. You can see these options in Figure 4.3.

---

1. http://www.digitaltrends.com/computing/ddos-attacks-hit-record-numbers-in-q2-2015/

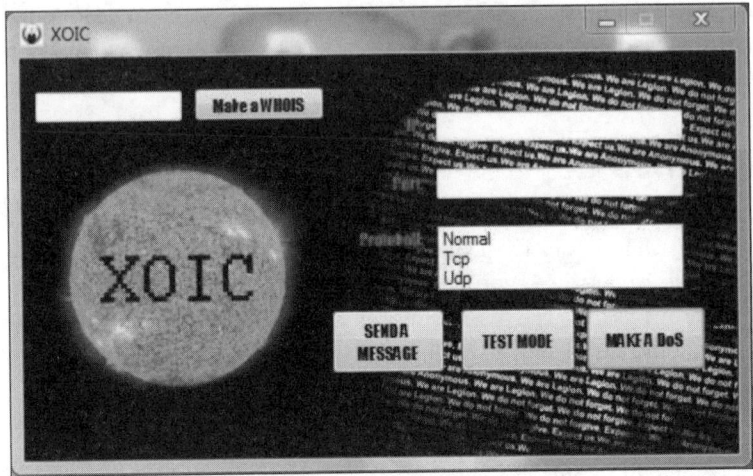

FIGURE 4.3    XOIC.

Like LOIC, XOIC is very easy to use. It is just a point-and-click graphical user interface. This allows even attackers with minimal skill to launch a DoS attack.

## TFN and TFN2K

TFN, also known as Tribal Flood Network, and TFN2K have been around for many years and are still in use today. TFN2K is a newer version of TFN that supports both Windows Server and UNIX platforms (and can easily be ported to additional platforms). It has some features that make detection more difficult than its predecessor, including sending decoy information to avoid being traced. Experts at using TFN2K can use the resources of a number of agents to coordinate an attack against one or more targets. Additionally, TFN and TFN2K can perform various attacks such as UDP flood attacks, ICMP flood attacks, and TCP SYN flood attacks (all discussed later in this chapter).

TFN2K works on two fronts. First, there is a command-driven client on the master system. Second, there is a daemon process operating on an agent system. The attack works like this:

1. The master instructs its agents to attack a list of designated targets.

2. The agents respond by flooding the targets with a barrage of packets.

With this tool, multiple agents, coordinated by the master, can work together during the attack to disrupt access to the target. Additionally, there are a number of "safety" features for the attacker that significantly complicate development of effective and efficient countermeasures for TFN2K.

- Master-to-agent communications are encrypted and may be mixed with any number of decoy packets.

- Both master-to-agent communications and the attacks themselves can be sent via randomized TCP, UDP, and ICMP packets.

- The master can falsify its IP address (spoof).

### Stacheldraht

This tool is not as widely known as the previously mentioned DoS tools. Stacheldraht, which is German for "barbed wire," is a DDoS attack tool that combines features of the Trinoo DDoS tool (another common tool) with the source code from the TFN DDoS attack tool. Like TFN2K, it adds encryption of communication between the attacker and the Stacheldraht masters. It also adds an automatic updating of the agents.

Stacheldraht can perform a variety of attacks including UDP flood, ICMP flood, TCP SYN flood, and Smurf attacks. It also detects and automatically enables source address forgery.

## DoS Weaknesses

The weakness in any DoS attack, from the attacker's point of view, is that the flood of packets must be sustained. As soon as the packets stop sending, the target system is back up. A DoS/DDoS attack, however, is very often used in conjunction with another form of attack, such as disabling one side of a connection in TCP hijacking or preventing authentication or logging between servers.

If the hacker is using a distributed attack, as soon as the administrators or owners of the infected machines realize their machine is infected, they will take steps to remove the virus and thus stop the attack. If a hacker attempts to launch an attack from her own machine, she must be aware that each packet has the potential to be traced back to its source. This fact means that a single hacker using a DoS will almost certainly be caught by the authorities. For this reason, the DDoS is quickly becoming the most common type of DoS attack. The specifics of DDoS attacks will be discussed later in this chapter.

## Specific DoS Attacks

The basic concept for perpetrating a DoS attack is not complicated. The real problem for the attacker is performing the attack without being caught. The next few sections of this chapter will examine some specific types of DoS attacks and look at specific case studies. This information should help you gain a deeper understanding of this particular Internet threat.

### TCP SYN Flood Attack

One popular version of the DoS attack is the SYN flood. This particular attack depends on the hacker's knowledge of how connections are made to a server. When a session is initiated between the client and server in a network using the TCP protocol, a packet is sent to the server with a 1-bit flag called a SYN flag set. SYN is short for synchronize. And this packet is asking the target server to please synchronize communications. The server will then allocate appropriate resources and then send to the client a packet with both the SYN (synchronize) and the ACK (acknowledge) flags set. The client machine is then supposed to respond with an ACK flag set. This is called the three-way handshake and is summarized as follows:

1. The client sends a packet with the SYN flag set.

2. The server allocates resources for the client and then responds with the SYN and ACK flags set.

3. The client responds with the ACK flag set.

There have been a number of well-known SYN flood attacks on web servers. The reason for the popularity of this attack type is that any machine that engages in TCP communication is vulnerable to it—and all machines connected to the Internet engage in TCP communications. Such communication is obviously the entire reason for web servers. The easiest way to block DoS attacks is via firewall rules. We will discuss firewalls in detail in Chapter 9, "Computer Security Technology." A properly configured firewall can prevent the SYN flood attack. There are, however, several methods and techniques you can implement on individual servers to protect against these attacks. The basic defensive techniques are as follows:

- Micro blocks

- SYN cookies

- RST cookies

- Stack tweaking

Some of these methods require more technical sophistication than others. These methods will be discussed in general here. When you are entrusted with defending a system against these forms of attacks, you can select the methods most appropriate for your network environment and your level of expertise and examine it further at that time. The specifics of how to implement any of these methods will depend on the operating system that your web server is using. You will need to consult your operating system's documentation, or appropriate websites, in order to find explicit instruction on how to implement methods.

### Micro Blocks

A *micro block* works by simply allocating a micro-record instead of allocating a complete connection object (an entire buffer segment) to the SYN object. In this way, an incoming SYN object can allocate as little as 16 bytes of space, making it significantly more difficult to flood a system. This method is a bit more obscure and not as widely used today as it once was. It also does not actually prevent a DoS attack; it merely mitigates the effects.

### SYN Cookies

This is another mitigation method, just like micro blocks. It should also be noted that many network administrators simply depend on their firewall to block DoS attacks and don't take any remediation steps on individual servers. I suggest you at least consider combining both approaches. Yes, have a well-configured firewall to block many DoS attacks, but also consider mitigating steps that can be taken on individual servers.

As the name *SYN cookies* suggests, this method uses cookies, not unlike the standard cookies used on many websites. With this method, the system does not immediately create a buffer space in memory for the handshaking process. Rather, it first sends a *SYN+ACK* (the acknowledgment signal that begins the handshaking process). The SYN+ACK contains a carefully constructed cookie, generated as a hash that contains the IP address, port number, and other information from the client machine requesting the connection. When the client responds with a normal ACK (acknowledgment), the information from that cookie will be included, which the server then verifies. Thus, the system does not fully allocate any memory until the third stage of the handshaking process. This enables the system to continue to operate normally; typically, the only effect seen is the disabling of large windows. However, the cryptographic hashing used in SYN cookies is fairly resource intensive, so system administrators that expect a great deal of incoming connections may choose not to use this defensive technique.

### FYI: Hashing

A hash value is a number generated from a string of text. The hash is significantly smaller than the text itself and is generated by a formula in such a way that it is extremely unlikely that some other text will produce the same hash value. Hashing plays a role in security when it is used to ensure that transmitted messages have not been tampered with. To do this, the sender generates a hash of the message, encrypts it, and sends it with the message itself. The recipient then decrypts both the message and the hash, produces another hash from the received message, and compares the two hashes. If they are the same, there is a very high probability that the message was transmitted intact. We will discuss hashing in more detail in Chapter 8, "Encryption."

### RST Cookies

Another cookie method that is easier to implement than SYN cookies is the *RST cookie*. In this method, the server sends a wrong SYN+ACK back to the client. The client should then generate an RST packet telling the server that something is wrong. Because the client sent back a packet notifying the server of the error, the server now knows the client request is legitimate and can now accept incoming connections from that client in the normal fashion. This method has two disadvantages. It might cause problems with older Windows machines or machines that are communicating from behind firewalls.

### Stack Tweaking

The method of *stack tweaking* involves altering the TCP stack on the server so that it will take less time to time out when a SYN connection is left incomplete. Unfortunately, this protective method will just make executing a SYN flood against that target more difficult; to a determined hacker, the attack is still possible.

> ### In Practice
>
> ## Stack Tweaking
>
> The process of stack tweaking is often quite complicated, depending on the operating system. Some operating systems' documentation provides no help on this subject. For these reasons, this method is usually only used by very advanced network administrators and is not recommended unless you have a very solid knowledge of the operating system with which you are working.

## Smurf IP Attack

The Smurf attack is a very popular version of the DoS attack. An ICMP (Internet Control Message Protocol) packet is sent out to the broadcast address of the network. Since it is broadcast, it responds by echoing the packet out to the network hosts, who then send it to the spoofed source address. Also, the spoofed source address can be anywhere on the Internet, not just on the local subnet. If the hacker can continually send such packets, she will cause the network itself to perform a DoS attack on one or more of its member servers. This attack is clever and rather simple. The only problem for the hacker is getting the packets started on the target network. This task can be accomplished via some software, such as a virus or Trojan horse, that will begin sending the packets.

In a Smurf attack, there are three people/systems involved: the attacker, the intermediary (who can also be a victim), and the victim. The attacker first sends an ICMP echo request packet to the intermediary's IP broadcast addresses. Since this is sent to the IP broadcast address, many of the machines on the intermediary's network will receive this request packet and will send an ICMP echo reply packet back. If all the machines on a network are responding to this request, the network becomes congested and there can be outages.

The attacker impacts the third party—the intended victim—by creating forged packets that contain the spoofed source address of the victim. Therefore, when all the machines on the intermediary's network start replying to the echo request, those replies will flood the victim's network. Thus, another network becomes congested and could become unusable. This attack is illustrated in Figure 4.4.

The Smurf attack is an example of the creativity that some malicious parties can employ. It is sometimes viewed as the digital equivalent of the biological process in an auto-immune disorder. With such disorders, the immune system attacks the patient's own body. In a Smurf attack, the network performs a DoS attack on one of its own systems. This method's cleverness illustrates why it is important that you attempt to work creatively and in a forward-thinking manner if you are responsible for system security in your network. The perpetrators of computer attacks are inventive and always coming up with new techniques. If your defense is less creative and clever than the attackers' defense, then it is simply a matter of time before your system is compromised.

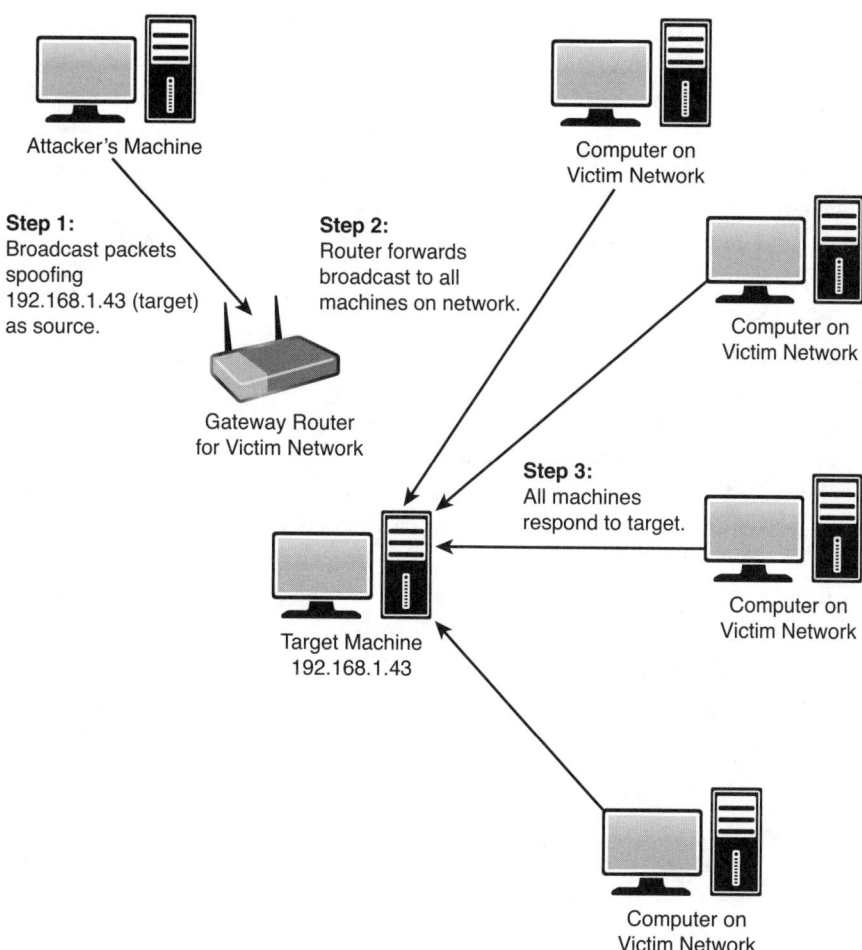

**FIGURE 4.4** Smurf

There are several ways to protect your system against this problem. One is to guard against Trojan horses. More will be said about the Trojan horse attack in later chapters; however, having policies prohibiting employees from downloading applications will help. Also, having adequate virus scanners can go a long way in protecting your system from a Trojan horse and, thus, a Smurf attack. It is also imperative that you use a proxy server, which was discussed in Chapter 2. If the internal IP addresses of your network are not known, then it is more difficult to target one in a Smurf attack. And, of course, the most obvious mitigation step you can take is to block all inbound broadcast packets at the firewall. Probably the best way to protect your system is to combine these defenses along with prohibiting directed broadcasts and patching the hosts to refuse to reply to any directed broadcasts.

## UDP Flood Attack

UDP, as you will recall from Chapter 2, is a connectionless protocol that does not require a connection setup procedure prior to transferring data. In a *UDP flood attack*, the attacker sends a UDP packet to a random port on a target system. When the target system receives a UDP packet, it automatically determines what application is waiting on the destination port. In this case, since there is no application waiting on the port, the target system will generate an ICMP packet of "destination unreachable" and attempt to send it back to the forged source address. If enough UDP packets are delivered to ports on the target, the system will become overloaded trying to determine awaiting applications (which do not exist) and then generating and sending packets back.

## ICMP Flood Attack

There are two basic types of *ICMP flood attacks*: floods and nukes. An ICMP flood is usually accomplished by broadcasting a large number of either pings or UDP packets. Like other flood attacks, the idea is to send so much data to the target system that it slows down. If it can be forced to slow down enough, the target will time out (not send replies fast enough) and be disconnected from the Internet. ICMP nukes exploit known bugs in specific operating systems. The attacker sends a packet of information that he knows the operating system on the target system cannot handle. In many cases, this will cause the target system to lock up completely.

This attack is far less effective against modern computers. Even a low-end desktop PC now will have 4 gigabytes (or more) of RAM and a dual core processor. That makes it difficult to generate enough pings to knock the machine offline. However, at one time this was a very common form of DoS attack.

## The Ping of Death

Recall from Chapter 2 that TCP packets are of limited size. In some cases, simply sending a packet that is too large can shut down a target machine. This action is referred to as the *ping of death (PoD)*. It works simply by overloading the target system. The hacker sends merely a single ping, but he does so with a very large packet and thus can shut down some machines.

This attack is quite similar to the classroom example discussed earlier in this chapter. The aim in both cases is to overload the target system and cause it to quit responding. PoD works to compromise systems that cannot deal with extremely large packet sizes. If successful, the server will actually shut down completely. It can, of course, be rebooted.

The only real safeguard against PoD is to ensure that all operating systems and software are routinely patched. This attack relies on vulnerabilities in the way a particular operating system (or application) handles abnormally large TCP packets. When such vulnerabilities are discovered, it is customary for the vendor to release a patch. The possibility of PoD is one reason, among many, why you must keep patches updated on all of your systems.

## Teardrop Attack

In a *teardrop attack*, the attacker sends a fragmented message. The two fragments overlap in ways that make it impossible to reassemble them properly without destroying the individual packet headers.

Therefore, when the victim attempts to reconstruct the message, the message is destroyed. This causes the target system to halt or crash. There are a number of variations on the basic teardrop attack that are available, such as TearDrop2, Boink, targa, Nestea Boink, NewTear, and SYNdrop.

## Land Attack

A *land attack* is probably the simplest in concept. The attacker sends a forged packet with the same source IP address and destination IP address (the target's IP address). The method is to drive the target system "crazy" by having it attempt to send messages to and from itself. The victim system will often be confused and will crash or reboot. More modern computers are not susceptible to this attack, but it is presented here just for historical purposes.

## DDoS

Perhaps the most common form of DoS today is the *DDoS*. This is accomplished by getting various machines to attack the target. A typical way this is done is by sending out a Trojan horse that will cause infected computers to attack a specified target at a particular date and time. This is a very effective way to execute a DDoS on any target. In this form of DDoS, the attacker does not have direct control of the various machines used in the attack. These machines are simply infected by some malware that causes them to participate in the attack on a particular date and time.

Another method is to use a botnet to orchestrate the attack. *Botnets* are networks of computers that have been compromised by the attacker, giving said attacker control of the infected system. This is often accomplished via delivery of a Trojan horse. However, unlike the previous DDoS example, the attacker will have direct control of the attacking machines in the botnet.

### Real-World Examples

A good deal of time has been spent discussing the basics of how various DoS attacks are conducted. By now, you should have a firm grasp of what a DoS attack is and have a basic understanding of how it works. It is now time to begin discussing specific, real-world examples of such attacks. This section will take the theoretical knowledge you have gained and give you real-world examples of its application.

### MyDoom

One of the most well-publicized DoS attacks was the MyDoom attack. While this attack is a few years old, it is an excellent one to study as it is a classic example of a virus being used to propagate a DDoS attack. This threat was a classically distributed DoS attack. The virus/worm would email itself to everyone in your address book and then, at a preset time, all infected machines would begin a coordinated attack on www.sco.com (Network World, 2004). Estimates put the number of infected machines between 500,000 and 1 million. This attack was successful and promptly shut down the SCO website. It should be noted that well before the day that the DoS attack was actually executed, network administrators and home users were well aware of what MyDoom would do. There were also several tools available free of charge on the Internet for removing the virus/worm. However, it appears that many people did not take the steps necessary to clean their machines of this virus/worm.

What is interesting is that MyDoom was still causing problems many years after its discovery. As late as July 2009, there was a DoS that utilized MyDoom as a backdoor to launch a DoS attack against South Korean and United States web servers.

---

**FYI: Virus or Worm?**

Definitions of the terms *virus* and *worm* are widely debated among the experts. And, depending upon the definition, what some would call a virus, others would call a worm. One general distinction that is accepted by many is that worms do not require direct human interaction to propagate, whereas viruses do. If you accept this definition, then both MyDoom and Slammer are worms. To avoid confusion on this issue, however, the term *virus/worm* will be used.

---

One thing that makes this attack so interesting is that it is clearly an example of domestic cyber terrorism (although it is certain that the creators of MyDoom would probably see it differently). (Cyber terrorism will be discussed further in Chapter 12, "Cyber Terrorism and Information Warfare.") For those readers who do not know the story, it will be examined here briefly. Santa Cruz Operations (SCO) makes a version of the UNIX operating system. Like most UNIX versions, their version is copyright protected. Several months before this attack, SCO began accusing certain Linux distributions of containing segments of SCO UNIX code. SCO sent demand letters to many Linux users demanding license fees. Many people in the Linux community viewed this request as simply an attempt to undermine the growing popularity of Linux, an open-source operating system. SCO went even further and filed suit against major companies that were distributing Linux (Software Patent Workgroup, 2003). This claim by SCO seemed unfounded to many legal and technology analysts. It was also viewed with great suspicion because SCO had close ties to Microsoft, which had been trying desperately to stop the growing popularity of Linux.

Many analysts feel that the MyDoom virus/worm was created by some individual (or group of individuals) who felt that the Santa Cruz Operations tactics were unacceptable. The hackers wished to cause economic harm to SCO and damage its public image. This probable motive makes this case clearly one of domestic economic terrorism: One group attacks the technological assets of another group based on an ideological difference. Prior to this virus/worm, there were numerous website defacements and other small-scale attacks that were part of ideological conflicts. However, this virus/worm was the first such attack to be so widespread and successful. This incident began a new trend in information warfare. As technology becomes less expensive and the tactics more readily available, you can expect to see an increase in this sort of attack in the coming years.

### Anonymous Uses DoS

On December 8, 2010, the infamous hacker group Anonymous launched multiple DDoS attacks on various financial companies, including Mastercard.com, PayPal, Visa.com, and PostFinance. These sites were brought down for over 16 hours. The attacks were launched because these sites refused to process donations for Wikileaks. The group Anonymous is a supporter of Wikileaks founder Julian Assange.

### DDoS Blackmail

In November 2015, the Australian company FastMail was the victim of a DDoS attack. First the system was attacked and knocked offline. After the second attack, the victim received a ransom demand. The attackers demanded 20 bit coins to call off the attack. A similar attack had been previously launched against Protonmail, also demanding ransom to stop the attacks.

### How to Defend Against DoS Attacks

There is no guaranteed way to prevent all DoS attacks, just as there is no sure way to prevent a hacking attack. However, there are steps you can take to minimize the danger. Some methodologies, such as SYN cookies and RST cookies, have already been mentioned. In this section, a few of the steps you can take to make your system less susceptible to a DoS attack will be examined.

One of the first things for you to consider is how these attacks are perpetrated. They may be executed via ICMP packets that are used to send error messages on the Internet or are sent by the `ping` and `traceroute` utilities. If you have a firewall (and you absolutely should have one), then simply configuring it to refuse ICMP packets from outside your network will be a major step in protecting your network from DoS attacks. Since DoS/DDoS attacks can be executed via a wide variety of protocols, you can also configure your firewall to disallow any incoming traffic at all, regardless of what protocol or port it occurs on. This step may seem radical, but it is certainly a secure one.

---

#### In Practice

#### Blocking ICMP Packets

There are very few legitimate reasons (and, some would argue, no good reasons) for an ICMP packet from outside your network to enter your network. Thus, blocking such packets is very often used as one part of the strategy to defend against DoS attacks. Incidentally, that will also make it more difficult for an attacker to scan your network (as we will see in Chapter 12).

---

It is also possible to detect some threats from certain DoS tools, such as TFN2K, by using information tools like NetStat. Many of these tools can be configured to look for the SYN_RECEIVED state, which could indicate a SYN flood attack.

If your network is large enough to have internal routers, then you can configure those routers to disallow any traffic that does not originate with your network. In that way, should packets make it past your firewall, they will not be propagated throughout the network. You should also consider disabling directed IP broadcasts on all routers. This strategy will prevent the router from sending broadcast packets to all machines on the network, thus stopping many DoS attacks. Additionally, you can install a filter on the router to verify that external packets actually have external IP addresses and that internal IPs have internal IP addresses.

Because many distributed DoS attacks depend on "unwitting" computers being used as launch points, one way to reduce such attacks is to protect your computer against virus attacks and Trojan horses. This problem will be discussed in more detail in a later chapter, but for now, it is important that you remember three things:

- Always use virus-scanning software and keep it updated.

- Always keep operating system and software patches updated.

- Have an organizational policy stating that employees cannot download anything onto their machines unless the download has been cleared by the IT staff.

As previously stated, none of these steps will make your network totally secure from either being the victim of a DoS attack or being the launch point for one, but they will help reduce the chances of either occurring. A good resource for this topic is the SANS Institute website, at www.sans.org/dosstep/. This site has some good tips on how to prevent DoS attacks.

# Summary

DoS attacks are among the most common attacks on the Internet. They are easy to perform, do not require a great deal of sophistication on the part of the perpetrator, and can have devastating effects on the target system. Only virus attacks are more common. (And, in some cases, the virus can be the source of the DoS attack.) In the exercises, you will practice stopping a DoS.

## Test Your Skills

### MULTIPLE CHOICE QUESTIONS

1. What is one of the most common and simplest attacks on a system?

    A. Denial of service

    B. Buffer overflow

    C. Session hacking

    D. Password cracking

2. Which of the following is not a valid way to define a computer's workload?

    A. Number of simultaneous users

    B. Storage capacity

    C. Maximum voltage

    D. Speed of network connection

3. What do you call a DoS launched from several machines simultaneously?

    A. Wide-area attack

    B. Smurf attack

    C. SYN flood

    D. DDoS attack

4. Leaving a connection half open is referred to as what?

    A. Smurf attack

    B. Partial attack

    C. SYN flood attack

    D. DDoS attack

5. What is the basic mechanism behind a DoS attack?

   A. Computers don't handle TCP packets well.

   B. Computers can only handle a finite load.

   C. Computers cannot handle large volumes of TCP traffic.

   D. Computers cannot handle large loads.

6. What is the most significant weakness in a DoS attack from the attacker's viewpoint?

   A. The attack is often unsuccessful.

   B. The attack is difficult to execute.

   C. The attack is easy to stop.

   D. The attack must be sustained.

7. What is the most common class of DoS attacks?

   A. Distributed denial of service

   B. Smurf attacks

   C. SYN floods

   D. Ping of death

8. What are three methods for protecting against SYN flood attacks?

   A. SYN cookies, RST cookies, and stack tweaking

   B. SYN cookies, DoS cookies, and stack tweaking

   C. DoS cookies, RST cookies, and stack deletion

   D. DoS cookies, SYN cookies, and stack deletion

9. Which attack mentioned in this chapter causes a network to perform a DoS on one of its own servers?

   A. SYN flood

   B. Ping of death

   C. Smurf attack

   D. DDoS

10. A defense that depends on a hash encryption being sent back to the requesting client is called what?

   A. Stack tweaking

   B. RST cookies

   C. SYN cookies

   D. Hash tweaking

11. What type of defense depends on sending the client an incorrect SYNACK?

   A. Stack tweaking

   B. RST cookies

   C. SYN cookies

   D. Hash tweaking

12. What type of defense depends on changing the server so that unfinished handshaking times out sooner?

   A. Stack tweaking

   B. RST cookies

   C. SYN cookies

   D. Hash tweaking

13. What type of attack is dependent on sending packets too large for the server to handle?

   A. Ping of death

   B. Smurf attack

   C. Slammer attack

   D. DDoS

14. What type of attack uses Internet routers to perform a DoS on the target?

   A. Ping of death

   B. Smurf attack

   C. Slammer attack

   D. DDoS

15. Which of the following is an example of a DDoS attack?

   A. MyDoom virus

   B. Bagle virus

   C. DoS virus

   D. Smurf virus

16. How can securing internal routers help protect against DoS attacks?

   A. Attacks cannot occur if your internal router is secured.

   B. Because attacks originate outside your network, securing internal routers cannot help protect you against DoS.

   C. Securing the router will only stop router-based DoS attacks.

   D. It will prevent an attack from propagating across network segments.

17. What can you do to your internal network routers to help defend against DoS attacks?

    **A.** Disallow all traffic that is not encrypted

    **B.** Disallow all traffic that comes from outside the network

    **C.** Disallow all traffic that comes from inside the network

    **D.** Disallow all traffic that comes from untrusted sources

18. Which of the following was rated by many experts to be the fastest growing virus on the Internet?

    **A.** MyDoom virus

    **B.** Bagle virus

    **C.** Slammer virus

    **D.** Smurf virus

19. What can you do with your firewall to defend against DoS attacks?

    **A.** Block all incoming traffic

    **B.** Block all incoming TCP packets

    **C.** Block all incoming traffic on port 80

    **D.** Block all incoming ICMP packets

20. Why will protecting against Trojan horse attacks reduce DoS attacks?

    **A.** Because many denial of service attacks are conducted by using a Trojan horse to get an unsuspecting machine to execute the DoS

    **B.** Because if you can stop a Trojan horse attack, you will also stop DoS attacks

    **C.** Because a Trojan horse will often open ports allowing a DoS attack

    **D.** Because a Trojan horse attacks in much the same way as a DoS attack

## EXERCISES

### EXERCISE 4.1: Executing a DoS

Note that Exercise 4.1 is best done in a laboratory setting where there are several machines available for this purpose.

1. Set up one machine (preferably a machine with very limited capacity) to run a small web server. (You can download Apache for free for either Windows or Linux from www.apache.org.)

2. Use the `ping` utility with various other computers to attempt to perform a simple DoS on that web server. This attempt is accomplished by getting other machines to begin a continuous

ping of that target machine using the previously mentioned `ping` command of `ping -l 65000 -w0 -t <insert target address here>`.

3. You should only add one to three lab machines to the "attack" at a time. (Start with one, add on a few more, and then a few more.)

4. As you add more machines, time how long it takes for another machine to bring up the home page of the target server. Also note the threshold (when that server quits responding completely).

## EXERCISE 4.2: **Stopping SYN Flood Attacks**

Note that this exercise is advanced. Some students may wish to work in groups.

1. Search the Web or your operating system's documentation for instructions on implementing either the RST cookie or the SYN cookie.

2. Follow those implementation instructions on either your own machine or on a machine designated by your instructor. The following websites might be of help to you in this matter:

   **Linux:** www.linuxjournal.com/article.php?sid=3554
   **Windows:** http://cr.yp.to/syncookies.html
   www.securityfocus.com/infocus/1729
   **Both Linux and Windows:** www.securiteam.com/tools/6D00K0K01O.html

## EXERCISE 4.3: **Using Firewall Settings**

This exercise is only for students with access to a lab firewall.

1. Use your firewall's documentation to see how to block ICMP packets.

2. Set your firewall to block those packets.

## EXERCISE 4.4: **Using Router Settings**

This exercise is only for students with access to a lab router.

1. Use your router's documentation to see how to block all traffic not originating on your own network.

2. Set your router to block that traffic.

## PROJECTS

### PROJECT 4.1: Employing Alternative Defenses

1. Using the Web or another research tool, search for alternative means of defending against either general DoS attacks or a specific type of DoS attack. This can be any defense other than the ones already mentioned in this chapter.

2. Write a brief paper concerning this defense technique.

### PROJECT 4.2: Defending Against Specific Denial of Service Attacks

1. Using the Web or other tools, find a DoS attack that has occurred in the last six months. You might find some resources at www.f-secure.com.

2. Note how that attack was conducted.

3. Write a brief explanation of how you might have defended against that specific attack.

### PROJECT 4.3: Hardening the TCP Stack Against DoS

Note that this project requires access to a lab machine. It is also a long project, requiring some research time on the part of the students.

1. Using manuals, vendor documentation, and other resources, find one method for altering TCP communications to help prevent DoS attacks.

2. Using this information, implement one of these methods on your lab computer.

---

### Case Study

Runa Singh is the network administrator in charge of network security for a medium-sized company. The firm already has a firewall, its network is divided into multiple segments separated by routers, and it has updated virus scanners on all machines. Runa wants to take extra precautions to prevent DoS attacks. She takes the following actions:

- She adjusts her firewall so that no incoming ICMP packets are allowed.
- She changes the web server so that it uses SYN cookies.

Now consider the following questions:

- Are there problems with any of her precautions? If so, what are the problems?
- What additional steps would you recommend to Runa?

## Chapter 5

# Malware

**After reading this chapter and completing the exercises, you will be able to do the following:**

- Understand viruses (worms) and how they propagate, including the Sobig and Sasser types
- Have a working knowledge of several specific virus outbreaks
- Understand how virus scanners operate
- Understand what a Trojan horse is and how it operates
- Have a working knowledge of several specific Trojan horse attacks
- Grasp the concept behind the buffer-overflow attack
- Have a better understanding of spyware and how it enters a system
- Defend against each of these attacks through sound practices, antivirus software, and antispyware software

## Introduction

In Chapter 4, "Denial of Service Attacks," we examined the denial of service attack. It is a very common attack and one that can easily be perpetrated. In this chapter, you will continue your examination of security threats by learning about several other types of attacks. First, you will learn about virus outbreaks. Our discussion will focus on information about how and why virus attacks work, including their deployment through Trojan horses. This chapter is not a "how to create your own virus" tutorial, but rather an introduction to the concepts underlying these attacks as well as an examination of some specific case studies.

This chapter will also explore buffer-overflow attacks, spyware, and several other forms of malware. Each of these brings a unique approach to an attack, and each needs to be considered when defending a system. Your ability to defend against such attacks will be enhanced by expanding your knowledge of how they work. In the exercises at the end of the chapter, you will have the opportunity to research preventive methods for viruses and to try out antivirus methods from McAfee and Norton.

# Viruses

By definition, a computer virus is a program that self-replicates. Generally, a virus will also have some other unpleasant function, but the self-replication and rapid spread are the hallmarks of a virus. Often this growth, in and of itself, can be a problem for an infected network. The last chapter discussed the MyDoom virus and the effects of its rapid, high-volume scanning. Any rapidly spreading virus can reduce the functionality and responsiveness of a network. Simply by exceeding the traffic load that a network was designed to carry, the network may be rendered temporarily nonfunctional. The infamous I Love You virus actually had no negative payload, but the sheer volume of emails it generated bogged down many networks.

## How a Virus Spreads

A virus will usually spread primarily in one of two ways. The first is to simply scan your computer for connections to a network and then copy itself to other machines on the network to which your computer has access. This is actually the most efficient way for a virus to spread. However, this method requires more programming skill than other methods. The more common method is to read your email address book and email itself to everyone in your address book. Programming this is a trivial task, which explains why it is so common.

The latter method is, by far, the most common method for virus propagation, and Microsoft Outlook may be the one email program most often hit with such virus attacks. The reason is not so much a security flaw in Outlook as it is the ease of working with Outlook. All Microsoft Office products are made so that a legitimate programmer who is writing software for a business can access many of the application's internal objects and thereby easily create applications that integrate the applications within the Microsoft Office suite. For example, a programmer could write an application that would access a Word document, import an Excel spreadsheet, and then use Outlook to automatically email the resulting document to interested parties. Microsoft has done a good job of making this process very easy, for it usually takes a minimum amount of programming to accomplish these tasks. Using Outlook, it takes less than five lines of code to reference Outlook and send out an email. This means a program can literally cause Outlook itself to send emails, unbeknownst to the user. There are numerous code examples on the Internet that show exactly how to do this, free for the taking. For this reason, it does not take a very skilled programmer to be able to access your Outlook address book and automatically send emails. Essentially, the ease of programming Outlook is why there are so many virus attacks that target Outlook.

While the overwhelming majority of virus attacks spread by attaching themselves to the victim's existing email software, some recent virus outbreaks have used other methods for propagation, such as their own internal email engine. Another virus propagation method is to simply copy itself across a network. Virus outbreaks that spread via multiple routes are becoming more common.

The method of delivering a payload can be rather simplistic and rely more on end-user negligence than on the skill of the virus writer. Enticing users to go to websites or open files they should not is a common method for delivering a virus and one that requires no programming skill at all. Regardless of the way a virus arrives at your doorstep, once it is on your system, it will attempt to spread and, in many cases, will also attempt to cause some harm to your system. Once a virus is on your system, it can do anything that any legitimate program can do. That means it could potentially delete files, change system settings, or cause other harm.

## Types of Viruses

There are many different types of viruses. In this section we will briefly look at some of the major virus types. Viruses can be classified by either their method for propagation or their activities on the target computers.

- **Macro:** Macro viruses infect the macros in office documents. Many office products, including Microsoft Office, allow users to write mini-programs called macros. These macros can also be written as a virus. A macro virus is written into a macro in some business application. For example, Microsoft Office allows users to write macros to automate some tasks. Microsoft Outlook is designed so that a programmer can write scripts using a subset of the Visual Basic programming language, called Visual Basic for Applications (VBA). This scripting language is, in fact, built into all Microsoft Office products. Programmers can also use the closely related VBScript language. Both languages are quite easy to learn. If such a script is attached to an email and the recipient is using Outlook, then the script can execute. That execution can do any number of things, including scanning the address book, looking for addresses, sending out email, deleting email, and more.

- **Multi-partite:** Multi-partite viruses attack the computer in multiple ways for example, infecting the boot sector of the hard disk and one or more files.

- **Memory Resident:** A memory-resident virus installs itself and then remains in RAM from the time the computer is booted up to when it is shut down.

- **Armored:** An armored virus uses techniques that make it hard to analyze. Code confusion is one such method. The code is written such that if the virus is disassembled, the code won't be easily followed. Compressed code is another method for armoring the virus.

- **Sparse infector:** A sparse infector virus attempts to elude detection by performing its malicious activities only sporadically. With a sparse infector virus, the user will see symptoms for a short period, then no symptoms for a time. In some cases the sparse infector targets a specific program but the virus only executes every 10th time or 20th time that target program executes. Or a sparse infector may have a burst of activity and then lie dormant for a period of time. There are a number of variations on the theme, but the basic principle is the same: to reduce the frequency of attack and thus reduce the chances for detection.

- **Polymorphic:** A polymorphic virus literally changes its form from time to time to avoid detection by antivirus software. A more advanced form of this is called the Metamorphic virus; it can completely change itself.

## Virus Examples

The threat from virus attacks cannot be overstated. While there are many web pages that give virus information, in my opinion, there are only a handful of web pages that consistently give the latest, most reliable, most detailed information on virus outbreaks. Any security professional will want to consult these sites on a regular basis. You can read more about any virus, past or current, at the following websites:

- http://www.pctools.com/security-news/top-10-computer-viruses/

- https://www.us-cert.gov/publications/virus-basics

- http://www.techrepublic.com/pictures/the-18-scariest-computer-viruses-of-all-time/

The following sections will look at several real-world virus outbreaks. We will examine very recent viruses as well as some examples from 10 or more years in the past. This should give you a fairly complete overview of how viruses behave in the real world.

## Rombertik

Rombertik wreaked havoc in 2015. This malware uses the browser to read user credentials to websites. It is most often sent as an attachment to an email. Perhaps even worse, in some situations Rombertik will either overwrite the master boot record on the hard drive, making the machine unbootable, or begin encrypting files in the user's home directory.

## Gameover ZeuS

Gameover ZeuS is a virus that creates a peer-to-peer botnet. Essentially, it establishes encrypted communication between infected computers and the command and control computer, allowing the attacker to control the various infected computers. In 2014 the U.S. Department of Justice was able to temporarily shut down communication with the command and control computers; then in 2015 the FBI announced a reward of $3 million for information leading to the capture of Evgeniy Bogachev for his alleged involvement with Gameover ZeuS.

A command and control computer is the computer used in a botnet to control the other computers. These are the central nodes from which a botnet will be managed.

## CryptoLocker and CryptoWall

One of the most widely known examples of ransomeware is the infamous CryptoLocker, first discovered in 2013. CryptoLocker utilized asymmetric encryption to lock the user's files. Several varieties of CryptoLocker have been detected.

CryptoWall is a variant of CryptoLocker first found in August 2014. It looked and behaved much like CryptoLocker. In addition to encrypting sensitive files, it would communicate with a command and control server and even take a screenshot of the infected machine. By March 2015 a variation of CryptoWall had been discovered that is bundled with the spyware TSPY_FAREIT.YOI and actually steals credentials from the infected system, in addition to holding files for ransom.

## FakeAV

This virus first appeared in July 2012. It affected Windows systems ranging from Windows 95 to Windows 7 and Windows server 2003. This was a fake antivirus (thus the name FakeAV) that would pop up fake virus warnings. This was not the first such fake antivirus malware, but it was one of the more recent ones.

## MacDefender

This virus is very interesting for multiple reasons. First, it specifically targets Macintosh computers. Most experts have long agreed that Apple products remained relatively virus free simply because their products did not have enough market share to attract the attention of virus writers. It has long been suspected that if Apple garnered a greater market share, it would also begin to get more virus attacks. That has proven to be true.

This virus was first seen in the early months of 2011. It is embedded in some web pages, and when a user visits those web pages, she is given a fake virus scan that tells her she has a virus and it needs to be fixed. The "fix" is actually downloading a virus. The point of the virus is to get end users to purchase the MacDefender "antivirus" product. This is the second reason this case is noteworthy. Fake antivirus attacks, also known as scareware, have been becoming increasingly common.

## Troj/Invo-Zip

This particular worm is a classic worm/Trojan horse that was first reported in mid-2010. It is transmitted as a zip file attached to an email. The email claims that the zip file contains data related to an invoice, tax issue, or similar urgent paperwork. This is a classic example of attempting to entice the recipient to open the attachment. And in this case, the recipients most likely to be enticed would be businesspeople.

If the recipient does open the attachment, then he will have installed spyware on his machine that would first disable the firewall and then start attempting to capture information including financial data. It even takes screenshots of the user's desktop.

## W32/Netsky-P

This worm was first found in 2006 and was still going around in 2011. It is a fairly typical virus in that it spreads primarily through email, but it also uses file sharing utilities to copy itself. It copies itself to various directories and shared folders. In one interesting twist, it attempts to copy itself to

C:\WINDOWS\FVProtect.exe. The name would make many people (including otherwise technically savvy people) think this program was actually part of some antivirus utility. It also copies itself to C:\WINDOWS\userconfig9x.dll. Again, it would appear to be a system file, thus making people less likely to delete it.

This is also a classic worm/virus in that the email it sends has a fairly generic title and content that attempts to get the recipient to open the attachment. For example, the body of the message might say something like, "Please see the attached file for details" or "Your file is attached."

## The Sobig Virus

This is obviously not a recent virus, as it was first found in 2003. However, it is an excellent virus to study because it received the most media attention and perhaps caused the most harm in 2003. The first interesting thing to study about this virus was how it utilized a multimodal approach to spreading. This means that it used more than one mechanism to spread and infect new machines. It would copy itself to any shared drives on your network and would email itself out to everyone in your address book. For these reasons, this virus was particularly virulent, which is also why it is important to study.

### FYI: Virulent Virus

The term *virulent* means essentially the same thing in reference to a computer virus as it does to a biological virus. It is a measure of how rapidly the infection spreads and how easily it infects new targets.

In the case of Sobig, if one person on a network was unfortunate enough to open an email containing the virus, not only would his machine be infected, but so would every shared drive on that network to which this person had access. However, Sobig, like most email-distributed virus attacks, had tell-tale signs in the email subject or title that could be used to identify the email as one infected by a virus. The email would have some enticing title such as "here is the sample" or "the document" to encourage you to be curious enough to open the attached file. The virus would then copy itself into the Windows System directory.

This particular virus spread so far and infected so many networks that the multiple copying of the virus alone was enough to bring some networks to a standstill. This virus did not destroy files or damage the system, but it generated a great deal of traffic that bogged down the networks infected by it. The virus itself was of moderate sophistication. Once it was out, however, many variants began to spring up, further complicating the situation. One of the effects of some variants of Sobig was to download a file from the Internet that would then cause printing problems. Some network printers would just start printing junk. The Sobig.E variant would even write to the Windows Registry, causing itself to be in the computer startup (F-Secure, 2003). These complex characteristics indicate that the creator knew how to access the Windows Registry, access shared drives, alter the Windows startup, and access Outlook.

This brings up the issue of virus variants and how they occur. In the case of a biological virus, mutations in the genetic code cause new virus strains to appear, and the pressures of natural selection allow some of these strains to evolve into entirely new species of viruses. Obviously, the biological method is not what occurs with a computer virus. With a computer virus, what occurs is that some intrepid programmer with malicious intent will get a copy of a virus (perhaps her own machine becomes infected) and will then reverse-engineer it. Since many virus attacks are in the form of a script attached to an email, unlike traditionally compiled programs, the source code of these attacks is readily readable and alterable. The programmer in question then simply takes the original virus code, introduces some change, and rereleases the variant. Frequently, the people who are caught for virus creation are actually the developers of the variants who lacked the skill of the original virus writer and therefore were easily caught.

## The Mimail Virus

This is another older virus that is still worth studying. The Mimail virus did not receive as much media attention as Sobig, but it had its intriguing characteristics. This virus not only collected email addresses from your address book, but also from other documents on your machine (Gudmundsson, 2004). Thus, if you had a Word document on your hard drive and an email address was in that document, Mimail would find it. This strategy meant that Mimail would spread farther than many other viruses. Mimail had its own built-in email engine, so it did not have to "piggy back" off your email client. It could spread regardless of what email software you used.

These two variations from most virus attacks made Mimail interesting to people who study computer viruses. There are a variety of techniques that allow you to programmatically open and process files on your computer; however, most virus attacks do not employ them. The scanning of the document for email addresses indicates a certain level of skill and creativity on the part of the virus writer. In this author's opinion, Mimail was not the work of an amateur, but rather a person with professional-level programming skill.

## The Bagle Virus

This is the last of the "historical viruses" that we will examine. It is noteworthy in that it combined email attachments along with the fake virus warning. The Bagle virus began to spread rapidly in the fourth quarter of 2003. The email it sent claimed to be from your system administrator. It would tell you that your email account had been infected by a virus and that you should open the attached file to get instructions. Once you opened the attached file, your system was infected. This virus was particularly interesting for several reasons. To begin with, it spread both through email and copying itself to shared folders. Second, it could scan files on your PC looking for email addresses. Finally, it would disable processes used by antivirus scanners. In biological terms, this virus took out your computer's "immune system." The disabling of virus scanners was a new twist that indicated at least moderate programming skills on the part of the virus creator.

## A Nonvirus Virus

Another new type of virus has been gaining popularity in the past few years, and that is the "nonvirus virus" or, put simply, a hoax. Rather than actually writing a virus, a hacker sends an email to every address he has. The email claims to be from some well-known antivirus center and warns of a new virus that is circulating. The email instructs people to delete some file from their computer to get rid of the virus. The file, however, is not really a virus but part of a computer's system. The jdbgmgr.exe virus hoax used this scheme (Rhode Island Soft Systems, Inc., 2003). It encouraged the reader to delete a file that was actually needed by the system. Surprisingly, a number of people followed this advice and not only deleted the file, but promptly emailed their friends and colleagues to warn them to delete the file from their machines.

---

**FYI: The Morris Internet Worm**

The Morris worm was one of the first computer worms ever to be distributed over the Internet. And it was certainly the first to gain any significant media attention.

Robert Tappan Morris, Jr., then a student at Cornell University, wrote this worm and launched it from an MIT system on November 2, 1988. Morris did not actually intend to cause damage with the worm. Instead, he wanted the worm to reveal bugs in the programs it exploited in order to spread. However, bugs in the code allowed an individual computer to be infected multiple times, and the worm became a menace. Each additional "infection" spawned a new process on the infected computer. At a certain point, the high number of processes running on an infected machine slowed down the computer to the point of being unusable. At least 6,000 UNIX machines were infected with this worm.

Morris was convicted of violating the 1986 Computer Fraud and Abuse Act and was sentenced to a $10,000 fine, 3 years probation, and 400 hours of community service. But perhaps the greatest impact of this worm was that it led to the creation of the Computer Emergency Response Team (CERT). CERT is an organization hosted at Carnegie Mellon University (www.cert.org/) that is a repository for security bulletins, information, and guidelines. CERT is a source that any security professional should be familiar with.

---

## Flame

No modern discussion of viruses would be complete without a discussion of Flame. This virus, which first appeared in 2012, targeted Windows operating systems. The first item that makes this virus notable is that it was specifically designed by the U.S. government for espionage. It was discovered in May 2012 at several locations, including Iranian government sites. Flame is spyware that can monitor network traffic and take screenshots of the infected system.

## Rules for Avoiding Viruses

You should notice a common theme with all virus attacks (except the hoax), which is that they want you to open some type of attachment. The most common way for a virus to spread is as an email attachment. This realization leads to some simple rules that will drastically reduce the odds of becoming infected with a virus.

- Use a virus scanner. McAfee and Norton (explored in the exercises at the end of this chapter) are the two most widely accepted and used virus scanners. However, Kaspersky and AVG are also good, reputable choices. Each costs about $30 per year to keep your virus scanner updated. Do it. Each antivirus has its proponents and detractors—I won't delve into the opinions on which is better. For most users, any of the four major antivirus programs would be effective. I rotate which one I use periodically, just so I can stay familiar with all of them.

- If you are not sure about an attachment, do not open it.

- You might even exchange a code word with friends and colleagues. Tell them that if they wish to send you an attachment, they should put the code word in the title of the message. Without seeing the code word, you will not open any attachment.

- Do not believe "security alerts" that are sent to you. Microsoft does not send out alerts in this manner. Check the Microsoft website regularly, as well as one of the antivirus websites previously mentioned.

These rules will not make your system 100% virus proof, but they will go a long way toward protecting your system.

# Trojan Horses

Recall from earlier chapters that *Trojan horse* is a term for a program that looks benign but actually has a malicious purpose. We have already seen viruses that are delivered via a Trojan horse. You might receive or download a program that appears to be a harmless business utility or game. More likely, the Trojan horse is just a script attached to a benign-looking email. When you run the program or open the attachment, it does something else other than or in addition to what you thought it would. It might

- Download harmful software from a website.

- Install a key logger or other spyware on your machine.

- Delete files.

- Open a backdoor for a hacker to use.

It is common to find combination virus plus Trojan horse attacks. In those scenarios, the Trojan horse spreads like a virus. The MyDoom virus opened a port on your machine that a later virus, doomjuice, would exploit, thus making MyDoom a combination virus and Trojan horse.

A Trojan horse could also be crafted especially for an individual. If a hacker wished to spy on a certain individual, such as the company accountant, he could craft a program specifically to attract that person's attention. For example, if he knew the accountant was an avid golfer, he could write a program that computed handicap and listed best golf courses. He would post that program on a free web server. He would then email a number of people, including the accountant, telling them about the free software.

The software, once installed, could check the name of the currently logged-on person. If the logged-on name matched the accountant's name, the software could then go out, unknown to the user, and download a key logger or other monitoring application. If the software did not damage files or replicate itself, then it would probably go undetected for quite a long time. There have been a number of Trojan horses through the years. One of the earliest and most widely known was Back Orifice.

---

**FYI: Virus or Worm?**

As noted in the previous chapter, there is disagreement among the experts as to the distinction between a virus and a worm. Some experts would call MyDoom (as well as Sasser, which will be discussed later) a worm because it spread without human intervention. However, I would define a virus as any file that can self-replicate, and a worm as any program that can propagate without human interference. This is also the most common definition you will find among security experts.

---

Such a program could be within the skill set of virtually any moderately competent programmer. This is one reason that many organizations have rules against downloading *any* software onto company machines. I am unaware of any actual incident of a Trojan horse being custom tailored in this fashion. However, it is important to remember that those creating virus attacks tend to be innovative people.

It is also important to note that creating a Trojan horse does not require programming skill. There are free tools on the Internet, such as EliteWrapper, that allow someone to combine two programs, one hidden and one not. So one could easily take a virus and combine it with, for example, a poker game. The end user would only see the poker game, but when it was run it would launch the virus.

Another scenario to consider is one that would be quite devastating. Without divulging programming details, the basic premise will be outlined here to illustrate the grave dangers of Trojan horses. Imagine a small application that displays a series of unflattering pictures of Osama Bin Laden. This application would probably be popular with many people in the United States, particularly people in the military, intelligence community, or defense-related industries. Now assume that this application simply sits dormant on the machine for a period of time. It need not replicate like a virus because the computer user will probably send it to many of his associates. On a certain date and time, the software connects to any drive it can, including network drives, and begins deleting all files. If such a Trojan horse were released "in the wild," within 30 days it would probably be shipped to thousands, perhaps millions, of people. Imagine the devastation when thousands of computers begin deleting files and folders.

This scenario is mentioned precisely to frighten you a little. Computer users, including professionals who should know better, routinely download all sorts of things from the Internet, such as amusing flash videos and cute games. Every time an employee downloads something of this nature, there is the chance of downloading a Trojan horse. One need not be a statistician to realize that if employees continue that practice long enough, they will eventually download a Trojan horse onto a company machine. If they do, hopefully the virus will not be as vicious as the theoretical one just outlined here.

Because Trojan horses are usually installed by users themselves, the security countermeasure for this attack is to prevent downloads and installations by end users. From a law enforcement perspective, the investigation of a crime involving a Trojan horse would involve a forensic scan of the computer hard drive, looking for the Trojan horse itself.

There are a number of tools, some free for download, that will help a person create a Trojan horse. One that I use in my penetration testing classes is eLiTeWrap. It is easy to use. Essentially, it can bind any two programs together. Using a tool such as this one, anyone can bind a virus or spyware to an innocuous program such as a shareware poker game. This would lead to a large number of people downloading what they believe is a free game and unknowingly installing malware on their own system.

The eLiTeWrap tool is a command line tool, but it is very easy to use. Just follow these steps:

1. Enter the file you want to run that is visible.

2. Enter the operation:

   - 1—Pack only

   - 2—Pack and execute, visible, asynchronously

   - 3—Pack and execute, hidden, asynchronously

   - 4—Pack and execute, visible, synchronously

   - 5—Pack and execute, hidden, synchronously

   - 6—Execute only, visible, asynchronously

   - 7—Execute only, hidden, asynchronously

   - 8—Execute only, visible, synchronously

   - 9—Execute only, hidden, synchronously

3. Enter the command line.

4. Enter the second file (the item you are surreptitiously installing).

5. Enter the operation.

6. When done with files, press Enter.

In Figure 5.1 you can see a demonstration that is appropriate for a classroom laboratory. In this example, two innocuous programs are combined into one Trojan horse. The programs chosen are simple Windows utilities that won't harm the computer. However, it illustrates how easy it would be to combine legitimate programs with malware, to deliver them to the target computer.

This is provided as an illustration of how easy it is to create a Trojan horse, not an encouragement for you to do so. It is important to understand just how easy this process is so you can understand the prevalence of malware. Any attachment or download should be treated with significant suspicion.

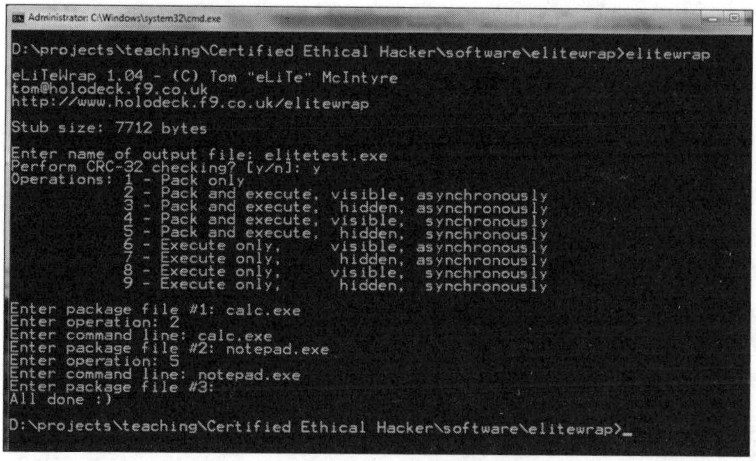

**FIGURE 5.1    eLiTeWrap.**

# The Buffer-Overflow Attack

You have become knowledgeable about a number of ways to attack a target system: denial of service, virus, and Trojan horse. While these attacks are probably the most common, they are not the only methods. Another method of attacking a system is called a buffer-overflow (or buffer-overrun) attack. A buffer-overflow attack happens when someone tries to put more data in a buffer than it was designed to hold (searchSecurity.com, 2004a). Any program that communicates with the Internet or a private network must take in some data. This data is stored, at least temporarily, in a space in memory called a *buffer*. If the programmer who wrote the application was careful, when you try to place too much information into a buffer, that information is then either simply truncated or outright rejected. Given the number of applications that might be running on a target system and the number of buffers in each application, the chances of having at least one buffer that was not written properly are significant enough to cause any prudent person some concern.

Someone who is moderately skilled in programming can write a program that purposefully writes more into the buffer than it can hold. For example, if the buffer can hold 1024 bytes of data and you try to fill it with 2048 bytes, the extra 1024 bytes is then simply loaded into memory. If that extra data is actually a malicious program, then it has just been loaded into memory and is thus now running on the target system. Or, perhaps the perpetrator simply wants to flood the target machine's memory, thus overwriting other items that are currently in memory and causing them to crash. Either way, the buffer overflow is a very serious attack.

Fortunately, buffer-overflow attacks are a bit harder to execute than a DoS or simple Microsoft Outlook script virus. To create a buffer-overflow attack, you must have a good working knowledge of some programming language (C or C++ is often chosen) and understand the target operating system/application well enough to know whether it has a buffer overflow weakness and how that weakness might be exploited.

It must be noted that modern operating systems and web servers are not generally susceptible to common buffer overflow attacks. Windows 95 was quite susceptible, but it has been many years since a Windows operating system was susceptible. Certainly Windows 7, 8, or 10 cannot be compromised with this type of buffer overflow. However, the same cannot be necessarily said for all the custom applications developed to run on various systems. It is always possible that an Internet-enabled application, including but not limited to web applications, might be susceptible to this attack.

Essentially, this vulnerability only exists if programmers fail to program correctly. If all programs truncate extra data, then a buffer overflow cannot be executed on that system. However, if the program does not check the boundaries of variables and arrays and allows excess data to be loaded, then that system is vulnerable to a buffer overflow.

# The Sasser Virus/Buffer Overflow

This is an older attack but one that demonstrates the use of a buffer-overflow attack. Sasser is a combination attack in that the virus (or worm) spreads by exploiting a buffer overrun.

The Sasser virus spreads by exploiting a known flaw in a Windows system program. Sasser copies itself to the Windows directory as avserve.exe and creates a Registry key to load itself at startup. In that way, once your machine is infected, you will start the virus every time you start the machine. This virus scans random IP addresses, listening on successive TCP ports starting at 1068 for exploitable systems—that is, systems that have not been patched to fix this flaw. When one is found, the worm exploits the vulnerable system by overflowing a buffer in LSASS.EXE, which is a file that is part of the Windows operating system. That executable is a built-in system file and is part of Windows. Sasser also acts as an FTP server on TCP port 5554, and it creates a remote shell on TCP port 9996. Next, Sasser creates an FTP script named cmd.ftp on the remote host and executes it. This FTP script instructs the target victim to download and execute the worm from the infected host. The infected host accepts this FTP traffic on TCP port 5554. The computer also creates a file named win.log on the C: drive. This file contains the IP address of the localhost. Copies of the virus are created in the Windows System directory as #_up.exe. Examples are shown here:

- c:\WINDOWS\system32\12553_up.exe

- c:\WINDOWS\system32\17923_up.exe

- c:\WINDOWS\system32\29679_up.exe

A side effect of this virus is that it causes your machine to reboot. A machine that is repeatedly rebooting without any other known cause may well be infected with the Sasser virus.

This is another case in which the infection can easily be prevented by several means. First, if you update your systems on a regular basis, your systems should not be vulnerable to this flaw. Second, if your network's routers or firewall block traffic on the ports mentioned (9996 and 5554), you will then prevent most of Sasser's damage. Your firewall should only allow traffic on specified ports; all other ports should be shut down. In short, if you as the network administrator are aware of security issues and are taking prudent steps to protect the network, your network will be safe. The fact that so many networks were affected by this virus should indicate that not enough administrators are properly trained in computer security.

# Spyware

In Chapter 1, "Introduction to Computer Security," spyware was mentioned as one of the threats to computer security. Using spyware, however, requires a great deal more technical knowledge on the part of the perpetrator than some other forms of malware. The perpetrator must be able to develop spyware for the particular situation or customize existing spyware for his needs. He must then be able to get the spyware on the target machine.

Spyware can be as simple as a cookie used by a website to record a few brief facts about your visit to that website, or it could be of a more insidious type, such as a key logger. Recall from Chapter 1 that key loggers are programs that record every keystroke you make on your keyboard; this spyware then logs your keystrokes to the spy's file. The most common use of a key logger is to capture usernames and passwords. However, this method can capture every username and password you enter and every document you type, as well as anything else you might type. This data can be stored in a small file hidden on your machine for later extraction or sent out in TCP packets to some predetermined address. In some cases, the software is even set to wait until after hours to upload this data to some server or to use your own email software to send the data to an anonymous email address. There are also some key loggers that take periodic screenshots from your machine, revealing anything that is open on your computer. Whatever the specific mode of operation, spyware is software that literally spies on your activities on a particular computer.

## Legal Uses of Spyware

There are some perfectly legal uses for spyware. Some employers have embraced such spyware as a means of monitoring employee use of company technology. Many companies have elected to monitor phone, email, or web traffic within the organization. Keep in mind that the computer, network, and phone systems are the property of the company or organization, not of the employee. These technologies are supposedly only used for work purposes; therefore, company monitoring might not constitute an invasion of privacy. While courts have upheld this monitoring as a company's right, it is critical to consult an attorney before initiating this level of employee monitoring as well as to consider the potential negative impact on employee morale.

Parents can also elect to use this type of software on their home computer to monitor the activities of their children on the Internet. The goal is usually a laudable application—protecting their children from online predators. Yet, as with employees in a company, the practice may illicit a strong negative reaction from the parties being spied upon (namely, their children). Parents have to weigh the risk to their children versus what might be viewed as a breach of trust.

## How Is Spyware Delivered to a Target System?

Clearly, spyware programs can track all activity on a computer, and that information can be retrieved by another party via a number of different methods. The real question is this: How does spyware get onto a computer system in the first place? The most common method is a Trojan horse. It is also possible that when you visit a certain website spyware may download in the background while you are simply perusing the website. Of course, if an employer (or parent) is installing the spyware, it can then be installed noncovertly in the same way that an organization would install any other application.

## Obtaining Spyware Software

Given the many other utilities and tools that have been mentioned as available from the Internet, you probably will not be surprised to learn that you can obtain many spyware products for free, or at very low cost, on the Internet. You can check the Counterexploitation (www.cexx.org) website, shown in Figure 5.2, for a lengthy list of known spyware products circulating on the Internet and for information about methods you can use to remove them. The SpywareGuide website (SpywareGuide, 2004) (www.spywareguide.com) lists spyware that you can get right off the Internet should you feel some compelling reason to spy on someone's computer activities. Figure 5.3 shows the categories of malware that are available from this site. Several key logger applications are listed on this site, as shown in Figure 5.4. These applications include well-known key loggers such as Absolute Keylogger, Tiny Keylogger, and TypO. Most can be downloaded for free or for a nominal charge from the Internet.

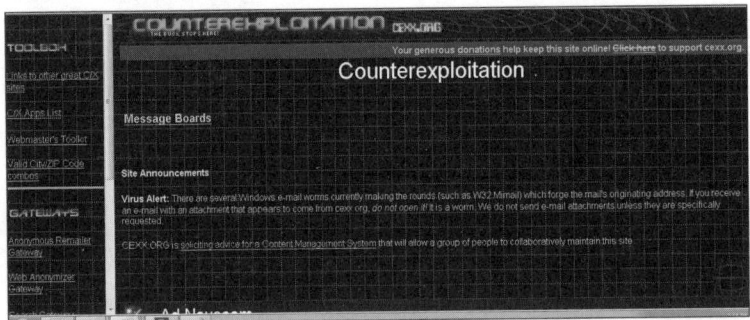

FIGURE 5.2   Counterexploitation website.

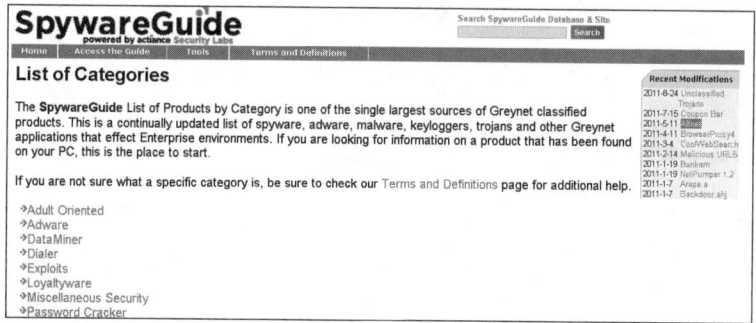

FIGURE 5.3    Malware categories at the SpywareGuide website.

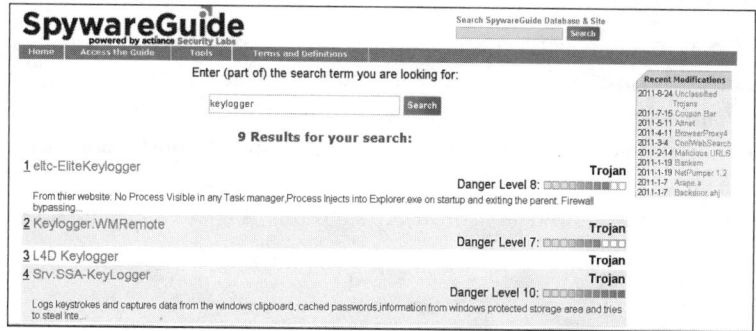

FIGURE 5.4    List of key loggers available through the SpywareGuide website.

Some well-known Trojan horses are also listed at this site (as shown in Figure 5.5), such as the 2nd Thought application that downloads to a person's PC and then blasts it with advertisements. This particular piece of spyware is one that downloads to your PC when you visit certain websites. It is benign in that it causes no direct harm to your system or files, nor does it gather sensitive information from your PC. However, it is incredibly annoying as it inundates your machine with unwanted ads. This sort of software is often referred to as adware. Frequently, these ads cannot be stopped by normal protective pop-up blockers because the pop-up windows are not generated by a website that you visit but rather by some rogue software running on your machine. Pop-up blockers only work to stop sites you visit from opening new windows. Websites use well-known scripting techniques to cause your browser to open a window, and pop-up blockers recognize these techniques and prevent the ad window from opening. However, if the adware launches a new browser instance, it bypasses the pop-up blocker's function.

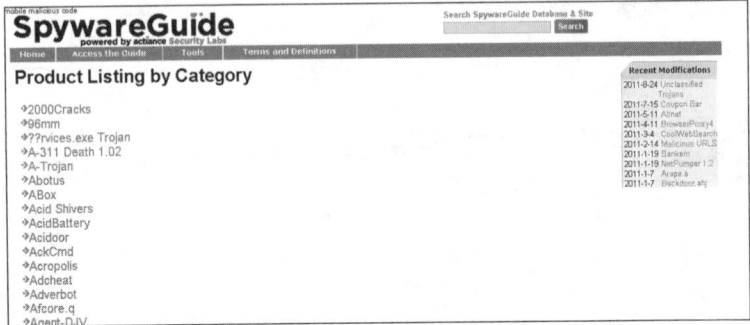

FIGURE 5.5     Trojan horses available at the SpywareGuide website.

# Other Forms of Malware

In this and preceding chapters, the most prominent forms of malware have been discussed. There are, however, many other forms of attack. It is beyond the scope of this book to explore each of these, but you should be aware of the existence of these other forms of malware. Simply being aware can go a long way toward enabling you to defend your system efficiently. This section will touch upon just a few other forms of malware. You should reference the websites discussed in the end-of-chapter exercises and projects often so that you can stay up-to-date with all current forms of attack and defenses.

## Rootkit

A *rootkit* is a collection of tools that a hacker uses to mask her intrusion and obtain administrator-level access to a computer or computer network. The intruder installs a rootkit on a computer after first obtaining user-level access, either by exploiting a known vulnerability or cracking a password. The rootkit then collects user IDs and passwords to other machines on the network, thus giving the hacker root or privileged access.

A rootkit may consist of utilities that also

- Monitor traffic and keystrokes

- Create a back-door into the system for the hacker's use

- Alter log files

- Attack other machines on the network

- Alter existing system tools to circumvent detection

The presence of a rootkit on a network was first documented in the early 1990s. At that time, Sun and Linux operating systems were the primary targets for a hacker looking to install a rootkit. Today, rootkits are available for a number of operating systems and are increasingly difficult to detect on any network (searchSecurity.com, 2004b).

## Malicious Web-Based Code

A *malicious web-based code*, also known as a *web-based mobile code*, simply refers to a code that is portable to all operating systems or platforms such as HTTP, Java, and so on. The "malicious" part implies that is it a virus, worm, Trojan horse, or some other form of malware. Simply put, the malicious code does not care what the operating system may be or what browser is in use. It infects them all blindly (Yakabovicz, 2003).

Where do these codes come from, and how are they spread? The first generation of the Internet was mostly indexed text files. However, as the Internet has grown into a graphical, multimedia user experience, programmers have created scripting languages and new application technologies to enable a more interactive experience. As with any new technology, programs written with scripting languages run the gamut from useful to poorly crafted to outright dangerous.

Technologies such as Java and ActiveX enable these buggy or untrustworthy programs to move to and execute on user workstations. (Other technologies that can enable malicious code are executables, JavaScript, Visual Basic Script, and plug-ins.) The Web acts to increase the mobility of code without differentiating between program quality, integrity, or reliability. Using available tools, it is quite simple to "drag and drop" code into documents that are subsequently placed on web servers and made available to employees throughout the organization or individuals across the Internet. If this code is maliciously programmed or just improperly tested, it can cause serious damage.

Not surprisingly, hackers have used these very useful tools to steal, alter, and erase data files as well as gain unauthorized access to corporate networks. A malicious code attack can penetrate corporate networks and systems from a variety of access points, including websites, HTML content in email messages, or corporate intranets.

Today, with billions of Internet users, new malicious code attacks can spread almost instantly through corporations. The majority of damage caused by malicious code happens in the first hours after a first-strike attack occurs—before there is time for countermeasures. The costs of network downtime or theft of IP make malicious code a top priority (finjan software, 2004).

## Logic Bombs

A *logic bomb* is a type of malware that executes its malicious purpose when a specific criteria is met. The most common factor is date/time. For example, a logic bomb might delete files on a certain date/time. An example is the case of Roger Duronio. In June 2006, Roger Duronio, a system administrator for UBS, was charged with using a logic bomb to damage the company's computer network. His plan was to drive the company stock down due to damage from the logic bomb, so he was charged with securities fraud. Duronio was later convicted and sentenced to 8 years and 1 month in prison and ordered to pay $3.1 million restitution to UBS.

Another good example of a logic bomb is the case of Michael Lauffenburger. In June 1992, Lauffenburger, who was an employee of defense contractor General Dynamics, was arrested for inserting a logic bomb into the company's systems. This logic bomb was designed to delete sensitive project data. Lauffenburger hoped the cause of the missing data would go unnoticed, and he could return as a consultant to "fix" the problem. Fortunately, another employee of General Dynamics uncovered the logic bomb before it was triggered, and a thorough investigation ensued. Lauffenburger was charged with computer tampering and attempted fraud. While statute allowed for fines of up to $500,000 as well as incarceration, he was only fined $5,000 and given no jail time.

Another example occurred at the mortgage company Fannie Mae. On October 29, 2008, a logic bomb was discovered in the company's systems.[1] This logic bomb had been planted by a former contractor, Rajendrainh Makwana, who had been terminated. The bomb was set to activate on January 31, 2009, and completely wipe all of the company's servers. Makwana was indicted in a Maryland court on January 27, 2009 for unauthorized computer access. On December 17, 2010 he was convicted and sentenced to 41 months in prison, followed by 3 years of probation after release. What is most interesting about this case is that Makwana planted the logic bomb between the time he was terminated and the time the network administrators cancelled his network access. This illustrates the importance of ensuring that the accounts of former employees are deactivated immediately when their employment is terminated. That applies whether it is an involuntary termination, retirement, or voluntary quit.

## Spam

Spam is something most readers are probably familiar with. *Spam* is unwanted and unsolicited email that is sent out to multiple parties. Often it is used for marketing purposes, but it can be used for much more malicious goals. For example, spam is a common way to spread a virus or worm. Spam is also used to send emails enticing recipients to visit phishing websites in order to steal the recipient's identity. Essentially, spam is, at best, an annoyance and, at worst, a vehicle for spyware, viruses, worms, and phishing attacks.

## Advanced Persistent Threats

Advanced persistent threats, often abbreviated APTs, is a relatively new term for a continuous process of attacking. It can involve hacking, social engineering, malware, or combinations of attacks. The issue is that the attack must be relatively sophisticated, thus the term *advanced*, and it must be ongoing, thus the term *persistent*.

The security firm Mandiant tracked several APTs over a period of 7 years, all originating in China—specifically, Shanghai and the Pudong region. These APTs were simply named APT1, APT2, and so on.

The attacks were linked to the UNIT 61398 of China's Military. The Chinese government regards this unit's activities as classified, but it appears that offensive cyber warfare is one of its tasks. Just one of the APTs from this group compromised 141 companies in 20 different industries. APT1 was able to maintain access to victim networks for an average of 365 days, and in one case for 1,764 days. APT1 is responsible for stealing 6.5 terabytes of information from a single organization over a 10-month time frame. We will discuss the Chinese attack in more detail in Chapter 12 as part of our discussion of cyber terrorism and information warfare.

---

1. https://www.fbi.gov/baltimore/press-releases/2010/ba121710.htm

# Detecting and Eliminating Viruses and Spyware

Once you understand the nature of malware, and just how devastating it can be, the next logical topic is how to detect and remove malware.

## Antivirus Software

In this chapter and throughout this book, the need for running virus-scanning software has been discussed. It is prudent at this point to provide you with some details on how virus scanners work and information on the major virus-scanning software packages. This information should help you better understand how a virus scanner might protect your system and help you make intelligent decisions regarding the purchase and deployment of some antivirus solution.

A virus scanner can work in one of two ways. The first is to look for a signature (or pattern) that matches a known virus. This is why it is important to keep your virus software updated so that you have the most recent list of signatures with which to work.

The other way in which a virus scanner might check a given PC is to look at the behavior of an executable. If that program behaves in a way consistent with virus activity, the virus scanner may flag it as a virus. Such activity could include the following:

- Attempting to copy itself
- Attempting to access the address book of the system's email program
- Attempting to change Registry settings in Windows

Figure 5.6 shows the Norton AntiVirus software in action. You can see that the virus definitions are up-to-date, virus scanning is enabled, auto-protection is enabled, and the Internet worm protection is enabled as well. The other popular virus scanners have many of the same features.

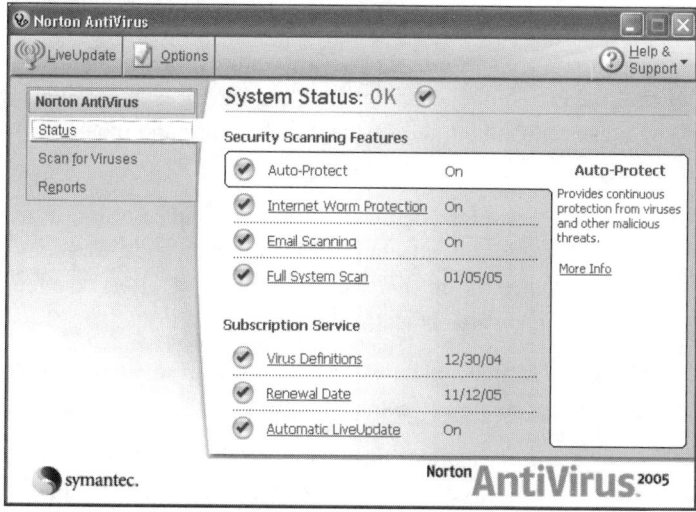

**FIGURE 5.6**   Norton AntiVirus interface.

Most antivirus software today offer additional features. Some of these features include warning the user of known phishing websites, detecting spyware as well as viruses, and even detecting likely phishing attempts. Any modern antivirus should be a comprehensive package, protecting against a variety of attacks, rather than just stopping viruses.

## Antispyware Software

Fortunately, just as there are many different spyware applications available, there are likewise many different software applications on the market that are designed specifically to detect and remove spyware. These applications are also usually available at extremely low cost. You can often get a free trial version to use for a limited time so that you can make a more intelligent purchasing decision. Of course, the most prudent course of action you can take to avoid getting spyware on your machine is to never download anything from the Internet that does not come from a very well-known and trusted website. However, in an organizational environment, you cannot simply rely on your employees to do the right thing. It is prudent as the company's computer security expert to take steps yourself to prevent the employees from compromising your system security.

One of the better known and more widely used antispyware applications includes Spector Pro from www.spectorsoft.com. Many of these types of applications can be obtained for anywhere from $20 to $50, and many offer a free trial version. Most modern antivirus software either includes antispyware, or it can be added as an option.

## Remediation Steps

Obviously, the first step is running up-to-date antivirus software. I don't endorse any particular antivirus program. McAfee, Norton, AVG, Kaspersky, and MalwareBytes are all reputable products. I do, however, recommend that if you are using both host-based antivirus and network antivirus you use products from two different vendors. Then what one misses, the other is likely to catch.

In addition to running antimalware software, there are specific steps security professionals can take to mitigate the risk from malware. Notice the goal is to mitigate the threat of malware. It is impossible to completely eliminate such threats, but you can reduce both the frequency of attacks and the severity of damage.

The first step is to educate end users. End users must be made aware of the prevalence of malware. The goal is for all users on your network to be suspicious of attachments and of downloads. Certainly, there are business needs that require the use of attached documents. But you can educate users on a few simple questions to ask themselves before opening any attachment:

- Was this attachment expected? Attachments from people you do not know or from whom you did not expect any attachment must always be treated as potential malware.

- Is the email specific, such as "These are the third-quarter sales reports we discussed in our meeting yesterday"? That indicates this is likely to be a real email with a real document attached. But generic-sounding emails such as, "Here is your document" or emails that try to convince the user that he must urgently open the attachment should be suspected of being malware.

- When in doubt, ask technical support. If you have significant doubts about the authenticity of an email attachment, don't open it. Ask technical support.

These simple steps would eliminate many malware outbreaks. There is another, more complicated step, but it would render your computers virtually immune to malware. First set up a virtual machine on your computer. There are a variety of virtual machine applications, such as VMware. Oracle Box is free. Then install into that virtual machine (VM) some operating system other than what the host computer runs. So if your host is Windows 10, then the VM should run Linux. If your host is Macintosh, then run Windows in the VM. Now if you surf the Internet inside the VM, it is almost impossible for you to get a virus on the host machine. To date, no virus has jumped the VM/host barrier, and no virus infects multiple operating systems. It should be noted that Java viruses or certain web page malware can infect browsers on different systems. However, as a general rule, a virus written for Windows won't affect a Macintosh computer and vice versa.

# Summary

Clearly, there are a number of ways to attack a target system: by denial of service, virus/worm, Trojan horse, buffer-overflow attacks, and spyware. Each type of attack comes in many distinct variations. It should be obvious by this point that securing your system is absolutely critical. In the upcoming exercises, you will try out the antivirus programs by Norton and McAfee. There are so many ways for a hacker to attack a system that securing your system can be a rather complex task.

Another theme that is driven home throughout this chapter is that many, if not most, attacks are preventable. The exercises ahead will give you practice in figuring out how to prevent the Sasser and Sobig viruses. In most cases, prompt and regular patching of the system, use of antivirus tools, and blocking unneeded ports would prevent the attack. The fact that so many systems do get infected is an indication of the very real problem of network professionals who are not skilled in computer security.

## Test Your Skills

## MULTIPLE CHOICE QUESTIONS

1. Which of the following is the best definition of virus?

    A. Program that causes harm on your computer

    B. Program used in a DoS attack

    C. Program that slows down networks

    D. Program that self-replicates

2. What is the most common damage caused by virus attacks?

    A. Slowing down networks by the virus traffic

    B. Deleting files

    C. Changing the Windows Registry

    D. Corrupting the operating system

3. What is the most common way for a virus to spread?

    A. By copying to shared folders

    B. By email attachment

    C. By FTP

    D. By downloading from a website

4. Which of the following is the primary reason that Microsoft Outlook is so often a target for virus attacks?

   A. Many hackers dislike Microsoft.

   B. Outlook copies virus files faster.

   C. It is easy to write programs that access Outlook's inner mechanisms.

   D. Outlook is more common than other email systems.

5. Which of the following virus attacks used a multimodal approach?

   A. Slammer virus

   B. Mimail virus

   C. Sobig virus

   D. Bagle virus

6. What factor about the Sobig virus made it most intriguing to security experts?

   A. It spread in multiple ways.

   B. It deleted critical system files.

   C. It was difficult to protect against.

   D. It was very sophisticated.

7. What was most interesting to security experts about the Mimail virus?

   A. It spread more rapidly than other virus attacks.

   B. It spread in multiple ways.

   C. It grabbed email addresses from documents on the hard drive.

   D. It deleted critical system files.

8. Which of the following reasons most likely made the Bagle virus spread so rapidly?

   A. The email containing it claimed to be from the system administrator.

   B. It copied itself across the network.

   C. It was a sophisticated virus.

   D. It was particularly virulent.

9. What made the Bagle virus so dangerous?

   A. It changed Windows Registry settings.

   B. It disabled antivirus software.

   C. It deleted key system files.

   D. It corrupted the operating system.

10. Which of the following is a way that any person can use to protect against virus attacks?

    A. Set up a firewall.

    B. Use encrypted transmissions.

    C. Use secure email software.

    D. Never open unknown email attachments.

11. Which of the following is the safest way to send and receive attachments?

    A. Use a code word indicating the attachment is legitimate.

    B. Only send spreadsheet attachments.

    C. Use encryption.

    D. Use virus scanners before opening attachments.

12. Which of the following is true regarding emailed security alerts?

    A. You must follow them.

    B. Most companies do not send alerts via email.

    C. You can trust attachments on security alerts.

    D. Most companies send alerts via email.

13. Which of the following is something a Trojan horse might do?

    A. Open a backdoor for malicious software.

    B. Change your memory configuration.

    C. Change ports on your computer.

    D. Alter your IP address.

14. What is a buffer-overflow attack?

    A. Overflowing a port with too many packets

    B. Putting more email in an email system than it can hold

    C. Overflowing the system

    D. Putting more data in a buffer than it can hold

15. What virus exploited buffer overflows?

    A. Sobig virus

    B. Mimail virus

    C. Sasser virus

    D. Bagle virus

16. What can you do with a firewall to help protect against virus attacks?

    A. There is nothing you can do on the firewall to stop virus attacks.

    B. Shut down all unneeded ports.

    C. Close all incoming ports.

    D. None of the above.

17. A key logger is what type of malware?

    A. Virus

    B. Buffer overflow

    C. Trojan horse

    D. Spyware

18. Which of the following is a step that all computer users should take to protect against virus attacks?

    A. Purchase and configure a firewall.

    B. Shut down all incoming ports.

    C. Use nonstandard email clients.

    D. Install and use antivirus software.

19. What is the primary way a virus scanner works?

    A. By comparing files against a list of known virus profiles

    B. By blocking files that copy themselves

    C. By blocking all unknown files

    D. By looking at files for virus-like behavior

20. What other way can a virus scanner work?

    A. By comparing files against a list of known virus profiles

    B. By blocking files that copy themselves

    C. By blocking all unknown files

    D. By looking at files for virus-like behavior

## EXERCISES

### EXERCISE 5.1: Using Norton Antivirus

1. Go to the Norton AntiVirus website (www.symantec.com/downloads) and download the trial version of its software.

2. Install and run its software.

3. Carefully study the application, noting features that you like and dislike.

### EXERCISE 5.2: Using McAfee Antivirus

1. Go to the McAfee antivirus website (http://us.mcafee.com/root/package.asp?pkgid= 100&cid=9901) and download the trial version of its software.

2. Install and run its software.

3. Carefully study the application, noting features you like and dislike.

### EXERCISE 5.3: Preventing Sasser

1. Using resources on the Web or in journals, carefully research the Sasser virus. You may find that www.f-secure.com and Symantec's Security Response center at https://www.symantec.com/security_response/ helpful in this exercise.

2. Write a brief essay about how Sasser spread, what damage it caused, and what steps could be taken to prevent it.

### EXERCISE 5.4: Preventing Sobig

1. Using resources on the Web or in journals, carefully research the Sobig virus. You may find that www.f-secure.com and Symantec's virus information center at www.sarc.com/avcenter/ are helpful in this exercise.

2. Write a brief essay about how Sobig spread, what damage it caused, and what steps could be taken to prevent it.

### EXERCISE 5.5: Learning About Current Virus Attacks

1. Using resources on the Web or in journals, find a virus that has been spreading in the last 90 days. You may find that www.f-secure.com and Symantec's virus information center at www.sarc.com/avcenter/ are helpful in this exercise.

2. Write a brief essay about how the virus spread, what damage it caused, and what steps could be taken to prevent it.

## PROJECTS

### PROJECT 5.1: **Antivirus Policies**

This activity can also work as a group project.

Considering what you have learned in this chapter and in previous chapters, as well as using outside resources, write an antivirus policy for a small business or school. Your policy should include technical recommendations as well as procedural guidelines. You may choose to consult existing antivirus policy guidelines that you find on the Web to give you some ideas.

However, you should not simply copy their antivirus policies. Rather, you should come up with your own.

### PROJECT 5.2: **The Worst Virus Attacks**

Using resources on the Web, books, or journals, find a virus outbreak that you consider to have been the worst in history. Write a brief paper describing this attack, and explain why you think it is the worst. Was it widely spread? How quickly did it spread? What damage did it do?

### PROJECT 5.3: **Why Write a Virus?**

A number of hypotheses have been formed regarding why people write a virus. These hypotheses range from the frankly conspiratorial to the academically psychological. Taking whatever position you feel is most likely, write a paper explaining why you think people take the time and effort to write a virus.

### Case Study

Chiao Chien manages IT security for a school. Given the wide range of people who use the school's computers, it is difficult for Chien to prevent virus attacks. Chien has a reasonably good budget and has installed antivirus software on every machine. He also has a firewall that has all unneeded ports blocked, and there is a school policy prohibiting the downloading of any software from the Web. Consider the following questions:

- How secure do you think Chien's network is from virus attacks?

- What areas has Chien not secured?

- What recommendations would you make to Chien?

## Chapter 6

# Techniques Used by Hackers

## *Chapter Objectives*

**After reading this chapter and completing the exercises, you will be able to do the following:**

- Understand the basic methodology used by hackers
- Be familiar with some of the basic hacking tools
- Understand the hacking mentality

## Introduction

In the preceding five chapters, we have explored computer security and various security breaches. In this chapter we will be exploring the techniques that hackers use to commit computer crimes. Before we go any further, it is important that you realize that many hackers are not criminals. A hacker is a person who wants to understand a system, often by probing its weaknesses. There are even hackers that work for organizations, testing the organization's system security. This is called *penetration testing*. This is also often referred to as *white hat hacking*. There are several certifications for penetration testing:

Offensive Security has several penetration testing certifications: https://www.offensive-security.com/information-security-certifications/

SANS Institute has a penetration testing certification: http://pen-testing.sans.org/certification

The EC Council (www.eccouncil.org) has a certification for this: the Certified Ethical Hacker.

And there is the Professional Penetration Tester certification: www.professionalpentester.com/

There is also a magazine for such people called *2600* (www.2600.com). Many computer security professionals attempt to learn hacking techniques either to enhance their security capabilities or to simply satisfy their curiosity. The techniques themselves are not criminal. However, there are people who use hacking techniques to breach systems to steal data, damage systems, or commit other cyber crimes. These people are usually referred to as *black hat hackers* or *crackers*.

The techniques presented in this chapter are not only presented to give the reader an understanding of how black hat hackers work, but also provide a method whereby a network administrator can perform a penetration test on his own network. By attempting some of these techniques on your network, you can assess your vulnerability. It should be pointed out that you should only do this once you are very comfortable with the techniques in this chapter, and only with permission from senior management.

# Basic Terminology

Before we can delve into the world of hacking, we need to discuss the basic terminology used in this community. We have already introduced you to the term *white hat hacker*, one who uses hacking techniques for legal/ethical purposes. And we have discussed the term *black hat hacker* or *cracker*, one who uses hacking techniques for illegal techniques.

There are a few other terms you should be familiar with. A *gray hat hacker* is one who was previously a black hat hacker and turned into a white hat hacker (basically, a former criminal now turned ethical). With the proliferation of tools on the Internet, there are also a lot of people who download some tools (we will examine some of these in this chapter) and perform some cyber attack, without really understanding it. These people are termed *script kiddies* (also sometimes spelled kiddy's). Another important term is *phreaking*. This refers to hacking into phone systems. Hacking of phone systems actually predates hacking computer systems.

# The Reconnaissance Phase

Any intelligent/experienced hacker is going to attempt to find out information about a target before actually attempting an attack. Just as a bank robber would want to know about a bank's alarm systems, number of guards, police response time, and so on, a black hat hacker will want to know about your system's security. What may surprise you is how much information can be found easily on the Internet, without even attaching to the target system.

## Passive Scanning Techniques

One of the easiest things a hacker can do is check the target organization's websites. It is common for businesses to put information up that can be very useful to an attacker. For example, let's assume company XYZ lists John Doe as its IT manager. An enterprising hacker scans bulletin boards and discussion groups for references to John Doe at XYZ. That attacker might find information useful in spear phishing attacks (phishing targeted at a specific individual or group of individuals), or the attacker might find information useful in social engineering. For example, a number of former employees complain that John Doe is demanding and quick to fire people. Then an enterprising hacker could call someone at

XYZ claiming to be working for John Doe. The hacker claims he is trying to log on remotely to that person's computer to update that person's system. After a few moments, the hacker tells the person he forgot the password John Doe gave him and is very concerned he will get fired if he doesn't complete this assignment; then he asks that person for his password. The information the attacker gleaned from the Web gave him enough information to make this social engineering attack plausible.

It is also possible for an attacker to scan bulletin boards, chat rooms, discussion groups, and more looking for questions from IT staff at the target organization. For example, if an administrator posts in a discussion group asking about a particular server problem, this can give the attacker valuable information about that target network.

Another way attackers can use the Web to find out information about a target is through job ads. For example, if a company routinely advertises for ASP.NET developers and never for PHP or Perl, then it is likely that the company's web applications are developed with ASP.NET running on a Windows web server (Internet Information Services). This can allow the attacker to focus only on a small group of possible attacks (those against ASP.NET/Windows). Other information can be garnered from job ads. For example, if a small company, less than 200 employees, has an advertisement for a network administrator twice a year, it is more likely that the last administrator is no longer with them. A small company would not need multiple administrators. Knowing the current administrator is new means she is not as familiar with her own systems. Also, if this trend of advertising for new administrators extends over a couple of years, it means the company has high turnover and there is some problem the attacker may be able to exploit.

There are also specific websites that provide information an attacker may find useful. The first such website is netcraft.com, shown in Figure 6.1. This website provides information about websites. For example, you can find out what kind of server a site is running, and in some cases how long it has been since it was last rebooted.

**FIGURE 6.1**  www.netcraft.com.

Another site that can be useful for attackers is https://archive.org. This site, shown in Figure 6.2, archives older versions of websites. The server scours the Web archiving sites. The frequency with which a site is archived depends on its popularity.

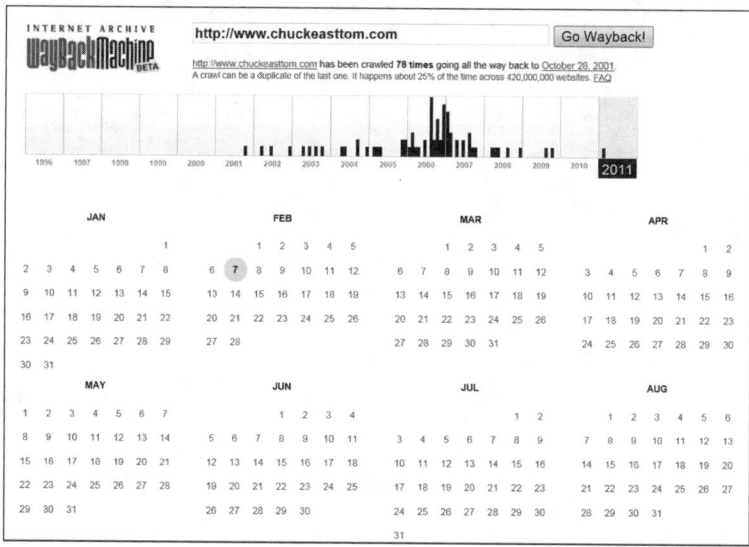

**FIGURE 6.2** www.archive.org.

# Active Scanning Techniques

The previously mentioned techniques are all considered passive, as they do not require the attacker to connect to the target system. Since the attacker is not actually connecting to the target system, it is impossible for an intrusion detection system (IDS) to detect the scan. Active scans are far more reliable but may be detected by the target system. There are a few types of active scans.

## Port Scanning

*Port scanning* is the process of attempting to contact each network port on the target system and see which ones are open. There are 1,024 well-known ports that are usually associated with specific services. For example, port 161 is associated with Simple Network Management Protocol. If an attacker detects port 161 open on the target system, he might decide to try SNMP-related attacks. Even more information can be derived from a port scan. For example, ports 137, 138, and 139 are all associated with NetBIOS, a very old Windows method of network communication, not used in Windows anymore. However, NetBIOS is often used for systems where Windows machines need to communicate with Linux machines. So discovering those ports open reveals something about the target network.

A simple Google search for *port scanner* will reveal a host of well-known, widely used, and often free port scanners. However, the most popular port scanner in the hacking and security community is the free tool Nmap (https://nmap.org/). There is a Windows version of it, shown in Figure 6.3.

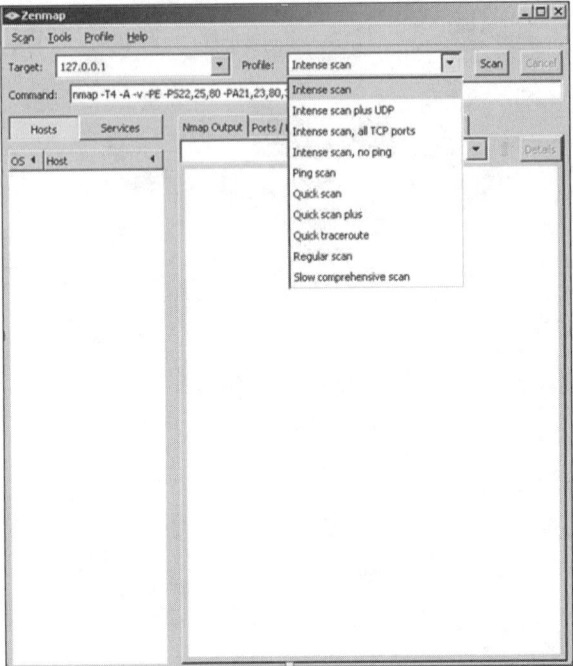

FIGURE 6.3   Nmap GUI

Nmap allows you to customize your scan making it more or less stealthy, and targeting certain systems. The most common types of scans are listed here:

- **Ping scan:** This scan simply sends a ping to the target port. Many network administrators block incoming ICMP packets for the purpose of stopping ping scans.

- **Connect scan:** This is the most reliable scan, but also the most likely to be detected. With this type of scan a complete connection is made with the target system.

- **SYN scan:** This scan is very stealthy. Most systems accept SYN (Synchronize) requests. This scan is similar to the SYN flood DoS attack described in Chapter 4, "Denial of Service Attacks." In this scan you send a SYN packet but never respond when the system sends a SYN/ACK. However, unlike the DoS SYN flood, you only send one packet per port. This is also called the *half-open scan*.

- **FIN scan:** This scan has the FIN flag, or connection finished flag set. This is also not an unusual packet for systems to receive, so it is considered stealthy.

Each of these scans provokes a different response on the target machine and thus provides different information to the port scanner:

- With a FIN scan or an XMAS scan, if the target port is closed, the system sends back an RST flag packet (RST means reset). If it is open, there is no response.

- With a SYN scan, if the port is closed, the response is an RST; if it is open, the response is a SYN/ACK.

- ACK scans and NULL scans only work on UNIX systems.

Nmap also lets you set a number of flags (either with the command-line version of Nmap or the Windows version) that customize your scan. The allowed flags are listed here:

| | |
|---|---|
| -O | Detects operating system |
| -sP | Is a ping scan |
| -sT | TCP connect scan |
| -sS | SYN scan |
| -sF | FIN scan |
| -sX | Xmas tree scan |
| -sN | NULL scan |
| -sU | UDP scan |
| -sO | Protocol scan |
| -sA | ACK scan |
| -sW | Windows scan |
| -sR | RPC scan |
| -sL | List/DNS scan |
| -sI | Idle scan |
| -Po | Don't ping |
| -PT | TCP ping |
| -PS | SYN ping |
| -PI | ICMP ping |
| -PB | TCP and ICMP ping |
| -PM | ICMP netmask |
| -oN | Normal output |
| -oX | XML output |
| -oG | Greppable output |
| -oA | All output |
| -T | Timing |

-T 0     Paranoid

-T 1     Sneaking

-T 2     Polite

-T 3     Normal

-T 4     Aggressive

-T 5     Insane

As you can see there are a number of options available to an attacker using Nmap. One can spend a lot of time just learning Nmap. There are, of course, a number of other port scanning tools. We have focused on Nmap because it is free and it is so widely used. It also is prominently figured on the EC Council Certified Ethical Hacker certification, GPEN (from SANS), and the Professional Penetration Tester Certification.

The settings are, for the most part, self-explanatory. Perhaps the timing warrants a bit more discussion. Timing involves how quickly to send scanning packets. Essentially, the faster you send packets, the more likely the scan is to be detected.

Here is the most basic Nmap scan:

```
nmap 192.168.1.1
```

Scan a range of IP addresses:

```
nmap 192.168.1.1-20
```

Scan to detect operating system, use TCP scan, and use sneaky speed:

```
nmap -O -PT -T1 192.168.1.1
```

## Vulnerability Assessment

Vulnerability assessment is checking a system to see if it is vulnerable to specific attacks. These tools can be used by attackers to assess your system; however, they are designed to allow you to assess your system. These tools are not particularly stealthy and thus will probably be detected by an intrusion detection system. In fact, vulnerability assessment tools are commonly used by network administrators to test their own networks. These tools will be covered in Chapter 11, "Network Scanning and Vulnerability Scanning."

## Enumeration

Another technique that is popular before the actual attack is enumeration. Enumeration is simply the process of finding out what is on the target system. If the target is an entire network, then the attacker is trying to find out what servers, computers, and printers are on that network. If the target is a specific computer, then the attacker is trying to find out what users and shared folders exist on that system.

A simple Google search will help you find a number of enumeration tools. One of the easiest to use is Cain and Abel, shown in Figure 6.4.

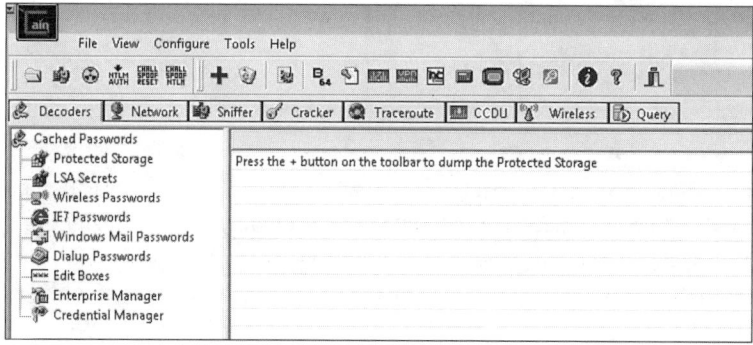

**FIGURE 6.4**   Cain and Abel.

Cain and Abel can do a lot more than just enumeration, but for our purposes that is what we are focusing on here. For enumeration, simply click on the Network tab and you will find all machines connected to the network you are on. This obviously requires some level of access before you can enumerate the target network.

A few other enumeration tools that are popular with hackers and can easily be found on the Internet are

- Sid2User
- Cheops (Linux only)
- UserInfo
- UserDump
- DumpSec
- Netcat
- NBTDump

This is not an exhaustive list, but it includes some of the most widely used enumeration tools.

To defend against scanning, you should use the following techniques:

- Be careful how much information you put on the Internet about your organization and its network.
- Make it a company policy that technical personnel who use bulletin boards, chat rooms, and so on for technical data must not use their real name or reveal the company's name.

- Use an IDS that detects many scans.

- Block incoming Internet Control Message Protocol (ICMP) packets.

These won't make scanning and reconnaissance impossible on your system, but they will make certain the attacker gathers significantly less information.

# Actual Attacks

Now that we have discussed how attackers scan a target system, let's look at a few attacks that are commonly used. Obviously this won't be an exhaustive list, but it will provide you some insight into the attack methodologies used. In Chapter 4 we discussed denial of service (DoS) attacks and some tools used to cause these attacks. In this section we will look at other sorts of attacks and the techniques and tools used to make them happen.

## SQL Script Injection

This may be the most popular attack on websites. In recent years, more websites have taken steps to ameliorate the dangers of this attack; unfortunately, all too many websites are susceptible. This attack is based on passing structured query language commands to a web application and getting the website to execute them.

Before we can discuss SQL injection, we must talk about SQL and relational databases. Relational databases are based on relations between various tables. The structure includes tables, primary and foreign keys, and relations. A basic description can be summarized with the following points:

- Each row represents a single entity.

- Each column represents a single attribute.

- Each record is identified by a unique number called a *primary key*.

- Tables are related by foreign keys. A *foreign key* is a primary key in another table.

You can see these relations in Figure 6.5.

All relational databases use Structured Query Language (SQL). SQL uses commands such as `SELECT`, `UPDATE`, `DELETE`, `INSERT`, `WHERE`, and others. At least the basic queries are very easy to understand and interpret.

The way the most basic SQL injection works is this. Many websites/applications have a page where users enter their username and password. That username and password will have to be checked against some database to see if they are valid. Regardless of the type of database (Oracle, SQL Server, MySQL), all databases speak SQL. SQL looks and functions a great deal like English. For example, to check a username and password, you might want to query the database and see if there is any entry in the users table that matches that username and password that was entered. If there is, then you have a match. The SQL statement might look something like this:

```
'SELECT * FROM tblUsers WHERE USERNAME = 'jdoe' AND PASSWORD = 'letmein'
```

| PK | LNAME | FNAME | JobCode | Hire Date |
|---|---|---|---|---|
| 1 | Smith | Jane | 2 | 1/10/2010 |
| 2 | Perez | Juan | 2 | 1/14/2011 |
| 3 | Kent | Clark | 1 | 3/2/2005 |
| 4 | Euler | Leonard | 3 | 3/5/2009 |
| 5 | Plank | Max | 3 | 4/2/2012 |

| PK | Job Name | Min Edu. | Min Salary | Max Salary |
|---|---|---|---|---|
| 1 | Super Hero | None | 100,000 | 1,000,000 |
| 2 | Programmer | BA/BS | 70,000 | 95,000 |
| 3 | Math/Scientist | Ph.D. | 80,000 | 110,000 |
| 4 | Manager | BA/BS | 140,000 | 220,000 |

FIGURE 6.5    Relations.

The problem with this, while it is valid SQL, is that we have hard coded the username and password. For a real website, we would have to take whatever the user entered into the username field and password field and check that. This can be easily done (regardless of what programming or scripting language the website is programmed in). It would look something like this:

```
'SELECT * FROM tblUsers WHERE USERNAME = '" + txtUsername.Text +' AND PASSWORD = '" +
txtPassword.Text +"'" .
```

If you enter username `'jdoe'` and password `'letmein'`, this code produces the following SQL command:

```
SELECT * FROM tblUsers WHERE USERNAME = 'jdoe' AND PASSWORD = 'letmein'
```

Now if there is a username jdoe in tblUsers, and the password for it is letmein, then this user will be logged on. If not, then an error will occur.

SQL injection works by putting some SQL into the username and password block that is always true. For example, suppose you enter `'OR X=X'` into the username and password boxes. This will cause the program to create this query:

```
SELECT * FROM tblUsers WHERE USERNAME = ''OR X=X' AND PASSWORD = ''OR X=X'
```

Notice that we start with a single quotation mark (`'`) before the OR X=X. This is to close the open quote the attacker knows must be in the code. And if you see `''`, that essentially is a blank or null. So what we are telling the database is to log us in if the username is blank, or if X=X, and if the password is blank, or if X=X. If you think about this for a second, you will see that X always equals X, so this will always be true.

There is no significance to `'OR X=X'`; it is simply a statement that will always be true. Attackers try other similar statements, such as the following:

```
' or 'a' ='a
' or '1' ='1
' or (1=1)
```

This is only one example of SQL injection; there are other methods, but this is the most common. The defense against this attack is to filter all user input before processing it. This is often referred to as *input validation*. This prevents an attacker from entering SQL commands rather than a username and password. Unfortunately, many sites do not filter user input and are still vulnerable to this attack.

The example given here is the most basic version of SQL injection. You can do far more with SQL injection. The attacker is limited only by her knowledge of SQL and the target database system.

Remember that earlier in the text when we first, briefly, mentioned SQL injection, it was suggested that filtering input would prevent this. For example, the programmer creating the website should write the code to first check for any common SQL injection symbols such as the single quote ('), percent sign (%), equal sign (=), or ampersand (&), and if those are found, stop processing and log an error. This would prevent many SQL injection attacks. There are methods to circumvent these security measures, but implementing them would stop many SQL injection attacks.

## Cross-Site Scripting

With cross-site scripting, an attacker injects client-side script into web pages viewed by other users. The key is that the attacker enters scripts into an area that other users interact with. When they go to that part of the site, the attacker's script is executed rather than the intended website functionality. For example, assume a shopping site allows users to review products. Rather than typing in a review, the attacker types in JavaScript that redirects the user to a phishing website. When another user views that "review," the script will execute and take him to the new site. Again, this can be prevented by simply filtering all user input. As of this writing, all the major online shopping portals, such as Amazon.com, do filter input and are not susceptible to this attack. However, many smaller sites are still susceptible.

This attack, as well as SQL injection, illustrates why it is critical that all IT personnel be familiar with security, not just security administrators. If more web developers were more familiar with security, these two attacks would not be widespread.

## Password Cracking

Doing password cracking is easiest when one can actually get physical access to a machine. This is not as difficult as it sounds. Many organizations (such as universities) have kiosk machines where someone can use the system with minimal/guest privileges. A skilled hacker can use this access to gain further access.

## OphCrack

A very popular tool for cracking Windows passwords is OphCrack. OphCrack can be downloaded from http://ophcrack.sourceforge.net. It is based on an understanding of how Windows passwords work. Windows passwords are stored in a hash file in one of the system directories, usually C:\WINDOWS\ system32\config\ in a SAM file. SAM is an acronym for Security Accounts Manager. The passwords are stored as a hash. (Hashes will be discussed in detail in Chapter 8, "Encryption.") What Windows does is hash the password you type in and compare it to the hash found in the SAM file. If there is a match, then you are logged in. To prevent someone from copying the SAM file and taking it off to try to brute force it, as soon as Windows begins the boot process, the operating system locks the SAM file. What OphCrack does is boot to Linux and then get the SAM file and look up the hashed passwords in a large table of hashed values it has, searching for a match. If it finds one, then the matching text in that table of hashed values is the password. You can see OphCrack in Figure 6.6.

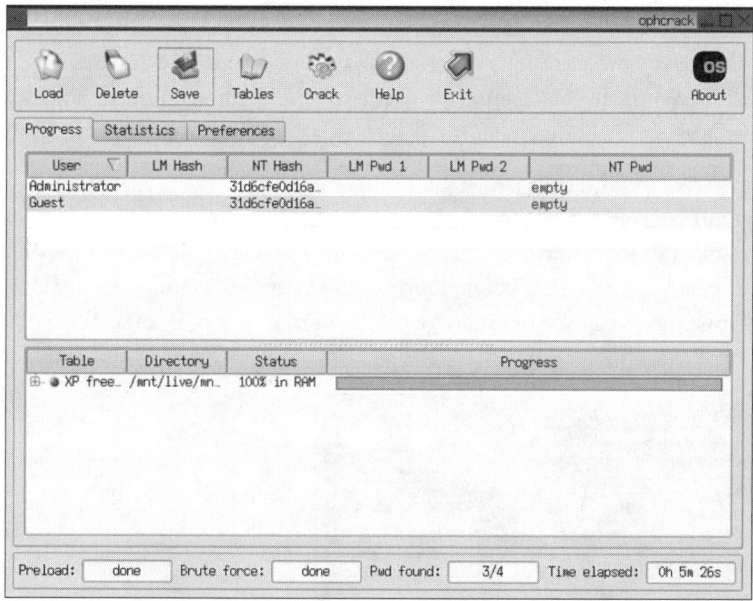

**FIGURE 6.6**   OphCrack.

This tool is remarkably easy to use. Just put the OphCrack CD into the machine and reboot. During the boot process you can press F12 for a boot menu and tell the system to boot from CD. You will then start OphCrack. It should be noted that longer passwords (as of this writing, longer than 10 characters) are usually not crackable by OphCrack.

Assuming OphCrack is successful (it isn't always), what can the attacker do with this? At best she simply got the local machine admin account, and not a domain account. Well, this can be used to then gain domain access. One simple technique is to create a script that will in turn create a domain admin account. The script is simple:

```
net user /domain /add localaccountname password
net group /domain "Domain Admins" /add localaccount
```

Obviously, if the attacker executes this script it will not work. One must be a domain admin for it to work. So the attacker saves this script to the All Users startup folder. The next time a domain admin logs on to this system, the script will successfully execute. But the attacker may not want to wait until that happens. In order to speed up the process, the attacker causes some minor problem in the system (changes settings, alters configuration, and so on). In many organizations, the tech support personnel are in the domain admins group. When a tech support person logs on to the system to correct the problem, the script will successfully run.

## Malware Creation

In this section we will briefly discuss how easy it is to create malware. Previously in Chapter 5, "Malware," you saw the tool eLiTeWrap. In this section you will see the methods used to actually create viruses. This is not in any way an encouragement for you to create such viruses. It is meant to educate you on why such malware is so common.

For many years, one needed significant programming skills in order to create a virus. However, in recent years there have been a number of tools developed that create viruses. These tools allow the end user to click a few buttons and create a virus. This is one reason viruses are becoming so prevalent. One such tool is the TeraBIT Virus Maker, shown in Figure 6.7.

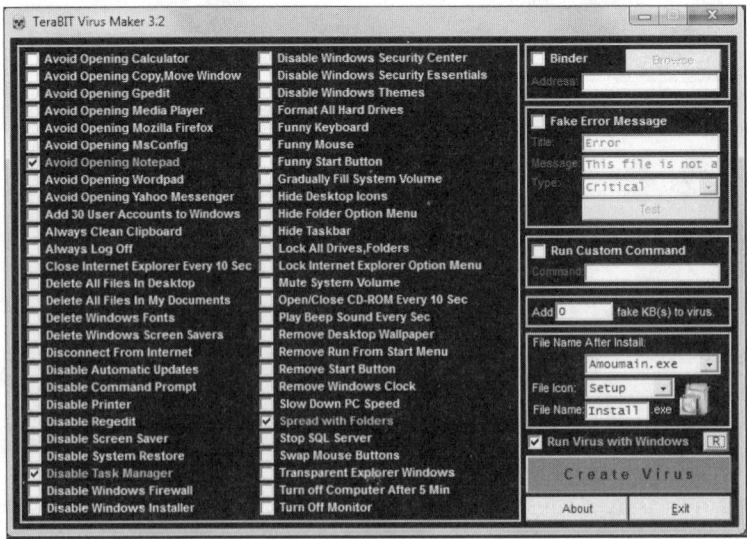

**FIGURE 6.7**   TeraBIT Virus Maker.

Tools like this make it very easy for even a novice to create a virus. When tools like this become prevalent, tools that automate some specific computer attack, then one can expect a great many more such attacks.

You can easily see from the options that TeraBIT Virus Maker can create some rather damaging malware. It is important to realize that this is only one option that a malware creator has. There are a number of tools on the Internet that help create viruses. There are even ransomware development kits.

In addition to these tools, there are websites that contain catalogs of malware code. Anyone with only moderate programming skills can download the code for a virus and modify that malware for his specific needs. You can think of this as a sort of cyber weapons proliferation.

This proliferation of cyber weapons is the primary reason for this section in this chapter. It is critical that security professionals, or aspiring security professionals, be aware of just how easy it is to create a virus. This means we should reasonably expect to see more viruses as time goes on. Of course, there are still custom written viruses, and these are in fact the most effective form of malware. But the proliferation of tools and source code means that even those with only minimal technical skills can create viruses.

## Windows Hacking Techniques

Given the ubiquitous nature of Microsoft Windows, it should be no surprise that there are a wide range of attacks specifically aimed at that operating system. In this section, we will briefly look at some of these.

### Pass the Hash

We will examine cryptographic hashes at some length in Chapter 8. For now just accept that many systems store passwords as a cryptographic hash. This is done because it is impossible to "unhash" something.

The pass the hash attack essentially realizes that the hash cannot be reversed; rather than trying to find out what the password is, the attacker just sends over the hash. If the attacker can obtain a valid username and user password hashes values (just the hash—the attacker does not know the actual password), then the hacker can use that hash, without ever knowing the actual password.

Windows applications ask users to type in their passwords; then they in turn hash them. Often this can be done with an API like LsaLogonUser, converting the password to either an LM hash or an NT hash. Pass the hash skips around the application and just sends the hash.

### Net User Script

This particular exploit first requires access to the target machine with at least guest-level privileges. It is based on the fact that many organizations put the technical support personnel in the domain admin's group.

The attacker writes the following two-line script (obviously the word *localaccountname* is replaced with an actual local account name.):

```
net user /domain /add localaccountname password
net group /domain "Domain Admins" /add Domain
```

Save that script in the All Users startup folder. The next time someone with domain admin privileges logs on to the machine, it will execute and that *localaccountname* will now be a domain admin. The only problem is that it may be quite some time before someone with such privileges logs onto that machine. To make this happen, the attacker will cause a problem with the system that would necessitate technical support fixing it, such as by disabling the network card. The next user to log in will not be able to access the network or Internet and will call technical support. There is a reasonably high chance that the person in technical support is a member of the domain administrators group. When that person logs on to the computer to fix the problem, unbeknownst to her the script will execute.

This particular exploit illustrates two different security issues. The first is the concept of least privileges. This means each user has the minimum privileges to do his job. This concept was discussed briefly in Chapter 1, "Introduction to Computer Security." Therefore, technical support personnel should not be in the domain admin group.

The second issue is that access to any of your machines should be controlled. This exploit only requires that the attacker have guest-level access and then only for a few minutes. From that minimum access, a skilled attacker can move forward and acquire domain admin privileges.

## Login as System

This particular attack requires physical access to one machine on your network. It does not require domain or even computer login credentials. To understand this attack, think about the last time you logged into any Windows computer, even a Windows server. Next to the login text boxes (Username and Password), there is an accessibility button that allows you to launch various tools to aid those users with disabilities. For example, you can launch the magnifier class in order to magnify text.

In this attack, the perpetrator will boot the system to any Linux live CD. Then, using the FDISK utility, the attacker will locate the Windows partition. Navigating to the Windows\System32 directory, the attacker can first take magnify.exe and make a backup, perhaps naming the backup magnify.bak. Then she can take command.exe (the command prompt) and rename it magnify.exe.

Now the attacker reboots to Windows. When the login screen appears, the perpetrator clicks Accessibility and then Magnify. Since command.exe was renamed to magnify.exe, this will actually launch the command prompt. No user has logged in yet, so the command prompt will have system privileges. At this point the attacker is only limited by her knowledge of commands executed from the command prompt.

This particular attack illustrates the need for physical security. If an attacker can get even 10 minutes alone with your Windows computer, she will likely find a way to breach the network.

# Penetration Testing

As was mentioned at the beginning of this chapter, these techniques can also be conducted as part of a penetration test. However, a penetration test is not simply the random application of a variety of hacking techniques. Usually a penetration test is done along with or subsequent to a vulnerability assessment. We will discuss vulnerability assessments in detail in Chapter 11.

The process is a methodical probing of a target network in order to identify weaknesses in the network. The theory behind penetration testing is that the only way to objectively determine the security level of a given network is to have a competent penetration tester attempt to breach security. There are a variety of standards that one can use to guide a penetration test.

## NIST 800-115

NIST 800-115 is the National Institute of Standards and Technology guideline for security assessments for Federal Information Systems. Assessments include penetration tests. NIST 800-115 describes security assessments and has four phases:

- **Planning:** During this phase the tester needs to set specific testing goals. Often these will be related to previous risk assessment evaluations of the target network.

- **Discovery:** This phase involves using a variety of tools, including port scanners, vulnerability scanners, and manual techniques to identify or discover any issues with the target network.

- **Attack:** Now the attacker can attempt to compromise the target network by exploiting the vulnerabilities found during the discovery phase. It is in this phase that the penetration tester applies the hacking techniques we have discussed in this chapter.

- **Reporting:** The final step is to prepare a detailed report and to deliver it to the person who hired the penetration tester. The report should provide details on what vulnerabilities were exploited, how they were exploited, and what remediation steps are recommended.

Even though this approach has only four phases, these are rather broad phases that include many substeps. It is not necessary for our purposes to delve into all the details of NIST 800-115. However, these broad steps provide a framework for penetration testing, even without delving into the details. Notice that there are two steps prior to the attack phase. Planning and discovery are critical, and you will see similar items in other penetration testing standards.

## National Security Agency Information Assessment Methodology

The National Security Agency (NSA) has primary responsibility for information security throughout the United States Federal government. For this reason, it formulated a methodology to be applied to any information systems assessment to include security audits, vulnerability tests, and penetration tests. That methodology is briefly described here:

- Pre-Assessment
    - Determine and manage the customer's expectations.
    - Gain an understanding of the organization's information criticality.
    - Determine customer's goals and objectives.
    - Determine the system boundaries.
    - Coordinate with customer.
    - Request documentation.

- On-Site Assessment
    - Conduct opening meeting.
    - Gather and validate system information (via interview, system demonstration, and document review).
    - Analyze assessment information.
    - Develop initial recommendations.
    - Present out-brief.

- Post-Assessment
    - Give additional review of documentation.
    - Get help understanding what you learned.
    - Report coordination (and writing).

This particular summary of steps is interesting. Let's begin with the pre-assessment. Managing customer expectations is a critical step. It is important that the customer know what a penetration test can and cannot do. Notice that this phase is all about deciding what will be done and what is expected.

The on-site assessment includes the process of examining the system and culminates in an out briefing to let the customer know the essence of what you found. Then it culminates with a report that is written and delivered in the third phase. It is also interesting to notice that in the final phase there is the substep to get additional expertise. If your penetration test or security audit found items that are outside your expertise, then it is wise to consult with an expert in that area.

## PCI Penetration Testing Standard

The Payment Card Industry Data Security Standards (PCI DSS) are standards used by companies that process credit cards. We will look at PCI standards in general in Chapter 10, "Security Policies." In this section we will briefly examine the penetration testing portion of those standards. PCI DSS

Requirement 11.3.4 mandates penetration testing to validate that segmentation controls and methods are operational, effective, and isolate all out-of-scope systems from systems in the cardholder data environment.

PCI standards recommend testing a separate environment, not on the live production environment during normal business hours.

It is recommended that pen testing include social engineering tests.

Per PCI DSS Requirements 11.3.1 and 11.3.2, penetration testing must be performed at least annually and after any significant change—for example, infrastructure or application upgrade or modification—or new system component installations. As with the previous models we examined, PCI DSS has some specific steps:

- **Pre-engagement:** Defining scope, documents, rules of engagement, success criteria, and review of past issues

- **The actual penetration test:** Where you apply the hacking techniques

- **Post-Engagement:** Reporting and recommending remediation steps

It is not critical that you memorize these standards. The point is to understand that hacking techniques are utilized in penetration testing, but that penetration testing is more than just random attempts to hack the target network. It is a methodical approach to verifying the security of a target network that happens to include real hacking techniques.

# Summary

In this chapter we have examined just a few techniques hackers utilize. But these techniques and tools have illustrated the need for a variety of security measures. The scanning techniques illustrate the need for blocking certain traffic at the firewall and for running an IDS. The SQL injection attack demonstrates why security must be part of application development. And the OphCrack tool illustrates why physical security is important and why the principle of least privileges is important. Putting tech support staff into the domain admins group violates the concept of least privileges and makes the privilege escalation script possible.

## Test Your Skills

### MULTIPLE CHOICE QUESTIONS

1. SQL injection is based on what?

    A. Having database admin privileges

    B. Creating an SQL statement that is always true

    C. Creating an SQL statement that will force access

    D. Understanding web programming

2. Which of the following is a vulnerability scanner specifically for Windows systems?

    A. Nmap

    B. OphCrack

    C. Nessus

    D. MBSA

3. How can you prevent cross-site scripting?

    A. Filter user input.

    B. Use an IDS.

    C. Use a firewall.

    D. It cannot be prevented.

4. What is an advantage of using Nessus? Use your favorite search engine to research Nessus to answer this question.

    A. It is free for businesses.

    B. It has a wide range of vulnerabilities it can check for.

    C. It is designed for Windows systems.

    D. It includes an IDS.

5. OphCrack depends on the attacker doing what?

   A. Getting physical access to the machine

   B. Getting domain admin privileges

   C. Using social engineering

   D. Using a scanning tool

6. If you wish to view items that have been removed from a website, what is the best way to do that?

   A. Use Nessus.

   B. Use Nmap.

   C. Use www.netcraft.com.

   D. Use www.archive.org.

7. Which of the following is a popular port scanner?

   A. Nessus

   B. OphCrack

   C. MBSA

   D. Nmap

8. Blocking incoming ICMP packets will prevent what type of scan?

   A. SYN

   B. Ping

   C. FIN

   D. Stealth

9. A person who uses hacking techniques for illegal activities is referred to as what?

   A. A hacker

   B. A gray hat hacker

   C. A phreaker

   D. A cracker

10. A person who hacks into phone systems is referred to as what?

   A. A hacker

   B. A gray hat hacker

   C. A phreaker

   D. A cracker

11. A person who uses tools to hack without understanding the underlying technology is called what?

    A. A script kiddy

    B. A gray hat hacker

    C. A novice

    D. A white hat hacker

12. Trying to list all the servers on a network is referred to as what?

    A. Port scanning

    B. Enumeration

    C. Vulnerability scanning

    D. Scouting

13. Which of the following is a popular enumeration tool?

    A. Nessus

    B. Nmap

    C. MBSA

    D. Cheops

14. Which of the following is considered the most stealthy port scan?

    A. SYN

    B. Connect

    C. Ping

    D. Nmap

15. What is the most stealthy way to find out what type of server a website is running?

    A. Use Nmap.

    B. Use Cain and Abel.

    C. Use www.netcraft.com.

    D. Use www.archive.org.

# EXERCISES

### EXERCISE 6.1: **Using www.archive.org**

This exercise gives you practice in using www.archive.org. Go to www.archive.org and pull up at least two previous versions of your college/university's website. What information can you find that is no longer on the website?

### EXERCISE 6.2: **Using Nmap**

This exercise introduces you to the Nmap tool. You should download and install Nmap. Then run at least three different scans on either your own computer or on a designated lab computer.

While it is not illegal to scan a computer, it may violate some security policies for some colleges and universities. Make certain you only scan a designated lab computer.

### EXERCISE 6.3: **Using OphCrack**

Download OphCrack to a CD. Then reboot your own machine to OphCrack and attempt to crack your own local passwords.

It is critical that you only use this on your own machine or a designated lab machine. Using it on other machines will probably violate security policies at your college/university/company.

### EXERCISE 6.4: **Using Netcraft.com**

Visit www.netcraft.com and do a search on at least three different websites of your choosing. Note what information you are able to gather about the website.

# PROJECTS

### PROJECT 6.1: **Passive Reconnaissance**

Select a local organization and conduct a passive reconnaissance. This should include searching job boards, the organization's own website, user groups/bulletin boards, social networking sites, www.archive.org, and more. Gather as much information about the target network as you can.

### PROJECT 6.2: **Port Scanners**

Use your favorite search engine to locate at least two other port scanners. Download and install them, and then try them on your own machine or a designated lab computer. Compare and contrast these tools to Nmap. Are they easier to use? More informative?

### PROJECT 6.3: **MBSA**

Download and install MBSA and run a vulnerability scan on your own computer or on a designated lab computer. What problems did you find? Was the tool easy to use?

## Case Study

Jane is a hacker intent on breaking into the XYZ Corporation. She uses a variety of passive reconnaissance techniques and gathers extensive information about the company. Jane finds out what model routers are being used from network administrator questions/comments in user groups. She finds a complete list of the IT staff and their phone numbers from a personnel directory on the company website. She also was able to find out what services are running by using a port scan.

From this scenario, consider the following questions:

1. What reasonable steps could the company have taken to prevent Jane from finding out about company hardware, like router models?

2. What steps should the company take to prevent or at least reduce the efficacy of port scans?

## Chapter 7

# Industrial Espionage in Cyberspace

## Chapter Objectives

**After reading this chapter and completing the exercises, you will be able to do the following:**

- Know what is meant by industrial espionage
- Understand the low-technology methods used to attempt industrial espionage
- Be aware of how spyware is used in espionage
- Know how to protect a system from espionage

## Introduction

When you hear the word *espionage*, perhaps you conjure up a number of exciting and glamorous images. Perhaps you have visions of a well-dressed man who drinks martinis, shaken but not stirred, traveling to glamorous locations with equally glamorous travel companions. Or perhaps you envision some exciting covert operation with high-speed car chases and guns blazing in faraway exotic lands. Contrary to popular media portrayals, espionage is often much less exciting than those visions. The ultimate goal of espionage is to obtain information that would not otherwise be made available. Generally, espionage is best done with as little fanfare as possible. Blazing gun battles and glamorous locations tend to be the antithesis of intelligence gathering. Rather, information is the goal. If possible, it is best to obtain that information without the target organization even realizing that its information has been compromised.

Many people assume that such spying is only engaged in by governments, intelligence agencies, and nefarious international organizations, such as Al Qaida or ISIS. While those entities do indeed engage in espionage, they are certainly not the only organizations that do so. The aforementioned organizations desire to acquire information for political and military goals. However, economic goals are also dependent on accurate and often sensitive data. With billions of dollars at stake, private companies can become engaged in industrial espionage as either a target or a perpetrator. What company would not like to know exactly what its competitor is doing? In fact, corporate or economic espionage is on the rise.

Corporate or economic espionage is a growing problem, but it can be difficult to accurately assess just how great a problem it is. Companies that perpetrate corporate espionage do not share the fact that they do it, for obvious reasons. Companies that are victims of such espionage often do not wish to reveal that fact either. Revealing that their security was compromised could have a negative impact on their stock value. It is also possible, in certain cases, that such a breach of security might open the company to liability claims from customers whose data may have been compromised. For these reasons, companies often are hesitant to disclose any industrial espionage activities. Because you will want to protect yourself and your company, it is important that you learn about espionage methods and protections. In the exercises at the end of this chapter, you will run antispyware, key loggers, and screen-capture software so that you are aware of how they work and, hence, will be cognizant of the risks they pose. While we did cover those in previous chapters, we will expand on that in this chapter's exercises.

# What Is Industrial Espionage?

*Industrial espionage* is simply the use of spying techniques to find out key information that is of economic value. Such data might include details on a competitor's new project, a list of a competitor's clients, research data, or any information that might give the spying organization an economic advantage. While the rationale for corporate espionage is different from military espionage, corporate techniques are often the same as those methods employed by intelligence agencies and can include electronic monitoring, photocopying files, or compromising a member of the target organization. Not only does economic espionage use the same techniques as intelligence agencies, but it often also uses the same people. There have been a number of incidents in which former intelligence agents were found working in corporate espionage. When such individuals bring their skills and training to the world of corporate espionage, the situation becomes much more difficult for computer security experts.

### In Practice

### Leaving with Sensitive Data

While various computer experts and government agencies attempt to estimate the impact and spread of corporate espionage, its very nature makes accurate estimates impossible. Not only do the perpetrators not wish to disclose their crimes, but often the victims will not disclose the event either. However, anecdotal evidence would suggest that the most common form of espionage is simply an employee who quits, takes a job with another firm, and leaves with sensitive data. In many cases, these employees choose data that is readily available within the company and, as such, the data is considered a "gray area" as to its confidentiality. For example, a salesperson may leave with a printout of contacts and customers so that he can solicit them on behalf of the next employer. It is critical that you have a very well-worded nondisclosure and noncompete agreement with all employees. It is best to solicit the services of an employment attorney to draw up this agreement. Additionally, you might consider limiting an employee's access to data prior to terminating his employment. You should also conduct exit interviews and consider confiscating items such as company phone books, which may at first seem insignificant but which could contain data useful to another company. It is also the case that thumb drives, smart phones, and other technologies provide a method for taking data out of a company. Some companies restrict the use of these devices.

# Information as an Asset

Many people are used to viewing tangible objects as assets but have difficulty appreciating how mere information can be a real asset. Companies spend billions of dollars every year on research and development. The discovered information is worth at least the amount of resources taken to derive the information plus the economic gain produced by the information. For example, if a company spends $200,000 researching a process that will in turn generate $1 million in revenue, then that data is worth at least $1.2 million. You can think of this economic gain as a simple equation:

```
VI (value of information) = C (cost to produce) + VG (value gained)
```

While some people are not yet fully cognizant of the concept, data does indeed represent a valuable asset. When we speak of the "information age" or our "information-based economy," it is important to realize that these terms are not just buzzwords. Information is a real commodity. It is as much an economic asset as any other item in the company's possession. In fact, it is most often the case that the data residing on a company's computer is worth far more than the hardware and software of the computer system itself. It is certainly the case that the data is much more difficult to replace than the computer hardware and software.

To help you truly appreciate the concept of information as a commodity, consider the process of earning a college degree. You spend four years sitting in various classrooms. You pay a significant amount of money for the privilege of sitting in a room and listening to someone speak at length on some topic. At the end of the four years, the only tangible product you receive is a single piece of paper. Surely you can get a piece of paper for far less cost and with much less effort. What you actually paid for was the information you received. The same is true of the value of many professions. Doctors, attorneys, engineers, consultants, managers, and so forth all are consulted for their expert information. Information itself is the valuable commodity.

The data stored in computer systems has a high value for two reasons. First, there is a great deal of time and effort that goes into creating and analyzing the data. If you spend six months with a team of five people gathering and analyzing information, then that information is worth at least an amount equal to the salaries and benefits of those people for that length of time. Second, data often has intrinsic value, apart from the time and effort spent acquiring those facts. If the facts are about a proprietary process, invention, or algorithm, its value is obvious. However, any data that might provide a competitive edge is inherently valuable. For example, insurance companies frequently employ teams of statisticians and actuaries who use the latest technology to try to predict the risks associated with any given group of potential insureds. The resulting statistical information might be quite valuable to a competing insurance company. Even a customer contact list has a certain inherent value.

Thus, as you work in the computer security field, always keep in mind that any data that might have economic value is an asset to your organization and that such data provides an attractive target for any competitors who may not have ethical inhibitions against using espionage. If your company management thinks that this threat is not real, then they are very much mistaken. Any company is a potential victim of corporate espionage. You should take steps to protect your valuable information—and the first critical step in this process is asset identification.

*Asset identification* is the process of listing the assets that you believe support your organization. This list should include things that impact direct day-to-day operations as well as those that are tied to your company's services or products. The CERT website (http://people.tuke.sk/dezider.guspan/security/___ bezpecnost%20OCTAVE%20CERT/Tutorial%20Workbook%20-tutorial-workbook.pdf) offers a very useful worksheet that you can use to itemize the assets in your organization. This workbook also offers a number of other useful worksheets for assuring information security within your organization. As the table of contents in Figure 7.1 shows, this workbook is also a tutorial that steps you through all the information security considerations.

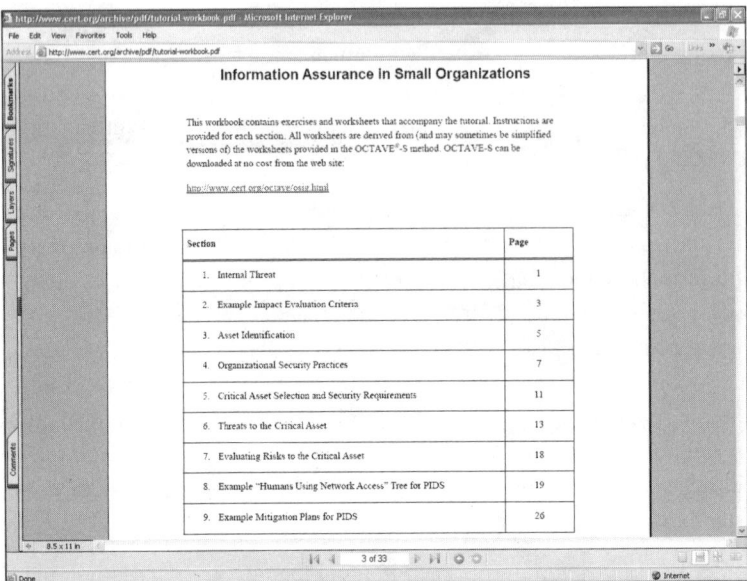

**FIGURE 7.1** Table of contents from the CERT Information Assurance in Small Organizations workbook.

Table 7.1 is a variation on the worksheet provided by CERT. Armed with this table and based on your knowledge and experience with the company, you can complete your asset identification following the steps outlined below.

**TABLE 7.1** Asset Identification Worksheet

| Information | Systems | Services and Applications | Other Assets | |
|---|---|---|---|---|
| | | | | |
| | | | | |
| | | | | |
| | | | | |
| | | | | |
| | | | | |
| | | | | |
| | | | | |
| | | | | |

1. In the first column of the table, list the information assets. You should list the types of information used by people in your company—the information people need to do their jobs. Examples are product designs, software programs, system designs, documentation, customer orders, and personnel data.

2. For each entry in the Information column, fill in the names of the systems on which the information resides. In each case, ask yourself which systems people need to perform their jobs.

3. For each entry in the Information column, fill in the names of the related applications and services. In each case, ask yourself what applications or services are needed for individuals to perform their jobs.

4. In the last column, list any other assets that may or may not be directly related to the other three columns. Examples are databases with customer information, systems used in production, word processors used to produce documentation, compilers used by programmers, and human resources systems.

Once you complete the proceeding steps and fill out the Asset Identification worksheet, you will have a good understanding of the critical assets for your organization. With this information, you will know how best to devote your defensive efforts. Some specific protective steps will be examined later in this chapter.

# Real-World Examples of Industrial Espionage

Now that you have been introduced to the concept of corporate espionage, let's look at five actual cases. These case studies are of real-world espionage found in various news sources. This section should give you an idea of what types of espionage activities actually occur. Note that while some of these cases are a bit old, they do illustrate the way industrial espionage is done. And it is frequently the case that details of an industrial espionage incident do not emerge until many years later, if at all.

## Example 1: Houston Astros

In 2015 the Houston Astros baseball team's scouting and team information database was stolen. It is alleged that it was stolen by members of the St. Louis Cardinals. The Houston Astros have a proprietary internal computer system they named Ground Control. It has notes on players and potential trading of players.

The Astros general manager, Jeff Luhnow, had previously worked for the Cardinals, and when he came to work for the Astros, he also brought along some of his staff. Initial reports are that either Mr. Luhnow or one of his staff used a password similar to what he had used with the Cardinals. This allowed someone associated with the Cardinals to guess the password and access the Houston Astros database.

## Example 2: University Trade Secrets

In May 2015, Professor Hao Zhang of Tianjin University and five other individuals were arrested and charged with stealing trade secrets for use by universities controlled by the Chinese government. The secrets stolen included research and development on thin-film bulk acoustic resonator (FBAR) technology.

The details of FBAR technology are not important for our discussion of this case of industrial espionage, but I will provide you with a brief description: It is essentially a device that has material located between two electrodes and acoustically isolated from the medium it is in. This is commonly used as a radio frequency filter in cell phones.

## Example 3: VIA Technology

VIA Technology actually provides two examples of industrial espionage. In the first instance, the chief executive officer (CEO) of the firm, which was based in Taipei, was indicted for copyright infringement for allegedly stealing technology from one of his own customers, a networking company called D-Link (Network World Fusion, 2003).

According to the allegations, VIA engineer Jeremy Chang left VIA to work for D-Link. For several months while at D-Link, Chang continued to receive a paycheck from VIA. Then he promptly resigned from D-Link and returned to VIA. Once Chang rejoined VIA, a D-Link document that detailed one of its simulation programs for testing integrated circuits was posted to an FTP server owned by VIA.

The prosecutors allege that Chang continued to receive a check from VIA because he had never really resigned. They allege that Chang was in fact a "plant" sent to D-Link to acquire D-Link's technology for VIA. VIA maintains that his continuation to receive a check was simply an oversight, and Chang denies that he posted the document in question. Whatever the truth of the case, it should make any employer think twice about hiring decisions and nondisclosure agreements.

To make matters worse for VIA, another company accused VIA of stealing code for its optical readers. In both cases, the story of the possible theft of technology alone has had a negative impact on the stock value of both companies.

## Example 4: General Motors

In 1993, General Motors (GM) and one of its partners began to investigate a former executive, Inaki Lopez. GM alleged that Lopez and seven other former GM employees had transferred GM proprietary information to Volkswagen (VW) in Germany via GM's own network (Brinks et al., 2003). The information allegedly stolen included component price data, proprietary construction plans, internal cost calculations, and a purchasing list.

In 1996, GM followed up the ongoing criminal investigation with civil litigation against Lopez, VW, and the other employees. In November 1996, GM expanded its legal battle by invoking the various Racketeer Influenced and Corrupt Organizations Act (RICO) statutes, originally intended to be used against organized crime conspiracies (*Economist,* 1996). By May 2000, a federal grand jury indicted Lopez on six counts related to fraud and racketeering. As of this writing, the case is not resolved (*USA Today,* 2000). At the time Lopez was indicted, he was residing in Spain, and the U.S. Justice Department was negotiating for his extradition. Thus, you can see that corporate espionage is neither new nor restricted to technology companies.

## Example 5: Bloomberg, Inc.

According to the *American Bar Association Journal* (2003), in August 2003, Oleg Zezev, a 29-year-old PC technician from Kazakhstan, broke into the Bloomberg Inc. computer system and used the alias Alex to obtain information and then blackmail the firm.

Zezev entered Bloomberg's computer system and accessed various accounts, including Michael Bloomberg's (CEO and founder of Bloomberg L.P.) personal account as well as accounts for other Bloomberg employees and customers. Zezev copied information from these accounts, including email inbox screens, Michael Bloomberg's credit card numbers, and screens relating to the internal functions of Bloomberg. He also copied internal information that was only accessible by Bloomberg employees.

Zezev then threatened to expose the data he had stolen to the public and, in essence, tell everyone exactly how he had broken into Bloomberg's network unless he received $200,000.

After deliberating for less than six hours, the jury in the U.S. District Court in Manhattan found the perpetrator guilty of all four charges: conspiracy, attempted extortion, sending threatening electronic messages, and computer intrusion. Although this is not industrial espionage in the classic sense, it does illustrate the compromising situations in which a company and its employees can be placed when security is breached.

## Example 6: Interactive Television Technologies, Inc.

On August 13, 1998, someone broke into the computer systems of Interactive Television Technologies, Inc. and stole the data for a project the company was working on (Secure Telecom, 1998). That project involved four years of intense research and a substantial financial investment. The product was to be a way whereby anyone with a television could have Internet access via the Web. This product, code named "Butler," would have been worth a substantial amount to its inventors. However, with all the research material stolen, it was only a matter of time before several other companies came out with competing products, thus preventing Interactive Television Technologies from pursuing a patent.

To date, no arrests have been made and no leads are available in this case. This situation was a case of very skillful hackers breaking into a computer system and taking exactly what they needed. One can only speculate about their motives. They may well have sold the research data to competitors of Interactive Television Technologies, or they may have simply put the data out in the open via the Internet. Whatever the motives or profits for the perpetrators, the outcome for the victim company was catastrophic.

## Trends in Industrial Espionage

While the cases just discussed range over a number of years, the problem is not abating. In fact, according to a CNN report, 2015 saw a 53% increase in cases of industrial espionage. The FBI conducted a survey of 165 companies and found that half of those companies had been the victim of industrial espionage of some type. A significant number of industrial espionage cases involve insider threats.

## Industrial Espionage and You

These cases notwithstanding, most companies will deny involvement in anything that even hints at espionage. However, not all companies are quite so shy about the issue. Larry Ellison, CEO of Oracle Corporation, has openly defended his decision to hire private investigators to sift through Microsoft garbage in an attempt to garner information (CNET News, 2001). Clearly, espionage is no longer a problem just for governments and defense contractors. It is a very real concern in the modern business world. The savvy computer security professional will be aware of this concern and will take the appropriate proactive steps.

# How Does Espionage Occur?

There are two ways that espionage can occur. An easy, low-technology avenue would be for current or former employees to simply take the data or for someone to use social engineering methods (discussed in Chapter 3, "Cyber Stalking, Fraud, and Abuse") to extract data from unsuspecting company employees. The second, more technology-oriented method is for the individuals to use spyware, which includes the use of cookies and key loggers. There are other technological methods we will discuss.

## Low-Tech Industrial Espionage

Corporate espionage can occur without the benefit of computers or the Internet. Disgruntled former (or current) employees can copy sensitive documents, divulge corporate strategies and plans, or perhaps reveal sensitive information. In fact, whether the method used is technological or not, disgruntled employees are the single greatest security risk to any organization. A corporate spy need not hack into a system in order to obtain sensitive and confidential information if an employee is willing to simply hand over the information. Just as with military and political espionage, the motives for the employee to divulge the information vary. Some engage in such acts for obvious financial gains. Others may elect to reveal company secrets merely because they are angry over some injustice (real or imagined). Whatever the motive, any organization has to be cognizant of the fact that it has any number of employees who may be unhappy with some situation and have the potential to divulge confidential information.

Certainly, one can obtain information without the benefit of modern technology; however, computer technology (and various computer-related tactics) can certainly assist in corporate espionage, even if only in a peripheral manner. Some incidents of industrial espionage are conducted with technology that requires little skill on the part of the perpetrator, as illustrated in Figures 7.2 and 7.3. This technology can include using universal serial bus (USB) flash drives, compact discs (CDs), or other portable media to take information out of the organization. Even disgruntled employees who wish to undermine the company or make a profit for themselves will find it easier to burn a wealth of data onto a CD and carry that out in their coat pocket rather than attempt to photocopy thousands of documents and smuggle them out. And the new USB flash drives, smaller than your average key chain, are a dream come true for corporate spies. These drives can plug into any USB port and store a tremendous amount of data. As of this writing, one can easily purchase small portable devices capable of holding 2 terabytes or more of data.

**FIGURE 7.2**    Low-tech espionage is easy.

**FIGURE 7.3**    Low-tech espionage is portable.

While information can be taken from your company without overt hacking of the system, you should keep in mind that if your system is unsecure, it is entirely possible that an outside party would compromise your system and obtain that information without an employee as an accomplice. In addition to these methods, there are other low-tech, or virtually "no-tech," methods used to extract information. *Social engineering*, which was discussed at length in Chapter 3, is the process of talking a person into giving up information she otherwise would not divulge. This technique can be applied to industrial espionage in a number of ways.

The first and most obvious use of social engineering in industrial espionage is in direct conversation in which the perpetrator attempts to get the targeted employee to reveal sensitive data. As illustrated in Figure 7.4, employees will often inadvertently divulge information to a supplier, vendor, or salesperson without thinking the information is important or that it could be given to anyone. This involves simply trying to get the target to talk more than they should. In 2009, there was a widely publicized case of a Russian spy ring working in the United States. One of their tactics was simply to befriend key employees in target organizations and, through ongoing conversations, slowly elicit key data.

Another interesting way of using social engineering would be via email. In very large organizations, one cannot know every member. This loophole allows the clever industrial spy to send an email message claiming to come from some other department and perhaps simply asking for sensitive data. A corporate spy might, for example, forge an email to appear to be coming from the legal office of the target company requesting an executive summary of some research project.

FIGURE 7.4 Social engineering used as low-tech espionage.

Computer security expert Andrew Briney (Information Security, 2003) places people as the number-one issue in computer security.

## Spyware Used in Industrial Espionage

Clearly, any software that can monitor activities on a computer can be used in industrial espionage. *Security IT World,* an online e-zine, featured an article in its October 2003 issue that dealt with the fact that monitoring a computer is an easy thing to do in the twenty-first century. The problem still persists to this day, with many security experts stating that spyware is at least as widespread as viruses. One method to accomplish monitoring is via spyware, which we discussed in detail in Chapter 5, "Malware." Clearly, software or hardware that logs key strokes or takes screenshots would be most advantageous to the industrial spy.

The application of this type of software to espionage is obvious. A spy could get screenshots of sensitive documents, capture logon information for databases, or in fact capture a sensitive document as it is being typed. Any of these methods would give a spy unfettered access to all data that is processed on a machine that contains spyware.

# Steganography Used in Industrial Espionage

Steganography is a different way of keeping messages secret. Rather than hide them through encryption, it protects communication via obscuring them. Messages are hidden within images. And in some cases other images are hidden within images. The word *steganography* comes from the Greek *steganos*, meaning covered or secret, and *graphy*, meaning writing or drawing. There are several technical means to accomplish this, but the most common is to conceal the data in the least significant bits of an image file. However, data can be concealed in any sort of digital file.

It should also be noted that historically there have been nontechnical means of hiding messages. A few notable examples include the following:

- The ancient Chinese wrapped notes in wax and swallowed them for transport.
- In ancient Greece a messenger's head might be shaved, a message written on his head, and then his hair was allowed to grow back.
- In 1518, Johannes Trithmeus wrote a book on cryptography and described a technique where a message was hidden by having each letter taken as a word from a specific column.

You might think that steganography requires a great deal of technical knowledge to accomplish; however, there are many software packages available that will perform the steganography for you. Quick Stego and Invisible Secrets are two very easy-to-use software tools that will do steganography for you. MP3Stego is a free tool that hides data inside MP4 files. These are just a few of the tools that one can find on the Internet. The widespread availability of cheap or free tools that are easy to use makes steganography a greater threat to any organization.

# Phone Taps and Bugs

Of course, there is always the possibility of using phone taps. A phone tap is simply the process of tying into the phone line at some point and intercepting calls. This is often done at some utility location inside the building one wishes to tap. Obviously, this sort of attack requires the attacker to enter on or near the premises, compromise phone equipment, and have the skill to tap into the phone line.

# Protecting Against Industrial Espionage

By now, you are aware that there are many ways that your organization's valuable information assets can be compromised. The question thus becomes this: What steps can you take to alleviate the danger? Note that I said "alleviate" the danger. There is nothing you can do to make any system, any information, or any person totally secure. Totally unbreakable security is simply a myth. The best you can do is work to achieve a level of security that makes the effort required to get information more costly than the value of the information.

One obvious protection is to employ antispyware software. As was mentioned earlier in this book, many antivirus programs also have antispyware capabilities. This software, coupled with other security measures such as firewalls and intrusion detection software (both examined in Chapter 9, "Computer Security Technology"), should drastically reduce the chance that an outside party will compromise your organization's data. Furthermore, implementing organizational policies (also discussed in Chapter 9) that help guide employees on safely using computer and Internet resources will make your system relatively secure. If you add to your protection arsenal the strategy of encrypting all transmissions, your system will be as secure as you can reasonably make it. (Chapter 8, "Encryption, is devoted to encryption.) However, all of these techniques (firewalls, company policies, antispyware, encryption, and so forth) will only help in cases in which the employee is not the spy. What do you do to ameliorate the danger of employees intentionally stealing or compromising information? Actually, there are several courses of action any organization can take to lessen risks due to internal espionage. Here are 12 steps you can use:

1. Always use all reasonable network security: firewalls, intrusion detection software, antispyware, patching and updating the operating system, and proper usage policies.

2. Give the personnel of the company access to only the data that they absolutely need to perform their jobs. This concept is referred to as *least privileges*. The employees are given the minimum privileges necessary to perform their job tasks. Use a need-to-know approach. One does not want to stifle discussion or exchange of ideas, but sensitive data must be treated with great care.

3. If possible, set up a system for those employees with access to the most sensitive data in which there is a rotation or a separation of duties. In this way, no one employee has access and control over all critical data at one time.

4. Limit the number of portable storage media in the organization (such as CD burners, and flash drives) and control access to these media. Log every use of such media and what was stored.

Some organizations have even prohibited cell phones because many phones allow the user to photograph items and send the pictures electronically.

5. Do not allow employees to take documents/media home. Bringing materials home may indicate a very dedicated employee working on her own time or a corporate spy copying important documents and information.

6. Shred documents and melt old disks/tape backups/CDs. A resourceful spy can often find a great deal of information in the garbage. If any storage media is disposed of, it should be completely wiped. Degaussing is a good technique for hard drives and USB drives.

7. Do employee background checks. You must be able to trust your employees, and you can only do this with a thorough background check. Do not rely on "gut feelings." Give particular attention to information technology (IT) personnel who will, by the nature of their jobs, have a greater access to a wider variety of data. This scrutiny is most important with positions such as database administrators, network administrators, and network security specialists.

8. When any employee leaves the company, scan the employee's PC carefully. Look for signs that inappropriate data was kept on that machine. If you have any reason to suspect inappropriate usage, then store the machine for evidence in subsequent legal proceedings.

9. Keep all tape backups, sensitive documents, and other media under lock and key, with limited access to them.

10. If portable computers are used, then encrypt the hard drives. Encryption prevents a thief from extracting useable data from a stolen laptop. There are a number of products on the market that accomplish this encryption, including the following:

    ■ TrueCrypt (see Figure 7.5) is one example of a free tool for encrypting drives, folders, or partitions. The tool is remarkably easy to use and can be found at www.truecrypt.org/. There are several other similar tools; most are low cost or free.

    ■ Microsoft Windows includes two types of encryption. Windows 7 Enterprise or Ultimate edition includes BitLocker for encrypting entire hard drives. BitLocker is also available on later versions of Windows (8, 8.1, 10). And all versions of Windows since Windows 2000 have included Encrypted File System for encrypting specific files or folders (see Figure 7.6).

    ■ This list is not exhaustive; therefore, it is highly recommended that you carefully review a variety of encryption products before making a selection.

11. Have all employees with access to any sensitive information sign nondisclosure agreements. Such agreements give you, the employer, a recourse should an ex-employee divulge sensitive data. It is amazing how many employers do not bother with this rather simple protection.

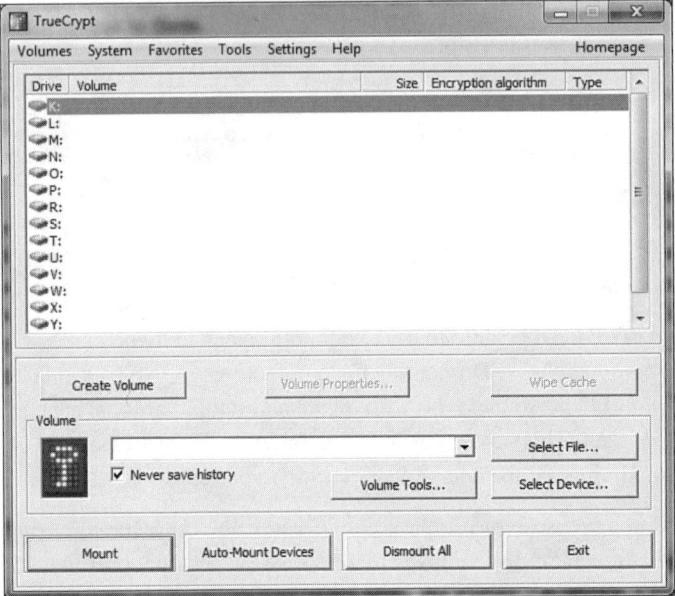

FIGURE 7.5    TrueCrypt.

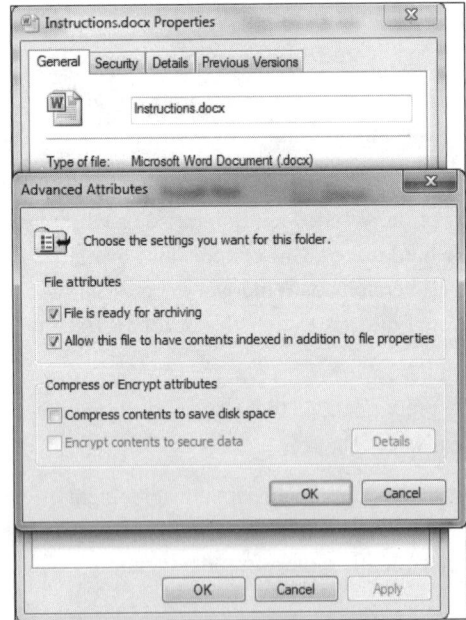

FIGURE 7.6    Windows EFS.

12. Have security awareness sessions. Clearly, employee education is one of the most important things you can do. An organization should have some method for routinely advising employees about security issues. An excellent way to do that is to have an intranet site that has security bulletins posted to it. It is also a good idea to have periodic training sessions for employees. These need not be lengthy or in depth. Most nontechnical employees only need an introduction to security concepts.

Unfortunately, following these simple rules will not make you totally immune to corporate espionage. However, using these strategies will make any such attempts much more difficult for any perpetrator; thus, you will improve your organization's data security.

# Industrial Espionage Act

The Industrial Espionage Act of 1996 was the first U.S. law to criminalize theft of commercial trade secrets. This law provides for significant penalties for violators. Quoting from the actual law:[1]

(a) Whoever, with intent to convert a trade secret, that is related to or included in a product that is produced for or placed in interstate or foreign commerce, to the economic benefit of anyone other than the owner thereof, and intending or knowing that the offense will injure any owner of that trade secret, knowingly—

(1) steals, or without authorization appropriates, takes, carries away, or conceals, or by fraud, artifice, or deception obtains such information;

(2) without authorization copies, duplicates, sketches, draws, photographs, downloads, uploads, alters, destroys, photocopies, replicates, transmits, delivers, sends, mails, communicates, or conveys such information;

(3) receives, buys, or possesses such information, knowing the same to have been stolen or appropriated, obtained, or converted without authorization;

(4) attempts to commit any offense described in paragraphs (1) through (3); or

(5) conspires with one or more other persons to commit any offense described in paragraphs (1) through (3), and one or more of such persons do any act to effect the object of the conspiracy, shall, except as provided in subsection (b), be fined under this title or imprisoned not more than 10 years, or both.

# Spear Phishing

*Phishing*, as you know, is the process of attempting to get personal information from a target in order to steal the target's identity or compromise the target's system. A common technique is to send out a mass email that is designed to entice recipients into clicking on a link that purports to be some financial institution's website but is actually a phishing website.

---

1. http://fas.org/irp/congress/1996_rpt/s104359.htm

*Spear phishing* is using the same technology in a targeted manner. For example, if an attacker wanted to get into the servers at a defense contractor, he might craft email and phishing websites specifically to target software and network engineers at that company. The emails might be made to appear of interest to that specific subgroup of people. Or the attacker might even take the time to learn personal details of a few of these individuals and target them specifically. This technique has been used against executives at various companies. In 2010 and 2011, this problem began to grow significantly.

This has since been expanded even more into the process of whaling. *Whaling* attempts to compromise information regarding a specific, but highly valuable, employee. It uses the same phishing techniques, but highly customized to increase the chances that the single individual target will be fooled and actually respond to the phishing attempt.

# Summary

A number of conclusions can be drawn from the examination of industrial espionage. The first conclusion: It does indeed occur. The case studies clearly demonstrate that industrial espionage is not some exotic fantasy dreamed up by paranoid security experts. It is an unfortunate, but quite real, aspect of modern business. If your firm's management chooses to ignore these dangers, then they do so at their own peril.

The second thing that can be concluded from this brief study of industrial espionage is that there are a variety of methods by which espionage can take place. An employee revealing confidential information is perhaps the most common. However, compromising information systems is another increasingly popular means of obtaining confidential and potentially valuable data. You will want to know the best way to protect your company and yourself. In the upcoming exercises at the end of this chapter, you will run screen-capture software, key loggers, and antispyware.

## Test Your Skills

## MULTIPLE CHOICE QUESTIONS

1. What is the ultimate goal of espionage?

    A. To subvert a rival government

    B. To obtain information that has value

    C. To subvert a rival business

    D. To obtain information not otherwise available

2. What is the best outcome for a spy attempting an espionage activity?

    A. To obtain information without the target even realizing he did so

    B. To obtain information with or without the target realizing he did so

    C. To obtain information and discredit the target

    D. To obtain information and cause harm to the target

3. What is the usual motivating factor for corporate/industrial espionage?

    A. Ideological

    B. Political

    C. Economic

    D. Revenge

4. Which of the following types of information would be a likely target for industrial espionage?

   A. A new algorithm that the company's IT department has generated

   B. A new marketing plan that the company has formulated

   C. A list of all the company's customers

   D. All of the above

5. Which of the following is a likely reason that an organization might be reluctant to admit it has been a victim of corporate espionage?

   A. It would embarrass the IT department.

   B. It would embarrass the CEO.

   C. It might cause stock value to decline.

   D. It might lead to involvement in a criminal prosecution.

6. What is the difference between *corporate* and *industrial* espionage?

   A. None; they are interchangeable terms.

   B. Industrial espionage only refers to heavy industry, such as factories.

   C. Corporate espionage only refers to executive activities.

   D. Corporate espionage only refers to publicly traded companies.

7. You can calculate the value of information by what formula?

   A. Resources needed to produce the information, plus resources gained from the information

   B. Resources needed to produce the information, multiplied by resources gained from the information

   C. Time taken to derive the information, plus money needed to derive the information

   D. Time taken to derive the information, multiplied by money needed to derive the information

8. If a company purchases a high-end UNIX server to use for its research and development department, what is probably the most valuable part of the system?

   A. The high-end UNIX server

   B. The information on the server

   C. The devices used to protect the server

   D. The room to store the server

9. Information is an asset to your company if it

    **A.** Cost any sum of money to produce

    **B.** Cost a significant sum of money to produce

    **C.** Might have economic value

    **D.** Might cost significant money to reproduce

10. What is the greatest security risk to any company?

    **A.** Disgruntled employees

    **B.** Hackers

    **C.** Industrial spies

    **D.** Faulty network security

11. Which of the following is the best definition for *spyware*?

    **A.** Software that assists in corporate espionage

    **B.** Software that monitors activity on a computer

    **C.** Software that logs computer keystrokes

    **D.** Software that steals data

12. What is the highest level of security you can expect to obtain?

    **A.** A level of security that makes the effort required to get information more than the value of the information

    **B.** A level of security comparable with government security agencies, such as the Central Intelligence Agency

    **C.** A level of security that has a 92.5% success rate in stopping intrusion

    **D.** A level of security that has a 98.5% success rate in stopping intrusion

13. In the context of preventing industrial espionage, why might you wish to limit the number of company CD burners and control access to them in your organization?

    **A.** An employee could use such media to take sensitive data out.

    **B.** An employee could use such media to copy software from the company.

    **C.** CDs could be a vehicle for spyware to get on your system.

    **D.** CDs could be a vehicle for a virus to get on your system.

14. Why would you want to scan an employee's computer when he leaves the organization?

   A. To check the work flow prior to leaving

   B. To check for signs of corporate espionage

   C. To check for illegal software

   D. To check for pornography

15. What is the reason for encrypting hard drives on laptop computers?

   A. To prevent a hacker from reading that data while you are online

   B. To ensure that data transmissions are secure

   C. To ensure that another user on that machine will not see sensitive data

   D. To prevent a thief from getting data off of a stolen laptop

## EXERCISES

### EXERCISE 7.1: Learning About Industrial Espionage

1. Using the Web, library, journals, or other resources, look up a case of industrial or corporate espionage not already mentioned in this chapter.

2. Write a brief essay describing the facts in the case. The parties in the case and the criminal proceeding are of interest, but most of your discussion should focus on the technical aspects of the case. Be sure to explain how the espionage was conducted.

### EXERCISE 7.2: Using Antispyware

Note that this exercise may be repeated with different antispyware products. It is a good idea for any person interested in computer security to be familiar with multiple antispyware products.

1. Go to the website of one of the antispyware utilities. (See Chapter 5 if you need more direction.)

2. Find instructions on the vendor's website.

3. Download the trial version of that software.

4. Install the software on your machine.

5. After installation, run the utility. What did it find? Record your results.

6. Let the utility remove or quarantine anything it found.

## EXERCISE 7.3: Learning About Key Loggers

Note that this exercise may only be completed on machines where you have explicit permission to do so (no public computers).

1. Using any website, find and download a key logger. The following websites might help you locate a key logger:

   www.kmint21.com/familykeylogger/
   www.blazingtools.com/bpk.html

2. Install the key logger on your PC.

3. Examine how the key logger behaves on your machine. Do you notice anything that might indicate the presence of illicit software?

4. Run the antispyware software you downloaded in Exercise 2. Does the antispyware software detect the key logger?

## EXERCISE 7.4: Screen-Capture Spyware

1. Using the Web, find and download a screen-capturing spyware application. The following website might be helpful to you in selecting an appropriate product. Warning: Since you are downloading spyware, it is likely that your system's antivirus/antispyware will give you a warning on some of these sites:

   http://en.softonic.com/s/screen-capture-spy-software

2. Install and configure the application on your computer.

3. Run the application and note what it finds.

4. Run the antispyware from Exercise 2 and see whether it detects your spyware program.

## EXERCISE 7.5: Learning About Hardware-Based Key Loggers

In this chapter, as well as in Chapter 5, we discussed software-based key loggers. However, there are also hardware-based key loggers.

1. Use the Internet to learn more about hardware-based key loggers. (You may wish to search for "Keykatcher" as a starting point.)

2. Write an essay outlining the way in which these key loggers work and how they could be implemented for either security or industrial espionage.

## PROJECTS

### PROJECT 7.1: **Preventing Corporate Espionage**

Using one of the websites listed in this book (you can also choose from the preferred resources in Chapter 1) or other resources, find a set of guidelines on general computer security. Write a brief essay comparing and contrasting those guidelines against the ones given in this chapter. Keep in mind that the guidelines in this chapter relate specifically to corporate espionage and not to general computer security.

### PROJECT 7.2: **Handling Employees**

Write a brief essay describing steps regarding the handling of employees. Include all steps that you believe an organization should take to prevent corporate espionage. It is important that you support your opinions with sources and reasons.

If possible, visit a company and talk with someone in either the IT or personnel departments to determine how that company handles issues such as employee termination, rotation of duties, control of access to data, and so forth. Compare and contrast your steps to those used by the company you visited.

### PROJECT 7.3: **Asset Identification in Your Organization**

Using the Asset Identification table found in this chapter or a similar table of your own design, identify the most valuable data in your organization (school or business) and what parties would most likely wish to access that data. Then write a brief guideline on how you might go about securing that data. In this project, you should tailor your security recommendations to the specific type of data you are trying to protect and against the most likely perpetrators of industrial espionage.

---

### Case Study

David Doe is a network administrator for the ABC Company. David is passed over for promotion three times. He is quite vocal in his dissatisfaction with this situation. In fact, he begins to express negative opinions about the organization in general. Eventually, David quits and begins his own consulting business. Six months after David's departure, it is discovered that a good deal of the ABC Company's research has suddenly been duplicated by a competitor. Executives at ABC suspect that David Doe has done some consulting work for this competitor and may have passed on sensitive data. However, in the interim since David left, his computer has been formatted and reassigned to another person. ABC has no evidence that David Doe did anything wrong.

What steps might have been taken to detect David's alleged industrial espionage? What steps might have been taken to prevent his perpetrating such an offense?

# Chapter | **8**

# Encryption

## Chapter Objectives

**After reading this chapter and completing the exercises, you will be able to do the following:**

- Explain the basics of encryption
- Discuss modern cryptography methods
- Select appropriate cryptography for your organization

## Introduction

There are many aspects of computer and information security. *Encryption*, the process of scrambling a message or other information so that it cannot be easily read, is one of the most critical parts to the security puzzle. If you have the best firewall, very tight security policies, hardened operating systems, virus scanners, intrusion detection software, antispyware, and every other computer security angle covered but send your data in raw, plain text, then you simply are not secure.

In this chapter, you will obtain what can be termed a "manager's understanding" of *cryptography* — the art of writing in or deciphering secret code. It is important to understand that this chapter will not make you a cryptographer. In fact, reading several volumes on encryption would not accomplish that lofty goal. Rather, this chapter is designed to give you a basic overview of what encryption is, some idea of how it works, and enough information so that you can make intelligent decisions about what sorts of encryption to incorporate in your organization. You will learn the basic history of encryption, the fundamental concepts, and after you have completed the exercises at the end of the chapter you'll have enough knowledge to at least be able to ask the right questions. Now, this does not mean we won't cover some technical details. We will. But the focus of this chapter is to give you a broad understanding of the relevant concepts.

We will go into the actual process of some of the cryptography algorithms presented. For example, we will show you the process of DES and RSA. It is beyond the scope of this book to go in depth into every cryptographic algorithm available, but it is useful for you to see a few of them described in detail.

As a security practitioner or aspiring security practitioner, it is not critical that you have an in-depth knowledge of cryptographic algorithms. In this chapter, some of the concepts we cover, particularly in regard to asymmetric cryptography, may be difficult to grasp. It is acceptable if you don't get 100% of those concepts, particularly the math-related concepts, on your first reading of the material. Some topics in this chapter are likely to require a bit more study and effort than other material in this book. In Chapter 9, "Computer Security Technology," you will see some applications of cryptography such as SSL/TLS, digital certificates, and virtual private networks.

# Cryptography Basics

The aim of cryptography is not to hide the existence of a message, but rather to hide its meaning—the process known as *encryption*. To make a message unintelligible, it is scrambled according to a particular algorithm, which is agreed upon beforehand between the sender and the intended recipient. Thus, the recipient can reverse the scrambling protocol and make the message comprehensible (Singh, 2001a). This reversal of the scrambling is referred to as *decryption*. The advantage of using encryption/decryption is that, without knowing the scrambling protocol, the message is difficult to re-create.

There are two basic types of cryptography in use today: *symmetric* and *asymmetric*. Symmetric means the same key is used to encrypt the message and to decrypt the message. With asymmetric cryptography, a different key is used to encrypt the message than is used to decrypt the message. That may sound a bit odd, and some readers may be pondering how that is possible. Later in this chapter, we will explore exactly how that works. For now the important point is to understand the basic concept of symmetric and asymmetric cryptography. But first, let's take a brief look at the history of encryption.

# History of Encryption

The idea of encryption is probably as old as written communication. The basic concept is actually fairly simple. Messages must be changed in such a way that the message cannot be easily read by an enemy, but they can be easily decoded by the intended recipient. In this section, you will examine a few historical methods of encryption. It should be noted that these are very old methods, and they cannot be used for secure communication today. The methods discussed in this section would be easily cracked, even by an amateur. However, they are wonderful for conveying the concepts of cryptography without having to incorporate a great deal of math, which is required of the more complex encryption methods.

> **FYI: Cryptographers**
>
> Encryption is a very broad and complex subject area. Even amateur cryptographers typically have some mathematical training and have studied cryptographic methods for several years.

If you are interested in learning more about the history of cryptography than what we touch upon here, you may wish to read one of the many books written on the subject. Or, you might consult the following websites, which are shown in Figure 8.1 and Figure 8.2. I have a cryptography website that may augment your reading in this chapter: www.cryptocorner.com.

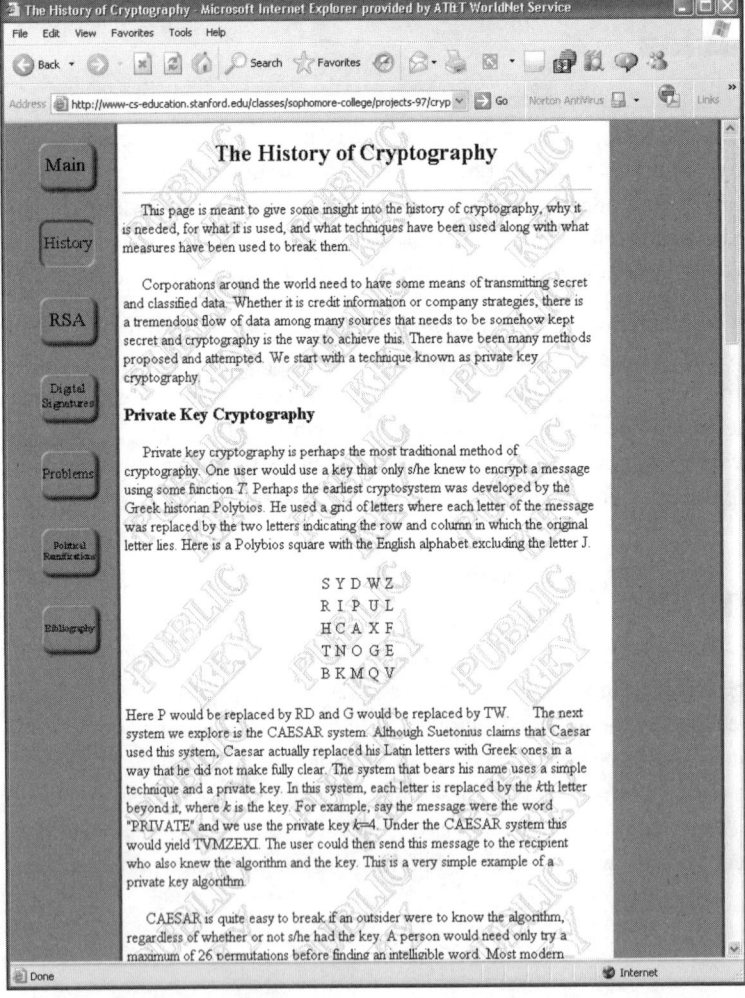

**FIGURE 8.1**   Stanford's cryptography history website.

- **The Stanford University History of Cryptography website:** http://cs.stanford.edu/people/ eroberts/courses/soco/projects/public-key-cryptography/history.html

- **Cryptography.org:** http://cryptography.org/

Understanding the simple methods described here and other methods listed on the aforementioned websites should give you a sense of how cryptography works as well as what is involved in encrypting a message. Regardless of whether you go on to study modern, sophisticated encryption methods, it is important for you to have some basic idea of how encryption works at a conceptual level. Having a basic grasp of how encryption works, in principle, will make you better able to understand the concepts of any encryption method you encounter in the real world.

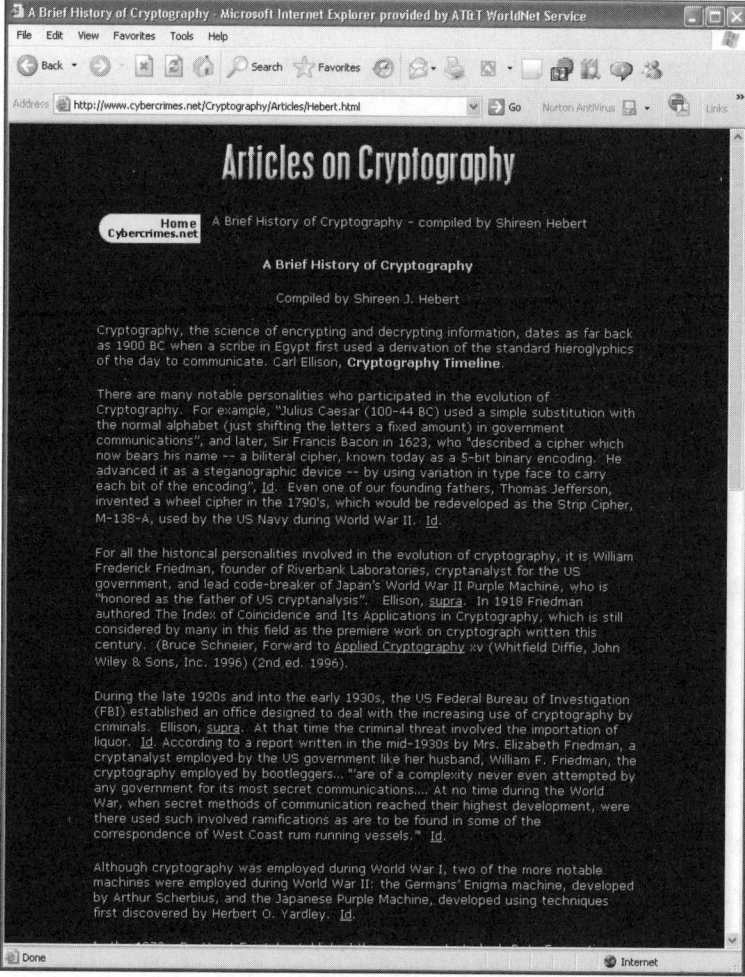

FIGURE 8.2    Hebert's cryptography history website.

## The Caesar Cipher

One of the oldest encryption methods is the *Caesar cipher*. This method is purported to have been used by the ancient roman Caesars—thus, the name. It is actually quite simple to do. You choose some number by which to shift each letter of a text. For example, if the text is

```
A cat
```

and you choose to shift by two letters, then the message becomes

```
C ecv
```

Or, if you choose to shift by three letters, it becomes

```
D fdw
```

Julius Caesar was reputed to have used a shift of three to the right. However, you can choose any shifting pattern you wish. You can shift either to the right or to the left by any number of spaces you like. Because this is a very simple method to understand, it makes a good place to start our study of encryption. It is, however, extremely easy to crack. You see, any language has a certain letter and word frequency, meaning that some letters are used more frequently than others (*Letter Frequency Distributions in the English Alphabet*, 2003). In the English language, the most common single-letter word is *A*. The most common three-letter word is *the*. Those two rules alone could help you decrypt a Caesar cipher. For example, if you saw a string of seemingly nonsense letters and noticed that a three-letter word was frequently repeated in the message, you might easily surmise that this word was *the*—and the odds are highly in favor of this being correct. Furthermore, if you frequently noticed a single-letter word in the text, it is most likely the letter *A*. You now have found the substitution scheme for *A, T, H*, and *E*. You can now either translate all of those letters in the message and attempt to surmise the rest or simply analyze the substitute letters used for *A, T, H*, and *E* and derive the substitution cipher that was used for this message. Decrypting a message of this type does not even require a computer. It could be done in less than 10 minutes using pen and paper by someone with no background in cryptography. There are other rules that will help make cracking this code even easier. For example, in the English language the two most common two letter combinations are *ee* and *oo*. That gives you even more to work on.

Another reason this algorithm can be easily cracked is an issue known as key space. The *key space* is the number of possible keys that could be used. In this case, when applied to the English alphabet, there are only 26 possible keys since there are only 26 letters in the English alphabet. That means that you could simply try each possible key (+1, +2, +3….+26) until one works. Trying all possible keys is referred to as a *brute force attack*.

The substitution scheme you choose (for example, +2, +1) is referred to as a *substitution alphabet* (that is, *B* substitutes for *A*, *U* substitutes for *T*). Thus, the Caesar cipher is also referred to as a *mono-alphabet substitution* method, meaning that it uses a single substitution for the encryption. There are other mono-alphabet algorithms, but the Caesar cipher is the most widely known.

## Atbash

In ancient times, Hebrew scribes used this substitution cipher to encrypt religious works such as the book of Jeremiah. Applying the Atbash cipher is fairly simple; just reverse the order of the letters of the alphabet. This is, by modern standards, a very primitive and easy-to-break cipher.

The Atbash cipher is a Hebrew code that substitutes the first letter of the alphabet for the last and the second letter for the second to the last, and so on. It simply reverses the alphabet. For example, in English:

>       *A* becomes *Z*, *B* becomes *Y*, *C* becomes *X*, and so on.

Of course, the Hebrews used a different alphabet, with *aleph* being the first letter and *tav* being the last letter. However, I will use English examples to demonstrate this:

>       Attack at dawn

Becomes

>       Zggzxp zg wzdm

As you can see, the *A* is the first letter in the alphabet and is switched with *Z*, the last letter in the alphabet. Then the *T* is the nineteenth letter (seventh from the end) and gets swapped with *G*, the seventh letter from the beginning. This process is continued until the entire message is enciphered.

To decrypt the message, you simply reverse the process and *Z* becomes *A*, *B* becomes *Y*, and so on. This is obviously a rather simple cipher and not used in modern times. However, it illustrates the basic concept of cryptography: to perform some permutation on the plain text to render it difficult to read by those who don't have the key to unscramble the cipher text. The Atbash cipher, like the Caesar cipher, is a single substitution cipher. That means each letter in the plain text has a direct, one-to-one relationship with each letter in the cipher text. This also means that the same letter and word frequency issues that can be used to crack a Caesar cipher can be used to crack the Atbash cipher.

## Multi-Alphabet Substitution

Eventually, a slight improvement on the Caesar cipher was developed, called *multi-alphabet substitution*. In this scheme, you select multiple numbers by which to shift letters (that is, multiple substitution alphabets). For example, if you select three substitution alphabets (12, 22, 13), then

```
A CAT
```

becomes

```
C ADV
```

Notice that the fourth letter starts over with another +2, and you can see that the first *A* was transformed to *C* and the second *A* was transformed to *D*. This makes it more difficult to decipher the underlying text. While this is harder to decrypt than a Caesar cipher, it is not overly difficult. It can be done with simple pen and paper and a bit of effort. It can be cracked very quickly with a computer. In fact, no one would use such a method today to send any truly secure message, for this type of encryption is considered very weak.

At one time multi-alphabet substitution was considered quite secure. In fact, a special version of this, called a *Vigenère cipher*, was used in the 1800s and early 1900s. The Vigenère cipher was invented in 1553 by Giovan Battista Bellaso. It is a method of encrypting alphabetic text by using a series of different Caesar ciphers based on the letters of a keyword. Figure 8.3 shows the Vigenère cipher.

| | A | B | C | D | E | F | G | H | I | J | K | L | M | N | O | P | Q | R | S | T | U | V | W | X | Y | Z |
|---|---|---|---|---|---|---|---|---|---|---|---|---|---|---|---|---|---|---|---|---|---|---|---|---|---|---|
| A | A | B | C | D | E | F | G | H | I | J | K | L | M | N | O | P | Q | R | S | T | U | V | W | X | Y | Z |
| B | B | C | D | E | F | G | H | I | J | K | L | M | N | O | P | Q | R | S | T | U | V | W | X | Y | Z | A |
| C | C | D | E | F | G | H | I | J | K | L | M | N | O | P | Q | R | S | T | U | V | W | X | Y | Z | A | B |
| D | D | E | F | G | H | I | J | K | L | M | N | O | P | Q | R | S | T | U | V | W | X | Y | Z | A | B | C |
| E | E | F | G | H | I | J | K | L | M | N | O | P | Q | R | S | T | U | V | W | X | Y | Z | A | B | C | D |
| F | F | G | H | I | J | K | L | M | N | O | P | Q | R | S | T | U | V | W | X | Y | Z | A | B | C | D | E |
| G | G | H | I | J | K | L | M | N | O | P | Q | R | S | T | U | V | W | X | Y | Z | A | B | C | D | E | F |
| H | H | I | J | K | L | M | N | O | P | Q | R | S | T | U | V | W | X | Y | Z | A | B | C | D | E | F | G |
| I | I | J | K | L | M | N | O | P | Q | R | S | T | U | V | W | X | Y | Z | A | B | C | D | E | F | G | H |
| J | J | K | L | M | N | O | P | Q | R | S | T | U | V | W | X | Y | Z | A | B | C | D | E | F | G | H | I |
| K | K | L | M | N | O | P | Q | R | S | T | U | V | W | X | Y | Z | A | B | C | D | E | F | G | H | I | J |
| L | L | M | N | O | P | Q | R | S | T | U | V | W | X | Y | Z | A | B | C | D | E | F | G | H | I | J | K |
| M | M | N | O | P | Q | R | S | T | U | V | W | X | Y | Z | A | B | C | D | E | F | G | H | I | J | K | L |
| N | N | O | P | Q | R | S | T | U | V | W | X | Y | Z | A | B | C | D | E | F | G | H | I | J | K | L | M |
| O | O | P | Q | R | S | T | U | V | W | X | Y | Z | A | B | C | D | E | F | G | H | I | J | K | L | M | N |
| P | P | Q | R | S | T | U | V | W | X | Y | Z | A | B | C | D | E | F | G | H | I | J | K | L | M | N | O |
| Q | Q | R | S | T | U | V | W | X | Y | Z | A | B | C | D | E | F | G | H | I | J | K | L | M | N | O | P |
| R | R | S | T | U | V | W | X | Y | Z | A | B | C | D | E | F | G | H | I | J | K | L | M | N | O | P | Q |
| S | S | T | U | V | W | X | Y | Z | A | B | C | D | E | F | G | H | I | J | K | L | M | N | O | P | Q | R |
| T | T | U | V | W | X | Y | Z | A | B | C | D | E | F | G | H | I | J | K | L | M | N | O | P | Q | R | S |
| U | U | V | W | X | Y | Z | A | B | C | D | E | F | G | H | I | J | K | L | M | N | O | P | Q | R | S | T |
| V | V | W | X | Y | Z | A | B | C | D | E | F | G | H | I | J | K | L | M | N | O | P | Q | R | S | T | U |
| W | W | X | Y | Z | A | B | C | D | E | F | G | H | I | J | K | L | M | N | O | P | Q | R | S | T | U | V |
| X | X | Y | Z | A | B | C | D | E | F | G | H | I | J | K | L | M | N | O | P | Q | R | S | T | U | V | W |
| Y | Y | Z | A | B | C | D | E | F | G | H | I | J | K | L | M | N | O | P | Q | R | S | T | U | V | W | X |
| Z | Z | A | B | C | D | E | F | G | H | I | J | K | L | M | N | O | P | Q | R | S | T | U | V | W | X | Y |

**FIGURE 8.3** Vigenère.

Match the letter of your keyword on the top with the letter of your plain text on the left to find the cipher text. For example, using the chart shown in Figure 8.3, if you are encrypting the word *cat* and your key is *horse*, then the cipher text is *jok*.

## Rail Fence

All the preceding ciphers we examined are substitution ciphers. Another approach to classic cryptography is the transposition cipher. The *rail fence* cipher may be the most widely known transposition cipher. You simply take the message you wish to encrypt and alter each letter on a different row. So "attack at dawn" is written as

```
A   t   c   a   d   w
  t   a   k   t   a   n
```

Next, you write down the text reading from left to right as one normally would, thus producing

atcadwtaktan

In order to decrypt the message, the recipient must write it out on rows:

```
A    t    c    a    d    w
     t    a    k    t    a    n
```

Then the recipient reconstructs the original message. Most texts use two rows as examples; however, this can be done with any number of rows you wish to use.

## Enigma

It is really impossible to have a discussion about cryptography and not talk about Enigma. Contrary to popular misconceptions, the Enigma is not a single machine, but rather a family of machines. The first version was invented by German engineer Arther Scherbius near the end of World War I. It was used by several different militaries, not just the Nazi Germans.

Some military texts encrypted using a version of Enigma were broken by Polish cryptanalysts Marrian Rejewsky, Jerzy Rozycki, and Henryk Zygalski. The three basically reverse engineered a working Enigma machine and used that information to develop tools for breaking Enigma ciphers, including one tool named the cryptologic bomb.

The core of the Enigma machine was the rotors, or disks that were arranged in a circle with 26 letters on them. The rotors were lined up. Essentially, each rotor represented a different single substitution cipher. You can think of the Enigma as a sort of mechanical poly-alphabet cipher. The operator of the Engima machine would be given a message in plain text and then type that message into Enigma. For each letter that was typed in, Enigma would provide a different cipher text based on a different substitution alphabet. The recipient would type in the cipher text, getting out the plain text, provided both Enigma machines had the same rotor settings. Figure 8-4 is a picture of an enigma machine.

**FIGURE 8.4**　An Enigma machine.

There were actually several variations of the Enigma machine. The Naval Enigma machine was eventually cracked by British cryptographers working at the now famous Bletchley Park. Alan Turing and a team of analysts were able to eventually break the Naval Enigma machine. Many historians claim this shortened World War II by as much as two years. This story is the basis for the 2014 movie *The Imitation Game*.

## Binary Operations

Most symmetric ciphers make use of a binary operation called Exclusive Or (XOR). Before we examine modern symmetric ciphers, we will review basic binary math. Various operations on *binary numbers* (numbers made of only 0s and 1s) are well known to programmers and programming students. But for those readers not familiar with them, a brief explanation follows. When working with binary numbers, there are three operations not found in normal math: AND, OR, and XOR operations. Each is illustrated next.

### AND

To perform the AND operation, you take two binary numbers and compare them one place at a time. If both numbers have a 1 in both places, then the resultant number is a 1. If not, then the resultant number is a 0, as you see here:

```
1 1 0 1
1 0 0 1
_____

1 0 0 1
```

### OR

The OR operation checks to see whether there is a 1 in either or both numbers in a given place. If so, then the resultant number is 1. If not, the resultant number is 0, as you see here:

```
1 1 0 1
1 0 0 1
_____

1 1 0 1
```

### XOR

The XOR operation impacts your study of encryption the most. It checks to see whether there is a 1 in a number in a given place, but *not* in both numbers at that place. If it is in one number but not the other, then the resultant number is 1. If not, the resultant number is 0, as you see here:

```
1 1 0 1
1 0 0 1
_____

0 1 0 0
```

XORing has a very interesting property in that it is reversible. If you XOR the resultant number with the second number, you get back the first number. And if you XOR the resultant number with the first number, you get the second number:

```
0 1 0 0
1 0 0 1
_____
1 1 0 1
```

Binary encryption using the XOR operation opens the door for some rather simple encryption. Take any message and convert it to binary numbers and then XOR that with some key. The key is some string of digits (1s and 0s) that should be random (or at least as random as possible). Converting a message to a binary number is really a simple two-step process. First, convert a message to its ASCII code, and then convert those codes to binary numbers. Each letter/number will generate an 8-bit binary number. Then you can use a random string of binary numbers of any given length as the key. Simply XOR your message with the key to get the encrypted text, and then XOR it with the key again to retrieve the original message. This method is easy to use and great for computer science students; however, it does not work well for truly secure communications because the underlying letter and word frequency remains. This exposes valuable clues that even an amateur cryptographer can use to decrypt the message. Yet, it does provide a valuable introduction to the concept of *single-key encryption*, which will be discussed in more detail in the next section. While simply XORing the text is not the method typically employed, single-key encryption methods are widely used today. And binary operations are often a part of the process.

Symmetric key cryptography often uses two processes: substitution and transposition. The substitution portion is accomplished by XORing the plain text message with the key. The transposition is done by swapping blocks of the text.

# Modern Methods

Modern cryptography methods, as well as computers, make cryptography a rather advanced science. What you have seen so far regarding cryptography is simply for educational purposes. As has been noted several times, you would not have a truly secure system if you implemented any of the previously mentioned encryption schemes. You may feel that this has been overstated in this text. However, it is critical that you have an accurate view of what encryption methods do and do not work. It is now time to discuss a few methods that are actually in use today.

Before we delve too deeply into this topic, let's start with some basic definitions you will need:

- **Key:** The bits that are combined with the plain text to encrypt it. In some cases this is random numbers; in other cases it is the result of some mathematical operation.

- **Plain text:** The unencrypted text.

- **Cipher text:** The encrypted text.

- **Algorithm:** A mathematical process for doing something.

# Single-Key (Symmetric) Encryption

Basically, single-key encryption means that the same key is used to both encrypt and decrypt a message. This is also referred to as symmetric key encryption. There are two types of symmetric algorithms: stream and block. A block cipher divides the data into blocks (often 64-bit blocks, but newer algorithms sometimes use 128-bit blocks) and encrypts the data one block at a time. Stream ciphers encrypt the data as a stream of bits, one bit at a time.

## Data Encryption Standard

*Data Encryption Standard*, or *DES* as it is often called, was developed by IBM in the early 1970s. It was finally published in 1976. DES is a block cipher. A *block cipher* is one that divides the plaintext into blocks and encrypts each block. In the case of DES, 64 bit blocks are used. The basic concept, however, is as follows (Federal Information Processing Standards, 2004):

---

### FYI: Block Ciphers and Stream Ciphers

When applying a key to plain text to encrypt it and produce the cipher text, you must also choose how to apply the key and the algorithm. In a block cipher, the key is applied to blocks (often 64 bits in size) at a time. This differs from a stream cipher that encrypts 1 bit at a time.

---

1. Data is divided into 64-bit blocks.

2. Those blocks are divided into two 32-bit halves.

3. One half is manipulated with substitution and XOR operations via a round function.

4. The two 32-bit halves are swapped.

5. This is repeated 16 times (16 rounds).

At the time DES was released, it was a marvelous invention. Even today the algorithm is still sound. However, the small key size, 56 bits, is not good enough to defend against brute force attacks with modern computers. The algorithm itself is quite sound. Many cryptography textbooks and university courses use this as the basic template for studying all block ciphers. We will do the same and give this algorithm more attention than most of the others in this chapter.

For those new to security and cryptography, the brief facts listed earlier are enough. However, for those who want to delve a bit deeper, let's examine the details of the DES algorithm. DES uses a 56-bit cipher key applied to a 64-bit block. There is actually a 64-bit key, but one bit of every byte is used for error correction, leaving just 56 bits for actual key operations.

DES is a Feistel cipher with 16 rounds and a 48-bit round key for each round. They are called Feistel ciphers (also Feistel functions) after Horst Feistel, the inventor of the concept, and the primary inventor of DES. All Feistel ciphers work in the same way: They divide the block into two halves, apply a round function to one of those halves, and then swap the halves. This is done each round. The primary difference between different Feistel ciphers is what exactly occurs within the round function.

The first issue to address is the key schedule. What is a key schedule? All block ciphers use one. A *key schedule* is a simple algorithm that will take the initial key the two parties derived and generate from that a slightly different key each round. DES does this by taking the original 56-bit key and slightly permuting it each round so that each round is applying a slightly different key but one that is based on the original cipher key. To generate the round keys, the 56-bit key is split into two 28-bit halves, and those halves are circularly shifted after each round by one or two bits. This will provide a different subkey each round. During the round key generation portion of the algorithm (recall that this is referred to as the key schedule) each round, the two halves of the original cipher key (the 56 bits of key that the two endpoints of encryption must exchange) are shifted a specific amount. The end result is that for each of the 16 rounds of DES, the key is actually a little different from the key used in the previous round. All modern symmetric ciphers do something like this. It improves the security of the cipher.

Once the round key has been generated for the current round, the next step is to address the half of the original block that is going to be input into the round function. Recall that the two halves are each 32 bit. The round key is 48 bits. That means that the round key does not match the size of the half block it is going to be applied to. You cannot really XOR a 48-bit round key with a 32-bit half block unless you simply ignore 16 bits of the round key. If you did so, you would basically be making the round key shorter and thus less secure, so this is not a good option. The 32-bit half needs to be expanded to 48 bits before it is XORd with the round key. This is accomplished by replicating some bits so that the 32-bit half becomes 48 bits.

This expansion process is actually quite simple. The 32 bits that are to be expanded are broken into 4-bit sections. The bits on each end are duplicated. If you divide 32 by 4, the answer is 8. So there are 8 of these 4-bit groupings. If you duplicate the end bits of each grouping, that will add 16 bits to the original 32, thus providing a total of 48 bits.

It is also important to keep in mind that it was the bits on each end that were duplicated. This will be a key item later in the round function. Perhaps this example will help you understand what is occurring at this point. Let us assume 32 bits as shown here:

 11110011010111111111000101011001

 Now divide that into 8 sections each of 4 bits, as shown here:

 1111 0011 0101 1111 1111 0001 0101 1001

 Now each of these has its end bits duplicated, as you see here:

 1111 becomes 111111

 0011 becomes 000111

 0101 becomes 001011

 1111 becomes 111111

1111 becomes 111111

0001 becomes 000011

0101 becomes 001011

1001 becomes 110011

The resulting 48-bit string is now XORd with the 48-bit round key. Now you are done with the round key. Its only purpose was to XOR with the 32-bit half. It is now discarded, and on the next round another 48-bit round key will be derived from the two 28-bit halves of the 56-bit cipher key, using the key schedule we previously described.

Now we have the 48-bit output of the XOR operation. But this still does not seem to work. Don't we need 32 bits rather than 48? That 48 bits is now split into 8 sections of 6 bits each. Each of those 6-bit sections is going to be input into an s-box (substitution box) and only 4 bits output.

The 6-bit section is used as the input to an s-box. An *s-box* is a table that takes input and produces an output based on that input. In other words, it is a substitution box that substitutes new values for the input. There are eight different s-boxes for DES, but below you can see one of them:

| | | Middle 4 bits of input | | | | | | | | | | | | | | | |
|---|---|---|---|---|---|---|---|---|---|---|---|---|---|---|---|---|---|
| | | 0000 | 0001 | 0010 | 0011 | 0100 | 0101 | 0110 | 0111 | 1000 | 1001 | 1010 | 1011 | 1100 | 1101 | 1110 | 1111 |
| Outer bits | 00 | 0010 | 1100 | 0100 | 0001 | 0111 | 1010 | 1011 | 0110 | 1000 | 0101 | 0011 | 1111 | 1101 | 0000 | 1110 | 1001 |
| | 01 | 1110 | 1011 | 0010 | 1100 | 0100 | 0111 | 1101 | 0001 | 0101 | 0000 | 1111 | 1010 | 0011 | 1001 | 1000 | 0110 |
| | 10 | 0100 | 0010 | 0001 | 1011 | 1010 | 1101 | 0111 | 1000 | 1111 | 1001 | 1100 | 0101 | 0110 | 0011 | 0000 | 1110 |
| | 11 | 1011 | 1000 | 1100 | 0111 | 0001 | 1110 | 0010 | 1101 | 0110 | 1111 | 0000 | 1001 | 1010 | 0100 | 0101 | 0011 |

An s-box is really just a hard coded lookup table. The two bits on either end are shown in the left column, and the four bits in the middle are shown in the top row. They are matched, and the resulting value is the output of the s-box. For example, with the previous demonstration numbers we were using, our first block would be 111111. So you find 1xxxx1 on the left and x1111x on the top. The resulting value is 3 in decimal or 0011 in binary.

Recall during the expansion phase we simply duplicated the outermost bits, so when we come to the s-box phase and drop the outermost bits, no data is lost.

Since each s-box outputs 4 bits and there are 8 s-boxes, the result is 32 bits. That 32 bits is now exclusively ORd with the other half of the original block. Recall that we did nothing with that half originally. Now the two halves are swapped.

If you are new to cryptography, all of this might be a bit confusing to you, even with the explanations provided. Many readers will need to reread this section a few times for it to become totally clear.

## 3DES

Triple DES was created as a replacement for DES. At the time, the cryptography community was searching for a viable alternative. While that was still being worked on, a stop-gap measure was created. It essentially applies DES three times with three different keys, thus the name 3DES.

There were variations of 3DES that used only two keys. The text was first encrypted with key A. The cipher text from that operation was then encrypted with key B. Then the cipher text from that operation was encrypted, this time reusing key A. The reason for this is that creating good cryptographic keys is computationally intensive.

## AES

*Advanced Encryption Standard (AES)* was the algorithm eventually chosen to replace DES. It is a block cipher that works on 128-bit blocks. It can have one of three key sizes of 128, 192, or 256 bits. This was selected by the United States government to be the replacement for DES and is now the most widely used symmetric key algorithm.

AES is also known as *Rijndael block cipher*. It was officially designated as a replacement for DES in 2001 after a 5-year process involving 15 competing algorithms. AES is designated as FIPS 197. Other algorithms that did not win that competition include such well-known algorithms as Twofish. The importance of AES cannot be overstated. It is widely used around the world and is perhaps the most widely used symmetric cipher. Of all the algorithms in this chapter, AES is the one you should give the most attention to.

AES can have three different key sizes: 128, 192, and 256 bits. The three different implementations of AES are referred to as AES 128, AES 192, and AES 256. The block size can also be 128, 192, or 256 bit. It should be noted that the original Rijndael cipher allowed for variable block and key sizes in 32-bit increments. However, the U.S. government uses these three key sizes with a 128-bit block as the standard for AES.

This algorithm was developed by two Belgian cryptographers, Joan Daemen and Vincent Rijmen. John Daeman is a Belgian cryptographer who has worked extensively on the cryptanalysis of block ciphers, stream ciphers, and cryptographic hash functions. For those new to security, this brief description given so far is sufficient. However, we will explore the AES algorithm in more detail. Just as with the details of DES, this may be a bit confusing to some readers at first glance and may require a few rereads.

Rijndael uses a substitution-permutation matrix rather than a Feistel network. The Rijndael cipher works by first putting the 128-bit block of plain text into a 4-byte x 4-byte matrix. This matrix is termed the *state* and will change as the algorithm proceeds through its steps. So the first step is to convert the plain text block into binary and then put it into a matrix, as shown in Figure 8.5.

| | | | |
|---|---|---|---|
| 11011001 | 01110010 | 10110000 | 11101010 |
| 01011111 | 00011001 | 11011001 | 10011001 |
| 10011100 | 11011101 | 00011001 | 11111101 |
| 11011001 | 10001001 | 11011001 | 10001001 |

**FIGURE 8.5**  The Rijndael matrix.

Once you have the original plain text in binary, placed in the 4-byte x 4-byte matrix, the algorithm consists of a few relatively simple steps that are used during various rounds. The steps are described here:

- **AddRoundKey:** In this step, each byte of the state is exclusively ORd with the round key. Just like DES, there is a key schedule algorithm that slightly changes the key each round.

- **SubBytes:** This involves substation of the input bytes (which are the output from the AddRoundKey phase). This is where the contents of the matrix are put through the s-boxes. Each of the s-boxes is 8 bits.

- **ShiftRows:** This is a transposition step where each row of the state is shifted cyclically a certain number of steps. In this step the first row is left unchanged. Every byte in the second row is shifted one byte to the left (with the far left wrapping around). Every byte of the third row is shifted two to the left, and every byte of the fourth row is shifted three to the left (again with wrapping around. This is shown in Figure 8.6.

Initial State

| 1a | 1b | 1c | 1d |
|---|---|---|---|
| 2a | 2b | 2c | 2d |
| 3a | 3b | 3c | 3d |
| 4a | 4b | 4c | 4d |

After Shift Rows

| 1a | 1b | 1c | 1d |
|---|---|---|---|
| 2b | 2c | 2a | 2a |
| 3c | 3d | 3a | 3b |
| 4d | 4a | 4b | 4c |

**FIGURE 8.6**  ShiftRows.

Notice that in Figure 8.6, the bytes are simply labeled by their row and then a letter, such as 1a, 1b, 1c, 1d.

- **MixColumns:** This is a mixing operation that operates on the columns of the state, combining the four bytes in each column. In the MixColumns step, each column of the state is multiplied with a fixed polynomial. Each column in the state (remember the matrix we are working with) is treated as a polynomial within the Galois Field ($2^8$). The result is multiplied with a fixed polynomial $c(x) = 3x^3 + x^2 + x + 2$ modulo $x^4 + 1$.

The MixColumns step can also be viewed as a multiplication by the shown particular MDS matrix in the finite field $GF(2^8)$.

With the aforementioned steps in mind, this is how those steps are executed in the Rijndael cipher. For 128-bit keys, there are 10 rounds. For 192-bit keys, there are 12 rounds. For 256-bit keys, there are 14 rounds.

These last few steps may be leaving you a bit confused if you don't have a background in number theory. You may be asking, what is a Galois field? What is a fixed polynomial? A general overview of the math needed to understand this is provided in the next section.

### AES Math

A group is an algebraic system consisting of a set, an identity element, one operation, and its inverse operation. Basically, groups are ways to take math operations, such as addition, and limit them to a specific set of numbers. There are several specialized types of groups briefly described here:

- An abelian group or commutative group has an additional axiom a + b = b + a if the operation is addition or ab = ba if the operation is multiplication.

- A cyclic group is one that has elements that are all powers of one of its elements.

- A ring is an algebraic system consisting of a set, an identity element, two operations, and the inverse operation of the first operation.

- A field is an algebraic system consisting of a set, an identity element for each operation, two operations, and their respective inverse operations.

This brings us to the Galois group or Galois field. GF(p) for any prime, p, this Galois field has p elements that are the residue classes of integers modulo p. That prime number p is the defining element for the field. Now, this is obviously a brief description and does not attempt to get into details. A thorough study of group theory would be needed to get into more detail.

### Blowfish

Blowfish is a symmetric block cipher. It uses a variable-length key ranging from 32 to 448 bits. Blowfish was designed in 1993 by Bruce Schneier. It has been analyzed extensively by the cryptography community and has gained wide acceptance. It is also a noncommercial (free of charge) product, thus making it attractive to budget-conscious organizations.

### RC4

All the other symmetric algorithms we have discussed have been block ciphers. RC4 is a stream cipher developed by Ron Rivest. The RC is an acronym for Ron's Cipher or sometimes Rivest's Cipher. There are other RC versions, such as RC5 and RC6.

### Serpent

Serpent has a block size of 128 bits and can have a key size of 128, 192, or 256 bits, much like AES. The algorithm is also a substitution-permutation network like AES. It uses 32 rounds working with a block of four 32-bit words. Each round applies one of eight 4-bit to 4-bit s-boxes 32 times in parallel. Serpent was designed so that all operations can be executed in parallel. This is one reason it was not selected as a replacement for DES. At the time many computers had difficulty with the parallel processing. However, modern computers have no problem with parallel processing, so Serpent is once again an attractive choice.

### Skipjack

Originally classified, this algorithm was developed by the NSA for the clipper chip. The clipper chip was a chip with built-in encryption; however, the decryption key would be kept in a key escrow in case law enforcement needed to decrypt data without the computer owner's cooperation. This feature made the process highly controversial. Skipjack uses an 80-bit key to encrypt or decrypt 64-bit data blocks. It is an unbalanced Feistel network with 32 rounds. Unbalanced Fiestel simply means a Feistel cipher wherein the two halves of plain text for each block are not the same size. For example, a 64-bit block might be divided into a 48-bit half and a 16-bit half rather than two 32-bit halves.

## Modification of Symmetric Methods

Just as important as understanding symmetric ciphers is understanding how they are implemented. There are some common modes that can affect how a symmetric cipher functions.

### Electronic Codebook

The most basic encryption mode is the electronic codebook (ECB) mode. The message is divided into blocks, and each block is encrypted separately. The problem is that if you submit the same plain text more than once, you always get the same cipher text. This gives attackers a place to begin analyzing the cipher to attempt to derive the key. Put another way, ECB is simply using the cipher exactly as it is described without attempts to improve its security.

### Cipher-Block Chaining

When using cipher-block chaining (CBC) mode, each block of plaintext is XORed with the previous ciphertext block before being encrypted. This means there is significantly more randomness in the final ciphertext, making it much more secure than electronic codebook mode. It is the most common mode.

There really is no good reason to use ECB over CBC if both ends of communication can support CBC. CBC is a strong deterrent to known plain text attacks, a cryptanalysis method we will examine later in this chapter.

The only issue with CBC is the first block. There is no preceding block of cipher text to XOR the first plaintext block with. It is common to add an initialization vector to the first block so that it has some-thing to be XORd with. The initialization vector is basically a pseudo random number, much like the cipher key. Usually an IV is only used once and is thus called a *nonce* (number used only once). The CBC mode is actually fairly old. It was introduced by IBM in 1976.

# Public Key (Asymmetric) Encryption

*Public key encryption* is essentially the opposite of single-key encryption. With any public key encryption algorithm, one key is used to encrypt a message (called the public key), and another is used to decrypt the message (called the private key). You can freely distribute your public key so that anyone can encrypt a message to send to you, but only you have the private key and only you can decrypt the message. The actual mathematics behind the creation and application of the keys will vary between different asymmetric algorithms. We will look at the math for RSA later in this section. It should be pointed out, however, that many public key algorithms are dependent, to some extent, on large prime numbers, factoring, and number theory.

It has become standard in cryptography to use the fictitious Alice and Bob to illustrate asymmetric cryptography. If Alice wants to send Bob a message, she will use Bob's public key to encrypt that message. It does not matter if every other person on the planet also has Bob's public key. That key cannot decrypt the message. Only Bob's private key can do that. This is shown in Figure 8.7.

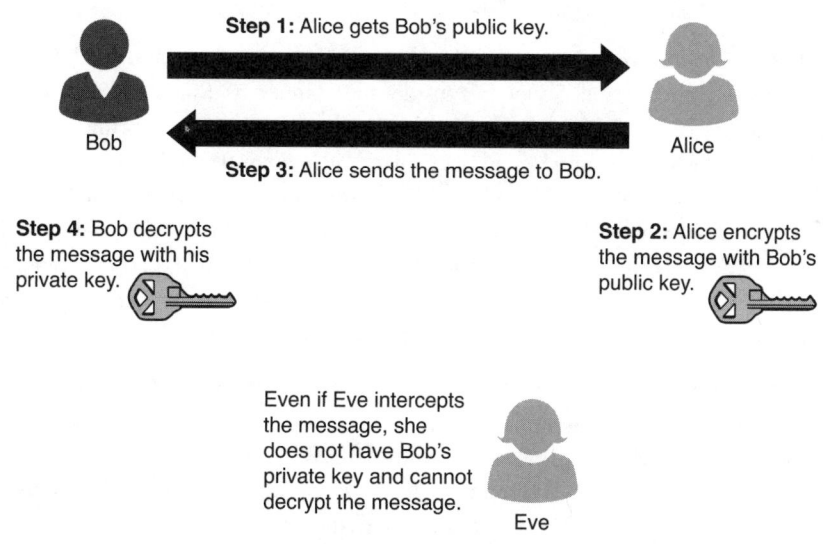

**FIGURE 8.7**   Public key cryptography.

Public key encryption is important because there are no issues to deal with concerning distribution of the keys. With symmetric key encryption, you must get a copy of the key to every person to whom you wish to send your encrypted messages. If that key were lost or copied, someone else might be able to decrypt all of your messages. With public key encryption, you can freely distribute your public key to the entire world, yet only you can decrypt messages encrypted with that public key.

## RSA

You cannot discuss cryptography without at least some discussion of RSA, which is a very widely used encryption algorithm. This public key method was developed in 1977 by three mathematicians: Ron Rivest, Adi Shamir, and Len Adlema. The name RSA is derived from the first letter of each mathematician's last name (Burnett and Paine, 2001). Let us take a look at the math involved in RSA. It should be pointed out that knowing the math behind this, or any other algorithm, is not critical for most security professionals. But some readers will have an interest in going deeper into cryptography, and this will be a good place to start.

Before we can delve into RSA, there are a few basic math concepts you need to know. Some (or even all) of this material may be a review.

- **Prime Numbers:** A prime number is divisible by itself and 1. So 2, 3, 5, 7, 11, 13, 17, and 23 are all prime numbers. (Note that 1 itself is considered a special case and is not prime.)

- **Co-prime:** This actually does not mean prime; it means two numbers have no common factors. So, for example, the factors of 8 (excluding the special case of 1) are 2 and 4. The factors of 9 are 3. The numbers 8 and 9 have no common factors. They are co-prime.

- **Euhler's Totient:** Pronounced "oilers" totient, or just the totient, this is the number of integers smaller than n that are co-prime with n. So let us consider the number 10. Since 2 is a factor of 10, it is not co-prime with 10. But 3 is co-prime with 10. The number 4 is not co-prime since both 4 and 10 have 2 as a factor. The number 5 is not since it is a factor of 10. Neither is 6 since both 6 and 10 have 2 as a cofactor. The number 7 is prime, so it is co-prime with 10. The number 8 is not because both 8 and 10 have 2 as a factor. The number 9 is co-prime with 10. So the numbers 3, 7, and 9 are co-prime with 10. We add in 1 as a special case, the Euler's totient of 10 is 4. Now it just so happens that Leonard Euler also proved that if the number n is a prime number, then its totient is always n − 1. So the totient of 7 is 6. The totient of 13 is 12.

- **Multiplying and co-prime:** Now we can easily compute the totient of any number. And we know automatically that the totient of any prime number n is just n − 1. But what if we multiply two primes? For example, we can multiply 5 and 7, getting 35. Well, we can go through all the numbers up to 35 and tally up the number that are co-prime with 35. But the larger the numbers get, the more tedious this process becomes. For example, if you have a 20-digit number, manually calculating the totient is almost impossible. Fortunately, Leonard Euler also proved that if you have a number that is the product of two primes (let's call them p and q), such as 5 and 7, then the totient of the product of those two numbers (in this case 35) is equal to p − 1 * q − 1 (in this case 4 * 6, or 24).

- **Modulus:** This is the last concept you need for RSA. There are a few approaches to explaining this concept. We will actually use two of them. First, from a programmer's perspective, the modulus operation is to divide two numbers but only give the remainder. Programmers often use the symbol % to denote modulo operations. So 10 % 3 is 1. The remainder of 10 divided by 3 is 1. Now, this is not really a mathematical explanation of modulo operations.

Basically, modulo operations take addition and subtraction and limit them by some value. You have actually done this all your life without realizing it. Consider a clock. When you say *2 p.m.*, what you really mean is 14 mod 12 (or 14 divided by 12; just give me the remainder). Or if it is 2 p.m. now (14 actually) and you tell me you will call me in 36 hours, what I do is 14 + 36 mod 12, or 50 mod 12, which is 2 a.m. ( a bit early for a phone call, but it illustrates our point).

Now if you understand these basic operations, then you are ready to learn RSA. If needed, reread the preceding section (perhaps even more than once) before proceeding.

To create the key, you start by generating two large random primes, $p$ and $q$, of approximately equal size. You need to pick two numbers so that when multiplied together the product will be the size you want (2048 bits, 4096 bits, and so on).

Now multiply $p$ and $q$ to get $n$.

Let $n = pq$

The next step is to multiply the Euler's totient for each of these primes. Basically, the Euler's totient is the total number of co-prime numbers. Two numbers are considered co-prime if they have no common factors. For example, if the original number is 7, then 5 and 7 would be co-prime. Remember that it just so happens that for prime numbers, this is always the number minus 1. For example 7 has 6 numbers that are co-prime to it. (If you think about this a bit you will see that 1, 2, 3, 4, 5, and 6 are all co-prime with 7.)

Let $m = (p - 1)(q - 1)$

Now we are going to select another number. We will call this number $e$. We want to pick $e$ so that it is co-prime to $m$.

Choose a small number $e$, co-prime to $m$.

We are almost done generating a key. Now we just find a number $d$ that when multiplied by $e$ and modulo $m$ would yield a 1. (Remember: *Modulo* means to divide two numbers and return the remainder. For example, 8 modulo 3 would be 2.)

Find $d$, such that $de \% m = 1$

Now you will publish $e$ and $n$ as the public key. Keep $d$ as the secret key. To encrypt, you simply take your message raised to the $e$ power and modulo $n$.

$= m^e \% n$

To decrypt, you take the cipher text and raise it to the $d$ power modulo $n$.

$P = C^d \% n$

The letter $e$ is for encrypt and $d$ for decrypt. If all this seems a bit complex to you, first you must realize that many people work in network security without being familiar with the actual algorithm for RSA (or any other cryptography for that matter). However, if you wish to go deeper into cryptography, then this is a very good start. It involves some fundamental number theory, particularly regarding prime numbers. There are other asymmetric algorithms that work in a different manner. For example, elliptic curve cryptography is one such example.

Let's look at an example that might help you understand. Of course, RSA would be done with very large integers. To make the math easy to follow, we will use small integers in this example. (Note that this example is from Wikipedia.)

Choose two distinct prime numbers, such as $p = 61$ and $q = 53$.

Compute $n = pq$ giving n = 61 * 53 = 3233.

Compute the totient of the product as $\Phi(n) = (p - 1)(q - 1)$ giving $\Phi(3233) = (61 - 1)(53 - 1) = 3120$.

Choose any number $1 < e < 3120$ that is co-prime to 3120. Choosing a prime number for $e$ leaves us only to check that $e$ is not a divisor of 3120. Let $e = 17$.

Compute $d$, the modular multiplicative inverse of yielding $d = 2753$.

The public key is $(n = 3233, e = 17)$. For a padded plaintext message $m$, the encryption function is $m^{17} \pmod{3233}$.

The private key is $(n = 3233, d = 2753)$. For an encrypted ciphertext $c$, the decryption function is $c^{2753} \pmod{3233}$.

For those readers new to RSA or new to cryptography in general, it might be helpful to see one more example, with even smaller numbers.

Select primes: $p = 17$ & $q = 11$

Compute $n = pq = 17 \times 11 = 187$

Compute $\emptyset(n) = (p - 1)(q - 1) = 16 \times 10 = 160$

Select e : $\gcd(e, 160) = 1$; choose $e = 7$

Determine d: $de = 1 \bmod 160$ and $d < 160$ Value is d = 23 since $23 \times 7 = 161 = 10 \times 160 + 1$

Publish public key (7 and 187)

Keep secret private key 23

## Diffie-Hellman

Diffie-Hellman was the first publically described asymmetric algorithm. This is a cryptographic protocol that allows two parties to establish a shared key over an insecure channel. In other words, Diffie-Hellman is often used to allow parties to exchange a symmetric key through some unsecure medium, such as the Internet. It was developed by Whitfield Diffie and Martin Hellman in 1976.

One problem with working in cryptology is that much of the work is classified. You could labor away and create something wonderful…that you cannot tell anyone about. Then to make matters worse, years later someone else might develop something similar and release it, getting all the credit. This is exactly the situation with Diffie-Hellman. It turns out that a similar method had been developed a few years earlier by Malcolm J. Williamson of the British Intelligence Service, but it was classified.

### Elliptic Curve

This algorithm was first described in 1985 by Victor Miller and Neil Koblitz. Elliptic Curve cryptography is based on the fact that finding the discrete logarithm of a random elliptic curve element with respect to a publicly known base point is difficult to the point of being impractical to do. The mathematics behind this algorithm are a bit much for an introductory book on security. However, if you are interested, there is a great tutorial at http://arstechnica.com/security/2013/10/a-relatively-easy-to-understand-primer-on-elliptic-curve-cryptography/.

There are a number of variations such as ECC-DH (ECC Diffie-Hellman), and ECC-DSA (ECC Digital Signature Algorithm). The real strength of ECC crypto systems is that you can get just as much security with a smaller key than with other systems, like RSA. For example, a 384-bit ECC key is as strong as 2048-bit RSA.

# PGP

*PGP*, a public key system, stands for *Pretty Good Privacy*. It is a widely used system that is considered very secure by most experts (International PGP website, 2004). There are several software implementations available as freeware for most desktop operating systems. There are PGP plug-ins for MSN Messenger and many other popular communications software packages (McCune, 2004). A simple Yahoo! or Google search for *PGP* will help you find many of these software products.

---

**FYI: "Old" Encryption**

PGP is quite old. Some readers might wonder whether it is old and outdated. Cryptography is unlike other technological endeavors in this regard: Older is better. It is usually unwise to use the "latest thing" in encryption for the simple reason that it is unproven. An older encryption method, provided it has not yet been broken, is usually a better choice because it has been subjected to years of examination by experts and to cracking attempts by both experts and less honorably motivated individuals. This is sometimes hard for computer professionals to understand since the newest technology is often preferred in the computer business.

---

PGP was invented by Phil Zimmerman (Zimmerman, 2004). Before creating PGP, Mr. Zimmerman had been a software engineer for 20 years and had experience with existing forms of cryptography. A great deal of controversy surrounded the birth of PGP because it was created without an easy means for government intrusion, and its encryption was considered too strong for export. This caused Mr. Zimmerman to be the target of a three-year government investigation. However, those legal matters are now resolved, and PGP is one of the most widely used encryption methods available.

The important things to know about PGP are that it is

- A public key encryption
- Considered quite secure
- Available free of charge

These facts make it well worth your time to investigate PGP as a possible solution for your organization's encryption needs.

# Legitimate Versus Fraudulent Encryption Methods

The encryption methods discussed earlier are just a few of the more widely used modern encryption methods. Dozens of other methods are released to the public for free or are patented and sold for profit every year. However, it is important to realize that this particular area of the computer industry is replete with frauds and charlatans. One need only scan a search engine for *encryption* to find a plethora of advertisements for the latest and greatest "unbreakable" encryption. If you are not knowledgeable about encryption, how do you separate legitimate encryption methods from frauds?

There are many fraudulent cryptographic claims out there. You do not have to be a cryptography expert to be able to avoid many of those fraudulent claims. Here are some warning signs:

- **Unbreakable:** Anyone with experience in cryptography knows that there is no such thing as an unbreakable code. There are codes that have not yet been broken. There are codes that are very hard to break. But when someone claims that his method is "completely unbreakable," you should be suspicious.

- **Certified:** Guess what? There is no recognized certification process for encryption methods. Therefore, any "certification" the company has is totally worthless.

- **Inexperienced people:** A company is marketing a new encryption method. What is the experience of the people working with it? Does the cryptographer have a background in math, encryption, or algorithms? If not, has he submitted his method to experts in peer-reviewed journals? Or, is he at least willing to disclose how his method works so that it can be fairly judged? Recall that PGP's inventor had decades of software engineering and encryption experience.

This can be formally expressed as Kerckhoff's principle. Auguste Kerckhoff first articulated this in the 1800s, stating that the security of a cipher depends only on the secrecy of the key, not the secrecy of the algorithm. Claude Shannon rephrased this stating that, "One ought to design systems under the assumption that the enemy will ultimately gain full familiarity with them." This is referred to as Shannon's maxim and states essentially the same thing Kerckhoff's principle states.

I would add to Kerckhoff's principle/Shannon's maxim something I will humbly call Easttom's corollary: "You should be very wary of any cryptographic algorithm that has not been published and thoroughly reviewed. Only after extensive peer review should you consider the use of any cryptographic algorithm." I first proposed this corollary in my book *Modern Cryptography: Applied Mathematics for Encryption and Information Security.*

# Digital Signatures

A digital signature is not used to ensure the confidentiality of a message but rather to guarantee who sent the message. This is referred to as nonrepudiation. Essentially, it proves who the sender is. Digital signatures are actually rather simple, but clever. They simply reverse the asymmetric encryption process. Recall that in asymmetric encryption, the public key (which anyone can have access to) is used to encrypt a message to the recipient, and the private key (which is kept secure, and private) can decrypt it. With a digital signature, the sender encrypts something with his private key. If the recipient is able to decrypt that with the sender's public key, then it must have been sent by the person purported to have sent the message. This process is shown in Figure 8.8.

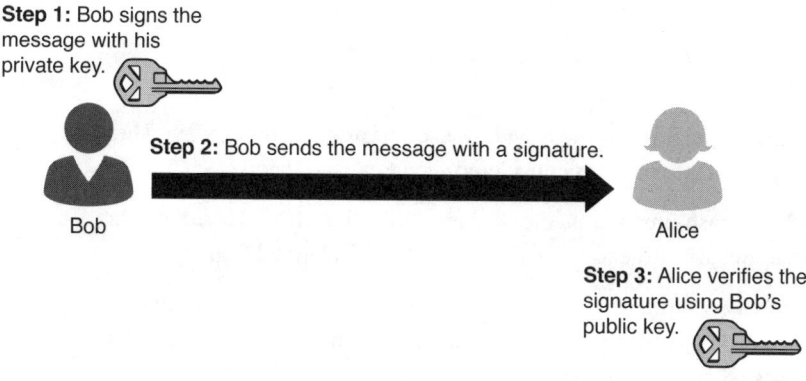

**Step 1:** Bob signs the message with his private key.

**Step 2:** Bob sends the message with a signature.

Bob

Alice

**Step 3:** Alice verifies the signature using Bob's public key.

**Figure 8.8**  *Digital signatures.*

# Hashing

A *hashing* is a type of cryptographic algorithm that has some specific characteristics. First and foremost, it is one way. That means you cannot unhash something. Second, you get a fixed-length output no matter what input is given. Third, there are no collisions. A collision occurs when two different inputs to the same hashing algorithm produce the same output (called a *hash* or *digest*). Ideally we would like to have no collisions. But the reality is that with a fixed-length output, a collision is possible. So the goal is to make it so unlikely as to be something we need not think about.

Hashes are exactly how Windows stores passwords. For example, if your password is *password*, then Windows will first hash it producing something like this:

0BD181063899C9239016320B50D3E896693A96DF

Windows will then store that in the SAM (Security Accounts Manager) file in the Windows System directory. When you log on, Windows cannot unhash your password (remember it is one-way). So, what Windows does is take whatever password you type in, hash it, and then compare the result with what is in the SAM file. If they match (exactly), then you can log in.

Storing Windows passwords is just one application of hashing. There are others. For example, in computer forensics it is common to hash a drive before you begin forensic examination. Then later you can always hash it again to see if anything was changed (accidently or intentionally). If the second hash matches the first, then nothing has been changed.

There are various hashing algorithms. The two most common are MD5 and SHA. (It was SHA-1, but since then later versions like SHA-256 are becoming more common.)

## MD5

This is a 128-bit hash that is specified by RFC 1321. It was designed by Ron Rivest in 1991 to replace an earlier hash function, MD4. MD5 produces a 128-bit hash or digest. It has been found not to be as collision resistant as SHA.

## SHA

The Secure Hash Algorithm is perhaps the most widely used hash algorithm today. There are now several versions of SHA. SHA (all versions) is considered secure and collision free.

- **SHA-1:** This is a 160-bit hash function that resembles the earlier MD5 algorithm. This was designed by the National Security Agency (NSA) to be part of the Digital Signature Algorithm.

- **SHA-2:** This is actually two similar hash functions, with different block sizes, known as SHA-256 and SHA-512. They differ in the word size; SHA-256 uses 32-byte (256 bits) words, whereas SHA-512 uses 64-byte (512 bits) words. There are also truncated versions of each standardized, known as SHA-224 and SHA-384. These were also designed by the NSA.

- **SHA-3:** This is the latest version of SHA. It was adopted in October 2012.

## RipeMD

RACE Integrity Primitives Evaluation Message Digest is a 160-bit hash algorithm developed by Hans Dobbertin, Antoon Bosselaers, and Bart Preneel. There exist 128-, 256-, and 320-bit versions of this algorithm, called RIPEMD-128, RIPEMD-256, and RIPEMD-320, respectively. All these replace the original RIPEMD, which was found to have collision issues.

# MAC and HMAC

Hashes are used for several security-related functions. One is to store passwords, which we have discussed already (and we will see more later in this chapter).

A hash of a message can be sent to see if accidental alteration occurred in transit. If a message is altered in transit, the recipient can compare the hash received against the hash the computer sent and detect the error in transmission. But what about intentional alteration of messages? What happens if someone alters the message intentionally, deletes the original hash, and recomputes a new one? Unfortunately, a simple hashing algorithm cannot account for this scenario.

A Message Authentication Code (or MAC) is one way to detect intentional alterations in a message. A MAC is also often called a *keyed cryptographic hash function*. That name should tell you how this works. One way to do this is the HMAC, or Hashing Message Authentication Code. Let us assume you are using MD5 to verify message integrity. To detect an intercepting party intentionally altering a message, both the sender and the recipient must previously exchange a key of the appropriate size (in this case, 128 bits). The sender will hash the message and then XOR that hash with this key. The recipient will hash what she receives and XOR that computed hash with the key. Then the two hashes are exchanged. Should an intercepting party simply recompute the hash, he will not have the key to XOR that with (and may not even be aware that it should be XORd); thus, the hash the interceptor creates won't match the hash the recipient computes and the interference will be detected.

There are other variations of the concept. Some use a symmetric cipher in CBC (Cipher Block Chaining mode) and then use only the final block as the MAC. These are called CBC-MAC.

## Rainbow Tables

Since Windows and many other systems store passwords as hashes, many people have had an interest in how to break hashes. As we've mentioned, since a hash is not reversible, there is no way to unhash something. In 1980, Martin Hellman described a cryptanalytic technique that reduces the time of cryptanalysis by using precalculated data stored in memory. This technique was improved by Rivest before 1982. Basically, these types of password crackers are working with precalculated hashes of all passwords available within a certain character space, be that a–z or a–zA–z or a–zA–Z0–9, and more. This is called a rainbow table. If you search a rainbow table for a given hash, whatever plaintext you find must be the text that was input into the hashing algorithm to produce that specific hash.

Clearly, such a rainbow table would get very large very fast. Assume that the passwords must be limited to keyboard characters. That leaves 52 letters (26 uppercase and 26 lowercase), 10 digits, and roughly 10 symbols, or about 72 characters. As you can imagine, even a 6-character password has a very large number of possible combinations. This means there is a limit to how large a rainbow table can be, and this is why longer passwords are more secure than shorter passwords.

Since the development of rainbow tables, there have been methods designed to thwart such attacks. The most common is salt. Random bits are added to further secure encryption or hashing. Most often encountered with hashing to prevent rainbow table attacks.

Essentially, the salt is intermixed with the message that is to be hashed. Consider this example. You have a password that is

pass001

In binary that is

01110000 01100001 01110011 01110011 00110000 00110000 00110001

A salt algorithm would insert bits periodically. Let's assume for our example that we insert bits every fourth bit, giving us

0111100001 0110100011 0111100111 0111100111 0011100001 0011100001 0011100011

If you convert that to text, you would get

xZ7◆◆#

All this is transparent to the end user. The end user doesn't even know that salting is happening or what it is. However, an attacker using a rainbow table to get passwords would get the wrong password.

# Steganography

*Steganography* is the art and science of writing hidden messages in such a way that no one, apart from the sender and intended recipient, suspects the existence of the message. It is a form of security through obscurity. Often the message is hidden in some other file such as a digital picture or audio file to defy detection.

The advantage of steganography over cryptography alone is that messages do not attract attention to themselves. If someone is aware the message is even there, she won't try to decipher it. In many cases messages are encrypted and hidden via steganography.

The most common implementation of steganography utilizes the least significant bits in a file in order to store data. By altering the least significant bit, you can hide additional data without altering the original file in any noticeable way.

There are some basic steganography terms you should know:

- *Payload* is the data to be covertly communicated. In other words, it is the message you wish to hide.
- The *carrier* is the signal, stream, or data file into which the payload is hidden.
- The *channel* is the type of medium used. This may be still photos, video, or sound files.

The most common way steganography is accomplished today is via least significant bits. In every file there are a certain number of bits per unit of the file. For example, an image file in Windows is 24 bits per pixel. If you change the least significant of those bits, then the change is not noticeable with the naked eye. And you can hide information in the least significant bits of an image file. With least significant bit (lsb) replacement, certain bits in the carrier file are replaced.

## Historical Steganography

In modern times, steganography means digital manipulation of files to hide messages. However, the concept of hiding messages is not new. There have been many methods used throughout history.

- The ancient Chinese wrapped notes in wax and swallowed them for transport. This was a crude but effective method of hiding messages.

- In ancient Greece, a messenger's head might be shaved, a message written on his head, and then his hair was allowed to grow back. Obviously, this method required some time to be available.

- In 1518 Johannes Trithmeus wrote a book on cryptography and described a technique where a message was hidden by having each letter taken as a word from a specific column.

- During WW II the French Resistance sent messages written on the backs of couriers using invisible ink.

- Microdots are images/undeveloped film the size of a typewriter period, embedded in innocuous documents. These were said to be used by spies during the Cold War.

- Also during the Cold War, the U.S. Central Intelligence Agency used various devices to hide messages. For example, they developed a tobacco pipe that had a small space to hide microfilm but could still be smoked.

In more recent times, but before the advent of computers, other methods were used to hide messages.

## Methods and Tools

There are a number of tools available for implementing steganography. Many are free or at least have a free trial version. A few of these tools are listed here:

- **QuickStego:** Easy to use but very limited

- **Invisible Secrets:** Much more robust with both a free and a commercial version

- **MP3Stego:** Specifically for hiding payload in MP3 files

- **Stealth Files 4:** Works with sound files, video files, and image files

- **Snow:** Hides data in whitespace

- **StegVideo:** Hides data in a video sequence

- **Invisible Secrets:** A very versatile steganography tool that has several options.

# Cryptanalysis

Cryptanalysis is a daunting task. It is essentially the search for some means to break through some encryption. And, unlike what you see in the movies, it is a very time-consuming task that frequently leads to only partial success. Cryptanalysis involves using any method to decrypt the message that is more efficient than simple brute force attempts. Remember that brute force is simply trying every possible key.

A cryptanalysis success is not necessarily breaking the target cipher. In fact, finding any information about the target cipher or key is considered a success. There are several types of cryptographic success:

- **Total break:** The attacker deduces the secret key.

- **Global deduction:** The attacker discovers a functionally equivalent algorithm for encryption and decryption but without learning the key.

- **Instance (local) deduction:** The attacker discovers additional plaintexts (or ciphertexts) not previously known.

- **Information deduction:** The attacker gains some Shannon information about plaintexts (or ciphertexts) not previously known.

- **Distinguishing algorithm:** The attacker can distinguish the cipher from a random permutation.

Entire books have been written on cryptanalysis. The purpose of this section is just to give you some basic concepts from the field so that you have a general understanding at a basic level. There are certainly other methods not discussed in this section.

## Frequency Analysis

This is the basic tool for breaking most classical ciphers. It is not useful against modern symmetric or asymmetric cryptography. It is based on the fact that some letters and letter combinations are more common than others. In all languages, certain letters of the alphabet appear more frequently than others. By examining those frequencies, you can derive some information about the key that was used. Remember in English that the words *the* and *and* are the two most common three-letter words. The most common single-letter words are *I* and *a*. If you see two of the same letters together in a word, it is most likely *ee* or *oo*.

## Modern Methods

Cracking modern cryptographic methods is quite daunting. The level of success depends on a combination of resources. Those resources are computational power, time, and data. If you had an infinite amount of any of these, you could crack any modern cipher. But you won't have an infinite amount.

### Known Plaintext Attack

This method is based on having a sample of known plain texts and their resulting cipher texts and then using this information to try to ascertain something about the key used. It is easier to obtain known plain text samples than you might think. Consider email. Many people, myself included, use a standard signature block. If you have ever received an email from me, you know what my signature block is.

Then if you intercept encrypted emails I send, you can compare the known signature block to the end of the encrypted email. You would then have a known plain text and the matching cipher text to work with. This requires many thousands of known plaintext samples to be successful.

### Chosen Plaintext Attack

This is closely related to the known plain text attack, the difference being that the attacker has found a method to get the target to encrypt messages the attacker chooses. This can allow the attacker to attempt to derive the key used and thus decrypt other messages encrypted with that key. The method can be difficult but is not impossible. It requires many thousands of chosen plaintext samples to be successful.

### Ciphertext-Only

The attacker only has access to a collection of cipher texts. This is much more likely than known plaintext, but also the most difficult. The attack is completely successful if the corresponding plaintexts can be deduced, or even better, if the key can. The ability to obtain any information at all about the underlying plaintext is still considered a success.

### Related-Key Attack

This is like a chosen-plaintext attack, except the attacker can obtain ciphertexts encrypted under two different keys. This is actually a very useful attack if you can obtain the plain text and matching cipher text.

These are the basic approaches used to attack block ciphers. There are other methods that are beyond the scope of this book, such as differential cryptanalysis and linear cryptanalysis. For the purposes of understanding basic computer security, it is not necessary that you master these techniques.

# Cryptography Used on the Internet

What sort of encryption is used on bank websites and e-commerce? In general, symmetric algorithms are faster and require a shorter key length to be as secure as asymmetric algorithms. However, there is the problem of how to securely exchange keys. So most e-commerce solutions use an asymmetric algorithm to exchange symmetric keys and then use the symmetric keys to encrypt the actual data.

When visiting websites that have an HTTPS at the beginning rather than HTTP, the *S* denotes *secure*. That means traffic between your browser and the web server is encrypted. This is usually done with either SSL (Secure Sockets Layer) or TLS (Transport Layer Security). SSL, the older of the two technologies, was developed by Netscape. Both SSL and TLS are asymmetric systems.

# Summary

A basic element of computer security is encryption. Sending sensitive data that is not encrypted is simply foolish. This chapter provided the basic information on how cryptography works. The most important thing to remember is that, ultimately, it is not your computer or your network that will be compromised but rather your data. Encrypting the data when transmitting it is an integral part of any security plan.

In the exercises at the end of this chapter, you will practice using different cipher methods and learn more about a number of encryption methods.

## Test Your Skills

## MULTIPLE CHOICE QUESTIONS

1. Which of the following most accurately defines encryption?

   A. Changing a message so it can only be easily read by the intended recipient

   B. Using complex mathematics to conceal a message

   C. Changing a message using complex mathematics

   D. Applying keys to a message to conceal it

2. Which of the following is the oldest encryption method discussed in this text?

   A. PGP

   B. Multi-alphabet encryption

   C. Caesar cipher

   D. Cryptic cipher

3. What is the main problem with simple substitution?

   A. It does not use complex mathematics.

   B. It is easily broken with modern computers.

   C. It is too simple.

   D. It maintains letter and word frequency.

4. Which of the following is an encryption method using two or more different shifts?

   A. Caesar cipher

   B. Multi-alphabet encryption

   C. DES

   D. PGP

5. Which binary mathematical operation can be used for a simple encryption method?

   A. Bit shift

   B. OR

   C. XOR

   D. Bit swap

6. Why is binary mathematical encryption not secure?

   A. It does not change letter or word frequency.

   B. It leaves the message intact.

   C. It is too simple.

   D. The mathematics of it is flawed.

7. Which of the following is most true regarding binary operations and encryption?

   A. They are completely useless.

   B. They can form a part of viable encryption methods.

   C. They are only useful as a teaching method.

   D. They can provide secure encryption.

8. What is PGP?

   A. Pretty Good Privacy, a public key encryption method

   B. Pretty Good Protection, a public key encryption method

   C. Pretty Good Privacy, a symmetric key encryption method

   D. Pretty Good Protection, a symmetric key encryption method

9. Which of the following methods is available as an add-in for most email clients?

   A. DES

   B. RSA

   C. Caesar cipher

   D. PGP

10. Which of the following is a symmetric key system using 64-bit blocks?

    A. RSA

    B. DES

    C. PGP

    D. Blowfish

**11.** What advantage does a symmetric key system using 64-bit blocks have?

    **A.** It is fast.

    **B.** It is unbreakable.

    **C.** It uses asymmetric keys.

    **D.** It is complex.

**12.** What size key does a DES system use?

    **A.** 64 bit

    **B.** 128 bit

    **C.** 56 bit

    **D.** 256 bit

**13.** What type of encryption uses different keys to encrypt and decrypt the message?

    **A.** Private key

    **B.** Public key

    **C.** Symmetric

    **D.** Secure

**14.** Which of the following methods uses a variable-length symmetric key?

    **A.** Blowfish

    **B.** Caesar

    **C.** DES

    **D.** RSA

**15.** What should you be most careful of when looking for an encryption method to use?

    **A.** Complexity of the algorithm

    **B.** Veracity of the vendor's claims

    **C.** Speed of the algorithm

    **D.** How long the algorithm has been around

**16.** Which of the following is most likely to be true of an encryption method that is advertised as unbreakable?

    **A.** It is probably suitable for military use.

    **B.** It may be too expensive for your organization.

    **C.** It is likely to be exaggerated.

    **D.** It is probably one you want to use.

17. Which of the following is most true regarding certified encryption methods?

    A. These are the only methods you should use.

    B. It depends on the level of certification.

    C. It depends on the source of the certification.

    D. There is no such thing as certified encryption.

18. Which of the following is most true regarding new encryption methods?

    A. Never use them until they have been proven.

    B. You can use them, but you must be cautious.

    C. Only use them if they are certified.

    D. Only use them if they are rated unbreakable.

## EXERCISES

### EXERCISE 8.1: Using the Caesar Cipher

This exercise is well suited for group or classroom exercises.

1. Write a sentence in normal text.

2. Use a Caesar cipher of your own design to encrypt it.

3. Pass it to another person in your group or class.

4. Time how long it takes that person to break the encryption.

5. (Optional) Compute the mean time for the class to break Caesar ciphers.

### EXERCISE 8.2: Using Multi-Alphabet Ciphers

This exercise also works well for group settings and is best used in conjunction with the preceding exercise.

1. Write a sentence in normal text.

2. Use a multi-alphabet cipher of your own design to encrypt it.

3. Pass it to another person in your group or class.

4. Time how long it takes that person to break the encryption.

5. (Optional) Compute the mean time for the class to break these and compare that to the mean time required to break the Caesar ciphers.

## EXERCISE 8.3: Using PGP

1. Download a PGP attachment for your favorite email client. Doing a web search for PGP and your email client (that is, PGP and Outlook or PGP and Eudora) should locate both modules and instructions.

2. Install and configure the PGP module.

3. Send encrypted messages to and from a classmate.

## EXERCISE 8.4: Finding Good Encryption Solutions

1. Scan the Web for various commercial encryption algorithms.

2. Find one that you feel may be "snake oil."

3. Write a brief paper explaining your opinion.

# PROJECTS

## PROJECT 8.1: RSA Encryption

Using the Web or other resources, write a brief paper about RSA, its history, its methodology, and where it is used. Students with a sufficient math background may choose to delve more deeply into the RSA algorithm's mathematical basis.

## PROJECT 8.2: Programming Caesar Cipher

This project is for those students with some programming background.

Write a simple program in any language you prefer (or your instructor dictates) that can perform a Caesar cipher. In this chapter, you not only saw how this cipher works, but were also given some ideas on how to use ASCII codes to make this work in any standard programming language.

## PROJECT 8.3: Other Encryption Methods

Write a brief essay describing any encryption method not already mentioned in this chapter. In this paper, describe the history and origin of that algorithm. You should also provide some comparisons with other well-known algorithms.

### Case Study

Jane Doe is responsible for selecting an encryption method that is suitable for her company, which sells insurance. The data the company sends is sensitive but is not military or classified in nature. Jane is looking at a variety of methods. She ultimately selects a commercial implementation of RSA. Was this the best choice? Why or why not?

## Chapter 9

# Computer Security Technology

## *Chapter Objectives*

**After reading this chapter and completing the exercises, you will be able to do the following:**

- Evaluate the effectiveness of a scanner based on how it works
- Choose the best type of firewall for a given organization
- Understand antispyware methods
- Employ intrusion detection systems to detect problems on your system
- Understand honey pots

## Introduction

Throughout this book, various aspects of computer security have been discussed. At this point in your studies, you should have a good idea of what the real dangers are and what adequate security measures include, as well as a basic understanding of the various forms of computer attacks. However, if you are striving to secure your network, you will need more technical details on the various security devices and software you might choose to employ. This chapter reviews these items with enough detail to allow you to make intelligent decisions on which types of products you will see.

Most of these devices have been mentioned and briefly described in the preceding chapters. The intent of this chapter is to delve more deeply into details of how these devices work. This information is of particular value to those readers who intend to eventually enter the computer security profession. Simply having a theoretical knowledge of computer security is inadequate. You must have some practical skills. This chapter will be a good starting point for gaining those skills, and the exercises at the end of the chapter will give you a chance to practice setting up and evaluating various types of firewalls, intrusion detection systems (IDSs), and antivirus applications.

# Virus Scanners

A *virus scanner* is essentially software that tries to prevent a virus from infecting your system. This fact is probably abundantly obvious to most readers. Knowing how a virus scanner works, however, is another matter. This topic was discussed briefly in our previous discussions on viruses but will be elaborated on in this chapter.

In general, virus scanners work in two ways. The first method is that they contain a list of all known virus definitions. The virus definitions are simply files that list known viruses, their file size, properties, and behavior. Generally, one of the services that vendors of virus scanners provide is a periodic update of this file. This list is typically in a small file, often called a *.dat* file (short for data). When you update your virus definitions, what actually occurs is that your current file is replaced by the more recent one on the vendor's website.

The antivirus program can then scan your PC, network, and incoming email for known virus files. Any file on your PC or attached to an email is compared to the virus definition file to see whether there are matches. With emails, this can be done by looking for specific subject lines and content. The virus definitions often also include details on the file, file size, and more. This provides a complete signature of the virus.

The second way a virus scanner can work is to look for virus-like behavior. Essentially, the scanner is looking to see if the file in question is doing things that viruses typically do—things like manipulating the Registry or looking through your address book. Obviously, this second technique is essentially a best guess.

## How Does a Virus Scanner Work?

Let's take a more detailed look at how antivirus software works. An article in the July 2004 issue of *Scientific American* titled "How Does a Virus Scanner Work," stated that a virus scanner is essentially software that searches for the signature or pattern of known virus. Keep in mind that the scanner only works if you keep it updated. And, of course, it only works with known viruses. While that article may seem a bit dated now, it is still accurate.

Recall that the second way a virus scanner works is to watch for certain types of behaviors that are typical of a virus. This might include any program that attempts to write to your hard drive's boot sector, change system files, automate your email software, or self-multiply. Programs that attempt to modify the system Registry (for Windows systems) or alter any system settings may also be indicative of a virus.

Another feature that virus scanners search for is a file that will stay in memory after it executes. This is called a *Terminate and Stay Resident (TSR)* program. Some legitimate programs do this, but it is often a sign of a virus. Additionally, some virus scanners use more sophisticated methods, such as scanning your system files and monitoring any program that attempts to modify those files.

Whatever the behavior, antivirus software uses specific algorithms to evaluate the likelihood that a given file is actually a virus. It should be noted that modern virus scanners scan for all forms of malware, including Trojan horses, spyware, and viruses.

There is a third method, called heuristic scanning. This is basically examining the file itself and is similar to signature scanning. However, in this case the file need not exactly match the signature. Heuristics refers to functions that rank various alternatives using a branching step in the algorithm. So the Heuristic scan checks to see the likelihood of a given file being a virus. This is based on file characteristics rather than behavior.

It is important to differentiate between on-demand virus scanning and ongoing scanners. An *ongoing virus scanner* runs in the background and is constantly checking your PC for any sign of a virus. *On-demand virus scanners* run only when you launch them. Many modern antivirus scanners offer both options.

Keep in mind that any antivirus program will have some false positives and some false negatives. A false positive occurs when the virus scanner detects a given file as a virus, when in fact it is not. For example, a legitimate program may edit a Registry key or interact with your email address book. A false negative occurs when a virus is falsely believed to be a legitimate program.

Due to false positives, it is recommended that you do not set your antivirus to automatically delete suspected viruses. Rather, they should be quarantined and the computer user notified.

## Virus-Scanning Techniques

In general, there are five ways a virus scanner might scan for virus infections. Some of these were mentioned in the previous section, but they are outlined and defined here:

- **Email and attachment scanning:** Since the primary propagation method for a virus is email, email and attachment scanning is the most important function of any virus scanner. Some virus scanners actually examine your email on the email server before downloading it to your machine. Other virus scanners work by scanning your emails and attachments on your computer before passing it to your email program. In either case, the email and its attachments should be scanned prior to your having any chance to open them and release the virus on your system.

- **Download scanning:** Anytime you download anything from the Internet, either via a web link or through some FTP program, there is a chance you might download an infected file. Download scanning works much like email and attachment scanning but does so on files you select for downloading.

- **File scanning:** This is the type of scanning in which files on your system are checked to see whether they match any known virus. This sort of scanning is generally done on an on-demand basis instead of an ongoing basis. It is a good idea to schedule your virus scanner to do a complete scan of the system periodically. I recommend a weekly scan, preferably at a time when no one is likely to be using the computer.

- **Heuristic scanning:** This was briefly mentioned in the previous section. Perhaps the most advanced form of virus scanning, this uses rules to determine whether a file or program is behaving like a virus and is one of the best ways to find a virus that is not a known virus. A new virus will not be on a virus definition list, so you must examine its behavior to determine whether it is a virus. However, this process is not foolproof. Some actual virus infections will be missed, and some nonvirus files might be suspected of being a virus.

- **Sandbox:** Another approach is the sandbox approach. This basically means that you have a separate area, isolated from the operating system, in which a download or attachment is run. Then if it is infected, it won't infect the operating system.

One way to accomplish sandboxing is for the operating system to set aside a protected area of memory to open the suspected file and to monitor its behavior. This is not 100% effective, but it is far safer than simply opening files on your system and hoping there is no infection.

A related concept is called a "sheep dip" machine. This is useful in corporate networks. You set up a system that is identical in configuration to your standard workstations. However, this sheep dip machine is not networked. Suspect files are opened first on this system. Then the system is monitored for a period of time for signs of infection. Once the file has cleared this check, it can then be opened on normal workstations.

A simple way to do this in a home or small office is to set up a virtual machine on your computer and to open suspected attachments or downloads in the virtual machine first. This virtual machine can have virus scanners running on it. Also, you can change the time in the virtual machine in order to detect logic bombs. Allow the suspect file to reside on the VM for a period of time before bringing it to the host computer.

## FYI: How Most Commercial Scanners Work

Most commercial virus scanners use multiple methods, including most, if not all, of the methods listed here. Any virus scanner that uses only one scanning modality would be virtually worthless from a practical virus defense perspective. These modalities are how a scanner works regardless of whether it is using a heuristic scan, download scan, email scan, and so on.

- **Active code scanning:** Modern websites frequently embed active codes, such as Java applets and ActiveX. These technologies can provide some stunning visual effects to any website. However, they can also be a vehicle for malicious code. Scanning such objects before they are downloaded to your computer is an essential feature in any quality virus scanner.

- **False positives and false negatives:** Regardless of the type of virus scanner, any antivirus software will occasionally have an error. There are two types of errors that you should be concerned with. It is possible that your antivirus software will mistake a legitimate program for a virus. For example, you might have a program that is supposed to make some adjustment to the Windows Registry or to scan your email address book. Mistaking a legitimate program for a virus is referred to as a *false positive*. It is also possible that your antivirus will fail to recognize a virus. This is referred to as a *false negative*. The best way to minimize false negatives is to keep your antivirus software updated. For false positives, it is recommended that you simply quarantine suspected viruses and not automatically delete them.

## Commercial Antivirus Software

There are four brands of antivirus software that virtually dominate the antivirus market today and a number of companies that offer a commercial scanner also offer a free version that does not provide as many features as the commercial product. For example, AVG AntiVirus, available from www.grisoft.com, is a commercial product, but the company also offers the AVG AntiVirus Free Edition. McAfee, Norton, and Kapersky are three very well-known antivirus vendors. All three products are good choices and come with additional options, such as spam filters and personal firewalls. Any of these three products can be purchased for a home machine for about $30 to $60 (depending on options you add). This purchase price includes a one-year subscription to update the virus files so that your antivirus software will recognize all known virus attacks. Organizational licenses are also available to cover an entire network.

Malwarebytes is another popular product that has both free and commercial versions. Of course, there are other antivirus solutions available. Several free virus scanners can easily be found on the Internet. McAfee, Norton, AVG, Malwarebytes, and Kapersky are mentioned here because they are so commonly used, and it is likely that you will encounter them frequently. But that is not to indicate that I am discouraging you from using other systems. I do strongly recommend that you stick with widely used, well-supported antivirus products.

# Firewalls

A *firewall* is, in essence, a barrier between two computers or computer systems. The most common place to encounter a firewall is between your network and the outside world. However, firewalls on individual computers and between network segments are also quite common. At a minimum, a firewall will filter incoming packets based on certain parameters such as packet size, source IP address, protocol, and destination port. Linux and Windows (beginning with Windows XP and in all subsequent Windows versions) ship with a simple firewall. For Windows, the firewall in Windows 7 was expanded to handle filtering both inbound and outbound traffic. Windows 8 and Windows 10 have not significantly changed the firewall functionality in Windows. You should turn on and configure your individual computer firewalls in addition to perimeter firewalls.

In an organizational setting, you will want, at a minimum, a dedicated firewall between your network and the outside world. This might be a router that also has built-in firewall capabilities. (Cisco Systems is one company that is well known for high-quality routers and firewalls.) Or, it might be a server that is dedicated solely to running firewall software. Selecting a firewall, however, is an important decision. If you lack the expertise to make that decision, then you should arrange for a consultant to assist you in this respect.

## Benefits and Limitation of Firewalls

A firewall, no matter what type you get (types are described in the next section), is basically a tool to block certain traffic. A set of rules determine what traffic to allow in and what traffic to block. Obviously, a firewall is a critical piece of your security strategy. I cannot even conceive of a reason to run a system without one. However, it is not a panacea for security because it cannot block every attack. For example, a firewall won't stop you from downloading a Trojan horse. It also cannot stop internal attacks. But a firewall can be an excellent way to stop a denial of service (DoS) attack or to prevent a hacker from scanning the internal details of your network.

## Firewall Types and Components

There are numerous types of firewalls and variations on those types. But most firewalls can be grouped into one of the following three families of firewalls.

- Packet inspection

- Stateful packet inspection

- Application

The following sections will discuss each of these and assess the advantages and disadvantages of each.

### Packet Filtering

Basic packet filtering is the simplest form of firewall. It looks at packets and checks to see if each packet meets the firewall rules. For example, it is common for a packet filtering firewall to ask three questions:

1. Is this packet using a protocol that the firewall allows?

2. Is this packet destined for a port that the firewall allows?

3. Is the packet coming from an IP address that the firewall has not blocked?

Those are three very basic rules. Some packet filter firewalls have additional rules to check. But what is not checked is the preceding packets from that same source. Essentially, each packet is treated as a singular event without reference to the preceding conversation. That makes packet filtering firewalls quite susceptible to some DoS attacks, such as SYN floods.

### Stateful Packet Inspection

The Malwarebytes firewall will examine each packet, denying or permitting access based not only on the examination of the current packet, but also on data derived from previous packets in the conversation. This means that the firewall is aware of the context in which a specific packet was sent. This makes these firewalls far less susceptible to ping floods and SYN floods, as well as less susceptible to spoofing. For example, if the firewall detects that the current packet is an ICMP packet and a stream of several thousand packets have been continuously coming from the same source IP, it is clearly a DoS attack and the packets will be blocked.

The SPI firewall can also look at the actual contents of the packet, which allows for some very advanced filtering capabilities. Most high-end firewalls use the stateful packet inspection method; when possible, this is the recommended type of firewall.

### Application Gateway

An *application gateway* (also known as *application proxy* or *application-level proxy*) is a program that runs on a firewall. When a client program, such as a web browser, establishes a connection to a destination service, such as a web server, it connects to an application gateway, or proxy. The client then negotiates with the proxy server in order to gain access to the destination service. In effect, the proxy establishes the connection with the destination behind the firewall and acts on behalf of the client, hiding and protecting individual computers on the network behind the firewall. This process actually creates two connections. There is one connection between the client and the proxy server and another connection between the proxy server and the destination.

Once a connection is established, the application gateway makes all decisions about which packets to forward. Since all communication is conducted through the proxy server, computers behind the firewall are protected.

Essentially, an application firewall is one that is used for specific types of applications such as database or web server. It is able to examine the protocol being used (such as HTTP) for any anomalous behavior and block traffic that might get past other types of firewalls. It is common to have an application firewall that also includes stateful packet inspection.

## Firewall Configurations

In addition to the various types of firewalls, there are various configuration options. The type of firewall tells you how it will evaluate traffic and hence decide what to allow and not to allow. The configuration gives you an idea of how that firewall is set up in relation to the network it is protecting. Some of the major configurations/implementations for firewalls include the following:

- Network host–based
- Dual-homed host
- Router-based firewall
- Screened host

Each of these is discussed in the following sections.

### Network Host–Based

A *network host–based firewall* is a software solution installed on an existing machine with an existing operating system. The most significant concern in using this type of firewall is that no matter how good the firewall solution is, it is contingent upon the underlying operating system. In such a situation, it is absolutely critical that the machine hosting the firewall have a hardened operating system.

### Dual-Homed Host

A *dual-homed host* is a firewall running on a server with at least two network interfaces. The server acts as a router between the network and the interfaces to which it is attached. To make this work, the automatic routing function is disabled, meaning that an IP packet from the Internet is not routed directly to the network. You can choose what packets to route and how to route them. Systems inside and outside the firewall can communicate with the dual-homed host but cannot communicate directly with each other.

### Router-Based Firewall

As was previously mentioned, you can implement firewall protection on a router. In larger networks with multiple layers of protection, this is commonly the first layer of protection. Although you can implement various types of firewalls on a router, the most common type used is packet filtering. If you use a broadband connection in your home or small office, you can get a packet-filtering firewall router to replace the basic router provided to you by the broadband company. In recent years, router-based firewalls have become increasingly common and are in fact the most common firewall used today.

### Screened Host

A *screened host* is really a combination of firewalls. In this configuration, you use a combination of a bastion host and a screening router. The screening router adds security by allowing you to deny or permit certain traffic from the bastion host. It is the first stop for traffic, which can continue only if the screening router lets it through.

## Commercial and Free Firewall Products

There is a variety of commercial firewall products from which you can choose. If all you want is a basic packet-filtering solution, many software vendors offer this. Major antivirus software vendors (including those mentioned previously in this chapter) often offer the firewall software as a bundled option with their antivirus software. Other companies, such as Zone Labs, sell firewall and intrusion detection software (IDS). Zone Labs, for example, offers the ZoneAlarm Security Suite, which provides all the tools for complete Internet security. Major manufacturers of routers and hubs, such as Cisco Systems, also offer firewall products. How much security you need is a difficult question to answer. A bare minimum recommendation is to have a packet-filtering firewall/proxy server between your network and the Internet—but that is a bare minimum. There are also many free firewall applications available. Zone Labs, mentioned earlier for their commercial product, also offers a free download of the ZoneAlarm firewall protection.

Outpost Firewall, available from www.agnitum.com/products/outpost/, is a product designed for the home or small office user. Like the Zone Labs product, it has both a free version and an enhanced commercial version. Information on this product is shown in Figure 9.1. Note that the free version is an older version of the software and does not include many of the enhancements of the commercial version. But it may be sufficient for your needs.

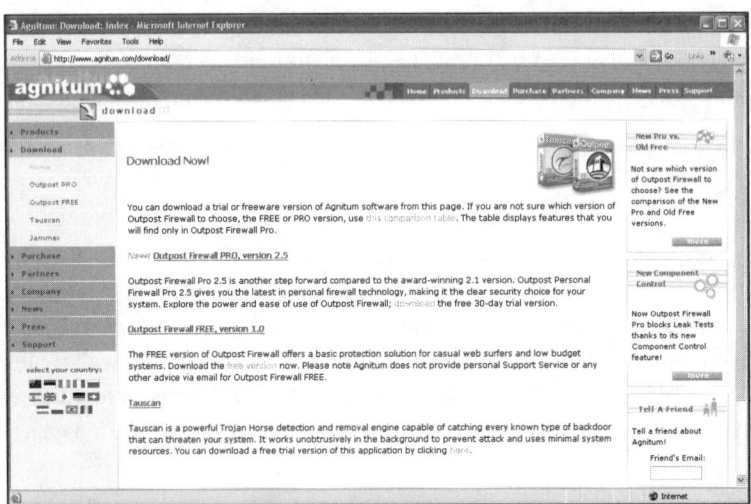

**FIGURE 9.1**    Firewall protection from Agnitum.

Listed and shown next are other sources for information on free firewall protection. Each of these websites offers links to a number of sources for free firewall protection as well as to other useful security tools. You may want to explore these sites as well as add them to your list of resource sites:

- http://www.zonealarm.com/software/free-firewall/
- https://www.comodo.com/home/internet-security/firewall.php

## Firewall Logs

Firewalls are also excellent tools when attempting to ascertain what has happened after an incident occurs. Almost all firewalls, regardless of type or implementation, will log activity. These logs can provide valuable information that can assist in determining the source of an attack, methods used to attack, and other data that might help either locate the perpetrator of an attack or at least prevent a future attack using the same techniques. Any security-conscious network administrator should make it a routine habit to check the firewall logs.

# Antispyware

Antispyware, as discussed earlier in this book, scans your computer to see whether there is spyware running on your machine. This is an important element of computer security software that was at one time largely ignored. Even today, not enough people take spyware seriously or guard against it. Most antispyware works by checking your system for known spyware files. Each application must simply be checked against a list of known spyware. This means that you must maintain some sort of subscription service so that you can obtain routine updates to your spyware definition list. Most antivirus solutions now also check for spyware.

In today's Internet climate, running antispyware is as essential as running antivirus software. Failing to do so can lead to serious consequences. Personal data, and perhaps sensitive business data, could easily be leaking out of your organization without your knowledge. And, as was pointed out earlier in this book, it is entirely possible for spyware to be the vehicle for purposeful industrial espionage.

Barring the use of antispyware, or even in conjunction with such software, you can protect yourself via your browser's security settings as was discussed in a previous chapter. Additionally, several times throughout this book, you have been warned to be cautious about attachments and Internet downloads. You would also be well advised to avoid downloading various Internet "enhancements," such as "skins" and "toolbars." If you are in an organization, prohibiting such downloads should be a matter of company policy. Unfortunately, many websites today require some sort of add-in such as Flash in order to function properly. The best advice for this situation is to only allow add-ins on trusted, well-known sites.

# IDS

IDS has become much more widely used in the last few years. Essentially, an IDS will inspect all inbound and outbound port activity on your machine/firewall/system and look for patterns that might indicate an attempted break-in. For example, if the IDS finds that a series of ICMP packets were sent to each port in sequence, this probably indicates that your system is being scanned by network-scanning software, such as Cerberus. Since this is often a prelude to an attempt to breach your system security, it can be very important to know that someone is performing preparatory steps to infiltrate your system.

Entire volumes have been written on how IDS systems work. This chapter cannot hope to cover that much information. However, it is important that you have a basic idea of how these systems work.

The sections that follow will first examine the broad categories in which IDS systems tend to be viewed and then will also look at some specific approaches to IDS. While this information is not all inclusive, it does address the more common terminology used.

## IDS Categorization

There are a number of ways in which IDS systems can be categorized. The most common IDS categorizations are as follows:

- Passive IDS

- Active IDS (also called Intrusion Prevention System, or IPS)

### Passive IDS

A passive IDS just monitors suspicious activity and then logs it. In some cases it may notify the administrator of the activity in question. This is the most basic type of IDS. Any modern system should have, at a minimum, a passive IDS along with the firewall, antivirus, and other security measures taken.

### Active IDS

An active IDS or IPS takes the added step of shutting down the suspect communication. Just like antivirus, it is possible for an IDS to have a false positive. It might suspect something is an attack when in fact it is legitimate traffic. Whether one uses an IDS or IPS is a decision that must be made after a thorough risk analysis.

Imagine an IDS that is looking at threshold monitoring to determine if an attack is occurring. A particular user normally works between the hours of 8 a.m. and 5 p.m. and uses a relatively small amount of bandwidth. The IDS detects the user at 10 p.m. using 10 times his normal bandwidth. This seems like it might be an attack, and the active IDS (IPS) shuts down the offending traffic. However, it is later found that this was a legitimate user working late on a critical project that was due to a client the next day, and your IPS prevented that from happening.

This is an excellent place to consider risk analysis. You have to weigh the hazards of false positives against the risk of allowing an attack to proceed undetected before deciding if a passive IDS or an IPS is appropriate for your organization. It is often the case that different network segments will have different risk profiles. You may find that a passive IDS is appropriate for most of your network but that an IPS is needed for the most sensitive network segments.

## Identifying an Intrusion

There are really two ways of identifying an intrusion. The first method is signature based. This is similar to the signatures used by antivirus. However, IDS signatures cover issues beyond malware. For example, certain DoS attacks have specific signatures that can be recognized.

The second method is statistical anomaly. Essentially, any activity that seems outside normal parameters and far enough said parameters to be a likely attack is identified as a probable attack. Any number of activities can trigger this type of alert. An example can be a sudden increase in bandwidth utilization or user accounts accessing resources they have never accessed before.

Most IDSs will use both forms of attack recognition. The two real issues for selecting an IDS are its ease of use and its signature database. There are certainly other considerations such as price, but those two are the most central to deciding on an IDS.

## IDS Elements

Whether it is an active IDS or a passive IDS, and regardless of whether it is commercial or open source, certain elements/terms are common to all IDSs.

- A *sensor* is the IDS component that collects data and passes it to the analyzer for analysis.
- The *analyzer* is the component or process that analyzes the data collected by the sensor.
- The *manager* is the IDS interface used for management. It is a software component to the IDS.
- The *operator* is the person primarily responsible for the IDS.

- *Notification* is the process or method by which the IDS manager makes the operator aware of an alert.

- An *activity* is an element of a data source that is of interest to the operator. It may or may not be a possible attack.

- An *event* is any activity that is deemed to be suspicious and a possible attack.

- An *alert* is a message from the analyzer indicating that an event has occurred.

- The *data source* is the raw information that the IDS is analyzing to determine if there has been an event.

All these elements are part of an IDS and function together to capture traffic, analyze that traffic, and report anomalous activity to the operator of the IDS. An IPS will have additional elements capable of shutting down offending traffic.

## Snort

There are a number of vendors who supply IDS systems, each with its own strengths and weaknesses. Which system is best for your environment is contingent on many factors including the network environment, security level required, budget constraints, and skill level of the person who will be working directly with the IDS. One popular open-source IDS is Snort, which can be downloaded for free from www.snort.org/.

We will examine Snort briefly in this section. While it is not the only IDS available, it is free, and that makes it an attractive option for many people. We will walk through the basic configuration of Snort for Windows.

First you must visit www.snort.org and register. It is free. Then download the Snort installation program and the latest rules. Make certain you download the installer that has an .exe extension. The .rpm extensions are for Linux. Also, I have found that certain versions of Microsoft Internet Explorer do not work well with the Snort website, so it is recommended that you use an alternative browser such as Mozilla Firefox.

Once you have downloaded both the rules and the installation, start the installation. Most of it is quite simple. There is a screen that asks you if you wish to support database connectivity. For most live situations, you would want to dump your Snort records to some database. However, for demonstration purposes, choose "I do not plan to log to a database," as shown in Figure 9.2.

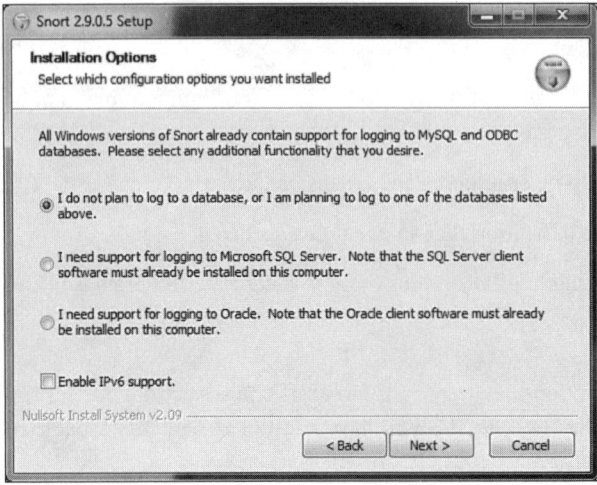

FIGURE 9.2 Snort database selection.

Other than this, simply use all default settings. At the end of the install, it will also attempt to install WinPCAP. If for some reason this fails, you will need to download and install it separately. WinPCAP is an open source tool for capturing packets. All IDSs depend on packet capturing.

Now copy rules you downloaded from wherever you saved them to C:\snort\rules. Then copy the configuration file from C:\snort\rules\etc\snort.conf to C:\snort\etc. Open that configuration file using WordPad, not Notepad. Notepad does not support word wrap, and it will be difficult to read the configuration file in Notepad.

The first step is to change the HOME_NET *any* to your machine's IP address, as shown in Figure 9.3. In a live situation, we would also set the other IP addresses (web server, SQL server, DNS server, and so on).

```
####################################################
# Step #1: Set the network variables.  For more information, see
README.variables
####################################################

# Setup the network addresses you are protecting
var HOME_NET any

# Set up the external network addresses.  A good start may be
"any"
var EXTERNAL_NET any

# List of DNS servers on your network
var DNS_SERVERS $HOME_NET

# List of SMTP servers on your network
var SMTP_SERVERS $HOME_NET

# List of web servers on your network
var HTTP_SERVERS $HOME_NET

# List of sql servers on your network
var SQL_SERVERS $HOME_NET
```

FIGURE 9.3 HOME_NET address.

Now you need to find and change the rules paths. They will have Linux-style paths, as shown in Figure 9.4.

```
# Path to your rules files (this can be a relative path)
# Note for Windows users:  You are advised to make this an
absolute path,
# such as:  c:\snort\rules
var RULE_PATH ../rules
var SO_RULE_PATH ../so_rules
var PREPROC_RULE_PATH ../preproc_rules
```

**FIGURE 9.4**   Linux-style paths.

You will need to change them to Windows-style paths, as shown in Figure 9.5.

```
var RULE_PATH c:\snort\rules
var SO_RULE_PATH c:\snort\rules\so_rules
var PREPROC_RULE_PATH c:\snort\rules\preproc_rules
```

**FIGURE 9.5**   Windows-style paths.

You will now need to find and change the library paths. This is a bit harder because the names of the paths and the files are a bit different in Windows. The Linux style library paths will appear as the ones shown in Figure 9.6.

```
# path to dynamic preprocessor libraries
dynamicpreprocessor directory
/usr/local/lib/snort_dynamicpreprocessor/

# path to base preprocessor engine
dynamicengine /usr/local/lib/snort_dynamicengine/libsf_engine.so

# path to dynamic rules libraries
# dynamicdetection directory /usr/local/lib/snort_dynamicrules
```

**FIGURE 9.6**   Linux-style library paths.

You can find your Windows pathnames and filenames by looking in the folder shown in Figure 9.7.

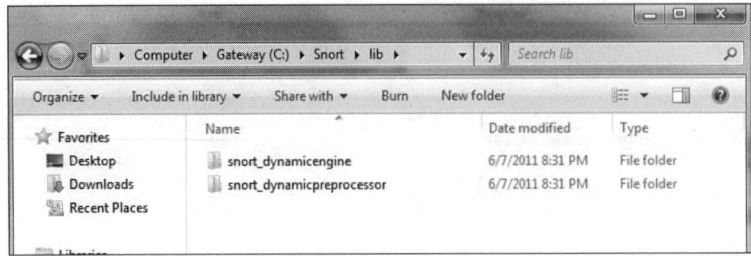

**FIGURE 9.7**   Windows-style library paths.

Note: If you find that you do not have a particular file or path in your system, just make sure it is commented out in the configuration file.

You must find the reference data and change it from Linux-style paths to Windows-style paths, as shown in Figure 9.8.

```
# metadata reference data.  do not modify these lines
include C:\Snort\etc\classification.config
include C:\Snort\etc\reference.config
```

**FIGURE 9.8**   Reference paths.

You are almost done. Now search for

```
#output log_tcp dump
```

and after that put this line

```
output alert_fast: alert.ids
```

Note: the pound sign (#) indicates a comment.

Now you will need to use the command line to start Snort. Simply navigate to C:\snort\bin. There are several different ways to start Snort. Many of the common ones are shown here in Table 9.1. I recommend you try the simplest first.

**TABLE 9.1**   Snort Commands

| Command | Purpose |
| --- | --- |
| `snort -v` | Start Snort as just a packet sniffer. |
| `snort -vd` | Start Snort as a packet sniffer, but have it sniff packet data rather than just the headers. |
| `snort -dev -l ./log` | Start Snort in logging mode so it logs packets. |
| `snort -dev -l ./log -h 192.168.1.1/24 -c snort.conf` (Put your IP address where you see italics.) | Start Snort in IDS mode. |

Snort is free and open source, but many people have a great deal of difficulty working with it the first time. The slightest error in your configuration file or the command-line startup will cause it to not run correctly. The purpose of this section is just to introduce you to Snort. For more information on Snort, try the following:

- **Snort Manual:** http://manual-snort-org.s3-website-us-east-1.amazonaws.com/

- **Writing your own Snort rules:** http://paginas.fe.up.pt/~mgi98020/pgr/writing_snort_rules.htm

## Honey Pots

A honey pot is an interesting technology. Essentially, it assumes that an attacker is able to breach your network security. And it would be best to distract that attacker away from your valuable data. Therefore, one creates a server that has fake data—perhaps an SQL server or Oracle server loaded with fake data, and just a little less secure than your real servers. Then, since none of your actual users ever access this server, monitoring software is installed to alert you when someone does access this server.

A honey pot achieves two goals. First, it will take the attacker's attention away from the data you wish to protect. Second, it will provide what appears to be interesting and valuable data, thus leading the attacker to stay connected to the fake server, giving you time to try to track them. There are commercial solutions, like Specter (www.specter.com). These solutions are usually quite easy to set up and include monitoring/tracking software. You may also find it useful to check out www.honeypots.org for more information on honey pots in general, and on specific implementations.

## Database Activity Monitoring

Database activity monitoring (DAM) is monitoring and analyzing database activity that operates independently of the database management system (DBMS). It is separate from the DBMS auditing, logging, and monitoring. Database activity monitoring and prevention (DAMP) is an extension to DAM that goes beyond monitoring and alerting to also block unauthorized activities.

## Other Preemptive Techniques

Besides IDS, antivirus, firewalls, and honey pots, there are a variety of preemptive techniques an administrator can use to attempt to reduce the chances of a successful attack being executed against her network.

### Intrusion Deflection

This method is becoming increasingly popular among the more security-conscious administrators. The essence of it is quite simple. An attempt is made to attract the intruder to a subsystem set up for the purpose of observing him. This is done by tricking the intruder into believing that he has succeeded in accessing system resources when, in fact, he has been directed to a specially designed environment. Being able to observe the intruder while he practices his art will yield valuable clues and can lead to his arrest.

This is often done by using what is commonly referred to as a *honey pot*. Essentially, you set up a fake system, possibly a server that appears to be an entire subnet. You make that system look very attractive by perhaps making it appear to have sensitive data, such as personnel files, or valuable data, such as account numbers or research. The actual data stored in this system is fake. The real purpose of the system is to carefully monitor the activities of any person who accesses the system. Since no legitimate user ever accesses this system, it is a given that anyone accessing it is an intruder.

### Intrusion Deterrence

This method involves simply trying to make the system seem like a less palatable target. In short, an attempt is made to make any potential reward from a successful intrusion attempt appear more difficult than it is worth. This approach includes tactics such as attempting to reduce the apparent value of the current system's worth through camouflage. This essentially means working to hide the most valuable aspects of the system. The other tactic in this methodology involves raising the perceived risk of a potential intruder being caught. This can be done in a variety of ways, including conspicuously displaying warnings and warning of active monitoring. The perception of the security of a system can be drastically improved, even when the actual system security has not been improved.

## Authentication

When a user logs on to a system, the system needs to authenticate her (and sometimes the user needs to authenticate the system). There are many authentication protocols. A few of the more common are briefly described here:

- **PAP:** Password Authentication Protocol is the simplest form of authentication and the least secure. Usernames and passwords are sent unencrypted, in plain text. This is obviously a very old method that is not used anymore. However, in the early days of computing, there were no widely available packet sniffers, and security was far less of a concern.

- **SPAP:** Shiva Password Authentication Protocol is an extension to PAP that does encrypt the username and password that is sent over the Internet.

- **CHAP:** Challenge Handshake Authentication Protocol calculates a hash after the user has logged in. Then it shares that hash with the client system. Periodically the server will ask the client to provide that hash. (This is the challenge part.) If the client cannot, then it is clear that the communications have been compromised. MS-CHAP is a Microsoft-specific extension to CHAP. The steps are basically these:

  1. After the handshake phase is complete, the authenticator (often the server) sends a "challenge" message to the peer.

  2. The peer responds with a value calculated using a "one-way hash" function.

  3. The authenticator checks the response against its own calculation of the expected hash value. If the values match, the authentication is acknowledged; otherwise, the connection should be terminated.

4. At random intervals, the authenticator sends a new challenge to the peer and repeats steps 1 to 3.

The entire goal of CHAP is to not only authenticate, but periodically reauthenticate, thus preventing session hijacking attacks.

- **EAP:** A framework frequently used in wireless networks and point-to-point connections. It was originally defined in RFC 3748 but updated since then. It handles the transport of keys and related parameters. There are several versions of EAP. It has many variations, including these:

  - **LEAP:** Lightweight Extensible Authentication protocol was developed by Cisco and has been used extensively in wireless communications. LEAP is supported by many Microsoft operating systems including Windows 7 and later versions. LEAP uses a modified version of MS-CHAP.

  - **Extensible Authentication Protocol—Transport Layer Security:** This utilizes TLS in order to secure the authentication process. Most implementations of EAP-TLS utilize X.509 digital certificates to authenticate the users.

  - **Protected Extensible Authentication Protocol (PEAP):** This encrypts the authentication process with an authenticated TLS tunnel. PEAP was developed by a consortium including Cisco, Microsoft, and RSA Security. It was first included in Microsoft Windows XP.

- **Kerberos:** Kerberos is used widely, particularly with Microsoft operating systems. It was invented at MIT and derives its name from the mythical three-headed dog that was reputed to guard the gates of Hades. The system is a bit complex, but the basic process is as follows:

When a user logs in, the authentication server verifies the user's identity and then contacts the ticket-granting server. (These are often on the same machine.) The ticket-granting server sends an encrypted "ticket" to the user's machine. That ticket identifies the user as being logged in. Later when the user needs to access some resource on the network, the user's machine uses that ticket-granting ticket to get access to the target machine. There is a great deal of verification for the tickets, and these tickets expire in a relatively short time.

## More on Kerberos

Since Kerberos is so widely used, it bears a bit closer look than the other authentication methods. In this section we will look a bit more in depth at Kerberos. If this is your first exposure to Kerberos, you may need to read this section more than once to really digest. While there are variations, the basic process is shown in Figure 9.9.

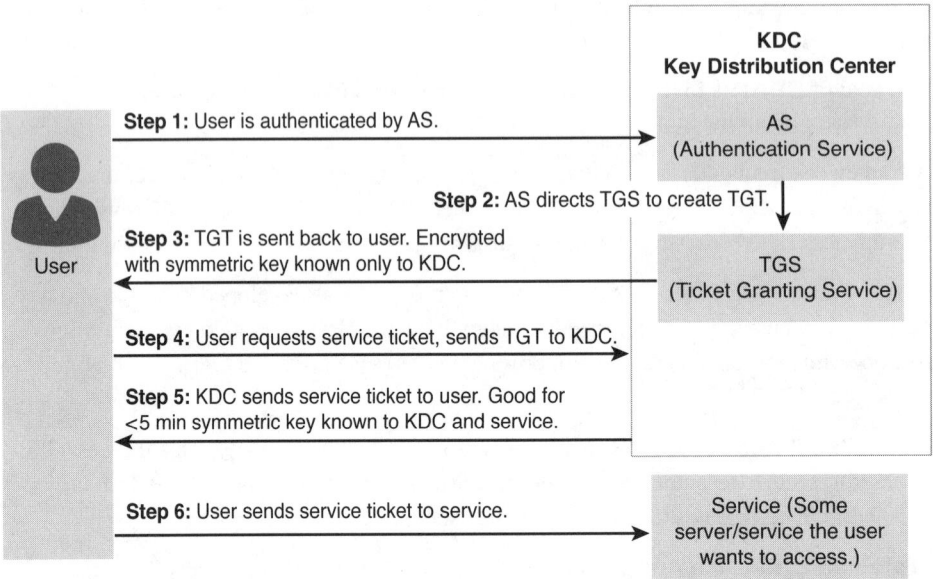

**FIGURE 9.9**    Kerberos

The elements of Kerberos follow:

- **Principal:** A server or client that Kerberos can assign tickets to.

- **Authentication server (AS):** Server that authorizes the principal and connects it to the ticket-granting server.

- **Ticket-granting server (TGS):** Provides tickets.

- **Key distribution center (KDC):** A server that provides the initial ticket and handles TGS requests. Often it runs both AS and TGS services. It must be noted that Kerberos is one of the most widely used authentication protocols. Europe often uses an alternative SESAME Secure European System for Applications in a multivendor environment.

# Digital Certificates

It seems very likely that you have heard the term *digital certificate* previously. The first thing you may wonder is what does a digital certificate do? First recall our discussions of asymmetric cryptography in Chapter 8, "Encryption." We mentioned that the public key can be disseminated widely since it can only be used to encrypt messages to us. Well, how does one provide people with a public key? The most common method is via a digital certificate. The digital certificate contains the user's public key, along with other information. However, a digital certificate can provide much more. It can provide a means for authenticating that the holder of the certificate is who she claims to be.

X.509 is an international standard for the format and information contained in a digital certificate. X.509 is the most common type of digital certificate in the world. It is a digital document that contains a public key signed by the trusted third party that is known as a certificate authority, or CA.

The following are the basic items in an X.509 certificate. There can be other optional information:

- **Version:** This is the version of X.509 that this certificate complies with.

- **Certificate holder's public key:** This is the primary way of getting someone's public key from his X.509 certificate.

- **Serial number:** This is a unique identifier for this certificate.

- **Certificate holder's distinguished name:** This is often a domain name or email associated with a certificate.

- **Certificate's validity period:** One year is the most common validity period.

- **Unique name of certificate issuer:** This is the certificate authority that issued this certificate.

- **Digital signature of issuer:** This field, and the next, are used to verify the certificate itself.

- **Signature algorithm identifier:** Identifies the actual digital signature algorithm used.

Let us see how this works in a common scenario. You visit your bank's website. In order to get the bank's public key, your browser will download that bank's digital certificate. But there is a problem. Could someone have set up a fake site, claiming to be your bank? Could that person have also generated a fake certificate claiming to be the bank? Yes, it's possible. This is one place digital certificates help us out. Your browser will look at the certificate issuer listed on the certificate and first ask if that is a CA that your browser trusts. Assuming it is, then your browser communicates with that CA to get that CA's public key. (Recall from Chapter 8 that a digital signature is created with a private key and verified with the public key.) The browser uses that CA public key to verify the CA signature on the certificate. If this is a fake certificate, the digital signature won't be recognized. This means a certificate not only provides you with the certificate holder's public key, but also gives you a method of verifying that entity with a trusted third party.

It should be noted that unlike X.509 certificates, PGP (Pretty Good Privacy) certificates are not issued by a CA and don't have a mechanism for third-party verification. They are usually only used for email communication. That is because it is assumed that you know who you are emailing, and verifying that identity is not required.

There are some other terms and concepts in digital certificates you need to be familiar with. Let us begin with a CA, the entity that issues you a digital certificate. For example, Comodo, Symantec, Digicert, GoDaddy, Verisign, and Thawte are all well-known certificate authorities. When you purchase a certificate from one of these vendors, they first verify who you are. (That can be as simple as matching your credit card with the domain you are buying the certificate for, or it can be far more involved.)

Since verifying a certificate user can be time consuming, many CAs offload that process to a registration authority (RA), who will then notify the CA to issue the certificate (or not to).

A CRL (certificate revocation list) is a list of certificates issued by a CA that are no longer valid. CRLs are distributed in two main ways: In the push model, the CA automatically sends the CRL out a regular interval. In the pull model, the CRL is downloaded from the CA by those who want to see it to verify a certificate. The problem is that CRL is not real-time checking. Thus, the newer answer is "Online Certificate Status Checking Protocol" OCSP; the idea is to have a protocol that checks in real time if the certificate is still valid.

# SSL/TLS

What sort of encryption is used on bank websites and e-commerce? In general, symmetric algorithms are faster and require a shorter key length to be as secure as asymmetric algorithms. However, there is the problem of how to securely exchange keys. Most e-commerce solutions use an asymmetric algorithm to exchange symmetric keys and then use the symmetric keys to encrypt the actual data.

When visiting websites that have an HTTPS at the beginning, rather than HTTP, the *S* denotes *secure*. That means traffic between your browser and the web server is encrypted. This is usually done with either SSL (Secure Sockets Layer) or TLS (Transport Layer Security). SSL, the older of the two technologies, was developed by Netscape. SSL and TLS are both asymmetric systems.

SSL is a technology employed to allow for transport-layer security via public key encryption. SSL was developed by Netscape for transmitting private documents via the Internet. By convention, URLs that require an SSL connection start with https instead of http. There have been several versions:

- Unreleased v1 (Netscape)
- Version 2 released in 1995 but had many flaws
- Version 3 released in 1996 RFC 6101
- Standard TLS1.0 RFC 2246 released in 1999
- TLS 1.1 was defined in RFC 4346 in April 2006
- TLS 1.2 was defined in RFC 5246 in August 2008. It is based on the earlier TLS 1.1 spec
- TLS 1.3 July 2014

The basic process of establishing an SSL/TLS connection is shown in Figure 9.10.

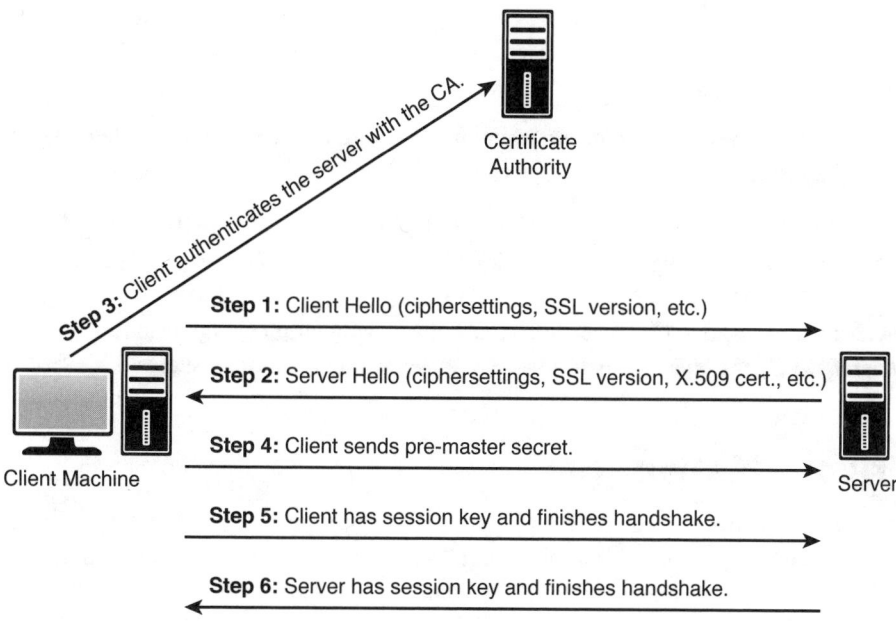

Step 3: Client authenticates the server with the CA.

Certificate
Authority

**Step 1:** Client Hello (ciphersettings, SSL version, etc.)

**Step 2:** Server Hello (ciphersettings, SSL version, X.509 cert., etc.)

**Step 4:** Client sends pre-master secret.

Client Machine

**Step 5:** Client has session key and finishes handshake.

**Step 6:** Server has session key and finishes handshake.

Server

**FIGURE 9.10   SSL/TLS.**

The process involves several complex steps, as defined here:

1. The client sends the server information regarding the client's cryptographic capabilities. That includes what algorithms it is capable of, what hashing algorithms it can use for message integrity, and related information.

2. The server responds by selecting the best encryption and hashing that both client and server are capable of and sends this information to the client. The server also sends its own certificate, and if the client is requesting a server resource that requires client authentication, the server requests the client's certificate.

3. The client uses the information sent by the server to authenticate the server. This means authenticating the digital certificate with the appropriate CA. If this fails the browser warns the user that the certificate cannot be verified. If the server can be successfully authenticated, the client proceeds to the next step.

4. Using all data generated in the handshake thus far, the client creates the pre-master secret for the session, encrypts it with the server's public key that it received from the server's X.509 certificate, and then sends the encrypted pre-master secret to the server.

5. If the server has requested client authentication, then the server will also authenticate the client's X.509 certificate. This does not happen in most e-commerce and banking websites.

6.  Both the client and the server use the master secret to generate the session keys. These are symmetric keys (such as AES) that will be used throughout the session to encrypt information between the client and the server.

7.  The client sends a message to the server informing it that future messages from the client will be encrypted with the session key.

8.  The server sends a message to the client informing it that future messages from the server will be encrypted with the session key.

This process provides a process to not only securely exchange a symmetric key, but also to verify the server and (optionally) verify the client. This is how secure web traffic is accomplished.

# Virtual Private Networks

A *VPN* is a *virtual private network*. This is essentially a way to use the Internet to create a virtual connection between a remote user or site and a central location. The packets sent back and forth over this connection are encrypted, thus making it private. The VPN must emulate a direct network connection.

There are three different protocols that are used to create VPNs:

- Point-to-Point Tunneling Protocol (PPTP)

- Layer 2 Tunneling Protocol (L2TP)

- Internet Protocol Security (IPsec)

These are each discussed in more depth in the following sections.

## Point-to-Point Tunneling Protocol

*Point-to-Point Tunneling Protocol (PPTP)* is the oldest of the three protocols used in VPNs. It was originally designed as a secure extension to Point-to-Point Protocol (PPP). PPTP was originally proposed as a standard in 1996 by the PPTP Forum—a group of companies that included Ascend Communications, ECI Telematics, Microsoft, 3Com, and U.S. Robotics. It adds the features of encrypting packets and authenticating users to the older PPP protocol. PPTP works at the data link layer of the OSI model (discussed in Chapter 2, "Networks and the Internet").

PPTP offers two different methods of authenticating the user: Extensible Authentication Protocol (EAP) and Challenge Handshake Authentication Protocol (CHAP). EAP was actually designed specifically for PPTP and is not proprietary. CHAP is a three-way process whereby the client sends a code to the server, the server authenticates it, and then the server responds to the client. CHAP also periodically reauthenticates a remote client, even after the connection is established.

PPTP uses Microsoft Point-to-Point Encryption (MPPE) to encrypt packets. MPPE is actually a version of DES. DES is still useful for many situations; however, newer versions of DES, such as DES 3, are preferred.

## Layer 2 Tunneling Protocol

*Layer 2 Tunneling Protocol (L2TP)* was explicitly designed as an enhancement to PPTP. Like PPTP, it works at the data link layer of the OSI model. It has several improvements to PPTP. First, it offers more and varied methods for authentication—PPTP offers two, whereas L2TP offers five. In addition to CHAP and EAP, L2TP offers PAP, SPAP, and MS-CHAP.

Besides more authentication protocols available for use, L2TP offers other enhancements. PPTP will only work over standard IP networks, whereas L2TP will work over X.25 networks (a common protocol in phone systems) and ATM (asynchronous transfer mode, a high-speed networking technology) systems. L2TP also uses IPsec for its encryption.

## IPsec

*IPsec* is the latest of the three VPN protocols. One of the differences between IPsec and the other two methods is that it encrypts not only the packet data (recall the discussion of packets in Chapter 2), but also the header information. It also has protection against unauthorized retransmission of packets. This is important because one trick that a hacker can use is to simply grab the first packet from a transmission and use it to get their own transmissions to go through. Essentially, the first packet (or packets) has to contain the login data. If you simply resend that packet (even if you cannot crack its encryption), you will be sending a valid logon and password that can then be followed with additional packets. Preventing unauthorized retransmission of packets prevents this from happening.

IPsec operates in one of two modes: Transport mode, in which only the payload is encrypted, and Tunnel mode, in which both data and IP headers are encrypted. Following are some basic IPsec terms:

- Authentication Headers (AHs) provide connectionless integrity and data origin authentication for IP packets.

- Encapsulating Security Payloads (ESPs) provide origin authenticity, integrity, and confidentiality protection of packets. These have encryption-only and authentication-only configurations.

- Security Associations (SAs) provide the parameters necessary for AH or ESP operations. SAs are established using the Internet Security Association and Key Management Protocol.

- The Internet Security Association and Key Management Protocol (ISAKMP) provides a framework for authentication and key exchange.

- Internet key exchange (IKE and IKEv2) is used to set up a security association (SA) by handling negotiation of protocols and algorithms and to generate the encryption and authentication keys to be used.

Essentially during the initial establishment of an IPsec tunnel, security associations (SAs) are formed. These SAs have information such as what encryption algorithm and what hashing algorithms will be used in the IPsec tunnel. Recall that we discussed encryption in some depth in Chapter 8. IKE is primarily concerned with establishing these SAs. ISAKMP allows the two ends of the IPsec tunnel to authenticate to each other and to exchange keys.

# Wi-Fi Security

With wireless networks being so prevalent, it is important to consider wireless network security. There are three Wi-Fi security protocols, ranging from the oldest and least secure (WEP) to the most recent and most secure (WPA2). They are each briefly described here.

## Wired Equivalent Privacy

Wired Equivalent Privacy (WEP) uses the stream cipher RC4 to secure the data and a CRC-32 checksum for error checking. Standard WEP uses a 40-bit key (known as WEP-40) with a 24-bit initialization vector (IV) to effectively form 64-bit encryption. 128-bit WEP uses a 104-bit key with a 24-bit IV.

Because RC4 is a stream cipher, the same traffic key must never be used twice. The problem with WEP is that the committee who created it was composed of very good computer professionals who thought they knew enough about cryptography, but did not. They reuse the IV. That defeats the entire purpose of an IV and leaves the protocol open to attacks. A simple search of YouTube for "how to crack WEP" will yield a deluge of videos on techniques for cracking WEP.

## Wi-Fi Protected Access

Wi-Fi Protected Access (WPA) was definitely an improvement over WEP. First, WPA uses AES, which is a very good encryption algorithm. Then WPA uses Temporal Key Integrity Protocol. TKIP dynamically generates a new key for each packet. So even if you crack a WPA key, there will be a different key for the next packet.

## WPA2

This is the most modern form of Wi-Fi security, and if it is at all possible, this is what you should be using. Thus, we will give it a bit more attention. WPA2 is based on the IEEE 802.11i standard. It provides the Advanced Encryption Standard (AES) using the Counter Mode-Cipher Block Chaining (CBC)-Message Authentication Code (MAC) Protocol (CCMP) that provides data confidentiality, data origin authentication, and data integrity for wireless frames. Some of these terms you should recall from Chapter 8. The Cipher Block Chaining prevents known plain text attacks.

The MAC preserves message integrity and ensures that packets were not altered in transit, either accidentally or intentionally. This means that WPA2 uses very strong encryption along with message integrity.

# Summary

It is absolutely critical that any network have a firewall and proxy server between the network and the outside world. It is critical that all machines in the network (servers and workstations alike) have updated virus protection. It is also a good idea to consider IDS and antispyware. In the upcoming exercises, you will have an opportunity to practice setting up various types of firewalls and IDS systems.

## Test Your Skills

### MULTIPLE CHOICE QUESTIONS

1. Which of the following is the most common way for a virus scanner to recognize a virus?

    A. To compare a file to known virus attributes

    B. To use complex rules to look for virus-like behavior

    C. To only look for TSR programs

    D. To look for TSR programs or programs that alter the Registry

2. What is one way of checking emails for virus infections?

    A. Block all emails with attachments.

    B. Block all active attachments (for example, ActiveX, scripting).

    C. Look for subject lines that are from known virus attacks.

    D. Look for emails from known virus sources.

3. What are TSR programs?

    A. Terminal Signal Registry programs that alter the system Registry

    B. Terminate and System Remove programs that erase themselves when complete

    C. Terminate and Scan Remote programs that scan remote systems prior to terminating

    D. Terminate and Stay Resident programs that actually stay in memory after you shut them down

4. What is the name for scanning that depends on complex rules to define what is and is not a virus?

    A. Rules-based scanning (RBS)

    B. Heuristic scanning

    C. TSR scanning

    D. Logic-based scanning (LBS)

5. Which of the following is not one of the basic types of firewalls?

    **A.** Screening firewall

    **B.** Application gateway

    **C.** Heuristic firewall

    **D.** Circuit-level gateway

6. Which of the following is the most basic type of firewall?

    **A.** Screening firewall

    **B.** Application gateway

    **C.** Heuristic firewall

    **D.** Circuit-level gateway

7. Which of the following is a disadvantage to using an application gateway firewall?

    **A.** It is not very secure.

    **B.** It uses a great deal of resources.

    **C.** It can be difficult to configure.

    **D.** It can only work on router-based firewalls.

8. What is SPI?

    **A.** Stateful packet inspection

    **B.** System packet inspection

    **C.** Stateful packet interception

    **D.** System packet interception

9. What is the term for a firewall that is simply software installed on an existing server?

    **A.** Network host based

    **B.** Dual-homed

    **C.** Router based

    **D.** Screened host

10. What is a major weakness with a network host–based firewall?

    **A.** Its security is dependent on the underlying operating system.

    **B.** It is difficult to configure.

    **C.** It can be easily hacked.

    **D.** It is very expensive.

11. What is the term for blocking an IP address that has been the source of suspicious activity?

    **A.** Preemptive blocking

    **B.** Intrusion deflection

    **C.** Proactive deflection

    **D.** Intrusion blocking

12. What is the term for a fake system designed to lure intruders?

    **A.** Honey pot

    **B.** Faux system

    **C.** Deflection system

    **D.** Entrapment

13. Which of the following is the correct term for simply making your system less attractive to intruders?

    **A.** Intrusion deterrence

    **B.** Intrusion deflection

    **C.** Intrusion camouflage

    **D.** Intrusion avoidance

14. What method do most IDS software implementations use?

    **A.** Anomaly detection

    **B.** Preemptive blocking

    **C.** Intrusion deterrence

    **D.** Infiltration

15. How do most antispyware packages work?

    **A.** By using heuristic methods

    **B.** By looking for known spyware

    **C.** The same way antivirus scanners work

    **D.** By seeking out TSR cookies

## EXERCISES

### EXERCISE 9.1: Setting Up a Firewall

Microsoft Windows (every version since XP, including Windows 10) and Linux both offer built-in packet-filtering firewalls of some sort.

1. Using the documentation for whichever operating system you have, decide what packets you wish to block.

2. Set your firewall to filter those packets.

Note: Ideally, if you have access to both operating systems, the best exercise is to experiment setting up firewalls for both.

### EXERCISE 9.2: Router-Based Firewalls

Note: This exercise is for those labs with access to a lab router-based firewall.

1. Consult your router documentation for instructions on how to configure the firewall.

2. Configure your router-based firewall to block the same items you chose to block in Exercise 1.

### EXERCISE 9.3: Evaluating Firewalls

Write a brief essay explaining whether you think the router-based solution or the built-in operating system solution is best. Explain your reasons.

### EXERCISE 9.4: Active Code

Using the Web or other resources, find out why blocking active code (for example, ActiveX scripts) might or might not be a good idea for some situations. Write a brief essay explaining your position.

### EXERCISE 9.5: Hardware Used by a Company

Visit the IT department of a company and ascertain what hardware they use in their computer system's defense. Do they use a hardware firewall in addition to a software firewall? What form of intrusion detection software do they use? Do they use antivirus and antispyware on the workstations within the company? Write a brief report summarizing your findings.

# PROJECTS

## PROJECT 9.1: **How Does the Microsoft Firewall Work?**

Using Microsoft documentation, the Web, and other resources, find out what methodologies the Microsoft Windows (whichever version you are using) firewall uses. Write a brief essay explaining the strengths and weaknesses of that approach. Also discuss situations in which you feel that approach is adequate and those in which it might be inadequate.

## PROJECT 9.2: **How Does Antivirus Software Work?**

Using documentation from the vendor, the Web, or other resources, find out what methodology Norton AntiVirus uses, as well as the methods that McAfee uses. Armed with this information, write a brief essay comparing and contrasting any differences. Also discuss situations in which one might be recommended over the other.

## PROJECT 9.3: **Using Snort**

Note: This is a longer project and appropriate for groups.

Go to the Snort.org website (www.snort.org/) and download Snort. Using the vendor documentation or other resources, configure Snort. Then use port scanners on the machine that has Snort configured and note whether Snort detects the scan.

## Case Study

Jane Smith is responsible for security at the ABC Company. She has a moderate budget with which to purchase security solutions. To date, she has installed a router-based firewall between the network and the outside world. She also has a commercial virus scanner on every machine on the network. What other actions might you recommend to her? Would you recommend a different firewall? Why or why not?

## Chapter 10

# Security Policies

## *Chapter Objectives*

**After reading this chapter and completing the exercises, you will be able to do the following:**

- Recognize the importance of security policies.
- Understand the various policies and the rationale for them.
- Know what elements go into good policies.
- Create policies for network administration.
- Evaluate and improve existing policies.

## Introduction

So far in this book we have explored various threats to networks. And in Chapter 9, "Computer Security Technology," we examined a variety of technical defenses against such attacks. However, the fact is that technology by itself cannot solve all network security problems. There are some issues that technology cannot stop. Examples of this include the following:

- Virus software won't prevent a user from manually opening an attachment and releasing a virus.
- A technologically secured network is still very vulnerable if former employees (perhaps some unhappy with the company) still have working passwords or if passwords are simply put on Post-it notes on computer monitors.
- A server is not secure if it is in a room that nearly everyone in the company has access to.
- Your network is not secure if end users are vulnerable to social engineering.

Another reason that technology alone is not the answer is that technology must be appropriately applied. Policies are used to guide you in how to implement and manage security, including security technology. In this chapter, we will examine computer security policies, including the elements that go into creating good security policies as well as examples of how to establish a network security policy.

# What Is a Policy?

A security policy is a document that defines how an organization will deal with some aspect of security. There can be policies regarding end-user behavior, IT response to incidents, or policies for specific issues and incidents.

Security policies can also be created to deal with regulatory requirements. These types of policies direct members of the organization as to how to comply with certain regulations. A good example would be a policy informing healthcare workers how to comply with HIPAA when using electronic medical records software.

Or policies can simply be advisory, suggesting to employees how they should handle certain items, but not requiring compliance. For example, a policy might advise users that emailing from a smart phone using a Wi-Fi hotspot can be unsecure, but not forbid it.

# Defining User Policies

When discussing user policies, there is one rule you must keep in mind: You should have a policy for every foreseeable situation. Failure to have policies that address a given problem will usually result in that problem being exacerbated. Something may seem like common sense to you but may not be to someone with no training or experience in computer networks or network security.

The misuse of systems is a major problem for many organizations. A large part of the problem comes from the difficulty in defining exactly what is misuse. Some things might be obvious misuse, such as using company time and computers to search for another job or to view illicit websites. However, other areas are not so clear, such as an employee using her lunchtime to look up information about a car she is thinking of buying. Generally, good user policies will outline specifically how people are to use the system and how they should not. For a policy to be effective, it needs to be very clear and quite specific. Vague statements such as "computers and Internet access are only for business use" are simply inadequate. I would recommend something more clear and perhaps more enforceable, perhaps something like "computers and Internet access are only for business purposes during business hours. However, employees may use the computer/Internet access for personal use during nonwork time such as breaks, lunch, and before work. However, such use must be in compliance with Internet usage policies." That is clear, direct, and enforceable.

Other areas for potential misuse are also covered by user policies, including password sharing, copying data, leaving accounts logged on while employees go to lunch, and so on. All of these issues ultimately have a significant impact on your network's security and must be clearly spelled out in your user policies. We will now examine several areas that effective user policies must cover:

- Passwords
- Internet use
- Email usage
- Installing/uninstalling software
- Instant messaging
- Desktop configuration
- Bring Your Own Device

## Passwords

Keeping passwords secure is critical. In Chapter 8, "Encryption," appropriate passwords were discussed as part of operating system hardening. A good password is at least eight characters long, uses numbers and special characters, and has no obvious relevance to the end user. For example, a Dallas Cowboys fan would be ill advised to use a password like *cowboys* or *godallas* but might be well advised to use a password such as *%trEe987* or *123DoG$$* since those don't reflect the person's personal interests and therefore would not be easily guessed. Issues such as minimum password length, password history, and password complexity come under administrative policies, not user policies. User policies dictate how the end user should behave. For reliable security, I recommend a passphrase that has been altered to include numbers and special characters. This can be something easy to remember but altered so that it will not be vulnerable to guessing or brute-force attacks. An example would be taking the phrase "I like double cheese burgers" and altering it to be IliK3double3ch33$eburg3r$. Notice the Es were changed to 3s, the Ss to $s, and two random letters were capitalized. You now have a 25-character password that is also complex. It is easy to remember and very difficult to break.

However, no password is secure, no matter how long or how complex, if it is listed on a sticky note stuck to the user's computer monitor. This may seem obvious, but it is not at all uncommon to go into an office and find a password either on the monitor or in the top drawer of the desk. Every janitor or anyone who simply passes by the office can get that password.

It is also not uncommon to find employees sharing passwords. For example, Bob is going to be out of town next week, so he gives Juan his password so that Juan can get into his system, check email, and more. The problem is that now two people have that password. And what happens if during the week Bob is gone, Juan gets ill and decides he will share the password with Shelly so that she can keep checking that system while Juan is out sick? It does not take long for a password to get to so many people that it is no longer useful at all from a security perspective.

Issues like minimum length of passwords, password age, and password history are ones of administrative policies. System administrators can force these requirements. However, none of that will be particularly helpful if the users don't manage their passwords in a secure fashion.

All of this means you need explicit policies regarding how users secure their passwords. Those policies should specify the following:

- Passwords are never to be kept written down in an accessible place. The preference is that they not be written down at all, but if they are, they should be in a secure area such as a lock box at your home (not in the office right next to your computer).

- Passwords must never be shared with another person for any reason.

- If an employee believes his password has been compromised, he should immediately contact the IT department so his password can be changed and so that logon attempts with the old password can be monitored and traced.

## Internet Use

Most organizations provide their users with some sort of Internet access. There are several reasons for this. The most obvious reason is email. However, that is hardly the only reason to have Internet access in a business or academic setting. There is also the Web, and even chat rooms. (Believe it or not, they can, and in some cases are being used for business communications.) The Internet can be used for legitimate purposes within any organization, but it can also bring about serious security problems. Appropriate polices must be in place to govern the use of Internet technologies.

The World Wide Web is a wonderful resource for a tremendous wealth of data. Throughout this book, we have frequently referenced websites where one can find valuable security data and useful utilities. The Internet is also replete with useful tutorials on various technologies. However, even non-technology-related business interests can be served via the Web. Here are a few examples of legitimate business uses of the Web:

- Sales staff checking competitor's websites to see what products or services they offer, in what areas, perhaps even getting prices

- Creditors checking the business's AM Best or Standard and Poor's rating to see how their business financial rating is doing

- Business travelers checking weather conditions and getting prices for travel

- Online training with webinars

- Web meetings

- Online bill payment or in some cases even filing regulatory and government documents

Of course, there are other web activities that are clearly not appropriate on a company's network:

- Using the Web to search for a new job

- Any pornographic use

- Any use that violates local, state, or federal laws

- Use of the Web to conduct your own business (you have another enterprise you are involved in other than the company's business)

In addition, there are gray areas. Some activities might be acceptable to some organizations, but not to others. Such activities might include

- Online shopping during the employee's lunch or break time

- Reading news articles online during lunch or break time

- Viewing humorous websites

What one person might view as absurdly obvious might not be to another. It is critical that any organization have very clear policies detailing specifically what is and what is not acceptable use of the Web at work. Giving clear examples of what is acceptable use and what is not is also important. You should also remember that most proxy servers and many firewalls can block certain websites. This will help prevent employees from misusing the company's web connection.

## Email Usage

Most business and even academic activity now occurs via email. As we have discussed in several previous chapters, email also happens to be the primary vehicle for virus distribution. This means that email security is a significant issue for any network administrator.

Clearly, you cannot simply ban all email attachments. However, you can establish some guidelines for how to handle email attachments. Users should only open an attachment if it meets the following criteria:

- It was expected. (Someone requested documents from a colleague or client.)

- If it was not expected, did it come from a known source? If so, first send that person an email (or phone them) and ask if she sent the attachment. If so, open it.

- It appears to be a legitimate business document (a spreadsheet, a document, a presentation, and so on).

It should be noted that some people might find such criteria unrealistic. There is no question they are inconvenient. However, with the prevalence of viruses, often attached to email, these measures are prudent. Many people choose not to go to this level to try to avoid viruses, and that may be your choice as well. Just bear in mind that millions of computers are infected with some sort of virus every single year.

No one should ever open an attachment that meets any of the following criteria:

- It comes from an unknown source.

- It is some active code or executable.

- It is an animation/movie.

■ The email itself does not appear legitimate. (It seems to entice you to open the attachment rather than simply being a legitimate business communication that happens to have an attachment.)

If the end user has any doubt whatsoever, then she should not open the email. Rather, she should contact someone in the IT department who has been designated to handle security. That person can then either compare the email subject line to known viruses or can simply come check out the email personally. Then if it appears legitimate the user can open the attachment.

---

**FYI: About Attachments**

I frequently follow the "better safe than sorry" axiom on this matter. This means that when forwarded some joke, image, flash animation, and so on circulating the Internet, I simply delete it. That may mean that I will miss many humorous images and stories, but it also means I will miss many viruses. You would do well to consider emulating this practice.

---

## Installing/Uninstalling Software

This is one matter that does have an absolute answer. End users should not be allowed to install anything on their machine. This includes wallpapers, screensavers, utilities—anything. The best approach is to limit their login privileges so that they cannot install anything. However, this should be coupled with a strong policy statement prohibiting the installation of anything on their PC. If they wish to install something, it should first be scanned by the IT department and approved. This process might be cumbersome, but it is necessary. Some organizations go so far as to remove or at least disable media drives (CD, USB, and so on) from end-user PCs, so installations can only occur from files that the IT department has put on some network drive. This is usually a more extreme measure than most organizations will require, but it is an option you should be aware of. In fact, Windows allows the administrator to disable allowing new USB devices. So the admin can install some USB devices that are approved for corporate use and then disallow any additional devices being added.

## Instant Messaging

Instant messaging is also widely used and abused by employees in companies and organizations. In some cases, instant messaging can be used for legitimate business purposes. However, it does pose a significant security risk. There have been viruses that specifically propagated via instant messaging. In one incident, the virus would copy everyone on the user's buddy list with the contents of all conversations. Thus, a conversation you thought was private was being broadcast to everyone you knew and had messaged with.

Instant messaging is also a threat from a purely informational security perspective. Nothing stops an end user from instant messaging trade secrets or confidential information without the traceability of email going through the corporate email server. It is recommended that instant messaging simply be banned from all computers within an organization. If you find you absolutely must have it, then you must establish very strict guidelines for its use, including the following:

- Instant messaging can only be used for business communications, no personal conversations. Now, this might be a bit difficult to enforce. Rules like this often are. More common rules, such as prohibiting personal web browsing, are also quite difficult to enforce. However, it is still a good idea to have those rules in place. Then if you find a person violating them, you do have a company policy that you can refer to that prohibits such actions. However, you should be aware that in all likelihood you won't catch most violations of this rule.

- No confidential or private business information should be sent via instant messaging.

## Desktop Configuration

Many users like to reconfigure their desktop. This means changing the background, screensaver, font size, and resolution. Theoretically speaking, this is not a security hazard. Simply changing your computer's background image cannot compromise your computer's security. However, there are other issues involved.

The first issue is where the background image comes from. Frequently, end users will download images from the Internet. This means there is a chance of getting a virus or Trojan horse, particularly one using a hidden extension (that is, it appears to be a mypic.jpg but is really mypic.jpg.exe). There are also human resources/harassment issues if an employee uses a backdrop or screensaver that is offensive to other employees. Some organizations simply decide to prohibit any changes to the system configuration for this reason.

The second problem is technical. In order to give users access to change screensavers, background images, and resolution, you must give them rights that will also allow them to change other system settings you might not want changed. The graphical display options are not separated from all other configuration options. This means that allowing users to change their screensaver might open the door for them to alter other settings (such as the network card configuration or the Windows Internet Connection Firewall) that would compromise security.

## Bring Your Own Device

Bring your own device (BYOD) has become a significant issue for most organizations. Most, if not all, of your employees will have their own smart phones, tablets, smart watches, and Fitbits that they will carry with them into the workplace. When they connect to your wireless network, this introduces a host of new security concerns. You have no idea what networks that device previously connected to, what software was installed on them, or what data might be exfiltrated by these personal devices.

In highly secure environments, the answer may be to forbid personally owned devices. However, in many organizations, such a policy is impractical. A workaround for that is to have a Wi-Fi network that is dedicated to BYOD and is not connected to the company's main network. Another approach, albeit more technologically complex, is to detect the device on connection, and if it is not a company-issued device, significantly limit its access.

Whatever approach you take, you must have some policy regarding personal devices. They are already ubiquitous. Just a few years ago smart phones were around, but smart watches were not. It is difficult to predict what new smart devices might loom on the horizon.

## Final Thoughts on User Policies

This section has provided an overview of appropriate and effective user policies. It is critical that any organization implement solid user policies. However, these policies will not be effective unless you have clearly defined consequences for violating them. Many organizations find it helpful to spell out specific consequences that escalate with each incident, such as the following:

- The first incident of violating any of these policies will result in a verbal warning.
- A second incident will result in a written warning.
- The third incident will result in suspension or termination. (In the case of academic settings, this would be suspension or expulsion.)

You must clearly list the consequences, and all users should sign a copy of the user policies upon being hired. This prevents employees claiming they were not aware of the policies.

---

**CAUTION**

### Termination or Expulsion

Any policy that can lead to expulsion from a school or termination from a job (or even a demotion) should first be cleared by your legal advisor. There can be significant legal ramifications for wrongful termination or expulsion. I am not an attorney or an expert in legal matters and cannot provide you with legal advice. It is imperative that you do consult an attorney about these matters.

---

It is also important to realize that there is another cost to misuse of corporate Internet access. That cost is lost productivity. How much time does the average employee spend reading personal email, doing nonbusiness web activities, or instant messaging? It is hard to say. However, for an informal view, go to www.yahoo.com on any given business day, during business hours, and click on one of the news stories. At the bottom of the story you will see a message board for this story. It lists date and time of posts. See how many posts are done during business hours. It is unlikely that all of those people are out of work, retired, or at home sick.

Let me be completely clear. The Internet is the single greatest communication tool in human history. And it can have a tremendous positive effect on any business. I conduct almost all of my business activities through the Web. However, many employees do abuse the Internet, and it does decrease productivity for those who cannot be self-disciplined. Here are just a few studies supporting this assertion:

- A 2008 study showed employees wasting an average of 5.3 hours a week on idle Internet surfing. While this study is a bit old, the problem persists to this day. It is often the case that widespread Internet access actually inhibits productivity rather than enhances it.

- Ohio State University researchers found regular Facebook users had a lower GPA than nonusers (http://researchnews.osu.edu/archive/facebookusers.htm).

- There have been multiple studies showing that Facebook at work has a negative impact on productivity. Most of these studies are a few years old, because it has become well established that social media at work hurts productivity.

  http://www.cnbc.com/2016/02/04/facebook-turns-12--trillions-in-time-wasted.html
  http://www.riskmanagementmonitor.com/the-risks-of-social-media-decreased-worker-productivity/
  http://www.shellypalmer.com/2011/05/social-media-use-drastically-reduces-work-productivity/

# Defining System Administration Policies

In addition to determining policies for users, you must have some clearly defined policies for system administrators. There must be a procedure for adding users, removing users, dealing with security issues, changing any system, and so on. There must also be standards for handling any deviation.

## New Employees

When a new employee is hired, the system administration policy must define specific steps to safeguard company security. New employees must be given access to the resources and applications their job function requires. The granting of that access must be documented (possibly in a log). It is also critical that the new employee receive a copy of the company's computer security/acceptable use polices and sign a document acknowledging receipt of such.

Before a new employee starts to work, the IT department (specifically network administration) should receive a written request from the business unit that person will be working for. That request should specify exactly what resources this user will need, when she will start, and have the signature of someone in the business unit with authority to approve such a request. Then the person who is managing network administration or network security should approve and sign the request. After you have implemented the new user on the system with the appropriate rights, you can file a copy of the request.

## Departing Employees

When an employee leaves, it is critical to make sure all of his logins are terminated and all access to all systems is discontinued immediately. Unfortunately, this is an area of security that all too many organizations do not give enough attention to. You cannot be certain which employees will bear the company ill will and which won't upon leaving the company. It is imperative to have all of the former employees' access shut down on their last day of work. This includes physical access to the building. If a former employee has keys and is disgruntled, nothing can stop him from returning to steal or vandalize computer equipment. When an employee leaves the company, you need to ensure that on his last day the following actions take place:

- All logon accounts to any server, VPN, network, or other resource are disabled.

- All keys to the facility are returned.

- All accounts for email, Internet access, wireless Internet, cell phones, and so on are shut off.

- Any accounts for mainframe resources are canceled.

- The employee's workstation hard drive is searched.

The last item might seem odd. But if an employee was gathering data to take with him (proprietary company data) or conducting any other improper activities, you need to find out right away. If you do see any evidence of such activity, you need to secure that workstation and keep it for evidence in any civil or criminal proceedings.

All of this might seem a bit extreme to some readers. It is true that with the vast majority of exiting employees you will have no issues to be concerned about. However, if you do not make it a habit of securing employees' access when they depart, you will eventually have an unfortunate situation that could have been easily avoided.

## Change Requests

The nature of information technology is change. Not only do end users come and go, but requirements change frequently. Business units request access to different resources, server administrators upgrade software and hardware, application developers install new software, and web developers change the website. Change is occurring all the time. Therefore, it is important to have a change control process. This process not only makes the change run smoothly, but it also allows the IT security personnel to examine the change for any potential security problems before it is implemented. A change control request should go through the following steps:

- An appropriate manager within the business unit signs the request, signifying approval of the request. In other words, there is no point in pursuing the change request process if the immediate supervisor of the requestor has not approved the request.

- The appropriate IT unit (database administration, network admin, email admin, cloud administration) verifies that the request is one it can fulfill technologically, fits within budget constraints, and does not violate IT policies.

- The IT security unit verifies that this change will not cause security problems. This is becoming more and more critical in modern times.

- The appropriate IT unit formulates a plan to implement the change and a plan to roll back the change in the event of some failure. That latter part is very critical and is often overlooked. There must be some mechanism to roll back the change should it cause any problems.

- The date and time for the change is scheduled, and all relevant parties are notified.

Your change control process might not be identical to this one; in fact, you might be much more specific. However, the key to remember is that in order for your network to be secure, you simply cannot have changes happening without some process for examining the impact of those changes prior to implementing them.

Change management activities are frequently managed through a Change Control Board (CCB) process, sometimes also called a Change Approval Board (CAB). The change process was detailed previously in this section, but the basic process can be summarized as follows:

- Initiated with RFC document (Request for Comments or Request for Change)

- RFC sent for approval

- Priority is set

- Assigned to whomever makes the change

- Document decisions

- Evaluate by CAB

- RFC scheduled

- Complete when change owner and requester verify successful implementation

- Review of RFC

This can be a process with a CAB meeting formally and documentation being extensive, or it can be informal and conducted via emails to the appropriate parties.

---

### In Practice

### Extremes of Change Control

Anyone with even a few years of experience in the IT profession can tell you that when it comes to change control there are all sorts of different approaches. The real problem is those IT groups that implement unreasonable extremes. I have seen both. Without using the real names of the companies involved, let's examine a real case of each extreme.

Software consultant Company X was a small company that did custom financial applications for various companies. It had a staff of less than 20 developers who frequently traveled to client locations around the country. It literally had

- No documentation for any of its applications—not even a few notes.

- No change control process. When someone did not like a setting on a server or some part of the network configuration, he simply changed it.

- No process for handling former employee access. In one case, a person had been gone for six months and still had a valid logon account.

Now, clearly this is alarming from several perspectives, not just from a security viewpoint. However, that is one extreme, one that makes for a chaotic environment that is very unsecure. Security-minded network administrators tend to move toward the opposite extreme, one that can have a negative impact on productivity.

Company B had over 2,000 employees, with an IT staff of about 100 people. In this company, however, the bureaucracy had overwhelmed the IT department to the point that their productivity was severely impacted. In one case, a person was a web server administrator, and the decision had been made that he also needed database administration rights on a single database server. The process, however, took three months with one face-to-face meeting between his manager and the CIO, as well as two phone conferences and a dozen emails between his manager and the manager of the database group.

The company's convoluted change control process had a severely negative impact on productivity. Some employees informally estimated that even the low-level IT supervisors spent 40% of their time in meetings/conferences, reporting on meetings/conferences, or preparing for meetings/conferences. And the further one went up the IT ladder, the more one's time became consumed in bureaucratic activities.

Both of these examples are meant to illustrate two extremes in change control management that you should try to avoid. Your goal in implementing change control management is simply to have an orderly and safe way of managing change, not to be an impediment to productivity.

## Security Breaches

Unfortunately, the reality is that your network will probably, at some point, have a security breach of some kind. This could mean that you are the target of a denial of service (DoS) attack, your system is infected with a virus, or perhaps a hacker gains entrance and destroys or copies sensitive data. You must have some sort of plan for how to respond should any such event occur. This book cannot tell you specifically how to deal with each and every event that might occur; however, we can discuss some general guidelines for what to do in certain, general, situations. We will look at each of the main types of security breaches and what actions you should take for each.

## Virus Infection

When a virus strikes your system, immediately quarantine the infected machine or machines. This means literally unplugging the machines from the network. If it is a subnet, then unplug its switch or disconnect wireless access. Isolate the infected machines (unless your entire network is infected, in which case simply shut down your router/ISP connection to close you off from the outside world and prevent spread beyond your network). After implementing the quarantine, you can safely take the following steps.

- Scan and clean each and every infected machine. Since the machines are now off the network, this will be a manual scan.

- Log the incident, the hours/resources taken to clean the systems, and the systems that were affected.

- When you are certain the systems are clean, bring them online in stages (a few at a time). With each stage, check all machines to see that they are patched, updated, and have properly configured/running antivirus.

- Notify the appropriate organization leaders of the event and the actions you have taken.

- After you have dealt with the virus and notified the appropriate people, you should then have a meeting with appropriate IT staff to discuss what can be learned from this breach and how you might prevent it from occurring in the future.

## DoS Attacks

- If you have taken the steps outlined earlier in this book (such as properly configuring your router and your firewall to reduce the impact of any attempted DoS), then you will already be alleviating some of the damage from this type of attack. Use your firewall logs or IDS to find out which IP address (or addresses) originated the attacks. Note the IP addresses, and then (if your firewall supports this feature, and most do) deny that IP address access to your network.

- Use online resources (interNIC.net and so on) to find out who the address belongs to.

- Contact that organization and inform it of what is occurring.

- Log all of these activities and inform the appropriate organizational leaders.

- After you have dealt with the DoS and notified the appropriate people, you should have a meeting with appropriate IT staff to discuss what can be learned from this attack and how you might prevent it from occurring in the future.

## Intrusion by a Hacker

- Immediately copy the logs of all affected systems (firewall, targeted servers, and so on) for use as evidence.

- Immediately scan all systems for Trojan horses, changes to firewall settings, changes to port filtering, new services running, and so on. In essence, you are performing an emergency audit to see what damage has been done.

- Document everything. Of all of your documentation, this must be the most thorough. You must specify which IT personnel took what actions at what times. Some of this data may be part of later court proceedings, so absolute accuracy is necessary. It is probably a good idea to log all activities taken during this time and to have at least two people verify and sign the log.

- Change all affected passwords. Repair any damage done.

- Inform the appropriate business leaders of what has happened.

- After you have dealt with the breach and notified the appropriate people, you should have a meeting with appropriate IT staff to discuss what can be learned from this breach and how you might prevent it from occurring in the future.

These are just general guidelines, and some organizations may have much more specific actions they want taken in the event of some security breach. You should also bear in mind that throughout this book when we have discussed various sorts of threats to network security, we have mentioned particular steps and policies that should be taken. The policies in this chapter are meant to be in addition to any already outlined in this book. It is an unfortunate fact that some organizations have no plan for what to do in case of an emergency. It is important that you do have at least some generalized procedures you can implement.

# Defining Access Control

An important area of security policies that usually generates some controversy in any organization is access control. There is always a conflict between users' desire for unfettered access to any data or resources on the network and the security administrator's desire to protect that data and resources. This means that extremes in policies are not practical. You cannot simply lock down every resource as completely as possible since that would impede the user's access to those resources. Conversely, you cannot simply allow anyone and everyone complete access to everything. The core of access control is the concept introduced in Chapter 1, "Introduction to Computer Security": least privileges. Each person is given the minimum privileges necessary to do her job. No more and no less.

This is where the least privileges concept comes into play. The idea is simple. Each user, including IT personnel, gets the least access he can have and still effectively do his job. Rather than ask the question, "why not give this person access to X?" you should ask, "why give this person access to X?" And if you don't have a very good reason, then don't. This is one of the fundamentals of computer security. The more people that have access to any resource, the more likely some breach of security is to occur.

Along with, and related to, least privileges is the concept of implicit deny. Implicit deny means that all users are implicitly denied access to network resources until an administrator explicitly grants them.

Separation of duty, job rotation, and mandatory vacations are also important and related concepts. Separation of duty means that no one person can perform critical tasks; at least two individuals are needed. This prevents one person from accidently, or intentionally, causing some security breach via inappropriate use of critical functions. Both job rotation and mandatory vacations are used to make sure that, periodically, the person performing a given job changes. This makes it more difficult for one person to exploit her position to breach security.

Obviously, trade-offs must be made between access and security. Examples abound. One common example involves sales contact information. Clearly, a company's marketing department needs access to this data. However, what happens if your competitors get all of your company's contact information? That could allow them to begin targeting your current client list. This requires a trade-off between security and access. In this case, you would probably give salespeople access only to the contacts that are within their territory. No one other than the sales manager should have complete access to all the marketing data.

# Developmental Policies

Many IT departments include programmers and web developers. Unfortunately, many security policies do not address secure programming. No matter how good your firewalls, proxy server, virus scanning, and policies are, if your developers create code that is flawed, you will have security breaches. Clearly, the topic of secure programming requires a separate volume to explore thoroughly. Nonetheless, we can consider a brief checklist for defining secure development policies. If your company currently has no secure programming initiatives, this checklist is certainly better than developing in a vacuum. It can also serve as a starting point to get you thinking and talking about secure programming:

- All code, especially code done by outside parties (contractors, consultants, and so on) must be checked for backdoors/Trojan horses.

- All buffers must have error handling that prevents buffer overruns.

- All communication (such as using TCP sockets to send messages) must adhere to your organization's secure communications guidelines.

- Any code that opens any port or performs any sort of communication is thoroughly documented, and the IT security unit is apprised of the code, what it will do, and how it will be used.

- All input is filtered for items that might facilitate an attack, such as an SQL injection attack.

- All vendors should supply you with a signed document verifying that there are no security flaws in their code.

Following these guidelines will not guarantee that flawed code is immune from being introduced into your system, but it will certainly lower the odds significantly. And the unfortunate fact is that these simple steps alone are more than most organizations are taking. A very good place to look at security policies is the SANS Institute (www.sans.org/security-resources/policies/).

# Standards, Guidelines, and Procedures

Related to policies are standards, guidelines, and procedures. All of these documents are related to security policies and in fact support those policies. A *standard* is a general statement of the desired level of operation. For example, requiring 99.5% network uptime would be a standard. A *guideline* is a general suggestion on how to achieve some standard. Guidelines are broad and are sometimes optional (not mandatory). *Procedures* are specific instructions on how to handle a specific issue.

# Data Classification

It is critical to classify information within your organization. This process is common in defense department–related agencies and organizations. It is less common in the civilian sector. Classifying information provides employees with guidance on how to handle data. Classification can be as simple as two categories:

- *Public information* is information that can be disseminated publically to anyone. There are no restrictions on who can view the data.

- *Private information* is intended only for use internally in the organization. This type of information can potentially embarrass the company, disclose trade secrets, reveal corporate strategy, expose private personal data of employees or customers, or otherwise reveal information that your organization does not want revealed.

This two-tier approach to data classification is rather elementary. Most organizations will have multiple tiers. Each tier is defined by the damage that information disclosure could cause. We will take a look at Department of Defense clearance levels. These provide some insight into varying security classifications. Even if you work in an entirely civilian environment, reviewing the DoD approach can give you some suggestions on how to classify your data and how to properly evaluate which personnel should have access.

## DoD Clearances

The terms *secret* and *top secret* have specific meanings. The United States has a specific hierarchy of classification. The lowest is *confidential*. This is information that might damage national security if disclosed. *Secret* information is data that might cause serious damage to national security if disclosed. *Top secret* information is data that could be expected to cause exceptionally grave damage to national security if disclosed. There is another designation: *Top Secret SCI* or *Sensitive Compartmented Information*.

Each of these clearances requires a different level of investigation. For a secret clearance, a complete background check including criminal, work history, credit check, and check with various national agencies (Department of Homeland Security, Immigration, State Department, and so on) is required. This is referred to as an NACLC or National Agency Check with Law and Credit. The check for employment will cover the last 7 years. The secret clearance may or may not include a polygraph.

The top secret clearance is more rigorous, as you may imagine. It uses a Single Scope Background Investigation (SSBI). This means a complete NACL for the subject and spouse that goes back at least 10 years. It will also involve a subject interview conducted by a trained investigator. Direct verification of employment, education, birth, and citizenship are also required. At least four references are necessary, and at least two of those will be interviewed by investigators. A polygraph is also used. The SSBI is repeated every 5 years.

Sensitive Compartmented Information is assigned only after a complete SSBI has been completed. An SCI may have its own process for evaluating access; therefore, a standard description of what is involved is not available.

# Disaster Recovery

Before we can discuss disaster recovery, we have to define what a disaster is. A *disaster* is any event that significantly disrupts your organization's operations. A hard drive crash on a critical server is a disaster. Other examples would include fire, earthquake, your telecom provider being down, a labor strike that affects shipping to and from your business, and a hacker deleting critical files. Just keep in mind that any event that can significantly disrupt your organization's operations is a disaster.

## Disaster Recovery Plan

A disaster recovery plan (DRP) is the plan you have in place to return business to normal operations. This must include a number of items. You must address personnel issues, including being able to find temporary personnel if needed and being able to contact the personnel you have employed. It also includes having specific people assigned to specific tasks. If there is a disaster, who in your organization is tasked with the following:

- Locating alternative facilities
- Getting equipment to those facilities
- Installing and configuring software
- Setting up the network at the new facility
- Contacting staff, vendors, and customers

These are just a few questions that a disaster recovery plan must address.

## Business Continuity Plan

A business continuity plan (BCP) is similar to a DRP but with a different focus. The DRP is designed to get the organization back to full functionality as quickly as possible. A BCP is designed to get minimal business functions back up and running at least at some level so you can conduct some type of business. An example would be a retail store whose credit card processing system is down. Disaster recovery is concerned with getting the system back up and running, and business continuity is concerned with simply getting a temporary solution, such as processing credit cards manually.

To successfully formulate a BCP, you must consider those systems that are most critical for your business and have an alternative plan in case those systems are down. The alternative plan need not be perfect, just functional.

## Impact Analysis?

Before you can create a realistic DRP or BCP, you have to do an impact analysis of what damage to your organization a given disaster might be. This is called a *business impact analysis* or *business impact assessment* (BIA). Consider a web server crash. If your organization is an e-commerce business, then a web server crash is a very serious disaster. However, if your business is an accounting firm and the website is just a way for new customers to find you, then a web server crash is less critical. You can still do business and earn revenue while the web server is down. You should make a spreadsheet of various likely or plausible disasters and do a basic BIA for each.

A few things go into your BIA. One item to consider is the maximum tolerable downtime (MTD). How long can a given system be down before the effect is catastrophic and the business is unlikely to recover? Another item to consider is the mean time to repair (MTTR). How long is it likely to take to repair a given system if it is down? These factors help you determine the business impact of a given disaster.

## Fault Tolerance

The fact is that equipment fails. At some point all equipment fails. So fault tolerance is important. At the most basic level, fault tolerance for a server means a backup. If the server fails, did you back up the data so you can restore it? While database administrators may use a number of different types of data backups, from a security point of view there are three primary backup types we are concerned with:

- **Full:** All changes

- **Differential:** All changes since last full backup

- **Incremental:** All changes since last backup of any type

Consider a scenario where you do a full backup at 2 a.m. each morning. But you are concerned about the possibility of a server crash before the next full backup, so you want to do a backup every two hours. Well, the type of backup you choose will determine the efficiency of doing those frequent backups and the time needed to restore. So let's consider each scenario and what would happen if the system crashes at 10:05 a.m.

**Full:** In this scenario, you do a full backup at 4 a.m., 6 a.m., …10 a.m., and then the system crashes. Well, to restore, you just have to restore the last full backup, done at 10 a.m. This makes restoration much simpler. However, running a full backup every 2 hours is very time consuming and resource intensive and will have a significant negative impact on your server's performance.

**Differential:** In this scenario, you do a differential backup at 4 a.m., 6 a.m., …10 a.m., and then the system crashes. To restore, you will need to restore the last full backup done at 2 a.m. and the most recent differential backup done at 10 a.m. This is just a little more complicated than the full backup strategy. However, those differential backups are going to get larger each time you do them, and thus more time consuming and resource intensive. While they won't have the impact of the full backups, they will still slow down your network.

**Incremental:** In this scenario, you do an incremental backup at 4 a.m., 6 a.m., …10 a.m., and then the system crashes. To restore, you need to restore the last full backup done at 2 a.m. and then each incremental backup done since then, and they must be restored in order. This is much more complex to restore, but each incremental backup is small and does not take much time or consume many resources.

There is no "best" backup strategy. Which one you select will depend on your organization's needs. Whatever backup strategy you choose, you must periodically test it. The only effective way to test your backup strategy is to actually restore the backup data to a test machine.

The other fundamental aspect of fault tolerance is RAID, or redundant array of independent disks. RAID allows your servers to have more than one hard drive, so that if the main hard drive fails, the system keeps functioning. The primary RAID levels are described here:

- RAID 0 (striped disks) distributes data across multiple disks in a way that gives improved speed at any given instant. There is no fault tolerance.

- RAID 1 mirrors the contents of the disks, making a form of 1:1 ratio real-time backup. This is also called mirroring.

- RAID 3 or 4 (striped disks with dedicated parity) combines three or more disks in a way that protects data against loss of any one disk. Fault tolerance is achieved by adding an extra disk to the array and dedicating it to storing parity information. The storage capacity of the array is reduced by one disk.

- RAID 5 (striped disks with distributed parity) combines three or more disks in a way that protects data against the loss of any one disk. It is similar to RAID 3, but the parity is not stored on one dedicated drive; instead, parity information is interspersed across the drive array. The storage capacity of the array is a function of the number of drives minus the space needed to store parity.

- RAID 6 (striped disks with dual parity) combines four or more disks in a way that protects data against loss of any two disks.

- RAID 1+0 (or 10) is a mirrored data set (RAID 1) that is then striped (RAID 0), hence the "1+0" name. A RAID 1+0 array requires a minimum of four drives: two mirrored drives to hold half of the striped data, plus another two mirrored for the other half of the data.

A server without at least RAID level 1 is gross negligence on the part of the network administrator. RAID 5 is actually very popular with servers.

While RAID and backup strategies are the fundamental issues of fault tolerance, any backup system provides additional fault tolerance. This can include uninterruptable power supplies, backup generators, and redundant Internet connections.

# Important Laws

There are a number of computer laws in various countries, states, and provinces. It is important to be familiar with the laws that are relevant to your jurisdiction. However, there are a few laws that are most critical in the United States. We will discuss each of those here.

# HIPAA

The *Health Insurance Portability and Accountability Act (HIPAA)* is a regulation that mandates national standards and procedures for the storage, use, and transmission of personal medical information. Passed into law in 1996, HIPAA has caused a great deal of change in healthcare record keeping.

HIPAA covers three areas—confidentiality, privacy, and security of patient records—and was implemented in phases to make the transition easier. Confidentiality and privacy of patient records had to be implemented by a set date, followed by security of patient records. Standards for transaction codes in medical record transmissions had to be completed by a given date as well.

The penalties for HIPAA violations are very stiff: They can be as high as $250,000 based on the circumstances. Medical practices are required to appoint a security officer. All related parties, such as billing agencies and medical records storage facilities, are required to comply with these regulations.

# Sarbanes-Oxley

The legislation came into force in 2002 and introduced major changes to the regulation of financial practice and corporate governance. Named after Senator Paul Sarbanes and Representative Michael Oxley, this law is designed to make publically traded corporations more accountable.

The legislation focuses primarily on financial issues, but it also affects the IT departments whose job it is to store a corporation's electronic records. The Sarbanes-Oxley Act states that all business records, including electronic records and electronic messages, must be saved for "not less than five years." The consequences for noncompliance are fines, imprisonment, or both.

# Payment Card Industry Data Security Standards

While not a law, the Payment Card Industry Data Security Standards (PCI DSS) are certainly something any IT security professional who works for a company that handles credit cards and debit cards should be familiar with. PCI DSS is a proprietary information security standard for organizations that handle branded credit cards from the major card schemes including Visa, MasterCard, American Express, and Discover.

# Summary

In this chapter, you learned that technology is not enough to ensure a secure network. You must have clear and specific policies detailing procedures on your network. Those policies must cover employee computer resource use, new employees, outgoing employees, access rights, how to respond to an emergency, and even how secure code in applications and websites is.

User policies must cover all aspects of how the user is expected to use company technology. In some cases, such as instant messaging and web use, policies may be difficult to enforce, but that does not change the fact that they must still be in place. If your user policies fail to cover a particular area of technology use, then you will have difficulty taking any action against an employee who performs that particular misuse.

We also learned that it is not just the end user who will need policies. The IT staff needs clearly delineated policies covering how to handle various situations. Of particular concern will be policies dictating how to handle new users or exiting users. You also need a carefully considered change management policy.

## Test Your Skills

## MULTIPLE CHOICE QUESTIONS

1. Which of the following does not demonstrate the need for policies?

    A. Antivirus software cannot prevent a user from downloading infected files.

    B. The most secure password is not at all secure if it's posted on a note by the computer.

    C. End users are generally not particularly bright and must be told everything.

    D. Technological security measures are dependent upon the employees' implementation.

2. Which of the following is not an area that user policies need to cover?

    A. Minimum length of passwords

    B. What websites one can or cannot visit

    C. If and when to share passwords

    D. What to do if you believe your password has been compromised

3. Which of the following is not an example of a user password policy?

    A. Users may not keep copies of passwords in their office.

    B. Passwords must be eight characters long.

    C. Users may only share passwords with their assistant.

    D. Passwords may not be shared with any employee.

4. What should an employee do if she believes her password has been revealed to another party?

   A. If it is a trusted employee or friend, just ignore it.

   B. Change your own password immediately.

   C. Notify the IT department.

   D. Ignore it.

5. Which of the following should not be recommended as acceptable email attachments?

   A. Flash animations

   B. Excel spreadsheets from a colleague

   C. Attachments you were expecting

   D. Plain text attachments from known sources

6. Which of the following is the best reason users should be prohibited from installing software?

   A. They may not install it correctly, which could cause security problems for the work-station.

   B. They may install software that circumvents security.

   C. Software installation is often complex and should be done by professionals.

   D. If a user's account does not have privileges to install, then it is likely that a Trojan horse will not be inadvertently installed under their account.

7. Which of the following is not a significant security risk posed by instant messaging?

   A. Employees may send harassing messages.

   B. Employees might send out confidential information.

   C. A virus or worm might infect the workstation via instant messaging.

   D. An instant messaging program could actually be a Trojan horse.

8. What must all user policies have in order to be effective?

   A. They must be reviewed by an attorney.

   B. They must have consequences.

   C. They must be notarized.

   D. They must be properly filed and maintained.

9. Which of the following is the appropriate sequence of events for a new employee?

    A. IT is notified of the new employee and the requested resources > employee is granted access to those resources > employee is briefed on security/acceptable use > employee signs acknowledging receipt of a copy of security rules.

    B. IT is notified of the new employee and the requested rights > employee is given access to those resources > employee signs acknowledging a receipt of a copy of security rules.

    C. IT is notified of the new employee and assigns default rights > employee is briefed on security/acceptable use > employee signs acknowledging receipt of a copy of security rules.

    D. IT is notified of the new employee and assigns default rights > employee signs acknowledging receipt of company security rules.

10. Which of the following is the appropriate sequence of events for a departing employee?

    A. IT is notified of the departure > all logon accounts are shut down > all access (physical and electronic) is disabled.

    B. IT is notified of the departure > all logon accounts are shut down > all access (physical and electronic) is disabled > the employee's workstation is searched/scanned.

    C. IT is notified of the departure > all physical access is shut down > all electronic access is shut down.

    D. IT is notified of the departure > all electronic access is shut down > all physical access is shut down.

11. Which of the following is the appropriate sequence for a change request?

    A. Business unit manager requests change > IT unit verifies request > request is implemented.

    B. Business unit manager requests change > IT unit verifies request > security unit verifies request > request is scheduled with rollback plan > request is implemented.

    C. Business unit manager requests change > IT unit verifies request > request is scheduled with rollback plan > request is implemented.

    D. Business unit manager requests change > IT unit verifies request > security unit verifies request > request is implemented.

12. What is the first step when discovering a machine(s) has been infected with a virus?

    A. Log the incident.

    B. Scan and clean infected machine(s).

    C. Notify appropriate management.

    D. Quarantine infected machine(s).

13. What is the rule in access control?

  A. The most access you can securely give

  B. The least access job requirements allow

  C. Standard access for all users

  D. Strictly limited access for most users

14. After dealing, on a technical level, with any security breach, what is the last thing to be done for a security breach?

  A. Quarantine infected machines.

  B. Study the breach to learn how to prevent a recurrence.

  C. Notify management.

  D. Log the incident.

15. Which of the following is a list of items that should be implemented in all secure code?

  A. All code checked for backdoors or Trojans, all buffers have error handling to prevent buffer overruns, all communication activity thoroughly documented

  B. All code checked for backdoors or Trojans, all buffers have error handling to prevent buffer overruns, all communication adheres to organizational guidelines, all communication activity thoroughly documented

  C. All code checked for backdoors or Trojans, all buffers have error handling to prevent buffer overruns, all communication adheres to organizational guidelines

  D. All code checked for backdoors or Trojans, all communication adheres to organizational guidelines, all communication activity thoroughly documented

## EXERCISES

Each of these exercises is intended to give the student experience writing limited portions of a policy. Taken together, the exercises represent a complete policy for a college campus computer network.

### EXERCISE 10.1: User Policies

Using the guidelines provided in this chapter (and other resources as needed), create a document that defines user policies. The policies should clearly define acceptable and unacceptable use for all personnel. You may require some separate policies for administration, faculty, and students.

### EXERCISE 10.2: New Student Policy

Using the guidelines provided in this chapter (and other resources as needed), create a step-by-step IT security policy for implementing a new user account for a student.

The policy should define what resources the student has access to, what she does not have access to, and for how long access is granted.

## EXERCISE 10.3: Leaving Student Policy

Using the guidelines provided in this chapter (and other resources as needed), create a step-by-step IT security policy for handling user accounts/rights for a student who is leaving prematurely (drops, is expelled, and so on).

You will need to consider specialized student scenarios, such as a student who works as an assistant to a faculty member or as a lab assistant in a computer lab and may have access to resources most students do not.

## EXERCISE 10.4: New Faculty/Staff Policy

Using the guidelines provided in this chapter (and other resources as needed), create a step-by-step IT security policy for implementing a new user account for a faculty or staff member.

The policy should define what resources the faculty or staff member has access to, what she does not have access to, and any restrictions. (Hint: Unlike student policies, you won't need to define time length since it should be indefinite.)

## EXERCISE 10.5: Leaving Faculty/Staff Policy

Write a policy for how to handle a faculty departure (quit, fired, retired, and so on). Use the guidelines in this chapter and any other resources you like to get you started.

Make certain you consider not only shutting down access but also the possibility of proprietary research material existing on the faculty/staff member's workstation.

## EXERCISE 10.6: Student Lab Use Policy

Considering the material in this chapter, create a set of policies for acceptable use of computer lab computers.

Make sure to specify web use, email use, and any other acceptable uses.

Carefully spell out unacceptable usage. (Is game playing acceptable?)

## PROJECTS

### PROJECT 10.1: Examining Policies

1. Examine the following web resources that discuss security policies:

    - **EarthLink acceptable use policy:** www.earthlink.net/about/policies/use/
    - **SANS Institute policies:** www.sans.org/resources/policies/
    - **Information Security Policy World:** www.information-security-policies-and-standards.com/

2. Summarize the main theme of these policy recommendations. Pay particular attention to any area that these recommendations differ from or exceed the recommendations of this chapter.

3. Choose which policy recommendation you believe is the most secure, and state the reasons for your choice.

## PROJECT 10.2: **Real-World Security Policies**

Ask a local business or your college to let you see its security policies. Study the policies carefully.

1. Summarize the main theme of these policy recommendations. Pay particular attention to any area that these recommendations differ from or exceed the recommendations of this chapter.

2. Choose which policy recommendation you believe is the most secure and state the reasons for your choice.

## PROJECT 10.3: **Creating Security Policies**

Note: This works well as a group project.

At this point in the book, you have studied security including policies. After this chapter and the proceeding exercises and projects, you have examined several polices from various web resources and the policies of some actual organizations.

Take the brief policies you created for the exercises in this chapter and expand them to create an entire working security policy for your college. You will need to add administrative policies, developmental policies, and more.

---

### Case Study

Hector is a security administrator for a defense contractor. This business frequently works with highly sensitive, classified material. Hector has developed a policy for departing employees. This policy handles everything mentioned in this chapter:

- All logon accounts to any server, VPN, network, or other resource are disabled.
- All keys to the facility are returned.
- All accounts for email, Internet access, wireless Internet, cell phones, and so on are shut off.
- Any accounts for mainframe resources are canceled.
- The employee's workstation hard drive is searched.

Given the highly sensitive nature of the work at this company, what other actions might you add to this policy?

# Chapter | **11**

# Network Scanning and Vulnerability Scanning

## *Chapter Objectives*

**After reading this chapter and completing the exercises, you will be able to do the following:**

- Understand how to secure a system
- Probe a system for vulnerabilities
- Use vulnerability scanning tools
- Evaluate potential security consultants

## Introduction

At this point, it should be clear that it is necessary to assess any system periodically for vulnerabilities. The first part of this chapter will discuss the essential steps that you should follow in assessing a system for vulnerabilities. The purpose of this chapter is to get someone who is new to computer security to begin thinking about these issues. This chapter is not meant to be a comprehensive treatment of the subject or a substitute for getting an expert consultant. In fact, most security topics, such as disaster recovery, cryptography, and policies, have had entire volumes written on them. However, this chapter should give you a basic blueprint you can follow. Specific details will depend on your particular environment, budget, skills, and security needs. The second part of this chapter will discuss various tools you can use to scan your network for vulnerabilities.

In this book, you have thus far examined a number of threats to individual computers and networks. You have learned specific defenses against each of these dangers. However, you have not yet looked at a comprehensive approach to security. In the second part of this chapter, you will learn many of the security procedures that can be implemented to provide your environment with more secure computing.

Note that this chapter is about overall procedures that you need to perform in securing a system rather than specific step-by-step techniques.

# Basics of Assessing a System

Knowing where to begin with system security can be daunting for those new to security. To keep it simple and easy to remember, the stages of assessing a system's security can be separated into the six Ps:

- Patch
- Ports
- Protect
- Policies
- Probe
- Physical

## Patch

The first rule of computer security is to check patches. This is true for networks, home computers, laptops, tablets, smart phones, literally any computer. This means that the operating system, database management systems, development tools, Internet browsers, and so forth are all checked for patches. In a Microsoft environment, this should be easy, as the Microsoft website has a utility that will scan your system for any required patches to the browser, operating system, or Office products. It is a very basic tenet of security to ensure that all patches are up to date. This should be one of the first tasks when assessing a system.

It is also important to consider the types of patches. The most important are labeled *important* or *critical*. (Microsoft labels them critical, but other vendors may use another designation.) These must be applied; without them your system simply is not secure. Next are recommended patches. These should be applied unless you have some compelling reason not to. Finally, we have optional patches. Your system will not be vulnerable without these. These optional patches usually enhance or correct some minor functionality in the system but are not necessary for security.

---

### FYI: Patching and Applications

Whenever there is a patch to an operating system or application, there is also documentation (sometimes in a Read Me file, sometimes at the download site) that indicates what the patch is fixing. This documentation also lists any known adverse interactions with other applications. Therefore, you should always read this documentation before you install a patch. In most cases, the problems are minimal and often involve obscure situations. But it is always good to check first to make sure that a service or application upon which you are dependent is not adversely impacted.

> ### FYI: Ports on Routers
>
> One security flaw seen in many organizations that are otherwise security conscious is a failure to close ports on routers. This is particularly a problem for large organizations with wide area networks (WANs) spread over multiple locations. The router between each location should be filtered and too often is not.
>
> Once you have ensured that all patches are up to date, the next step is to set up a system to ensure that they are kept up to date. One simple method is to initiate a periodic patch review where, at a scheduled time, all machines are checked for patches. There are also automated solutions that will patch all systems in your organization. It is imperative that all machines be patched, not just the servers.
>
> The question becomes when to patch. For home users it is usually recommended that automatic patching is turned on so that their systems get patched as soon as the patch is available. However, this is not recommended for network administrators. It is entirely possible that a particular patch may not be compatible with some software on your network. A good example occurred in 2010 with McAfee AntiVirus Business Edition. In April 2010, an update to McAfee caused computers running Windows XP Service Pack 3 to shut down. This caused a great many problems for networks with Windows XP workstations. It is recommended that you install patches on a test machine that has an identical configuration to your network's workstations. Then after the patch has been tested, it can be pushed out to the network.

## Ports

As you learned in Chapter 2, "Networks and the Internet," all communication takes place via some port. Any port you do not explicitly need should be shut down. This means that those unused services on servers and individual workstations should be shut down. Both Windows (XP, Vista, 7, 8, and 10) and Linux have built-in port-filtering capability. Windows 2000 Professional was the first Windows operating system to include port-filtering capability. Windows XP expanded this to a fully functional firewall. And more recently, Windows 7 added a firewall that could block outgoing as well as incoming traffic. Shutting down a service in Windows and port filtering are both discussed in more detail later.

You should also shut down any unused router ports in your network. If your network is part of a larger WAN, then it is likely you have a router connecting you to that WAN. Every open port is a possible avenue of entry for a malware or intruder. Therefore, every port you can close is one less opportunity for such attacks to affect your system.

## In Practice

### Shutting Down a Service in Windows

For an individual machine that is not running firewall software, you do not directly close ports; instead, you shut down the service using that port. For example, if you do not use an FTP service but you see that port is on, chances are that you unknowingly have an FTP service running on that machine. In Windows (7 or later) or in Windows Server 2008 (or later), if you have administrative privileges, the following three steps can be taken to shut down an unneeded service.

1. Go to the Control Panel. Double-click Administrative Tools. (Note in Windows 7 and 8 that you first have to click on System and Security.)

2. Double-click Services. You should see a window similar to the one shown in Figure 11.1.

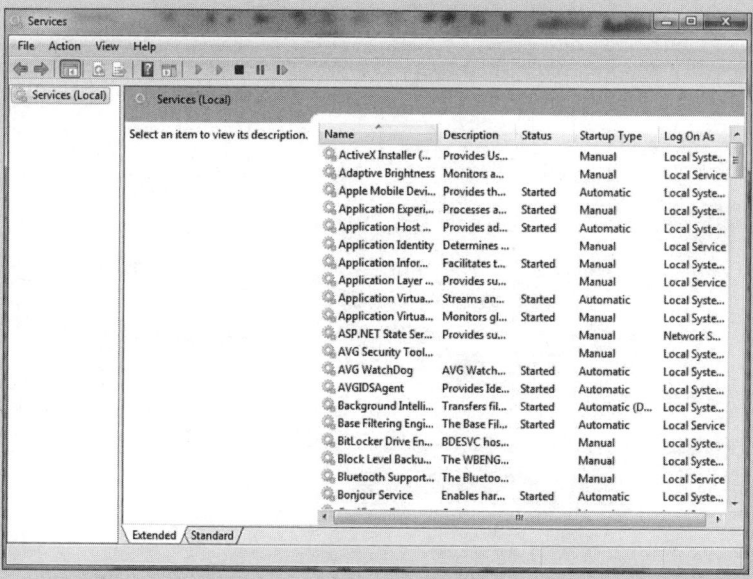

**FIGURE 11.1**   Services.

The window in Figure 11.1 shows all services installed on your machine, whether they are running or not. Notice that the window also displays information about whether a service is running, whether it starts up automatically, and so forth. In Windows XP, more information can be seen by selecting an individual service. When you double-click on an individual service in any version of Windows (Windows XP, Vista, 7, Server 2003, or Server 2008), you see a dialog box similar to Figure 11.2 that describes the details about that service.

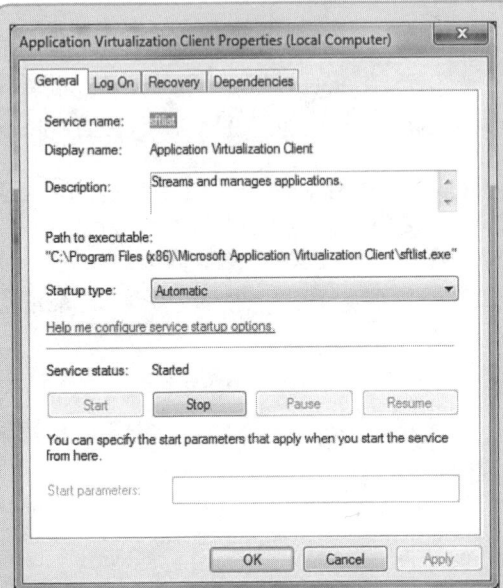

**FIGURE 11.2**    Disabled services.

In the example shown in Figure 11.1, you see a service on a machine that does not require it. To illustrate the procedure, this service is going to be disabled. Before you turn off any service, however, you need to check whether other services depend on the one you are about to shut off. If other services depend on the one you want to turn off and you proceed to turn it off, you will cause the other services to fail.

1. Click on the Dependencies tab. In our case, the service has no dependencies.

2. Click the General tab.

3. Change the Startup type to Disabled.

4. Click the Stop button in the Service status section, if necessary. Your dialog box should look similar to Figure 11.2. The fax service is now shut down.

5. Click OK to accept the edits made and close the Properties dialog box. Close the Services dialog box and the Administrative Tools dialog box.

Shutting down unneeded ports and services is an essential and very basic part of computer security. As mentioned, every port open (and every service running) is a possible avenue for a hacker or virus to get to your machine. Therefore, the rule is: If you don't need it, shut it down and block it.

It is best for you to first make a list of all software that you are running. Then look up the ports and protocols that you will need for that software and allow only those. It is important to keep in mind that these are ports for incoming traffic. If your machine is not used as a database server, web server, or other type of server and if your machine is a stand-alone one, you can (and should) close all ports. Workstations on networks may need some ports open for network utilities. We will examine some interesting utilities later in this chapter.

## Protect

The next phase of assessing a system's security is to ensure that all reasonable protective software and devices are employed. This means, at a minimum, a firewall between your network and the outside world. Firewalls were discussed in Chapter 2. You should also consider using an intrusion detection system (IDS) on that firewall and any web servers. Remember that we discussed Snort IDS in Chapter 9. An IDS is considered nonessential by some security experts; you can certainly have a secure network without one. However, an IDS is the only way to know of impending attacks, and there are free, open source IDSs available. For that reason, I highly recommend them. The firewall and IDS will provide basic security to your network's perimeter, but you also need virus scanning. Each and every machine, including servers, must have a virus scanner that is updated regularly. The point has already been made that a virus infection is the greatest threat to most networks. As also previously discussed, it is probably prudent to consider antispyware software on all of your systems. This will prevent users of your network from inadvertently running spyware on the network.

### In Practice

#### Finding a Firewall

When selecting a firewall to use, you have a number of options. You can purchase a very inexpensive router-based firewall for your high-speed Internet connection. You can get a router that is separate from your DSL or cable router. Or you can get one that includes the functions of your cable or DSL router with the firewall. The websites listed next should be helpful to you in finding more information on these options and determining which will best suit your needs.

- **Linksys:** http://www.linksys.com/us/ (Note: Linksys was purchased by Cisco.)
- **Home PC Firewall Guide:** www.firewallguide.com/
- **Broadband Guide:** www.firewallguide.com/broadband.htm

In addition to the information on the firewall options available, you can find many free or very inexpensive firewall packages on the Internet. Following is a list of some of the more popular firewalls available via the Internet.

- **Norton Personal Firewall:** This product is inexpensive and is available for multiple operating systems. A free trial download is available from www.symantec.com.
- **McAfee Personal Firewall:** This product is similar in price and basic function to Norton Personal Firewall. You can find out more about this product at http://us.mcafee.com.
- **Outpost Firewall:** This product is designed for the home or small office user. It has both a free version and an enhanced commercial version. You can find out more about this product at http://www.agnitum.com/index.php.

For medium-sized or larger networks, with more flexible budgets, you might consider the following:

- Citrix offers an application gateway specifically tailored for web servers. This solution is relatively inexpensive and can be ideal for companies whose primary function is to provide websites or web services. Information is available at https://www.citrix.com/products/netscaler-application-delivery-controller/tech-info.html

Finally, for Linux users, you have a built-in firewall called IP Tables; this is the successor to the earlier IP Chains. It is an excellent solution for any system using Linux.

## Policies

While policies were discussed in detail in Chapter 10, "Security Policies," we briefly review some aspects of policies here. It is absolutely essential that any organization have clearly written policies on computer security—and that those policies be strongly enforced by management. Those policies should cover acceptable use of organizational computers, the Internet, email, and any other aspect of the system. Policies should prohibit the installation of any software on the systems. Only IT personnel should install software, and only after they have verified its safety.

Policies should also advise users against opening unknown/unexpected attachments. Something that I recommend is for people within an organization or department to use a codeword. If that codeword does not appear in the body of the email (or in the subject line), then they do not open the attachment. Most virus attacks spread via email attachments. The subject line and body of such email messages are generated automatically by the virus itself. If all of your legitimate attachments have a codeword in the subject line, it is highly unlikely that this word would be in the subject line of an email sent by a virus. This alone could prevent your users from inadvertently opening a virus.

Polices should also be in place that clearly delineate who has access to what data, how backups are performed, and what to do to recover data in the case of a disaster (commonly called a *disaster recovery plan*). Data access must be limited to only those personnel with an actual need to access the data. For example, not everyone in the human resources department needs access to disciplinary files on all employees. Does your organization have a plan for what to do if a fire destroys your servers with all their data? Where do you get new machines? Who gets them? Is there an offsite copy of the data backup? All of these questions must be addressed in a disaster recovery plan.

There should be a policy regarding passwords: acceptable minimum length, lifetime of a password, password history, and passwords to be avoided, such as any word that has a direct connection to the user. For example, a user who is a big fan of the Dallas Cowboys should not use a password that has any relation to that sports team. Also, passwords that relate to personal data, such as spouse's birthday, children's names, or pet names, are poor choices. A password policy could also include recommendations or restrictions on a password.

## FYI: Good Passwords

Many sources claim a good password is at least 8 (preferably 15) characters long; contains letters, numbers, and characters; and combines upper- and lowercase. After learning about rainbow tables earlier in this book, you are probably aware that an even longer password might be needed. I usually recommend a passphrase. Start with something easy like "cheese burgers from Burger King." Now put it all together in one word, use some capitalization, and change some letters to numbers !!!k3ch33s3burg3rsfrombuRG3rk1ng.

You can memorize that with surprising ease, and it is very difficult to guess or even to crack with a rainbow table.

Additionally, a password should not be kept for long periods of time. A 90- or 180-day password replacement schedule is good for most situations. More secure environments might require 30 or even fewer days. Microsoft recommends 42 days (six weeks). This is referred to as *password age*. (This, of course, must be weighed against the user's access to sensitive information or data. A company financial officer might change her password weekly; a nuclear arms engineer might change his password daily; and a mail clerk might need to change her password on a much less frequent basis.)You can set many systems (including Windows) to force the user to get a new password after a certain period of time. You should also make sure the person does not merely reuse old passwords, referred to as *password history* and also referred to in some operating systems as uniqueness. A good rule of thumb is a history depth of five—meaning that the person cannot reuse any of her previous five passwords. Additionally, you may need to implement a minimum password age to prevent users from immediately changing their password five times to return to her current password. Generally, a minimum of one day is recommended.

## FYI: How Extensive Should Policies Be?

This question frequently arises: How extensive should policies be? Should they be a few brief pages or a lengthy manual? Various computer security experts will have differing opinions. My opinion is that the policies should be lengthy enough to cover your organizational needs but not so lengthy as to be unwieldy. In short, overly long policy manuals are likely to be left unread by employees and hence not be followed. If you absolutely must have a long policy manual, then create a few brief submanuals for specific employee groups so as to increase the chances of the policies being read and followed. It is probably a good idea to have new hires briefed on security polices by someone from the IT Security department.

## FYI: Checklists and Policies

For your convenience and to assist in getting you started in securing your systems and establishing good policies, the SANS Institute website contains examples of checklists and policies (www.sans.org/security-resources/policies/). Each of these is also available electronically through the companion website for this text.

Finally, policies should include specific instructions on what to do in case of an employee termination. It is imperative that all of that person's login accounts be immediately disabled and any physical access he has to any part of the system be immediately discontinued. Unfortunately, many organizations fail to address this properly and give an opportunity to a disgruntled former employee to inflict retribution on his former employer.

## Probe

An important step in assessing any network is to probe the network. We will look at several probes later in this chapter. The key is to periodically probe your own network for security flaws. This should be a regularly scheduled event—perhaps once a quarter. At a minimum, a complete audit of your security should be completed once per year. That would, of course, include probing your ports. However, a true security audit would also include a review of your security policies, your patching system, any security logs you maintain, personnel files of those in secure positions, and so forth.

## Physical

Lastly, you cannot ignore physical security. The most robustly secure computer that is left sitting unattended in an unlocked room is not at all secure. You must have some policy or procedure governing the locking of rooms with computers as well as the handling of laptops, PDAs, and other mobile computer devices. Servers must be in a locked and secure room with as few people as is reasonably possible having access to them. Backup tapes should be stored in a fireproof safe. Documents and old backup tapes should be destroyed before disposal (for example, by melting tapes, magnetizing hard disks, breaking CDs).

Physical access to routers and hubs should also be tightly controlled. Having the most hi-tech, professional information security on the planet but leaving your server in an unlocked room to which everyone has access is a recipe for disaster. One of the most common mistakes in the arena of physical security is co-locating a router or switch in a janitorial closet. This means that, in addition to your own security personnel and network administrators, the entire cleaning staff has access to your router or switch, and any one of them could leave the door unlocked for an extended period of time.

There are some basic rules you should follow regarding physical security:

- **Server rooms:** The room where servers are kept should be the most fire-resistant room in your building. It should have a strong door with a strong lock, such as a deadbolt. Only those personnel who actually have a need to go in the room should have a key. You might also consider a server room log wherein each person logs in when she enters or exits the room. There are actually electronic locks that record who enters a room, when she enters, and when she leaves. You may also wish to consider using biometric locks on critical areas such as server rooms. Consult local security vendors in your area for more details on price and availability.

- **Workstations:** All workstations should have an engraved identifying mark. You should also routinely inventory them. It is usually physically impossible to secure them as well as you secure servers, but you can take a few steps to improve their security. Some companies choose to attach the workstations to the desks with cables. This can be effective and affordable.

- **Miscellaneous equipment:** Projectors, CD burners, laptops, and so forth should be kept under lock and key. Any employee who wishes to use one should be required to sign it out, and it should be checked to see that it is in proper working condition and that all parts are present when it is returned.

# Securing Computer Systems

In this section, you will examine various security specifics for an individual workstation, a server, and a network. You should be aware, however, that you do not need to reinvent the wheel. A number of very reputable organizations have put together step-by-step guides, or security templates, that you can use in your network setting. These can be modified to fit your particular organization, or they can be used as a starting point for you in forming your own security strategy.

- The National Security Agency has a website with a number of specific network security guides: https://www.nsa.gov/ia/mitigation_guidance/security_configuration_guides/

- The Center for Internet Security offers a number of security guides and benchmarks: https://www.cisecurity.org/

- The SANS institute has a number of sample policies you can download and modify or use: www.sans.org/resources/policies/

There are also templates that can be applied to many operating systems and applications (such as Microsoft Windows and Microsoft Exchange) that will implement certain security precautions. These templates can be found for many products and then simply installed on the appropriate machine. Some security professionals prefer to handle the details of security themselves, but many administrators find these templates to be useful—and they can be invaluable for the beginner.

- Windows Security templates: https://support.microsoft.com/en-us/kb/816585

- MS Exchange templates: https://technet.microsoft.com/en-us/library/bb676692(v=exchg.80).aspx

- A collection of Windows templates: http://www.windowsecurity.com/articles-tutorials/misc_network_security/Understanding-Windows-Security-Templates.html. The use of these templates will at least give you a baseline of security on the applications to which they are applied.

## Securing an Individual Workstation

There are a number of steps that any prudent individual can take to make his own computer secure. These steps should be taken for both home computers and workstations on a network. In the former case, securing the individual computer is the only security option available. In the latter case, securing the individual computers as well as the perimeter allows for a layered approach to security. While some network administrators simply secure the perimeter via a firewall and/or proxy server, it is generally believed that you should also secure each machine in your organization. This is particularly vital in protecting against virus attacks and some of the distributed denial of service attacks that you learned about in Chapter 4, "Denial of Service Attacks."

### FYI: Hardening a System

The process of securing a computer system against hackers, malware, and other intruders is sometimes referred to as hardening a system. You may see the terms *server hardening* or *router hardening* commonly used.

The first step with an individual computer is to ensure that all patches are appropriately applied. Microsoft's website has utilities that will scan your machine for needed patches for both Windows and Microsoft Office. It is critical that you do this on a regular basis—once per quarter as a minimum. You should also check your other software vendors to see whether they have some similar mechanism to update patches for their products. It is amazing how many virus outbreaks have been widespread despite patches being available to secure the flaws they exploited. Too many people simply do not ensure that patches are applied regularly. For a home computer, this is the most critical step in your security strategy and will protect you from a number of attacks designed to exploit security flaws. For a networked workstation, this is still a vital piece of the overall security strategy and cannot be ignored.

The second step in securing an individual computer is restricting the ability to install programs or alter the machine configuration. In a network environment, this would mean that most users do not have permissions to install software or change system settings. Only network administrators and designated support staff should have that ability. In a home environment, this would mean that only a responsible party or parties (such as the parents) have access rights to install software.

One of the reasons for this particular precaution is to prevent users from accidentally installing a Trojan horse or other malware on their machine. If a person is prevented from installing any software, then there is no chance of inadvertently installing improper software such as a Trojan horse, adware, or other malware. Blocking users from altering the machine's configuration also prevents them from changing system security settings. Novice users may hear of some way to change some setting and will do so, not realizing the security risks they are exposing their system to.

A perfect example in which a novice might adversely alter security settings involves the Windows Messenger service. This is not used for chat rooms or instant messaging, as many novices incorrectly assume. It is instead used for network administrators to send a broadcast message to all people on a network. Unfortunately, some adware programs also use that service to circumvent pop-up blockers and inundate you with ads. Thus, a security-conscious person might disable that service. You would not want an inexperienced person to turn it back on by thinking it is needed for instant messaging.

It is absolutely critical in any network environment that limits be placed on what the average user can do to a machine's configuration. Without such limits, even well-meaning employees could eventually compromise security. This particular step is often met with some resistance from the organization. If you are in charge of a system's security, it is your job to educate the decision makers as to why this step is so critical.

The next step has been discussed previously in this book. Each and every computer must have antivirus and antispyware software. You must also set it to routinely automatically update its virus definitions. Updated, running antivirus software is an integral part of any security solution. The two-pronged approach of antispyware and antivirus software should be a major component in your individual computer security strategy. Some analysts feel that antispyware is a nice extra but not a critical component. Others contend that spyware is a rapidly growing problem and will probably eventually equal or surpass the dangers of virus attacks.

Of course, if your operating system has a built-in firewall, it is a good idea to configure it and have it turned on. Windows (7, 8, and 10) and Linux both come with built-in firewall features. Turn them on and configure them properly. The only significant problem you may encounter in implementing this step is that most networks require a certain amount of traffic between key servers (such as the DNS server) and individual computers. When you configure your firewall, make certain you are allowing appropriate traffic through. If you are at home, you can simply block all incoming traffic. If you are on a network, you must identify what traffic you need to allow.

Passwords and physical security, as discussed earlier in this chapter, are a critical part of computer security. You must ensure that all users utilize passwords that are at least eight characters long and consist of a combination of letters, numbers, and characters. In general, make sure that your password policy is complete and that all employees follow it. This will ensure that your physical security system is sound.

Following these guidelines will not make your computer totally impervious to danger, but these guidelines will make your workstation as secure as it reasonably can be. Remember that, even in a network environment, it is critical to also secure each computer as well as the perimeter.

## Securing a Server

The core of any network lies in its servers. This includes database servers, web servers, DNS servers, file and print servers, and so on. These computers provide the resources for the rest of the network. Generally, your most critical data will be stored on these machines. This means that these computers are an especially attractive target for intruders, and securing them is of paramount importance.

Essentially, to secure a server, you should apply the steps you would to any workstation and then add additional steps. There will not be a user on that machine routinely typing documents or using spreadsheets, so extra-tight restrictions are unlikely to cause the same difficulties for end users that they might on a workstation.

To begin with, you must follow the same steps you would for a workstation. Each and every server should have its software routinely patched. It should also have virus-scanning software and perhaps antispyware as well. It is critical that access to these machines, both via logging on and physical access, be limited to only those people with a clear need. There are, however, additional steps you should take with a server that you might not take with a standard workstation.

Most operating systems for servers (e.g., Windows 2008 Server, Linux) have the ability to log a variety of activities. These activities would include failed logon attempts, software installation, and other activities. You should make sure that logging is turned on and that all actions that might pose a security risk are logged. You then must make certain that those logs are checked on a periodic basis.

Remember that the data on a server is more valuable than the actual machine. For this reason, data must be backed up on a regular basis. A daily backup is usually preferred but, in some cases, a weekly backup might be adequate. The backup tapes should be kept in a secure offsite location (such as a bank safety deposit box) or in a fireproof safe. It is critical that you limit access to those backup tapes just as you would limit access to the servers themselves.

With any computer, you should shut down any service you do not need. However, with a server, you may wish to take the extra step of uninstalling any software or operating system components you do not need, meaning that anything not required for the server to function should be removed. But think carefully about this before proceeding. Clearly, games and office suites are not needed for a server. However, a browser might be necessary to update patches.

There is another step that should be taken with servers that is not necessary with workstations. Most server operating systems have built-in accounts. For example, Windows has built-in administrator, guest, and power user accounts. Any hacker who wants to try to guess passwords will begin by trying to guess the passwords that go with these standard users. In fact, there are utilities on the Web that will do this automatically for the would-be intruder. First, you should create your own accounts with names that do not reflect their level of permission. For example, disable the administrator account and create an account called basic_user. Set up basic_user as the administrator account, with appropriate permissions. (Of course, only give that username and password to those people you want to have administrator privileges.) If you do this, a hacker would not immediately guess that this account is the one that he wants to crack. Remember, hackers ultimately want administrative privileges on a target system; concealing which accounts have those privileges is a vital step in preventing the hacker from breaching your security.

---

### FYI: Handling Old Backup Media

Unfortunately, many network administrators simply throw old backup media in the trash. Persons with malicious intent who retrieve this discarded media could restore it to their own machine. This could give them access to your older data without breaking in to your system or could give them very valuable clues as to your current security practices, depending on what is found on that media. Old media (tapes, CDs, hard disks) should be thoroughly destroyed. For a CD, this means physically breaking it. For a tape, this means partially or completely melting it. Hard disks should be magnetized with a powerful magnet.

There are a variety of Registry settings in any version of Windows that can be altered to increase your security. If you use a scanning tool, such as Cerberus, it returns a report stating the weaknesses in your Registry settings. What items in the Registry settings might cause a security problem? A few items that are commonly examined include the following:

- **Logon:** If your Registry is set so that the logon screen shows the last user's name, you have done half of the hacker's work for her. Since she now has a username, she only needs to guess the password.

- **Default Shares:** Certain drives/folders are shared by default. Leaving them shared like this presents a security hazard.

These are just a few of the potential problems in the Windows Registry. A tool such as Cerberus will not only tell you what the problems are but will make recommendations for corrections. To edit your Registry, go to Start, select Run, and then key regedit. This will start the Registry editor.

## Securing a Network

Obviously, the first step in securing a network is to secure all computers that take part in that network, including all workstations and servers. However, this is just one part of network security. By now it should be clear that using a firewall and proxy server are also critical elements in network security. Chapter 12, "Cyber Terrorism and Information Warfare," will provide more details on these devices. For now, it is important to realize that you need to have them. Most experts also recommend using an IDS. There are a number of such systems available—some are even free. These systems can detect things, such as port scanning, which might indicate that a person is preparing to attempt a breach of your security perimeter.

If your network is at all large, then you might consider partitioning it into smaller segments with a firewall-enabled router between segments. Of course, "large" is a vague term, and you will have to decide if your network is large enough to require partitioning. In this way, if one segment is compromised, the entire network will not be compromised. In this system, you might consider putting your most important servers (database, file) on a secure segment.

Since web servers must be exposed to the outside world and are the most common point of attack, it then makes sense to separate them from the rest of the network. Many network administrators will put a second firewall between the web server and the rest of the network. This means that if a hacker exploits a flaw in your web server and gains access to it, then he will not have access to your entire network. This brings up the issue of what should be on your web server. The answer is: only what you need to post web pages. No data, documents, or other information should be stored on that server, and certainly no extraneous software. The operating system and web server software are all that are required. You may add a few other items (such as an IDS) if your situation requires it. Any other software running on that server is a potential security risk.

Another concept you should consider is the DMZ. A DMZ is a *demilitarized zone*. It essentially involves setting up two firewalls: one outer and one inner. Resources that must be accessible to the outside world are between the two firewalls. The outer firewall is more permissive, and the inner firewall is highly restrictive. There are even routers that include this functionality in a single box. By plugging into certain ports, you are adding a device either behind the inner firewall or in the DMZ. This is shown in Figure 11.3.

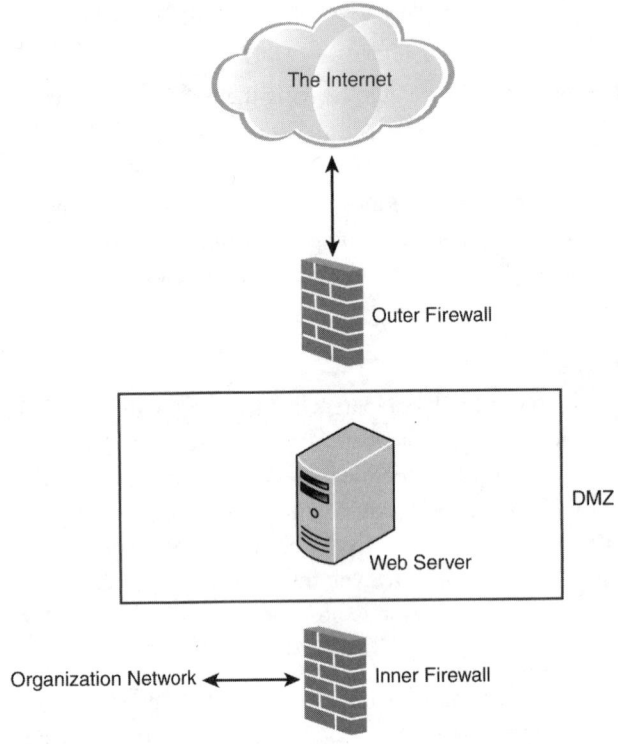

**FIGURE 11.3**    DMZ.

You must also have policies that guide users in how to use the system, as we discussed earlier in this chapter. The most robust security in the world will not be of much use if a careless user inadvertently compromises your security. Keep in mind that you must have policies in place that guide users in what is considered appropriate use of the system and what is not.

Just as you take steps to harden your servers (such as patching the operating system and shutting down unneeded services), you should also harden your router. The specifics of what needs to be done will be contingent on your particular router manufacturer and model, but a few general rules should be followed:

- **Use good passwords:** All routers are configurable. They can be programmed. Therefore, you must obey the same password policies on a router that you would use on any server, including minimum password length and complexity, age of password, and password history. If your router allows you to encrypt the password (as Cisco and other vendors do), then do it.

- **Use logging:** Most routers allow for logging. You should turn this on and monitor it just as you would monitor server logs.

- **Security rules:** Some basic router security rules should also be followed:

  - Do not answer to Address Resolution Protocol (ARP) requests for hosts that are not on the user local area network (LAN).

  - If no applications on your network use a given port, that port should be also shut down on the router.

  - Packets not originating from inside your LAN should not be forwarded.

These rules are simply a beginning. You will need to consult your vendor's documentation for additional recommendations. You must absolutely pay as much attention to securing your router as you do to securing your servers. The following links might be helpful:

- **Router security:** www.mavetju.org/networking/security.php

- **Cisco router hardening:** www.sans.org/rr/whitepapers/firewalls/794.php

# Scanning Your Network

The only way to be sure your network is secure is to actually check for vulnerabilities and flaws. In this section, we will look at some commonly used vulnerability scanners. These tools can be an invaluable asset for any network administrator.

## MBSA

Microsoft Baseline Security Analyzer is a free tool from Microsoft. (Just do a web search on the name to get the latest version.) It is also very simple to use. Critics point out that it is not as robust as other tools, and that is an accurate assessment. I am not claiming this is the best vulnerability assessment tool; it certainly is not. However, it is easy to use, free, and ideal for a Windows administrator who may not be well versed in security.

MBSA (version 2.2 as of this writing) will check one or more Windows machines to see if they have the latest patches, have good password policies, and generally have basic security in place.

Once you run the program, you choose whether you want to scan a single computer or multiple computers, as shown in Figure 11.4.

For demonstration purposes, we will scan a single computer. When you choose that option, you will see a screen that allows you to designate the computer to scan (it defaults to the computer you are on) and what scans to perform. This is shown in Figure 11.5.

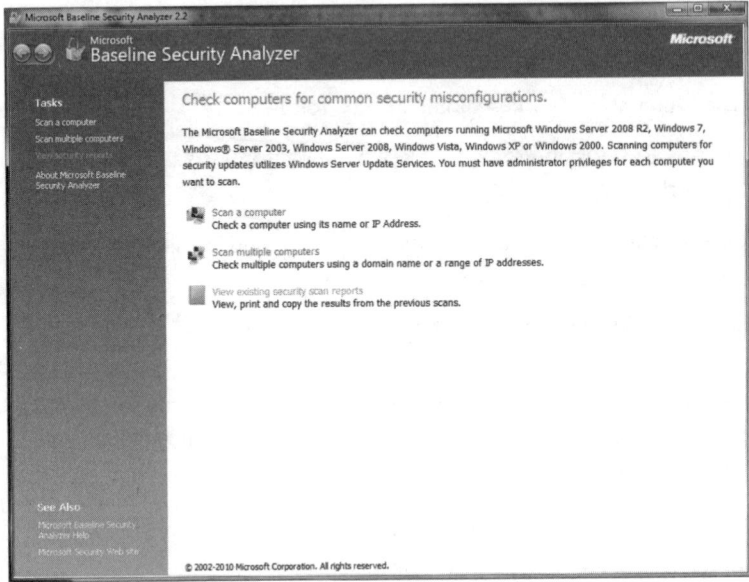

**FIGURE 11.4**    Starting MBSA.

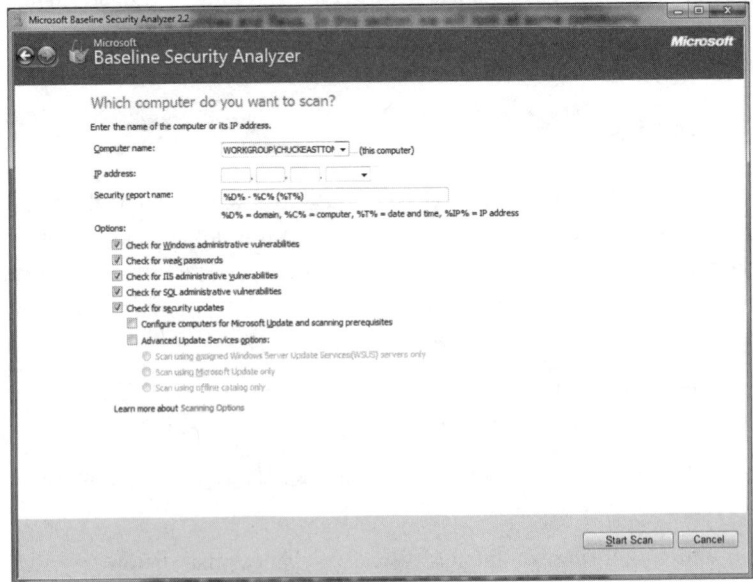

**FIGURE 11.5**    Scanning a single computer.

Then you simply start the scan. For a single computer, it won't take long, but for multiple computers it could take quite some time. When it is done, you will receive a report that details everything checked and if it was okay or not; it has links for deeper explanations if you need them. This is shown in Figure 11.6.

While I agree with critics that there are more robust scanning tools, I feel this particular tool is an excellent choice for someone who is a security novice. It is easy to use and will give you actionable information quickly.

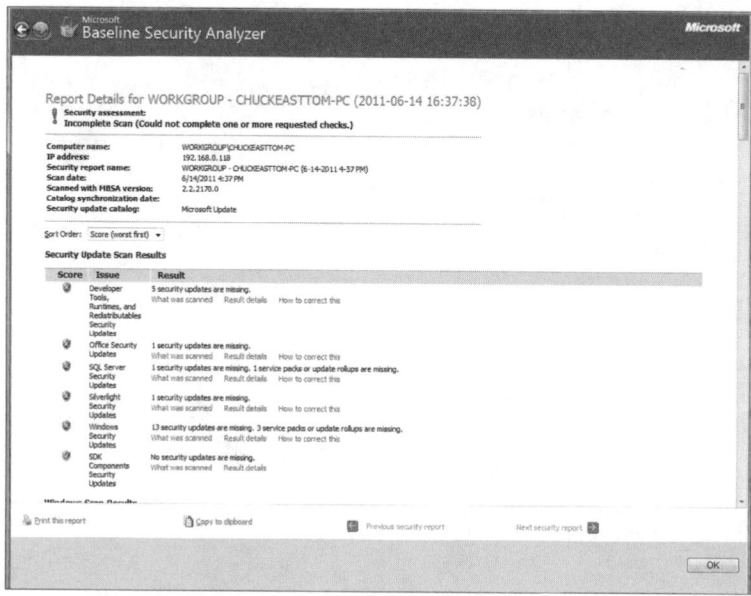

FIGURE 11.6   MBSA report.

## NESSUS

Nessus (www.Nessus.org) is the premiere network vulnerability scanner. There is a free version for personal use and a commercial version. This is perhaps the most widely used vulnerability scanner available today. It is not nearly as simple to use as MBSA but has many more capabilities. We will explore the basic functionality. If you have an interest in learning more about Nessus, then it is recommended that you consult the documentation available at the Nessus website.

Once you install Nessus, you will have two icons on your desktop. One is the Nessus server, and the other is the client. We will launch the server first, shown in Figure 11.7. The first thing you have to do is register it. The process is quick, easy, and free.

Once you register, it will take a few moments to download the latest plug-ins. When that is done, you will see the main Nessus server screen, shown in Figure 11.8.

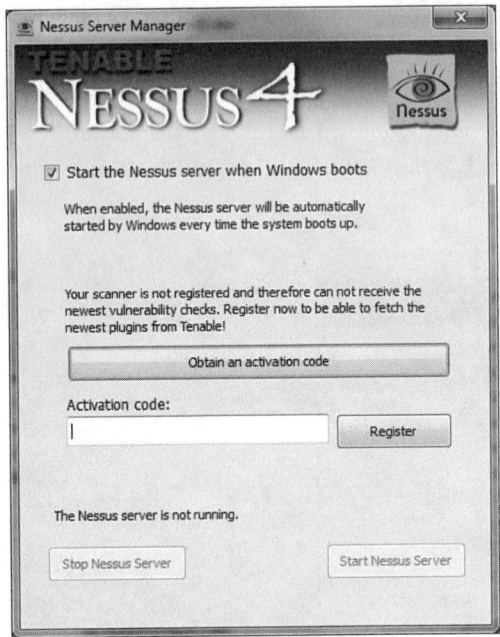

**FIGURE 11.7**　Starting the Nessus server.

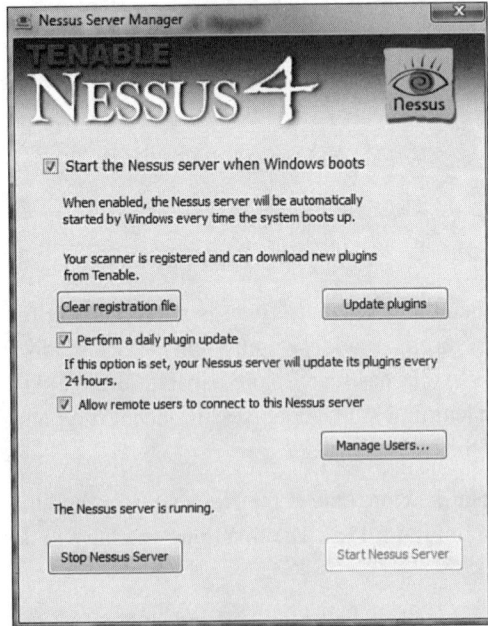

**FIGURE 11.8**　Nessus plugins.

You can leave the default settings for now. But you need to click on the Manage Users button and add a user. For demonstration purposes, it does not matter what name and password you give them. When you have done that, you will close out of the server and launch the client, shown in Figure 11.9.

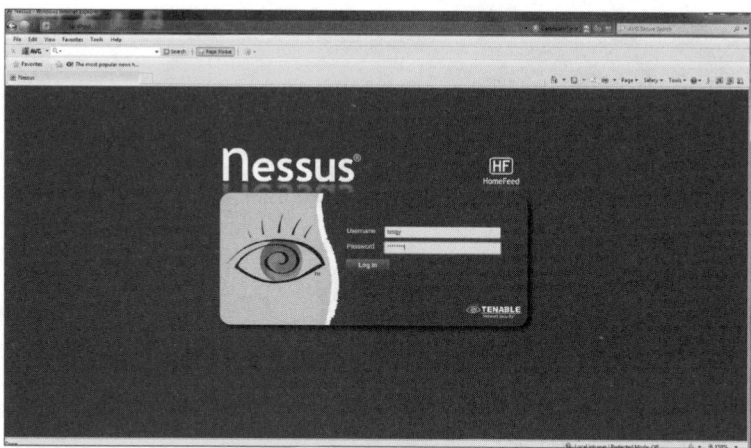

**FIGURE 11.9**    Nessus client login screen.

The Nessus client is actually a web interface. Once you log in, you will see a page with a toolbar at the top like the one shown in Figure 11.10.

**FIGURE 11.10**    Nessus client main screen.

It is important that you do things in a specific order. You first have to create a policy, then you can create a scan, and when the scan is done you will have a report. So we will start by creating a simple policy. When you click on Policy, you will see a screen like the one shown in Figure 11.11.

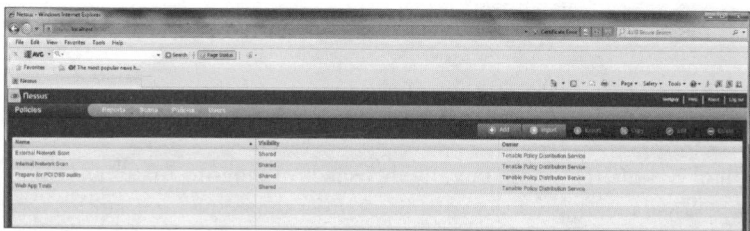

**FIGURE 11.11**    Policies.

As you can see, there are some default policies already there. But we will make our own simple policy just so you can see how it is done. If you click on the Add button, you will see a screen like the one shown in Figure 11.12.

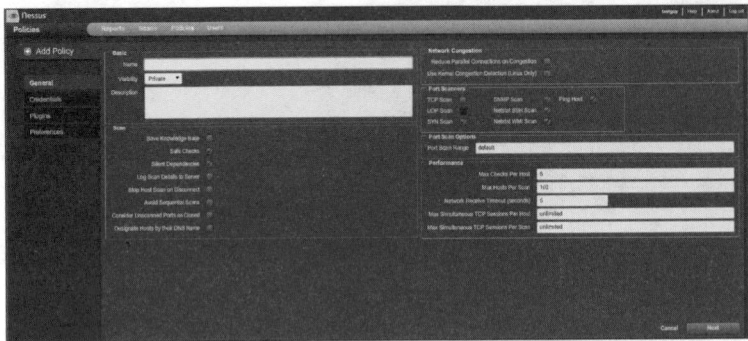

**FIGURE 11.12**    Add a new policy.

Give your new policy some meaningful name. For demonstration purposes, something like *test policy* might be appropriate. We will leave default settings on this screen, but take the time to review all the various items on this screen.

We are going to skip credentials for now. That is only necessary if, as part of the scan, you need Nessus to be able to log on to various systems. We are going to go to the plug-ins screen, shown in Figure 11.13.

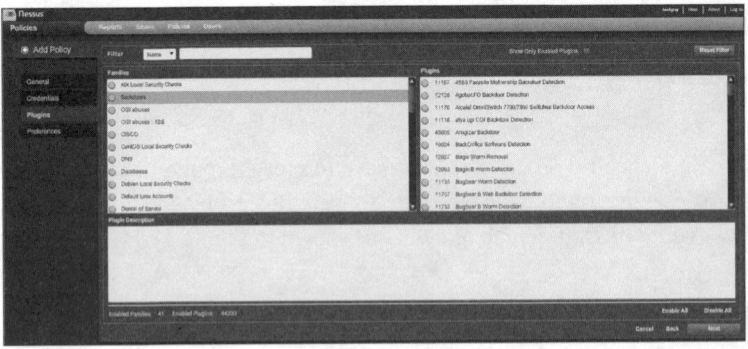

**FIGURE 11.13**    Selecting plug-ins.

The plug-ins are the real strength of Nessus. There are literally thousands of plug-ins for almost every conceivable type of vulnerability. When creating your own policies, they should be for specific types of scans. What you are scanning will determine the plug-in you select.

We are going to leave the default selection, but you should take time to review the options available to you. Nessus provides a truly impressive array of vulnerabilities it can scan for. For now, click the Next button, which will take you to Preferences, and then click Submit. You have just created a policy. Now click on the Scan option on the toolbar at the top. You will see a screen like the one depicted in Figure 11.14.

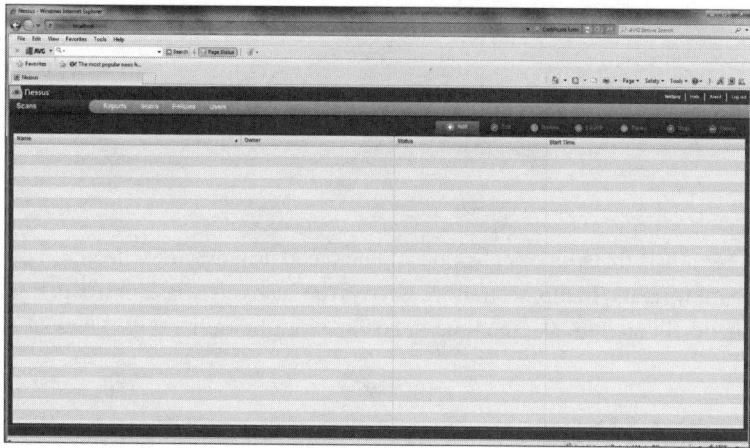

FIGURE 11.14   The Scan screen.

Now click the Add button and you will see a screen like the one shown in Figure 11.15.

FIGURE 11.15   Add a new scan.

Give your scan a meaningful name, select the policy to use for this scan, enter the IP addresses to scan in the targets text field (you can either enter a computer name or an IP address), and start your scan. When it is done, you will be notified and you can go to the Reports screen, shown in Figure 11.16.

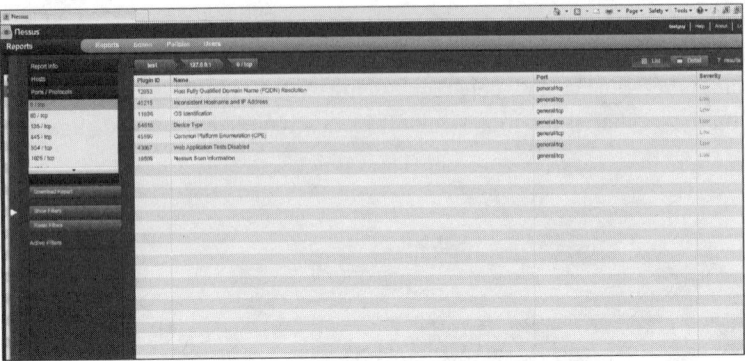

**FIGURE 11.16**   Reports.

The best thing about the Nessus reports is that you can click on any item and drill down for details. You can also export the report to several formats. In this section we have given just you a basic introduction to Nessus. It is strongly recommended that you take the time to become more familiar with Nessus.

# Getting Professional Help

You may decide that you need outside help to set up and test your system's security. This option is one that most security professionals would highly recommend if at all possible, particularly if you are new to security. It can be extremely helpful to get a professional consultant to assist you in setting up your initial security strategy and policies and perhaps do a periodic audit of your security. As mentioned in Chapter 1, "Introduction to Computer Security," there are a number of people who claim to be hackers who are not. Frankly, there are also a number of self-proclaimed security experts who simply do not have the requisite skills. The question here is: How do you determine whether an individual is qualified? Following are some guidelines to consider in making this decision.

Experience is the most important factor when looking for a security professional. You want someone with a minimum of five years of IT experience, with two years related to security. Often, this will be a network administrator or programmer who has moved into security. Note that this is a minimum level of experience. More experience is always better. It is certainly possible that someone with less experience might have the requisite skill, but it is unlikely. Everyone needs a place to start, but you do not want your systems to be the place where someone is learning.

The quality of the person's experience is as important as the length of experience. Ask details about the person's experience. For example, exactly what role did she play in computer security? Did she simply set up policies, or did she actually do hands-on security work? What was the result? Was her system free from virus infections and hacker breaches or not? Can you contact her references? In short, simply because a person states that she was responsible for information security on her resume is not enough. You need to find out exactly what she did and what the results were.

Another important aspect of a security professional is education. Remember that computer security is a very broad subject. One needs an understanding of networks, protocols, programming, and more. It is entirely possible for a person with no formal education to have these skills, but it is less likely than if they had a formal education. Generally, these skills will most likely be found in a person with experience and a degree in a computer- or math-related field. That may sound somewhat intellectually snobbish, but it is a fact. There are many people in IT who are self-taught, such as people with history degrees who are network administrators or psychology majors who are now programmers. However, the more areas a person focuses in, the harder it is to obtain mastery. This is not to say that a person cannot be a security professional without a computer science, math, or engineering degree. The point is simply that this is one factor you should consider. If someone has an unrelated degree but meets or exceeds all other qualifications, you might still consider him. Some colleges are beginning to offer security-specific curriculum, and a few even offer security degrees. Clearly, specific training in computer security would be the most preferable security background.

Certifications have become very controversial in the IT profession. Some people swear by them. You can easily find many job advertisements that demand certain certifications, such as the CNE (Certified Novel Engineer) or MCITP (Microsoft Certified Information Technology Professional). Cisco certifications are also common (Cisco Certified Network Associate through Cisco Certified Internetworking Engineer). On the other hand, you would have no problem finding some IT professionals who denigrate certifications and consider them utterly worthless. That second position stems from the fact that there are some people who hold certifications who don't have the skills one would expect. But that is true of any credential. There are medical doctors who are incompetent. But if you need medical help, your odds are much better if you consult someone who has a medical degree. Employers often take this approach to hiring. If they only interview those with certain degrees or certifications, then they have a higher chance of interviewing qualified candidates.

A more reasonable position is somewhat between the two extremes. A certification can be a good indicator of a candidate's knowledge of a specific product. For example, if you want someone to secure your Microsoft network, looking at people who are Microsoft certified is not a bad idea. You should balance that, however, by keeping in mind that it is entirely possible for someone with a good memory to use the various study guides available on the Internet and pass a test they don't actually understand. That is where experience comes in. A certification coupled with appropriate experience is a good indicator of skill. Put another way, a certification in and of itself is not enough. But a combination of one or more certifications with experience and perhaps a related degree can be a strong indicator of technical skills.

In addition to the certifications for network administrators, there are a number of security-related certifications. Some have more credibility than others. The Security+ exam from CompTIA and the CIW Security Analyst are both conceptual exams. This means that they test a candidate's knowledge of security concepts and not their ability to actually implement a security solution. By themselves, they may not indicate the skill level you need. But if, for example, you are securing a network using Novell, a candidate who is a CNE and has CIW Security Analyst or Security+ might be a good person to consider. It should be noted that CompTIA has recently added the Certified Advanced Security Practitioner (CASP), which is designed for those with 10 years of experience in security.

The most respected security certification is the CISSP (Certified Information Systems Security Professional). This test is a six-hour exam and can only be taken if you first verify four years of security-related experience (if you also have a degree) or five years of experience (if you do not have a degree). CISSP holders are also required to submit a recommendation from another CISSP or an officer of their company and to take continuing education credits to maintain the certification. This is probably the most respected security-related certification. The vendor who produces CISSP (ISC2) also has advanced, post CISSP certifications, such as the Information Systems Security Architecture Professional (ISSAP), Information Systems Security Engineering Professional (ISSEP), and Information Systems Security Management Professional (ISSMP).

The Certified Ethical Hacker certification is sponsored by the EC-Council (www.eccouncil.org/). This test has also been the subject of some controversy. Keep in mind that it tests basic hacking skills, not a mastery of hacking. It is good for an introduction to hacking/penetration testing.

Offensive Security (https://www.offensive-security.com/) specializes in penetration testing certifications. What makes their certification tests most interesting is that they all involve a hands-on component. You have to actually hack into their test systems. You don't simply take a test.

There is also the Professional Penetration Tester (http://www.professionalpentester.com/), which does cover hands-on hacking techniques but also covers penetration testing standards and methodologies.

There are a number of general forensics certifications. EC-Council has the Certified Hacking Investigator, ISC2 has the Certified Cyber Forensics Professional, and there are others. A good knowledge of basic forensics is useful for a security professional.

GIAC (www.giac.org/) has a number of security-related certifications. All have a very solid reputation in the security industry. They are, however, more expensive than other tests, and for that reason there are fewer security professionals who have them. GIAC has security certifications (GSEC), penetration testing certifications (GPEN), and forensics certifications (GCFA and GCFE).

All certifications get some critics. The fact is that some people do attend boot camps and cram in just enough information to pass a certification. However, the same can be said of any qualification. It is certainly the case that there are medical doctors who are incompetent, but I am certain that if you are sick or injured you seek out a medical doctor. The reason is that you are more likely to get qualified help than simply selecting some random person. The same is true of certifications. Keep in mind that certifications reflect a minimum skill level, not mastery. I would recommend having at least one general security certification (Security+, CASP, CISSP, and so on), one penetration testing certification (GPEN, CEH, Offensive Security, and so on), and one forensics certification (CCFP, GCFA, CHFI, and so on).

You should never hire a person based solely on certifications. Those certifications should simply be one element that you consider.

Finally, you should consider personal background. A security consultant or full-time employee will, by definition, have access to confidential information. Any legitimate security professional will not mind giving you any of the following:

- References

- Permission to check their credit history

- Permission to check their criminal background

Anyone who seems reluctant to provide any of these items should be avoided. Therefore, an ideal security consultant might be a person with five or more years of experience, a degree in a computer-related discipline, a certification in your organization's operating systems as well as one of the major security certifications, and a completely clean background, with references. As a rule, you simply cannot be too careful in hiring a security consultant.

Unless you have a highly trained security expert on staff, you should consider bringing in a security consultant to assess your system at least once. In our current legal environment, liability for security breaches is still being hotly debated. Companies are being sued for failing to practice due diligence in computer security. It is simply a wise move, both from a computer industry perspective as well as from a legal perspective, to do everything reasonable to ensure the security of your systems.

# Summary

This chapter has outlined some basic items to look for in any security assessment. You should periodically assess your network/system for security vulnerabilities. A general recommendation would be a quarterly assessment for noncritical/low-security sites and perhaps as frequently as a weekly assessment for high-security sites. In any case, what are outlined in this chapter are the basics of assessing the security of a network, and they should give you a start toward securing your own network.

Safe computing is a matter of securing your computer, your network, and your servers and using common sense on the Web. It is important to rigorously apply security practices and standards to all computers, whether they are home computers or part of an organizational network.

## Test Your Skills

## MULTIPLE CHOICE QUESTIONS

1. What are the six Ps of security?

   A. Patch, ports, personnel, privacy, protect, policies

   B. Ports, patch, protect, probe, policies, physical

   C. Physical, privacy, patch, ports, probe, protect

   D. Ports, patch, probe, physical, privacy, policies

2. What is the most basic rule of computer security?

   A. Keep systems patched.

   B. Always use an IDS.

   C. Install a firewall.

   D. Always use antispyware.

3. How might you ensure that system patches are kept up to date?

   A. Use an automated patching system.

   B. Patch anytime you receive a vendor notification of a new patch.

   C. Patch whenever a new threat is announced.

   D. Use periodic scheduled patching.

4. What is the rule about ports?

   A. Block all incoming ports.

   B. Block ICMP packets.

   C. Block all unused ports.

   D. Block all nonstandard ports.

5. Which of the following is a good reason to check dependencies before shutting down a service?

    A. To determine whether you will need to shut down other services as well

    B. To determine whether shutting down this service will affect other services

    C. To find out what this service does

    D. To find out whether this service is critical to system operations

6. If your machine is not used as a server and is not on a local network, what packet-filtering strategy should you use?

    A. Block all ports except 80.

    B. Do not block any ports.

    C. Block all ports.

    D. Do not block well-known ports.

7. Which of the following is the least essential device for protecting your network?

    A. Firewall

    B. Virus scanners on all machines

    C. IDS system

    D. Proxy server

8. What is the rule of thumb on data access?

    A. Data must be available to the widest range of people possible.

    B. Only administrators and supervisors should access sensitive data.

    C. Only those with a need for the specific data should have access.

    D. All employees should have access to any data used in their department.

9. What is password age?

    A. How long a user has had a password

    B. The length of the password history

    C. A reference to the sophistication (maturity) of the password

    D. A reference to a password's length

10. What is the minimum frequency for system probing and audits?

    A. Once per month

    B. Once per year

    C. Every other year

    D. Every other month

11. An audit should check what areas?

    A. Perform system patching, review polices, check personnel records of all managers, and probe for flaws

    B. Only probe for flaws

    C. Perform system patches, probe for flaws, check logs, and review policies

    D. Check all machines for illicit software, perform complete system virus scan, and review firewall polices

12. Which of the following is true of the room in which the server is located?

    A. It should be in the most fire-resistant room in the building.

    B. It should have a strong lock with a strong door.

    C. It should be accessible only to those who have a need for access.

    D. All of the above.

13. What would be most important to block end users from doing on their own machine?

    A. Running programs other than those installed by the IT staff

    B. Surfing the Web and using chat rooms

    C. Changing their screensaver and using chat rooms

    D. Installing software or changing system settings

14. What is the preferred method for storing backups?

    A. Near the server for quick restore if needed

    B. Offsite in a secure location

    C. In the IT manager's office for security

    D. At the home of one of the IT staff

15. Which of the following is a step you would definitely take with any server but might not be required for a workstation?

    A. Uninstall all unneeded programs/software.

    B. Shut down unneeded services.

    C. Turn off the screensaver.

    D. Block all Internet access.

16. Which of the following is a step you might take for large networks but not for smaller networks?

    A. Use an IDS.

    B. Segment the network with firewalls between the segments.

    C. Use antivirus software on all machines on the network.

    D. Do criminal background checks for network administrators.

17. Which of the following is a common way to establish security between a web server and a network?

    A. Block all traffic between the web server and the network.

    B. Place virus scanning between the network and the web server.

    C. Put a firewall between the web server and the network.

    D. Do not connect your network to the web server.

18. What is the rule on downloading from the Internet?

    A. Never download anything.

    B. Only download if the download is free of charge.

    C. Only download from well-known, reputable sites.

    D. Never download executables. Only download graphics.

19. Which of the following certifications is the most prestigious?

    A. CISSP

    B. PE

    C. MCSA

    D. Security+

20. Which of the following set of credentials would be best for a security consultant?

    A. Ten years of IT experience, one year in security, CIW Security analyst, MBA

    B. Eight years of IT experience, three years in security, CISSP, B.S. in computer science

    C. Eleven years of IT experience, three years in security, MCSE and CISSP, MS in information systems

    D. Ten years of experience as a hacker and cracker, MCSE/CIW and Security +, Ph.D. in computer science

## EXERCISES

### EXERCISE 11.1: Patching Systems

1. Using a lab system, find and apply all operating system patches.

2. Check with all vendors of software installed on that machine and apply patches for those applications as well (if available).

3. Note the time taken to fully patch a machine. Consider how long it would take to patch a 100-machine network.

4. Write an essay that answers the following questions: Are there ways you could speed the process of patching a 100-machine network? How might you approach such a task?

## EXERCISE 11.2: **Learning About Policies**

1. Using the resources given or other resources, find at least one sample security policy document.

2. Analyze that document.

3. Write a brief essay giving your opinion of that policy. Did it miss items? Did it include items you had not thought of?

## EXERCISE 11.3: **Learning About Disaster Recovery**

1. Using the resources given or other resources, find at least one sample disaster recovery plan.

2. Analyze that document.

3. Write a brief essay giving your opinion of that disaster recovery plan. Also note any changes you would recommend to that policy.

## EXERCISE 11.4: **Learning About Audits**

1. Using the resources given or other resources, find at least one sample security audit plan.

2. Analyze that document.

3. Write a brief essay giving your opinion of that plan. Do you feel the audit plan is adequate? What changes might you recommend?

---

### FYI: Helpful Resources

For Exercises 11.2, 11.3, and 11.4, you may find the following resources helpful:

- www.cert.org/
- www.sans.org/
- www.information-security-policies-and-standards.com/

---

## EXERCISE 11.5: **Securing Your Computer**

Using either your home computer or a lab computer, follow the guidelines given in this chapter to secure that computer. Those steps should include the following:

1. Scan for all patches and install them.

2. Shut down all unneeded services.

3. Install antivirus software. (A demo version can be used for this exercise.)

4. Install antispyware software. (A demo version can be used for this exercise.)

5. Set appropriate password permissions.

## EXERCISE 11.6: **Secure Passwords**

1. Using the Web or other resources, find out why longer passwords are harder to break.

2. Also find out what other things you should do to make a password harder to crack.

3. Write a brief essay describing what makes a perfect password.

## EXERCISE 11.7: **Securing a Server**

Note: This exercise is for those students with access to a lab server.

Using the guidelines discussed in this chapter, secure a lab server. The steps taken should include the following:

1. Scan for all patches and install them.

2. Shut down all unneeded services.

3. Remove unneeded software.

4. Install antivirus software. (A demo version can be used for this exercise.)

5. Install antispyware software. (A demo version can be used for this exercise.)

6. Set appropriate password permissions.

7. Enable logging of any security violations. (Consult your operating system documentation for instructions.)

## EXERCISE 11.8: **Backups**

Using the Web and other resources as a guide, develop a backup plan for a web server. The plan should cover how frequently to back up and where to store the backup media.

## EXERCISE 11.9: **User Accounts**

Note: This exercise is best done with a lab computer, not a machine actually in use.

1. Locate user accounts. (In Windows 8 or Windows 10, this is done by going to Start > Control Panel > Administrative Tools > Computer Management and looking for Groups and Users.)

2. Disable all default accounts (Guest, Administrator).

# PROJECTS

### PROJECT 11.1: Writing and Executing an Audit Plan

With the knowledge you have gained while studying six chapters of this text and in examining security policies in the preceding exercises, it is now time to devise your own audit plan. This plan should detail all the steps in an audit.

Note: The second part of this project is contingent upon getting permission from some organization to allow you to audit its security. It is also ideal for a group project.

Taking the audit plan you wrote, audit a network. This audit can be conducted for any sort of organization, but you should make your first audit one with a small network (fewer than 100 users).

### PROJECT 11.2: Forming a Disaster Recovery Plan

Using the knowledge you have gained thus far, create an IT disaster recovery plan for an organization. You may use a fictitious organization, but a real organization would be better.

### PROJECT 11.3: Writing a Security Policy Document

Note: This project is designed as a group project.

It is now time to bring all you have learned thus far together. Write a complete set of security policies for an organization. Again, you may use a fictitious company, but real organizations are better. This set of policies must cover user access, password policies, frequency of audits (both internal and external), minimum security requirements, guidelines for web surfing, and so on.

### PROJECT 11.4: Secure Web Servers

Using the information in this chapter as well as other resources, come up with a strategy specifically for securing a web server. This strategy should include the security of the server itself as well as securing the network from the server.

### PROJECT 11.5: Adding Your Own Guidelines

Note: This project is ideal for a group project.

This chapter has outlined some general procedures for security. Write an essay detailing your own additional guidelines. These can be guidelines for individual computers, servers, networks, or any combination thereof.

## Case Study

Juan Garcia is the network administrator for a small company that also maintains its own web server. He has taken the following precautions:

- All computers are patched, have antivirus software, and have unneeded services shut down.

- The network has a firewall with proxy server and IDS.

- The organization has a policy requiring passwords of ten characters in length, and they must be changed every 90 days.

Has Juan done enough to secure the network? What other actions would you recommend he take?

# Chapter | **12**

# Cyber Terrorism and Information Warfare

## *Chapter Objectives*

**After reading this chapter and completing the exercises, you will be able to do the following:**

- Explain what cyber terrorism is and how it has been used in some actual cases
- Understand the basics of information warfare
- Have a working knowledge of some plausible cyber terrorism scenarios
- Have an appreciation for the dangers posed by cyber terrorism

## Introduction

Throughout this book, various ways have been examined in which a person might use a computer to commit a crime. This book has also looked into specific methods to make a system more secure. One issue that has not been addressed is that of cyber terrorism. People in countries around the world have grown accustomed to the ever-present threat of a terrorist attack, which could come in the form of a bomb, a hijacking, release of a biological agent, or other means. Most people have not given much thought to the possibility of cyber terrorism.

The first question might be this: What is cyber terrorism? According to the FBI, *cyber terrorism* is the premeditated, politically motivated attack against information, computer systems, computer programs, and data that results in violence against noncombatant targets by subnational groups or clandestine agents (Dick, 2002). Cyber terrorism is simply the use of computers and the Internet connectivity between them in order to launch a terrorist attack. In short, cyber terrorism is just like other forms of terrorism—it is only the milieu of the attack that has changed. Clearly, the loss of life due to a cyber attack would be much less than that of a bombing. In fact, it is highly likely that there would be no loss of life at all. However, significant economic damage, disruptions in communications, disruptions in supply lines, and general degradation of the national infrastructure are all quite possible via the Internet.

The real question might be: What is the difference between cyber espionage and cyber terrorism? First and foremost, the goal of espionage is simply to gather information. It is preferable to the spy if no one is even aware that anything occurred. This is true for both corporate and international espionage. Cyber terrorism, on the other hand, seeks to cause damage, and it needs to be as public as possible. The idea is to strike fear into people. While some might find the topics related, they are actually quite different.

It is a strong possibility that, in time, someone or some group will try to use computer methods to launch a military or terrorist attack against our nation. Some experts make the case that the MyDoom virus (discussed in Chapter 4, "Denial of Service Attacks") was an example of domestic economic terrorism. However, an attack such as that may be only the tip of the iceberg. Sometime in the near future, our nation may be the target of a serious cyber terrorism attack. This chapter will examine some possible cyber terrorism scenarios, with the purpose of giving you a realistic assessment of just how serious a threat this is. In the exercises at the end of the chapter, you will have the opportunity to examine current acts of cyber terrorism, as well as potential threats, and the actions you can take to help prevent them.

The first edition of this book discussed cyber terrorism as well. That was in 2004. At that time, some may have thought that the coverage of that topic was almost fiction, that there was no real threat from cyber terrorism. That has proven to not be the case. One of the first indications that cyber terrorism is a real threat was that in November 2006 the Secretary of the Air Force announced the creation of the Air Force Cyber Command. This Command's primary function is to monitor and defend American interest in cyberspace. The AFCC draws upon the personnel resources of the 67th Network Warfare Wing as well as other resources. It seems that the United States Air Force takes the threat of cyber terrorism and cyber warfare seriously and has created an entire command to counter that threat.

# Actual Cases of Cyber Terrorism

Because some readers may wonder whether this is just fear mongering, let's look at some actual cases of cyber terrorism before we delve into the various aspects of it. How likely is a genuine cyber terrorist attack? Well, let's look at some real-world cases. Later in this chapter, we will examine some older, historical cases to get a sense of perspective. However, in this section, we will only look at recent attacks.

In May 2007, government offices of Estonia were subjected to a mass denial of service (DoS) attack. This attack was executed because some people opposed the government's removal of a Russian WWII memorial. While this was a relatively minor attack, it was politically motivated and thus qualifies as cyber terrorism.

CENTCOM, or Central Command, is the U.S. Military command responsible for operations in the Middle East and Near East. In 2008, CENTCOM was infected with spyware. A USB drive was left in the parking lot of a DoD facility in the Middle East. A soldier picked it up and plugged it into his work-station, thus introducing the spyware to the CENTCOM network. The worm was known as Agent.btz, a variant of the SillyFDC worm. This was a significant security breach, and we will probably never know how much data was lost or how much damage was caused.

The year 2009 brought a number of Internet-based attacks, specifically against U.S. government websites, such as the websites of the Pentagon and the White House (in the United States) and various government agencies in South Korea. These attacks coincided with increased tensions with North Korea. Clearly, these where examples of cyber terrorism, albeit relatively minor.

In December 2009, a far more disturbing story came out. Hackers broke into computer systems and stole secret defense plans of the United States and South Korea. Authorities speculated that North Korea was responsible. The information stolen included a summary of plans for military operations by South Korean and U.S. troops in case of war with North Korea, and the attacks traced back to a Chinese IP address. This case is clearly an example of cyber espionage and a very serious one at that.

In December 2010, a group calling itself the Pakistan Cyber Army hacked the website of India's top investigating agency, the Central Bureau of Investigation (CBI). This sort of cyber espionage is far more common than what is revealed to the public.

## The Chinese Eagle Union

No discussion of cyber terrorism would be complete without a discussion of the China Eagle Union. This group consists of several thousand Chinese hackers whose stated goal is to infiltrate western computer systems. There are a number of web resources regarding this group:

- www.thedarkvisitor.com/2007/10/china-eagle-union/
- https://news.hitb.org/node/6164

Members and leaders of the group insist that not only does the Chinese government have no involvement in their activities, but they are breaking Chinese law and are in constant danger of arrest and imprisonment. Many analysts find this claim dubious. Whether the Chinese government is involved in these attacks or not, some experts consider a state of cyber warfare to currently exist between China and the United States.

## China's Advanced Persistent Threat

An Advanced Persistent Threat (APT), as the name suggests, is a series of advanced cyber attacks that are sustained over a period of time, thus being *persistent*. The security firm Mandiant tracked several APTs over a period of 7 years, all originating in China, specifically Shanghai and the Pudong region. These APTs were simply named APT1, APT2, and so on.

The attacks were linked to the UNIT 61398 of China's military. The Chinese government regards this unit's activities as classified, but it appears that offensive cyber warfare is one of its tasks. Just one of the APTs from this group compromised 141 companies in 20 different industries. APT1 was able to maintain access to victim networks for an average of 365 days, and in one case for 1,764 days. APT1 is responsible for stealing 6.5 terabytes of information from a single organization over a 10-month time frame.

## India and Pakistan

These two nations have had deep enmity for each other for quite some time. It should be no surprise that, in recent years, this has involved cyber operations.

One India published an article in August 2015 titled "Pakistan Wants to Launch Cyber War on India."[1] In that article, the author stated, "The cyber wing of the Intelligence Bureau has warned that government websites could be hacked by the Pakistan Cyber Army in this ongoing proxy war against India...." As per the latest alert, Pakistan's ISI has directed its cyber army to declare an Internet war on India.

## Russian Hackers

According to ISight Partners, a cyber intelligence firm, in 2014 hackers from Russia were spying on computers used in NATO and the European Union. The spying was accomplished by exploiting bugs in Microsoft Windows. The hackers were also reported to have been targeting sites in the Ukraine for spying.

# Weapons of Cyber Warfare

In cyber warfare and cyber terrorism, malware is still the primary weapon. Whether it is spyware, a virus, a Trojan horse, a logic bomb, or some other sort of malware, it is still the malware that is the essential vehicle for conducting a cyber conflict. In this section, we will look at some well-known malware that has been used in conflicts.

## Stuxnet

Stuxnet is a classic example of weaponized malware. Stuxnet first spread via infected USB drives; however, once it was on an infected machine, it would spread over the entire network and even over the Internet. The Stuxnet virus then searched for a connection to a specific type of Programmable Logic Controller (PLC), specifically the Siemens Step7 software. If that particular PLC was discovered, Stuxnet would load its own copy of a specific DLL for the PLC in order to monitor the PLC and then alter the PLC's functionality.

Stuxnet was designed to target centrifuge controllers involved in Iran's uranium enrichment. But the virus spread beyond its intended target and thus became publically known. While many users reported no significant damage from Stuxnet, outside the Iranian reactors, it was detected on numerous machines.

Stuxnet employed a classic virus design. Stuxnet has three modules: a worm that executes routines related to the attack; a link file that executes the propagated copies of the worm; and a rootkit responsible for

---

1. http://www.oneindia.com/india/pakistan-wants-to-launch-cyber-war-on-india-1831947.html

hiding files and processes, with the goal of making it more difficult to detect the presence of Stuxnet. It is not the purpose of this discussion to explore the intricacies of Stuxnet. Rather, Stuxnet is introduced as both an example of state-sponsored malware attacks and at least an attempt to target such attacks.

## Flame

No modern discussion of cyber warfare and espionage would be complete without a discussion of Flame. This virus first appeared in 2012 and was targeting Windows operating systems. The first item that makes this virus notable is that it was specifically designed for espionage. It was first discovered in May 2012 at several locations, including Iranian government sites. Flame is spyware that can monitor network traffic and take screenshots of the infected system.

It was spyware that recorded keyboard activity and network traffic, took screen shots, and is even reported to have recorded Skype conversations. It also would turn the infected computer into a Bluetooth beacon attempting to download information from nearby Bluetooth-enabled devices.

Kaspersky labs reported that the Flame file contained an MD5 hash that only appeared on machines in the Middle East. This indicates the possibility that the virus authors intended to target the malware attack to a specific geographical region. The Flame virus also appears to have had a kill function allowing someone controlling it to send a signal directing it to delete all traces of itself. These two items indicate an attempt to target the malware, though the outcome of that targeting seems to have been a failure, or we would not be aware of its existence.

## StopGeorgia.ru Malware

During the conflict between Russia and Georgia, a number of hacking incidents played a role. The StopGeorgia.ru forum was an online forum designed to facilitate attacks against key network targets within Georgia. The online forum would advertise specific targets, give tutorials (and in some cases tools) for helping even low-skilled attackers engage the targets, and even provided links to proxy servers to help facilitate the attack by hiding the attacker's true IP address and location.

As an example of what the website StopGeorgia.ru offered, there was a tool named DoSHTTP that automated DoS attacks and a list of websites and IP addresses within Georgia that would be good targets. This encouraged anyone sympathetic to Russia's position in this conflict, who had even minimal computer skills, to embark on cyber attacks against Georgia.

## FinFisher

FinFisher (spyware) was designed for law enforcement agencies with a warrant, to collect evidence on suspects. However, the software was released by WikiLeaks. It is now available on the Internet for anyone who wishes to use it.

## BlackEnergy

BlackEnergy theoretically manipulates water and power systems, including causing blackouts and water supply disruptions. The software, BlackEnergy, has been traced to the Russian group SandWorm. In January, a blackout at the Kiev airport was linked to the BlackEnergy malware.[2]

## NSA ANT Catalog

This is reported to be a catalog that NSA makes available to agencies within the U.S. government that have clearance. It is a catalog of malware, including spyware, that has been developed by the National Security Agencies Tailored Access Operations group. A number of sources purport to have lists of items in the catalog as well as screenshots from the catalog. Given the classified nature of this catalog, if it actually exists, any website claiming to have details of the catalog should be treated with some skepticism.

# Economic Attacks

There are a variety of ways that a cyber attack can cause economic damage. Lost files and lost records are one way. Chapter 9, "Computer Security Technology," discussed cyber espionage and mentioned the inherent value of data. In addition to stealing that data, it could simply be destroyed, in which case the data is gone and the resources used to accumulate and analyze the data are wasted. To use an analogy, consider that a malicious person could choose to simply destroy your car rather than steal it. In either case, you are without the car and will have to spend additional resources acquiring transportation.

In addition to simply destroying economically valuable data (remember that there is very little data that does not have some intrinsic value), there are other ways to cause economic disruption. Some of those ways include stealing credit cards, transferring money from accounts, and committing fraud. But it is a fact that anytime IT staff is involved with cleaning up a virus rather than developing applications or administering networks and databases, there is economic loss. The mere fact that companies now need to purchase antivirus software and intrusion detection software and hire computer security professionals means that computer crime has already caused economic damage to companies and governments around the world. However, the general damage caused by random virus outbreaks, lone hacking attacks, and online fraud is not the type of economic damage that is the focus of this chapter. This chapter is concerned with a concerted and deliberate attack against a particular target or targets for the exclusive purpose of causing direct damage.

A good way to get a firm grasp on the impact of this type of attack is to walk through a scenario. Group X (which could be an aggressive nation, a terrorist group, an activist group, or literally any group with the motivation to damage a particular nation) decides to make a concerted attack on our country. It finds a small group of individuals (in this case, six) who are well versed in computer security, networking, and programming. These individuals, motivated either by ideology or monetary needs, are

---

2. http://www.theregister.co.uk/2016/01/18/blackenergy_power_outage_malware_kiev_airport/

organized to create a coordinated attack. There are many possible scenarios under which they could execute such an attack and cause significant economic harm. The example outlined next is just one of those possible attack modalities. In this case, each individual has an assignment, and all assignments are designed to be activated on the same specific date:

- Team member one sets up several fake e-commerce sites. Each of these sites is up for only 72 hours and pretends to be a major stock brokerage site. During the brief time it is up, the site's real purpose is only to collect credit card numbers, bank account numbers, and so forth. On the predetermined date, all of those credit card and bank numbers will be automatically, anonymously, and simultaneously posted to various bulletin boards/websites and newsgroups, making them available for any unscrupulous individual who wishes to use them.

- Team member two creates a virus that is contained in a Trojan horse. Its function is to delete key system files on the predetermined date. In the meantime, it shows a series of business tips or motivational slogans, making it a popular download with people in business.

- Team member three creates another virus. It is designed to create distributed denial of service (DDoS) attacks on key economic sites, such as those for stock exchanges or brokerage houses. The virus spreads harmlessly and is set to begin its DDoS attack on the predetermined date.

- Team members four and five begin the process of footprinting major banking systems, preparing to crack them on the predetermined date. *Footprinting* is the process of gathering information—some from public sources, others by scanning the target system/network.

- Team member six prepares a series of false stock tips to flood the Internet on the predetermined date.

If each of these individuals is successful in his mission, on the predetermined date several major brokerages and perhaps government economic sites are taken down, viruses flood networks, and files are deleted from the machines of thousands of businesspeople, economists, and stockbrokers. Thousands of credit cards and bank numbers are released on the Internet, guaranteeing that many will be misused. It is also highly likely that the cracking team members four and five will have some success—meaning that possibly one or more banking systems are compromised. It does not take an economist to realize that this would easily cost hundreds of millions of dollars, perhaps even billions of dollars. A concerted attack of this nature could easily cause more economic damage to our country than most traditional terrorists attacks (bombings) have ever done. This is illustrated in Figure 12.1.

You could extrapolate on this scenario and imagine not just one group of six cyber terrorists, but five groups of six—each group with a different mission and each mission designed to be committed approximately two weeks apart. In this scenario, the nation's economy would literally be under siege for two and one-half months.

This scenario is not particularly far-fetched when you consider that, in past decades, nuclear scientists were sought after by various nations and terrorist groups. More recently, experts in biological weapons have been sought by these same groups. It seems extremely likely that these groups will see the possibilities of this form of terrorism and seek out computer security/hacking experts. Given that there are thousands of people with the requisite skills, it seems likely that a motivated organization could find a few dozen people willing to commit these acts.

FIGURE 12.1   A team member of Group X?

# Military Operations Attacks

When computer security and national defense are mentioned together, the obvious thought that comes to mind is the possibility of some hacker breaking into ultra-secure systems at the Department of Defense, Central Intelligence Agency (CIA), or National Security Agency (NSA). However, such an intrusion into one of the most secure systems in the world is very unlikely—not impossible, but very unlikely. The most likely outcome of such an attack would be that the attacker is promptly captured. Such systems are hyper-secure, and intruding upon them is not as easy as some movies might suggest. However, there are a number of scenarios in which breaking into less secure systems could jeopardize our national defense or put military plans at risk.

Consider less sensitive military systems for a moment—systems that are responsible for basic logistical operations (such as food, mail, fuel). If someone cracks one or more of these systems, he could perhaps obtain information that several C-141s (an aircraft often used for troop transports and parachute operations) are being routed to a base that is within flight distance of some city—a city that has been the focal point of political tensions. This same cracker (or team of crackers) also finds that a large amount of ammunition and food supplies, enough for perhaps 5,000 troops for two weeks, is simultaneously being routed to that base. Then, on yet another low-security system, the cracker (or team of crackers) notes that a given unit, such as two brigades of the 82nd Airborne Division, has had all military leaves canceled. It does not take a military genius to conclude that these two brigades are preparing to drop in on the target city and secure that target. Therefore, the fact that a deployment is going to occur, the size of the deployment, and the approximate time of that deployment have all been deduced without ever attempting to break into a high-security system.

Taking the previous scenario to the next level, assume the hacker gets deep into the low-security logistical systems. Then assume that he does nothing to change the routing of the members of the brigades or the transport planes—actions that might draw attention. However, he does alter the records for the shipment of supplies so that the supplies are delivered two days late and to the wrong base. So there would be two brigades potentially in harm's way, without a resupply of ammunition or food en route. Of course, the situation could be rectified, but the units in question may go for some time without resupply—enough time, perhaps, to prevent them from successfully completing their mission.

These are just two scenarios in which compromising low-security/low-priority systems can lead to very significant military problems. This further illustrates the serious need for high security on all systems. Given the interconnectivity of so many components of both business and military computer systems, there are no truly "low-priority" security systems.

# General Attacks

The previously outlined scenarios involve specific targets with specific strategies. However, once a specific target is attacked, defenses can be readied for it. There are many security professionals who work constantly to thwart these specific attacks. What may be more threatening is a general and unfocused attack with no specific target. Consider the various virus attacks of late 2003 and early 2004. With the exception of MyDoom, which was clearly aimed at the Santa Cruz Organization, these attacks were not aimed at a specific target. However, the sheer volume of virus attacks and network traffic did cause significant economic damage. IT personnel across the globe dropped their normal projects to clean infected systems and shore up the defenses of systems. While these attacks are several years old, they are typical and thus worthy of study.

This leads to another possible scenario in which various cyber terrorists continuously release new and varied viruses, perform denial of service attacks, and work to make the Internet in general, and e-commerce in particular, virtually unusable for a period of time. Such a scenario would actually be more difficult to combat, as there would not be a specific target to defend or a clear ideological motive to use as a clue to the identity of the perpetrators.

# Supervisory Control and Data Acquisitions (SCADA)

These are industrial systems used to operate and monitor large-scale equipment (for example, power generators, civil defense alarms, water treatment plants). These systems are very attractive targets for cyber terrorism. In 2009, *60 Minutes* did a report on the vulnerability of power systems. It showed that penetration testers working for the Department of Energy were able to take over a power generator and potentially overload it, causing permanent damage and taking it offline. The famous Stuxnet virus that infected Iranian nuclear facilities was exploiting a vulnerability in SCADA systems.

These systems are of particular concern because damage to them is not simply an economic attack. It is entirely possible for lives to be lost as a result of cyber attacks on SCADA systems.

# Information Warfare

*Information warfare* certainly predates the advent of the modern computer and, in fact, may be as old as conventional warfare. In essence, information warfare is any attempt to manipulate information in pursuit of a military or political goal. When you attempt to use any process to gather information on an opponent or when you use propaganda to influence opinions in a conflict, these are both examples of information warfare. Chapter 7, "Industrial Espionage in Cyberspace," discussed the role of the computer in corporate espionage. The same techniques can be applied to a military conflict in which the computer can be used as a tool in espionage. Although information gathering will not be reexamined in this chapter, it is only one part of information warfare. Propaganda is another aspect of information warfare. The flow of information impacts troop morale, citizens' outlooks on a conflict, the political support for a conflict, and the involvement of peripheral nations and international organizations.

## Propaganda

Computers and the Internet are very effective tools that can be used in the dissemination of propaganda. Many people now use the Internet as a secondary news source, and some even use it as their primary news source. This means that a government, terrorist group, political party, or any activist group could use what appears to be an Internet news website as a front to put its own political spin on any conflict. Such a website does not need to be directly connected to the political organization whose views are being disseminated; in fact, it is better if it is not directly connected. The Irish Republican Army (IRA), for example, has always operated with two distinct and separate divisions: one that takes paramilitary/terrorist action and another that is purely political. This allows the political/information wing, called Sinn Féin, to operate independently of any military or terrorist activities. In fact, Sinn Féin now has its own website, shown in Figure 12.2, where it disseminates news with its own perspective (www.sinnfein.org). In this situation, however, it is fairly clear to whomever is reading the information that it is biased toward the perspective of the party sponsoring the site. A better scenario (for the party concerned) occurs when there is an Internet news source that is favorably disposed to a political group's position without having any actual connection. This makes it easier for the group to spread information without being accused of obvious bias. The political group (be it a nation, rebel group, or terrorist organization) can then "leak" stories to this news agency.

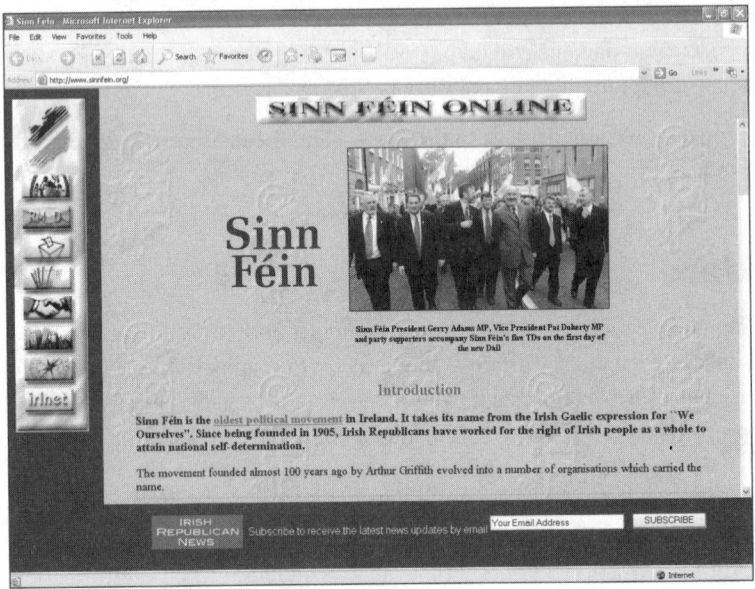

**FIGURE 12.2**   The Sinn Féin website.

## Information Control

Since World War II, control of information has been an important part of political and military conflicts. Following are just a few examples:

- Throughout the Cold War, Western democracies invested time and money for radio broadcasts into communist nations. This well-known campaign was referred to as Radio Free Europe. The goal was to create dissatisfaction among citizens of those nations, hopefully encouraging defection, dissent, and general discontent. Most historians and political analysts agree that this was a success.

- The Vietnam War was the first modern war in which there was strong and widespread domestic opposition. Many analysts believe that opposition was due to the graphic images being brought home via television.

- Today, the government and military of every nation are aware of how the phrases they use to describe activities can affect public perception. They do not say that innocent civilians were killed in a bombing raid. Rather, they state that there was "some collateral damage." Governments do not speak of being the aggressor or starting a conflict. They speak of "preemptive action." Dissenters in any nation are almost always painted as treasons or cowards.

Public perception is a very important part of any conflict. Each nation wants its own citizens to be totally in support of what it does and to maintain a very high morale. High morale and strong support lead to volunteers for military service, public support for funding the conflict, and political success for the nation's leader. At the same time, you want the enemy to have low morale—to doubt not only their ability to be successful in the conflict but also their moral position relative to the conflict. You want them to doubt their leadership and to be as opposed to the conflict as possible. The Internet provides a very inexpensive vehicle for swaying public opinion.

Web pages are just one facet of disseminating information. Having people post to various discussion groups can also be effective. One full-time propaganda agent could easily manage 25 or more distinct online personalities, each spending time in different bulletin boards and discussion groups, espousing the views that his political entity wants to espouse. These can reinforce what certain Internet news outlets are posting, or they could undermine those postings. They can also start rumors. Rumors can be very effective even when probably false. People often recall hearing something with only a vague recollection of where they heard it and whether it was supported by data.

Such an agent could have one personality that purports to be a military member (it would take very little research to make this credible) and could post information "not seen in newscasts" that would cast the conflict in either a positive or a negative light. She could then have other online personas that entered the discussion who would agree with and support the original position. This would give the initial rumor more credibility. Some people suspect this is already occurring in Usenet newsgroups and Yahoo! discussion boards. Obviously, Usenet and Yahoo! are just two examples. The Internet is replete with various blogs, community sites, boards, and more.

## FYI: Cyber Information Warfare Now

Anyone familiar with Yahoo! news boards (this is just one example; there are certainly many more) has probably noticed an odd phenomenon. At certain times, there will be a flood of posts from anonymous users, all saying essentially the same things—even using the same grammar, punctuation, and phrasing—and all in support of some ideological perspective. These flurries often happen in times when influence of public opinion is important, such as when an election is nearing. Whether or not these postings are coordinated by a well-known or official organization is debatable. However, they are an example of information warfare. One person or group of people attempt to sway opinion by flooding one particular media (Internet groups) with various items advocating one view. If they are lucky, some individuals will copy the text and email it to friends who do not participate in the newsgroups, thus crossing over to another media and spreading opinions (in some cases entirely unfounded) far and wide.

> ### FYI: Disinformation—A Historical Perspective
>
> While disinformation campaigns are certainly easier to conduct since the advent of mass communication, particularly the Internet, such activities did exist prior to the Internet, or even television. For example, in the weeks leading up the famous D-Day invasion of World War II, the Allied forces used a number of disinformation techniques:
>
> - They created documents and communiqués listing fictitious military units that would invade from an entirely different location than the real invasion was planned.
>
> - They used Allied double agents to spread similar disinformation to the Germans.
>
> - A few small groups simulated a large-scale invasion to distract the German army.

## Disinformation

Another category of information warfare that is closely related to propaganda is disinformation. It is a given that a military opponent is attempting to gather information about troop movements, military strength, supplies, and so forth. A prudent move would be to set up systems that had incorrect information and were just secure enough to be credible but not secure enough to be unbreakable. An example would be to send an encrypted coded message such that, when the message is decrypted, it seems to say one thing, but to those who can complete the code it has a different message. The actual message is "padded" with "noise." That noise is a weakly encrypted false message, whereas the real message is more strongly encrypted. In this way, if the message is decrypted, there exists a high likelihood that the fake message will be decrypted and not the real one. General Gray, USMC, put it best when he said, "Communications without intelligence is noise; intelligence without communications is irrelevant" (*Information Warfare*, 2004).

The goal of any military or intelligence agency is to make certain our communications are clear and that the enemy can only receive noise.

## Actual Cases

There have been several cases already mentioned in this chapter. In this section we will look at other cases briefly. We will examine incidents over a 20-year period from 1996 to 2016. It should be noted that there are voices in the computer security industry that think cyber terrorism or cyber war are simply not realistic scenarios. Marcus Ranum of *Information Security* magazine states as much in the April 2004 issue. He and others claim that there is no danger from cyber terrorism and that, in fact, "The whole notion of cyberwarfare is a scam" (*Information Security*, 2004). However, computer warfare and cyber terrorism have already been used on a small scale. It seems quite plausible that, in a matter of time, it will be seen on a much larger scale.

Even if you believe that the scenarios outlined in the earlier sections of this chapter are merely the product of an overactive imagination, you should consider that there have already been a few actual incidents of cyber terrorism, although much less severe than the theoretical scenarios. This section examines some of these cases to show you how such attacks have been carried out in the past.

The incidents listed next were reported in testimony before the Special Oversight Panel on Terrorism Committee on Armed Services U.S. House of Representatives (Cyberterrorism, 2000). Earlier in this chapter, we listed more recent attacks, but these older attacks are important to illustrate just how long this problem has been going on.

- In 1996, a computer hacker allegedly associated with the white supremacist movement temporarily disabled a Massachusetts ISP and damaged part of the ISP's record-keeping system. The ISP had attempted to stop the hacker from sending out worldwide racist messages under the ISP's name. The hacker signed off with the threat, "You have yet to see true electronic terrorism. This is a promise."

- In 1998, ethnic Tamil guerrillas swamped Sri Lankan embassies with 800 emails a day over a two-week period. The messages read, "We are the Internet Black Tigers and we're doing this to disrupt your communications." Intelligence authorities characterized it as the first known attack by terrorists against a country's computer systems.

- During the Kosovo conflict in 1999, NATO computers were blasted with email bombs and hit with DoS attacks by *hacktivists* (the name applied to individuals who work for their causes using cyber terrorism) protesting the NATO bombings. In addition, according to reports, businesses, public organizations, and academic institutes received highly politicized virus-laden emails from a range of Eastern European countries. Web defacements were also common. After the Chinese embassy was accidentally bombed in Belgrade, Chinese hacktivists posted messages such as, "We won't stop attacking until the war stops!" on U.S. government websites.

- Lest you think all attacks cause no real damage, in 2009 the United States Pentagon admitted that it had spent $100 million over a six-month period, responding to and repairing damage from cyber attacks.

- In August 2010, the United States publically warned that the Chinese military was targeting American companies as well as government agencies. The United States further warned that the Chinese government was utilizing civilian experts in these attacks. In this report a Chinese computer spying network named GhostNet was revealed.

- In 2013, the *New York Times* reported multiple cyber attacks, all targeting financial institutions within the United States. All appear to have been instigated from Iran.

- Also in 2013, several media companies including *Huffington Post*, Twitter, and *New York Times* were targeted by the Syrian Electronic Army. Visitors to the compromised sites were redirected to sites chosen by the hackers.

The good news is that most of these attacks caused little damage and were clearly the product of amateurs. However, it may only be a matter of time before more damaging attacks are perpetrated by far more skilled cyber terrorists. Yet it is clear that cyber terrorism, at least on a low-intensity scale, is already beginning. These warnings can be heeded and the issues taken seriously, or they can simply be ignored until disaster strikes. We will also be looking at other items of concern, such as the recruiting of terrorists via the Internet, later in this chapter.

In addition to those cases just listed, there have been other credible threats or actual incidents of cyber attacks in the past several years:

- In 2002, Counterpane Internet Security reported (as shown in Figure 12.3) a credible threat of a Chinese-backed, all-out cyber attack planned on the United States and Taiwan (2002). A private group of Chinese hackers, called the Chinese Eagle Union, planned to attack routers and web servers across the United States and Taiwan. The attack never materialized, but unconfirmed reports suggested that the CIA took the threat seriously.

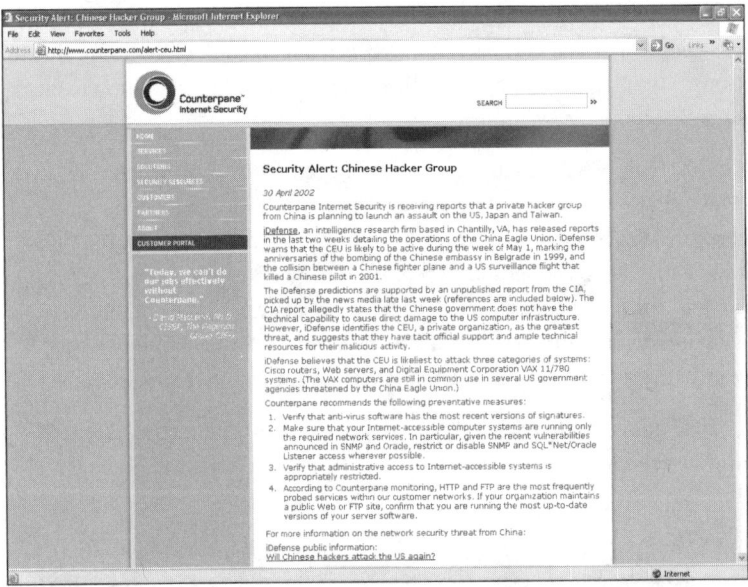

**FIGURE 12.3**　Counterpane Internet Security report on a planned cyber attack.

- In June 2000, Russian authorities arrested a man they accused of being a CIA-backed hacker. As shown in Figure 12.4, this man allegedly hacked into systems of the Russian Domestic Security Service (FSB) and gathered secrets that he then passed on to the CIA (BBC Report, 2000). This example illustrates the potential for a skilled hacker using her knowledge to conduct espionage operations. This espionage is likely occurring much more often than is reported in the media, and many such incidents may never come to light.

**FIGURE 12.4**   BBC report on an arrested hacker.

■ Operation Ababil was a hacktivist-led attack in 2012 that executed DoS attacks on the New York Stock Exchange and various banks. The hactivist group Qassam Cyber Fighters claimed credit.

■ Perhaps most disconcerting was the 2015 breach of the United States Office of Personnel Management. It is estimated that over 21 million records were stolen, including detailed background checks of persons with security clearances.

Alternative media sources have been reporting that both the CIA and the NSA have employed hackers for some time. This might be easily dismissed as false were it not for the fact that such hackers have actually been caught, as in the Russian story. One might even go so far as to say that, in our modern age, for intelligence gathering agencies not to employee cyber intelligence-gathering techniques would be a dereliction of their duty.

What is also frightening to consider are reports that our satellites, used for communication, weather, and military operations, could be vulnerable to hacking (InfoWorld, 2002). Such vulnerabilities seem less likely simply because of the skill level required to execute such an attack. As previously mentioned, hacking/cracking is like any other human endeavor—by the law of averages, most people are mediocre. The level of skill required to compromise security on a satellite system is far greater than that required to compromise the security of a website. Of course, that does not mean that such an attack is impossible, but simply that it is less likely.

# Future Trends

By carefully analyzing what is occurring presently in cyber crime and terrorism along with the recent history of that field, you can extrapolate and make reasonably accurate estimates for what trends will dominate in the near future. This section will endeavor to do that. There are certainly positive and negative trends that should be considered.

## Positive Trends

It does seem that various governments are beginning to take notice of this problem and are taking some steps to ameliorate the dangers. For example, then Senator John Edwards (D-NC) proposed two bills in 2002 aimed at allocating $400 million for cyber security efforts. The first measure, called the Cyberterrorism Preparedness Act of 2002 (Tech Law, 2002), a portion of which is shown in Figure 12.5, allocated $350 million over five years for improving network security, first for federal systems and then for the private sector. It would also create a group assigned to gather and distribute information about the best security practices. The Cybersecurity Research and Education Act of 2002 (The Orator, 2002), a portion of which is shown in Figure 12.6, would provide $50 million over four years for fellowships that would be used to train IT specialists in cyber security. It also calls for the creation of a web-based university where administrators can get updated training. The Cybersecurity Research and Education act was passed and became Public Law 107-305. The Cyberterrorism Preparedness Act of 2002 was not passed. However, many of its goals were addressed by the PATRIOT Act.

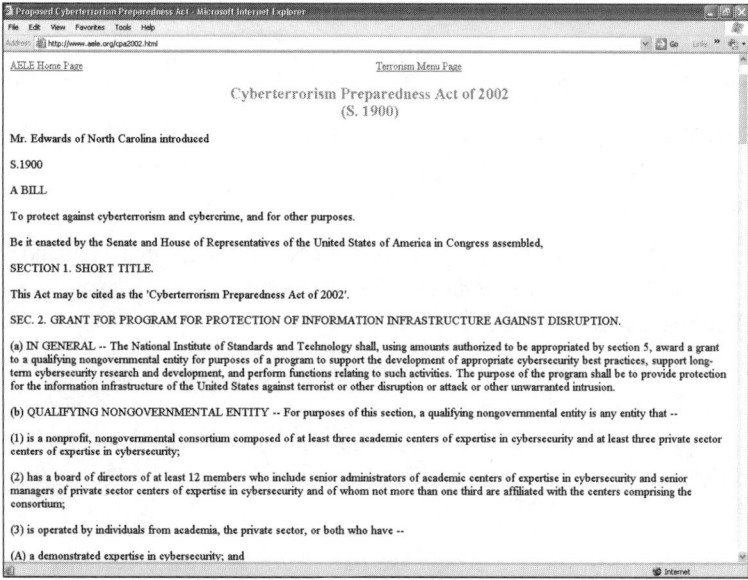

**FIGURE 12.5**   The Cyberterrorism Preparedness Act of 2002.

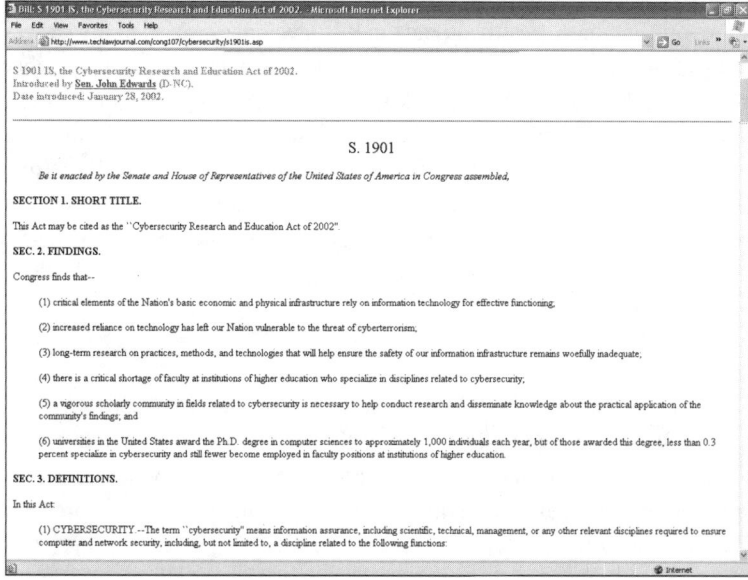

**FIGURE 12.6**   The Cybersecurity Research and Education Act of 2002.

Title VIII of the U.S. PATRIOT Act specifically deals with cyber terrorism. The number of cyber attacks included in that definition of *cyber terrorism* is expansive, including attempts to damage or alter medical records and releasing a virus in a target system. Penalties are also clearly set out.

More recently, in 2010 the United States Department of Defense established the U.S. Cyber Command (USCYBERCOM). This unit is based in Ft. Meade, Maryland, and is a joint task force representing components of all four U.S. armed services.

In 2011 the Dutch Ministry of Defense formulated and published a cyber strategy that included a joint cyber defense military unit. The Dutch ministry of defense has also established an offensive and defensive cyber force named Defensie Cyber Command (DCC).

In 2013 Germany revealed that IT had a Computer Network Operations unit. Some public reports suggested the unit was rather small with about 60 members, but the nature of the unit makes it difficult to get accurate numbers. It was reported that the German Intelligence Agency (Federal Intelligence Service in English, Bundesnachrichtendienst in German, commonly known as simply BND) began in 2013 to hire a number of hackers.

What we see are more and more nations treating cyber defense like any other area of defense and establishing the appropriate military and intelligence organizations to deal with it.

In the second edition of this book, I stated, "It is unreasonable to ask every police department to have a computer-crime specialist on staff. However, state-level investigative agencies should be able to hire such personnel." I am thrilled to report that many positive trends in this area have exceeded my expectations. First, many law enforcement agencies, even small local agencies, do indeed now have cyber forensic detectives. There are also a number of cybercrime task forces that bring together state, local, and federal resources. For example, the U.S. Secret Service had established Electronic Crimes Task Forces around the country that bring together state, local, and federal resources to combat cybercrime and terrorism. The Department of Homeland Security has set up regional Fusion Centers to assist in coordinating the sharing of information between intelligence agencies and law enforcement agencies, at all levels.

## Negative Trends

Unfortunately, as legislative bodies become aware of this problem and focus some resources on the issue, the threats continue to grow. In a paper commissioned by the Rand Corporation (Hoffman, 2003), it is noted that even groups such as Al Qaeda—who have not used cyber terrorism as one of their attack modalities as of this writing—have used Internet and computer technology resources to plan their various activities and coordinate training.

As early as 2000, the U.S. General Accounting Office warned of several possible cyber terrorism scenarios (*The Tech Law Journal*, 2000). As shown in Figure 12.7, their concerns involved far more lethal attackers than any of the scenarios that have been outlined in this chapter. They proposed possible attack scenarios in which the computer-controlled machinery in a chemical plant was altered in order to cause a release of toxic chemicals into the environment. This could be done in a variety of ways, including simply causing the machinery to drastically overproduce, overheat, or perhaps prematurely shut down equipment. The panel also contemplated scenarios in which water and power supplies were interrupted or compromised via computer systems. In essence, their focus was on the potential for massive casualties as a direct result of a cyber-based attack rather than the economic damage on which this chapter's scenarios focused.

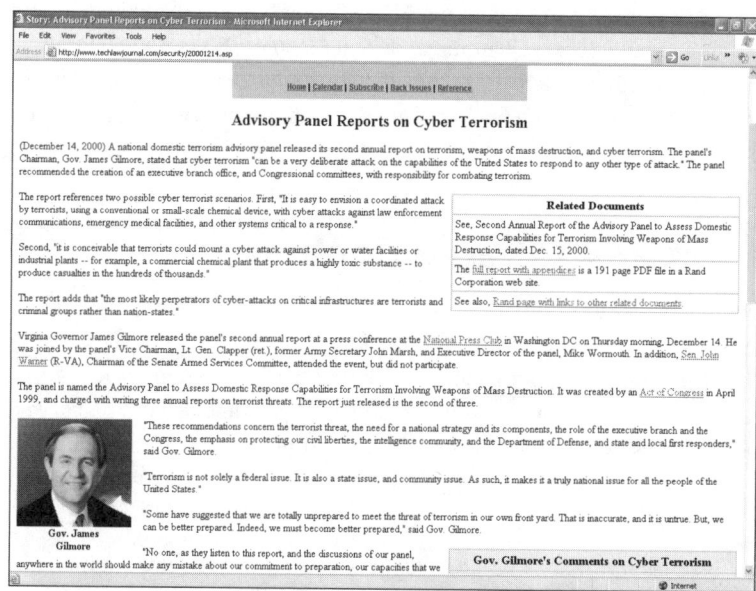

**FIGURE 12.7** Rand report on cyber terrorism.

# Defense Against Cyber Terrorism

As the world becomes more dependent upon computer systems, the danger of cyber terrorism will grow. Clearly, there must be a much stronger emphasis on computer security. In addition to the basic security measures already recommended in this book, there are some recommendations for preparing for and protecting systems against cyber terrorism:

- Major academic institutions must begin dedicated research and academic programs that are devoted solely to computer security.

- Computer crime must be treated far more seriously, with stronger punishments and more active investigation of suspected crimes.

- Rather than take law enforcement officers and train them in basic computer crime, I have always recommended that it is more appropriate to take highly skilled computer professionals and train them in law enforcement. To adequately combat cyber terrorism, one absolutely must first and foremost be a highly qualified computer expert.

- An emergency reporting system may need to be implemented so that security professionals from various industries have a single source where they can report attacks on their systems and can view the issues with which other security professionals are dealing. This could enable security professionals as a group to more quickly recognize when a coordinated attack is occurring.

In addition, you can make some additions to and variations on your existing security measures. For example, you should have a recovery process in place so that data can be quickly recovered should someone delete important files. You should also, as recommended in Chapter 9, assess what data is of most value and focus your attention on that data. But, as this chapter points out, you must consider how data that would at first appear to be of less value may actually reveal more information about you personally or your company than is prudent.

# Terrorist Recruiting and Communication

The Internet is an incredible communication tool. But it also serves as a communications and recruiting tool for terrorist groups. Internet chat rooms are perfect meeting places where terrorists can communicate and plan. One can easily set up a private chat room or bulletin board. Members of a terrorist group can then use public terminals to log in to that chat room or bulletin board and discuss plans. The terror network in the Netherlands that was responsible for the killing of filmmaker Theo van Gogh met regularly on Yahoo! to devise and discuss its plans. This is just one example of a terrorist group using the Internet to plan attacks.

The Internet's ubiquitous nature enables terrorists who are geographically separated to communicate and coordinate. Websites allow terrorist groups to spread propaganda, raise funds, and recruit new members. And, as discussed, the Internet will even enable extremist groups to inspire lone individuals to act on their own, but in the interests of the group.

It is also a fact that various terrorist groups have been using social media for recruiting purposes. Social media can be used to locate and entice those likely to be sympathetic to the terrorist organization. Then a grooming process can occur (not unlike that used by pedophiles). If needed, the terrorist group can even provide the new terrorist with training on topics like bomb making, via the Internet. The advantage to the terrorist organization is that if the fledgling terrorist is caught, he has no knowledge of the terrorist organization. He has never even met any of the members, so he cannot give any information.

# TOR and the Dark Web

TOR, or The Onion Router, may not seem like a military application of cryptography; however, it is appropriate to cover this topic in this chapter for two reasons:

- The TOR project is based on an earlier Onion Routing protocol developed by the United States Navy, specifically for military applications. So TOR is an example of military technology being adapted to civilian purposes.

- TOR is used by privacy advocates every day. But it is also used by terrorist groups and organized criminals.

TOR consists of thousands of volunteer relays spread around the world. Each relay uses encryption to conceal the origin and even final destination of the traffic passing through it. Each relay is only able to decrypt one layer of the encryption, revealing the next stop in the path. Only the final relay is aware of the destination, and only the first relay is aware of the origin. This makes tracing network traffic practically impossible.

The basic concepts for onion routing were developed at the U.S. Naval Research Laboratory in the mid-1990s and later refined by the Defense Advanced Research Projects Agency (DARPA). The goal was to provide secure intelligence communication online.

Onion routers communicate using TLS (covered in depth in Chapter 13, "Cyber Detective") and ephemeral keys. Ephemeral keys are so called because they are created for one specific use and then destroyed immediately after that use. 128-bit AES is often used as the symmetric key.[3]

While the TOR network is a very effective tool for maintaining privacy, it has also become a way to hide criminal activity. There exist markets on the TOR network that are used expressly to sell and distribute illegal products and services. Stolen credit card numbers and other financial data are a common product on TOR markets. The images in Figures 12.8 and 12.9 give you some insight into what is on the Dark Web. These are actual screen shots. It must be noted that neither I nor the publisher endorses these sites. In fact, I work with law enforcement regularly and am opposed to what is done on these websites. However, if you are going to learn cyber security, you should know what is out there.

**FIGURE 12.8**   Fake passports on the Dark Web.

3. Dingledine, R., N. Mathewson, P. Syverson. "Tor: The Second-Generation Onion Router." http://www.onion-router.net/Publications/tor-design.pdf.

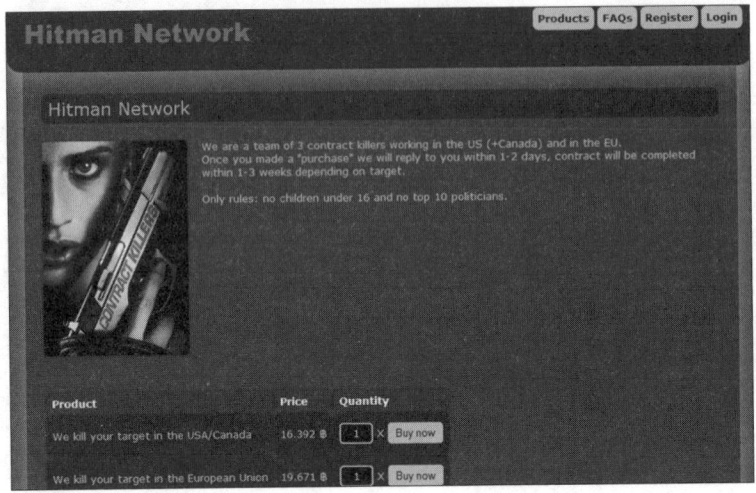

**FIGURE 12.9**   Murder for hire on the Dark Web.

Are some sites on the Dark Web fake? Of course. Some are simply scamming people out of their money and not delivering the nefarious service or money. But many are real—particularly those selling stolen credit cards, drugs, and child pornography.

In 2015, the founder of Silk Road, Ross Ulbricht, the most well-known of the TOR markets, was sentenced to life in prison. Many people on various news outlets are claiming this sentence is draconian. And one can certainly argue the merits of any sentence. But allow me to give you food for thought. Silk Road was not simply a venue for privacy or even for marijuana exchanges. It became a hub for massive drug dealing, including heroin, cocaine, and meth. It was also used to traffic in arms, stolen credit cards, child pornography, and even murder for hire. The venue Mr. Ulbricht created was a hub for thousands of very serious felonies.

# Summary

It is clear that there are a variety of ways in which cyber terrorist attacks could be used against any industrialized nation. Many experts, including various government panels, senators, and terrorism experts, believe that this is a very real threat. This means that it is more important than ever to be extremely vigilant in securing your computer systems. You must also look beyond the obvious uses of data and see how someone with an intent to harm or cause economic hardship could use seemingly unimportant information. In the exercises at the end of this chapter, you will have a chance to explore various cyber terrorism and information warfare threats.

## Test Your Skills

### MULTIPLE CHOICE QUESTIONS

1. What is the most likely damage from an act of cyber terrorism?

   A. Loss of life

   B. Military strategy compromised

   C. Economic loss

   D. Disrupted communications

2. Which of the following is not an example of financial loss due to cyber terrorism?

   A. Lost data

   B. Transferring money from accounts

   C. Damage to facilities including computers

   D. Computer fraud

3. Which of the following military/government systems would most likely be the target of a successful computer hack?

   A. The most sensitive systems of the CIA

   B. Nuclear systems at NORAD

   C. Low-security logistical system

   D. Military satellite control systems

4. Which of the following might be an example of domestic cyber terrorism?

   A. Sasser virus

   B. Mimail virus

   C. Sobig virus

   D. MyDoom virus

5. What differentiates cyber terrorism from other computer crimes?

   A. It is organized.

   B. It is politically or ideologically motivated.

   C. It is conducted by experts.

   D. It is often more successful.

6. Which of the following is a political group that has already used the Internet for political intimidation?

   A. Internet Black Tigers

   B. Al Qaeda

   C. Mafia

   D. IRA

7. What is information warfare?

   A. Only spreading disinformation

   B. Spreading disinformation or gathering information

   C. Only gathering information

   D. Spreading disinformation or secure communications

8. Which of the following would most likely be considered an example of information warfare?

   A. Radio Free Europe during the Cold War

   B. Radio political talk show

   C. Normal news reports

   D. Military press releases

9. Which of the following is a likely use of Internet newsgroups in information warfare?

   A. To spread propaganda

   B. To monitor dissident groups

   C. To send encoded messages

   D. To recruit supporters

10. Sending a false message with weak encryption, intending it to be intercepted and deciphered, is an example of what?

    A. Poor communications

    B. Need for better encryption

    C. Disinformation

    D. Propaganda

11. Which of the following best describes the communication goal of any intelligence agency?

   A. To send clear communications to allies and noise to all other parties

   B. To send clear communications to allies and noise only to the enemy

   C. To send disinformation to the enemy

   D. To send clear communications to allied forces

12. Which of the following conflicts had a cyber warfare component?

   A. 1989 invasion of Panama

   B. 1990 Kosovo crisis

   C. 1990 Somalia crisis

   D. Vietnam War

13. Which of the following agencies has allegedly had one of its cyber spies actually caught?

   A. NSA

   B. KGB

   C. FBI

   D. CIA

14. According to the October 2002 *InfoWorld* magazine article, which of the following systems may be vulnerable to attack?

   A. NORAD nuclear weapons control

   B. Low-level logistical systems

   C. Satellites

   D. CIA computers

15. Which of the following is a cyber attack that would likely cause imminent loss of life?

   A. Disruption of banking system

   B. Disruption of water

   C. Disruption of security systems

   D. Disruption of chemical plant control systems

## EXERCISES

### EXERCISE 12.1: **Finding Information Warfare**

1. Pick a current political topic.

2. Track that topic on multiple bulletin boards, Yahoo! newsgroups, or blogs.

3. Look for signs that might indicate an organized effort to sway opinion or information warfare. This might include posts allegedly made by separate individuals that have highly similar points, grammar, and syntax.

4. Write a brief essay discussing what you found and why you think it constitutes information warfare.

### EXERCISE 12.2: **Cyber Terrorism Threat Assessment**

1. Pick some activist group (political, ideological) that you find intriguing.

2. Using only the Web, gather as much information about that organization as you can.

3. Write a brief dossier on that group, including what you think is the likelihood that such a group would engage in information warfare or cyber terrorism and why.

### EXERCISE 12.3: **Finding Information Policies**

1. Using the Web or other resources, locate several examples of organizational policies regarding information dissemination.

2. Find points common to all such policies.

3. Write a brief essay explaining why these policies might be related to either propagating or preventing information warfare.

### EXERCISE 12.4: **How Companies Defend AGAINST Cyber Terrorism**

1. Interview the IT staff of a company to find out whether they take information warfare or cyber terrorism into direct account when they are securing their systems.

2. Find out what steps they take to protect their company's systems from these threats.

3. Write a brief essay explaining what you have found out.

### EXERCISE 12.5: **Pulling It All Together**

Pulling together what you have learned from previous chapters, what information can you apply to the protection of a system against cyber terrorism or information warfare? Write a brief outline of the steps you would take to secure a system against these threats.

## PROJECTS

### PROJECT 12.1: **Computer Security and Cyber Terrorism**

Consider the various security measures you have examined thus far in this book. Given the threat of cyber terrorism, write an essay discussing how those methods might relate to cyber terrorism. Also discuss whether or not the threat of computer-based terrorism warrants a higher security standard than you might have otherwise used, and explain why or why not.

### PROJECT 12.2: **The Law and Cyber Terrorism**

Note: This is meant as a group project.

Using the Web or other resources, find and examine laws that you feel relate to cyber terrorism. Then write an essay describing legislation you believe needs to be written regarding cyber terrorism. Essentially, your group should act as if it were technical advisors to a congressional committee drafting new legislation.

### PROJECT 12.3: **Cyber Terrorism Scenario**

Considering any of the theoretical cyber terrorism scenarios presented in this chapter, write a security and response plan that you feel addresses that scenario and protects against that specific threat.

### Case Study

Jane Doe is the network administrator responsible for security for a small defense contractor. Her company does handle some low-level classified material. She has implemented a strong security approach that includes the following:

- A firewall has all unneeded ports closed.
- Virus scanners are placed on all machines.
- Routers between network segments are secured.
- All machines have the operating systems patched monthly.
- Passwords are long, complex, and change every 90 days.

What other recommendations would you make to Jane Doe? Explain the reasons for each of your recommendations.

## Chapter 13

# Cyber Detective

## Chapter Objectives

**After reading this chapter and completing the exercises, you will be able to do the following:**

- Find contact information on the Web
- Locate court records on the Web
- Locate criminal records on the Web
- Use Usenet newsgroups to gather information

## Introduction

In the preceding chapters we have examined many facets of computer security. Three of those issues led us to the content of this chapter. The first is identity theft, the second is hacking, and the third is investigating potential employees for sensitive positions.

In order for a criminal to perpetrate identity theft, she has to take a small amount of information she finds on her target and use that to garner even more information. Perhaps a discarded credit card receipt or utility bill becomes the starting point from which the perpetrator finds enough information to assume the victim's identity. This chapter will show you some techniques that use the Internet to find additional information about a person. You need to be aware of how this is done in order to be better prepared to defend against it and so that you are aware of what information about you personally is available.

Hackers, at least skilled hackers, will want information about a target person, organization, and system in order to assist in compromising security. Whether the perpetrator is attempting to use social engineering or simply trying to guess a password, having information about the target will facilitate the task. Once you realize how easy it is to gain personal information about someone, you will realize why security experts are so adamant that you must not use passwords that are in any way associated with you, your profession, your hobbies, or anything that might be traced back to you.

Finally, when you are hiring employees that might have access to sensitive data, simply calling the references they provide is not an adequate method of checking into their background. And hiring a private investigator may be impractical. The information in this chapter might be of use to you in conducting some level of investigation on your own.

This may surprise some readers, but network administrators are of particular significance to be investigated before hiring. Most companies perform the same cursory check of network administrators as they do of any other person. That usually consists of verifying degrees/certifications and calling references. With some companies it might include a credit check and a local criminal check. However, a network administrator should be more thoroughly investigated. The reason is quite simple: Regardless of how tight your security is, it cannot keep out the person who sets it up and maintains it. If you are considering hiring a network administrator for your company, knowing that he has been affiliated with hacking groups might be of interest to you. Or simply knowing that he has had lapses in judgment might indicate a stronger possibility that he will have similar lapses in the future. This may seem a bit paranoid, but by this point in this book you should have developed a little healthy paranoia.

The Internet can be a valuable investigation tool. It can be used to find out about potential employees, babysitters, and more. Much of the information on the Internet is also free. Many states have court records online, and there are many other resources you can use to find information. In this chapter, we will examine some of the various resources you can use on the Internet to locate critical information.

Before beginning this discussion, a few points need to be made clear, the first being that this information is a two-edged sword. Yes, you can use it to find out if a potential business partner has previously been sued or declared bankruptcy or if your child's little league coach has a criminal record. However, as we briefly mentioned, a less scrupulous person can also use these techniques to gather detailed information about you, either for the purpose of identity theft or perhaps stalking. Some people have suggested to me that perhaps I should not put this information (and some other items that appear in various chapters) in this book. However, my opinion is that the hackers, crackers, and perpetrators of identity theft already know about these resources. My hope is to level the playing field. I would also warn all readers that invading other people's privacy is fraught with ethical, moral, and in many cases, legal ramifications. It would be advisable to obtain written permission before running a background check on any person—or, better yet, play it safe and only perform searches on your own name. It must also be stressed that I am neither an attorney nor a law enforcement officer. I am simply providing you with techniques and resources. If you have questions about legality, you should refer those questions to an attorney.

# General Searches

Sometimes you simply want to find an address, phone number, or email address for a person. Or perhaps that is the starting point for a more thorough investigation. There are a number of absolutely free services on the Web that will allow you to perform this sort of search. Some are better than others, and obviously the more common the name you are searching for the harder it will be to find the right one. If you do a search for John Smith in California, you might have a tough time dealing with all the results you get. No matter what search mechanism you utilize (LinkedIn, Facebook, and so on), the problem is the same.

A fairly easy-to-use service is the Yahoo! People Search. When you go to www.yahoo.com you see a number of options on the page. One option is the People Search shown in Figure 13.1. Or you can simply go directly to http://itools.com/tool/yahoo-people-search.

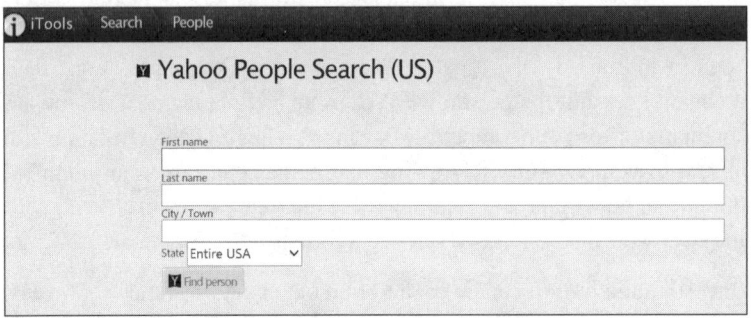

FIGURE 13.1   Yahoo! People Search.

When you select this option, you will see a screen similar to the one shown in Figure 13.2. In this screen, you enter a first and last name, as well as a city or state. You can then search for either a phone number/address or an email.

| First Name | Last Name (req'd) | City/Town | State | |
|---|---|---|---|---|
| Chuck | Easttom | | | Go |
| **Chuck Easttom** | WILLOW CREEK TRL MCKINNEY, TX 75071 | | | |
| **Chuck Easttom** | WILLOW CREEK TRL MCKINNEY, TX 75071 | | | |

FIGURE 13.2   Search options.

To illustrate how this works, I did a search on my own name, in Texas (where I live). The data shown in Figure 13.3 is an old address, not the new one. That illustrates that these searches are not perfect. This isn't demonstrated in the figure, but an inaccurate phone number also appears. You may also note that in some cases (as with mine) the search with options is the same as the search without. The issue is that I have a less common last name. If you are searching for someone with a common name, then the options can be very useful in refining your search.

| First Name | Last Name (req'd) | City/Town | State | |
|---|---|---|---|---|
| Chuck | Easttom | | | Go |

| | | |
|---|---|---|
| **Chuck Easttom** | WILLOW CREEK TRL | |
| | MCKINNEY, TX 75071 | |
| **Chuck Easttom** | WILLOW CREEK TRL | |
| | MCKINNEY, TX 75071 | |

**FIGURE 13.3** People Search results.

Another useful site for addresses and phone numbers around the world is www.infobel.com/en/ world. This site has the advantage of being international, allowing you to seek out phone numbers and addresses in a variety of countries. As you can see from Figure 13.4, the first step is to select a country to search in.

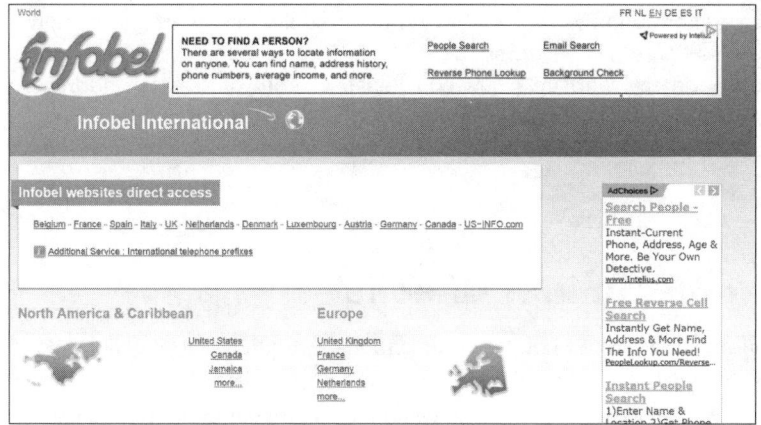

**FIGURE 13.4** Infobel home page.

Once you have selected your country, you can then narrow your search further by providing as much information as you can on the person you are trying to locate. A first and last name, however, is a minimum.

These are just two of the many sites that allow you to investigate and discover a person's home address or telephone number. Several other good sites you should consider are listed here:

- www.yellowpages.com
- www.theultimates.com/white/
- www.facebook.com
- www.whowhere.com

- www.switchboard.com

- www.LinkedIn.com

It is important to remember that the more information you can provide, and the more you narrow down your search, the greater the likelihood of finding what you are looking for. All of these websites can assist you in finding phone numbers and addresses, both current and past. For a background check on an employee, this can be useful in verifying previous addresses.

---

**FYI: Respecting Privacy**

You might wonder why I would be willing to put my home address and phone number in a published book. To begin with, the phone number and address displayed are not accurate. They are old and no longer valid. And, in order to illustrate the process, I needed a name to use. For the liability reasons mentioned earlier, I could not have used someone else's name. Anyone who wishes to find my current information would not have much trouble. I have an uncommon last name and am a semi-public figure. However, should readers wish to contact me, they are strongly encouraged to do so via my website (www.chuckeasttom.com) and email address (chuck@chuckeasttom.com) rather than via phone. I try to answer all my email but frequently avoid my phone. And I am certainly not encouraging anyone to make a surprise visit to my home!

---

# Court Records and Criminal Checks

A number of states are now putting a variety of court records online—everything from general court documents to specific records of criminal history and even lists of sex offenders. This sort of information can be critical before you hire an employee, use a babysitter, or send your child to little league. In the following sections, we discuss a variety of resources for this sort of information.

## Sex Offender Registries

First, you should become familiar with the online sex offender registries. The FBI maintains a rather exhaustive list of individual state registries. You can access this information at https://www.fbi.gov/scams-safety/registry. Every state that has an online registry is listed on this website, as shown in Figure 13.5.

Obviously, some states have done a better job of making accurate information public than have others. For example, Texas has a rather comprehensive site. You can find it at https://records.txdps.state.tx.us/DpsWebsite/index.aspx. This site allows you to either look up an individual person or to put in a ZIP code (or city name) and find out any registered sex offenders in that area. Figure 13.6 shows the search screen for the Texas site mentioned.

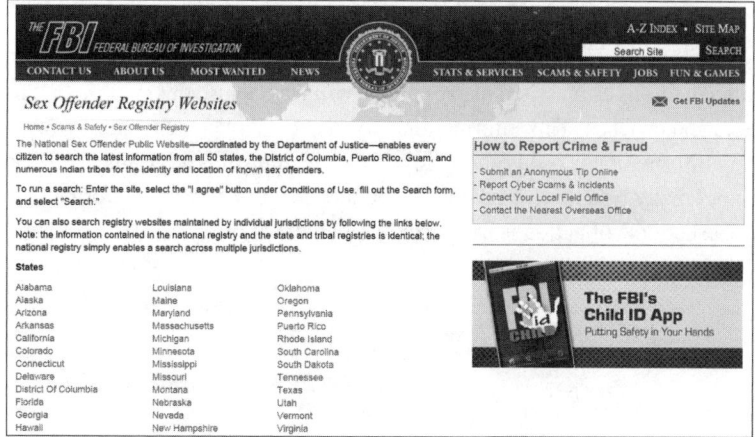

**FIGURE 13.5**   FBI state registry of sex offenders.

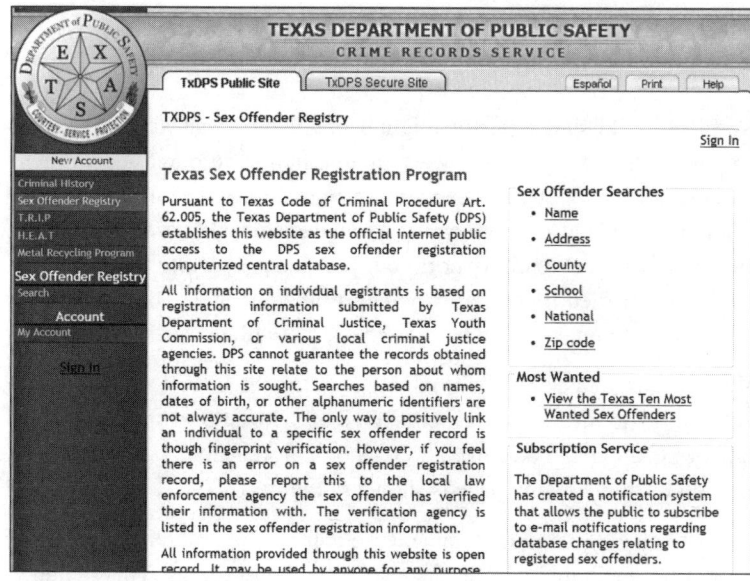

**FIGURE 13.6**   Texas sex offender search page.

One of the most compelling things about the Texas sex offender registry is that it lists the offense the person was convicted of as well as a photo of the offender. This is important since the term *sex offender* covers a wide variety of crimes. Some of these may not, for example, impact whether you should hire this person. It is important to know what a person was convicted of before you decide he is unsuitable to be interacting with your children or working in your organization.

It should also be noted that there in an app for the iPhone/iPad called Offender Locator that will take your GPS location and list registered sex offenders nearby.

Some sex offenders have committed heinous crimes, and many parents will want to use this information to find out about potential babysitters and coaches. This information may also be applicable to employment screenings. However, anytime any information is used for employment screening, it is advisable to check the laws in your area. You may not legally be able to base employment decisions on certain information. As with all legal questions, your best course of action is to consult a reputable attorney.

> **CAUTION**
>
> ### Mistaken Identity
>
> There have been cases of mistaken identity with sex offender lists. Any time you find negative information on a person you are investigating—whatever the source—you have an ethical responsibility to verify that information before you take any action on it.

## Civil Court Records

There are a variety of crimes, as well as civil issues, a person might be involved in that would make her unsuitable for a particular job. If you are hiring a person to work in your human resources department and oversee equal opportunity issues, knowing if she had been involved in domestic violence, racially motivated graffiti, or other similar issues might affect your employment decision. Or, if you are considering a business partnership, it would be prudent to discover if your prospective partner has ever been sued by other business partners or has ever filed for bankruptcy. Unfortunately, in any of these cases, you cannot simply rely on the other party's honesty. You need to check these things out for yourself.

Unfortunately, this area of legal issues has not been transferred to a web format as well as sex crimes. However, many states and federal courts do offer online records. One of the best organized and most complete on this issue is the state of Oklahoma. You can find Oklahoma's website at www.oscn.net/applications/oscn/casesearch.asp, and its home search page is shown in Figure 13.7.

This site allows you to search by last name, last and first name, case number, and more. You will get a complete record of any case you find, including current disposition and any filings. This includes both civil and criminal proceedings. Oddly enough, there are at least five different websites offering information on Oklahoma court cases for a fee—when all of that information is online and free. This illustrates a key point to keep in mind. There are a number of sites/companies that offer to do searches for you, for fees ranging from $9.95 to $79.95. It is true that they can probably do it faster than you. But it is also true that you can find the same information these people do, for free. And hopefully this chapter will equip you with the information you need to do that successfully.

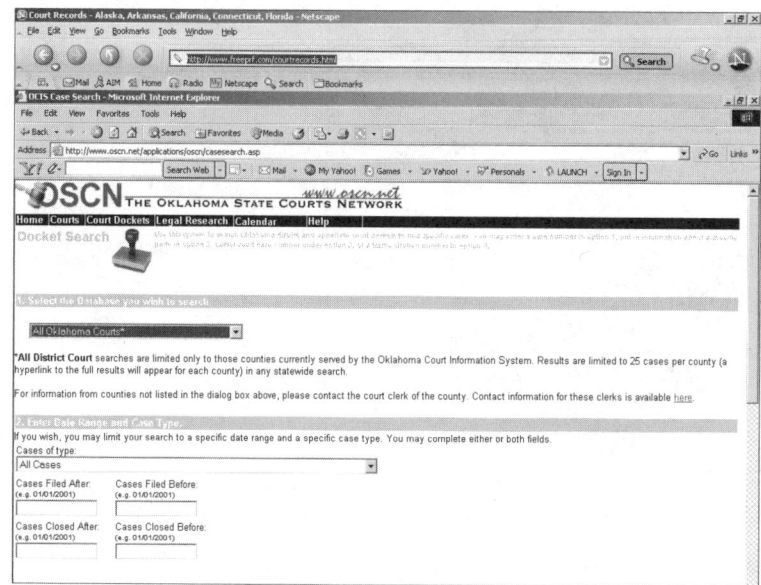

**FIGURE 13.7**   Oklahoma online court records.

## Other Resources

There are many other websites that can be quite helpful for your searches. There are a few that deserve particular attention. The National Center for State Courts has a website at http://www.ncsc.org/ that lists links to state courts all over the United States. It also lists several international courts in countries like Australia, Brazil, Canada, and the United Kingdom. This website, as shown in Figure 13.8, is an excellent starting point if you are seeking court records. There is a government access site that helps you find all federal courts. That website is www.uscourts.gov/court_locator.aspx.

The following list is designed to give you a starting point for online searches across the United States. These websites should help you start your search for court records:

- **Pacer:** www.pacer.psc.uscourts.gov/

- **Prison searches:** www.ancestorhunt.com/prison_search.htm

- **Federal prison records:** www.bop.gov/

- **Public records:** http://publicrecords.searchsystems.net/

- **The Bureau of Federal Prisons:** www.bop.gov/

As you begin searching the Internet, you will find other sites that appeal to you. This may be due to their ease of use, content, or other factors. When you do find such sites, bookmark them. In a short time, you will have an arsenal of online search engines. Also, your proficiency with using them will increase and you will learn which to use for which kind of information. This will allow you to become adept at quickly finding information that you need online.

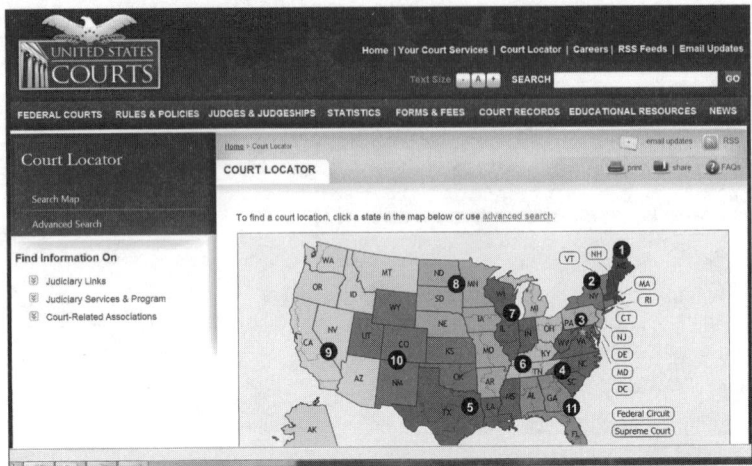

FIGURE 13.8    National Center for State Courts website.

# Usenet

Many readers who are new to the Internet (in the past five years) may not be familiar with Usenet. Usenet is a global group of bulletin boards that exist on any subject you can imagine. There are specific software packages used to view these newsgroups, but for some time now they have been accessible via web portals. The search engine Google has an option on its main page called Groups. When you click on that option, you are taken to Google's portal to Usenet newsgroups, as shown in Figure 13.9.

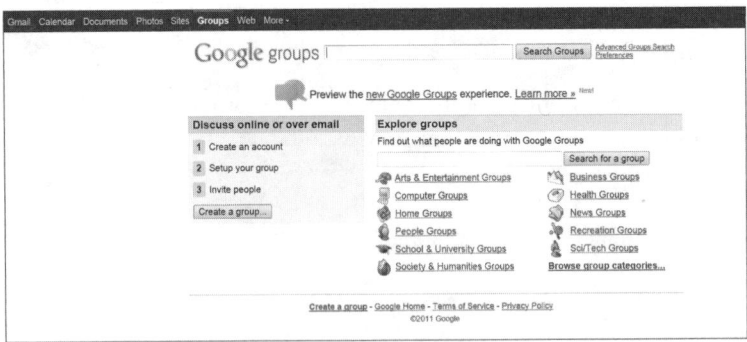

FIGURE 13.9    Google access to Usenet groups.

> **CAUTION**
>
> ## Usenet Information
>
> Anyone can post anything on Usenet. There are no restrictions. So simply because you find a negative comment about a person on Usenet, it is not wise to automatically assume that comment is true. These postings can only be viewed as part of an investigation and are only credible if other facets of the investigation also support the postings you find.

As you can see, newsgroups are divided into broad categories. For example, newsgroups devoted to science topics would be found under the heading sci. This includes groups like sci.anthropology, sci.logic, sci.math.stat, and more. The heading alt is a catchall for anything and everything. This category includes things ranging from alt.hacking to alt.adoption.

You may be thinking that, while all this is fascinating, it does not have anything to do with tracking down information. But actually it does. If, for example, you were hiring a network administrator, you could see if she had posted in various network administration groups and if those postings revealed key information about her network. This tool may be the single most important investigative tool you have if you are willing to take the time to ferret out the information you need.

# Summary

We have seen in this chapter that the Internet can be a valuable resource for any sort of investigation. It is often one of the tools that hackers and identity thieves use to gain information about their target. However, it can also be a valuable tool for you in researching a prospective employee or business partner. In addition, it can be invaluable for you to routinely find out what information is on the Internet about you. Seeing strange data that is not accurate can be an indication that you have already been the victim of identity theft.

## Test Your Skills

### MULTIPLE CHOICE QUESTIONS

1. How might an identity thief use the Internet to exploit his victim?

   A. He might find even more information about the target and use this information to conduct his crime.

   B. He could find out how much the target has in her savings account.

   C. The identity thief usually does not use the Internet to accomplish his task.

   D. He could use the Internet to intercept your email and thus get access to your personal life.

2. Which of the following is not an ideal place to seek out phone numbers and addresses?

   A. Yahoo! People Find

   B. People Search

   C. The international phone registry

   D. Infobel

3. Why do you not want too much personal data about you on the Internet?

   A. It might reveal embarrassing facts about you.

   B. It might be used by an identity thief to impersonate you.

   C. It might be used by a potential employer to find out more about you.

   D. There is no reason to worry about personal information on the Internet.

4. How could a hacker use information about you found through Internet searches?

   A. It could be used to guess passwords if your passwords are linked to personal information such as your birth date, address, or phone number.

   B. It could be used to guess passwords if your passwords are linked to your interests or hobbies.

C. It could be used in social engineering to ascertain more information about you or your computer system.

D. All of the above.

5. If you are hiring a new employee, which of the following should you do?

A. Verify degrees and certifications.

B. Call references.

C. Perform an Internet search to verify contact information and to check for a criminal record.

D. All of the above.

6. Which of the following would be *least* important to know about a potential business partner?

A. Past bankruptcies

B. A 15-year-old marijuana possession arrest

C. A lawsuit from a former business partner

D. A recent DUI

7. What information would provide the most accurate results for locating a person?

A. First name and state

B. First name, last name, and state

C. Last name and state

D. First name and last name

8. Of the websites listed in this chapter, which would be the most useful in obtaining the address and phone number of someone who does not live in the United States?

A. The FBI website

B. Yahoo!

C. Infobel

D. Google

9. Where would you go to find various state sex offender registries?

A. The FBI website

B. The national sex offender online database

C. The interstate online sex offender database

D. The special victims unit website

10. What is most important to learn about a person listed in a sex offender registry?

    A. The extent of his punishment

    B. How old she was when she committed her crime

    C. How long he has been out of prison

    D. The nature of her specific crime

11. Which web search approach is best when checking criminal backgrounds?

    A. Check primarily the person's state of residence.

    B. Check primarily federal records.

    C. Check the current and previous state of residence.

    D. Check as many places as might have information.

12. What advantages are there to commercial web search services?

    A. They can get information you cannot.

    B. They can get the information faster than you can.

    C. They can do a more thorough job than you can.

    D. They are legally entitled to do searches; you are not.

13. Which would you use to begin a search for information on a United States court case?

    A. The National Center for State Courts Website

    B. Infobel

    C. Yahoo! People Search

    D. Google Groups

14. Which of the following is the most accurate description of Usenet?

    A. A nationwide bulletin board

    B. A repository of computer security information

    C. A large-scale chat room

    D. A global collection of bulletin boards

15. Which of the following is the most helpful data you might get from Usenet on a person you are investigating?

    A. Postings by the individual you are investigating

    B. Security tips to help you investigate

    C. Criminal records posted

    D. Negative comments made by others about your target

# EXERCISES

For all exercises and projects in this chapter, you will concentrate your investigation on some person. It is best if you investigate yourself (which makes it easier to evaluate the accuracy of what you find) or someone in the class or the instructor who volunteers to be the target of the investigation. There are ethical issues with simply investigating random people without their knowledge or permission. It is also important to avoid embarrassing someone in the classroom. So the volunteer targets of the investigation should be certain they will not be embarrassed by whatever is found. Substitute the name of the person you are investigating for John Doe or Jane Doe in the projects and exercises.

## EXERCISE 13.1: Finding Phone Numbers

1. Beginning with Yahoo! People Search, seek out phone numbers and addresses for John Doe.

2. Use at least two other sources to look up John's phone number.

Did you get too little information or too much information? Were you able to determine the correct, current number?

## EXERCISE 13.2: Criminal Records Checks

1. Using sources listed in this chapter or other websites, look for criminal background information about John Doe. Start with the state John currently resides in, and then check other states, particularly those that might have shown up with John's name in Exercise 1.

2. Expand your search to check for federal crimes as well.

## EXERCISE 13.3: Checking Court Cases

1. Search court records for any court cases for Jane Doe's business.

2. Check state licensing agency websites, if applicable, for any history or complaints on John's business.

## EXERCISE 13.4: Finding Business Information on Usenet

1. Access Usenet.

2. Search bulletin boards and other groups that Jane Doe may have posted to in connection with her business.

Were you able to find out more about Jane's business through her postings to a Usenet group?

### EXERCISE 13.5: **Blocking Information**

This chapter illustrated the many ways you can access information about someone and pointed out the potential hazards of having too much personal information available on the Internet. So, what can you do to prevent unscrupulous individuals from finding out too much about you? Check the primary websites listed in this chapter (Yahoo! and Google) to see if they provide any means to block your information from being distributed. Are there any other means of blocking access to your personal information?

## PROJECTS

### PROJECT 13.1: **Investigating a Person**

Using all of the web resources in this chapter and any others you come across, do a complete investigation of Jane Doe. Try to determine her address, phone number, occupation, age, and any criminal history. You might even check Usenet postings and find out clues as to Jane's hobbies and personal interests. Create a brief report on Jane based on your findings.

### PROJECT 13.2: **Investigating a Company**

Using all of the web resources in this chapter and any others you come across, do a complete investigation of John Doe's business. How long has he been in business? Are there any complaints about the business with any regulatory agency? Any complaints on Usenet boards? Any business relationships? Any past court proceedings? Write a report discussing your analysis of this business based on your findings.

### PROJECT 13.3: **The Ethics of Investigation**

Write an essay discussing the ethics of online investigations. Do you feel these investigations are an invasion of privacy? Why or why not? If you do feel they are an invasion of privacy, what do you think can be done about it? Are there problems with getting inaccurate information?

## Case Study

Henry Rice, the owner and CEO of a small company, has been conducting a search for a new human resource administrator. After many rounds of interviews, he has narrowed his search down to two individuals whom he feels are the best candidates. Each has very similar qualifications, so Henry's decision may very well be based on the information he finds when he checks their references and performs a background check.

Henry has received written permission from each to conduct a background check. Where should Henry begin his search? What sites or sorts of information would be most critical for him to check? What type of information could weigh heavily for a person working in human resources? Write a brief essay outlining the steps Henry should take in conducting his research.

## Chapter 14

# Introduction to Forensics

## Chapter Objectives

**After reading this chapter and completing the exercises, you will be able to do the following:**

- Understand basic forensics principles
- Make a forensic copy of a drive
- Use basic forensics tools

## Introduction

In the preceding 13 chapters, you have been introduced to a variety of security topics: from concepts like the CIA triangle, to attacks such as session hijacking, to counter measures like IDS and honey pots. In this chapter, we are going to cover the basics of computer forensics. This is a very important topic for anyone involved in computer security or network administration. It is frequently the case that the first responder to a computer crime is the network administrator, not a law enforcement officer. And if you fail to handle the evidence properly, you may render it unusable in a court and ruin any chances of convicting the perpetrator.

Computer forensics is a comparatively new field. Widespread use of computers dates back to the 1970s and widespread computer crime to the 1990s. The field of computer forensics has evolved only in the past 20 to 25 years. The field of computer forensics, now often called cyber forensics, attempts to apply forensic science to computer devices.

CERT defines computer forensics in this manner:

> "If you manage or administer information systems and networks, you should understand computer forensics. Forensics is the process of using scientific knowledge for collecting, analyzing, and presenting evidence to the courts. (The word *forensics* means "to bring to

the court.") Forensics deals primarily with the recovery and analysis of latent evidence. Latent evidence can take many forms, from fingerprints left on a window to DNA evidence recovered from blood stains to the files on a hard drive."[1]

The goal of cyber forensics is to examine computer devices (laptops, servers, cell phones, tablets, and so on) using scientific methods to extract evidence in such a way that such evidence can be presented in a court. Now, there are certainly times when you will use forensics in scenarios that will never go to court. But the techniques were designed to satisfy the evidentiary requirements of courts.

It is important to keep in mind that a few jurisdictions have passed laws requiring that in order to extract the evidence, the investigator must be either a law enforcement officer or a licensed private investigator. This is a controversial law, given that normally private investigator training and licensing does not include computer forensics training. You should check with specifics in your state. However, many of those states will allow you to forensically examine a computer if you have the permission of the owner or if someone who is licensed seized the evidence. So this would not prohibit you from forensically examining computers in your company.

The purpose of this chapter is to give you a general introduction to the field of forensics. Clearly, each topic discussed in this chapter could be investigated in more depth.

# General Guidelines

There are some general guidelines you should always follow in any forensic examination. You want to have as little impact on the evidence as possible. This means you want to examine it and not alter it. You want to have a clear document trail for everything that is done. And, of course, you want to secure your evidence.

## Don't Touch the Suspect Drive

The first, and perhaps most important, precaution is to touch the system as little as possible. You do not want to make changes to the system in the process of examining it. Let's look at one possible way to make a forensically valid copy of a drive. Some of this depends on Linux commands, which you may or may not be familiar with. If you are not, I have had students with no Linux experience use these same commands and be able to accomplish the task of making a forensic copy of a drive. Later in this section I will show you how to image drives with other forensic tools, but first we will discuss how to do this without specialized tools.

You will need a bootable copy of Linux. Any Linux live CD will do. You will actually need two copies: one on the suspect machine and one on the target machine. Whichever version of Linux you use, the steps will be the same:

You have to completely wipe the target drive.

```
dd if=/dev/zero of=/dev/hdb1 bs=2048
```

---

1. CERT Forensics Definition: www.us-cert.gov/sites/default/files/publications/forensics.pdf

Now you need to set up that target forensics server to receive the copy of the suspected drive you wish to examine. The `Netcat` command helps with that. The specific syntax is as follows:

```
nc -l -p 8888 > evidence.dd
```

You are telling the machine to listen on port 8888 and put whatever it receives into `evidence.dd`.

On the suspect machine, you have to start sending the drive's information to the forensics server:

```
dd if=/dev/hda1 | nc 192.168.0.2 8888 -w 3
```

Of course, this assumes that the suspect drive is hda1. If not, then replace that part of the command with the partition you are using. This also assumes the server has an IP address of 192.168.0.2. If not, replace it with whatever your forensics server IP address is.

You will also want to create a hash of the suspect drive. Later you can hash the drive you have been working with and compare that to the hash of the original drive and confirm that nothing has been altered. You can make a hash using Linux shell commands:

```
md5sum /dev/hda1 | nc 192.168.0.2 8888 -w 3
```

When you are done, you have a copy of the drive. It is often a good idea to make two copies: One you will work with, and another will simply be stored. But in no case do you do your forensic analysis on the suspect drive.

## Image a Drive with Forensic Toolkit

AccessData is the maker of the Forensic Toolkit and the FTK Imager. The Forensic Toolkit is a commercial product that can be a bit expensive. The FTK Imager is a free download that can be used to make images of drives and to mount images that have been made. You begin by launching FTK Imager, as shown in Figure 14.1.

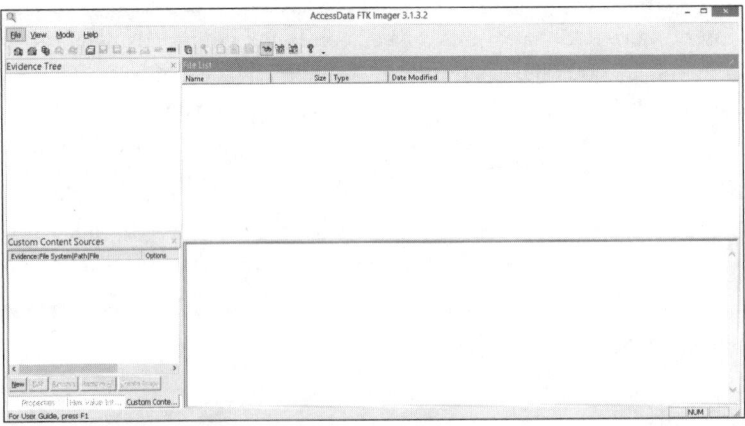

**FIGURE 14.1**    FTK Imager.

Choose File and select Create Disk Image, as you see in Figure 14.2.

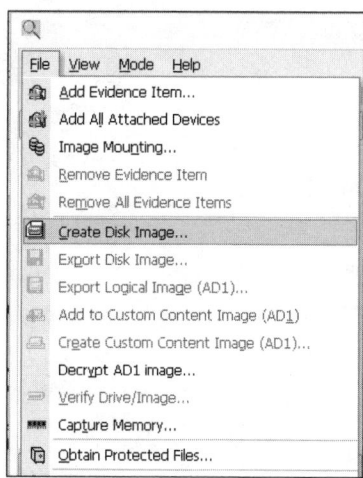

**FIGURE 14.2**   FTK Imager—Create Disk Image.

Next, you are prompted to select the type of drive you wish to image, as shown in Figure 14.3.

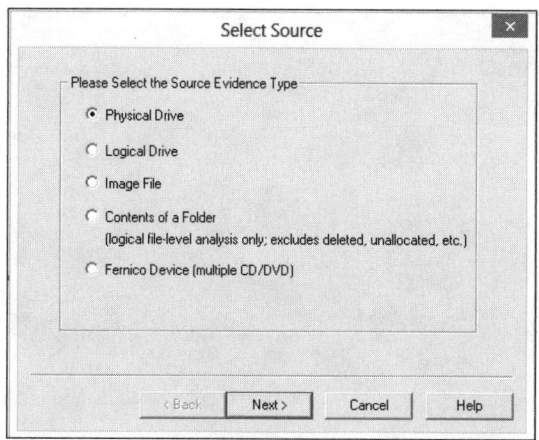

**FIGURE 14.3**   FTK Imager—Select Source.

Now, based on the source type you selected, you will need to make another choice. For example, if you selected Logical Drive, you now need to pick which logical drive, as shown in Figure 14.4.

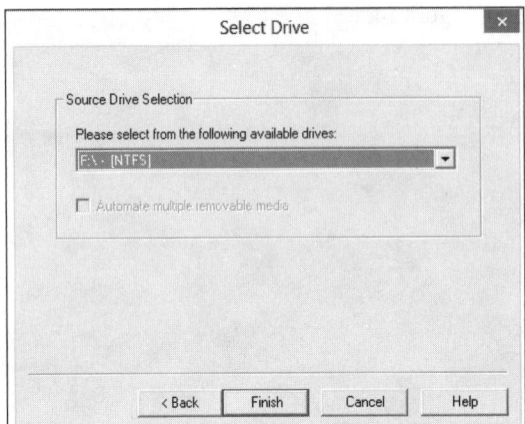

**FIGURE 14.4**   FTK Imager—Source Drive Selection.

Finally, select a destination for the image, as shown in Figure 14.5.

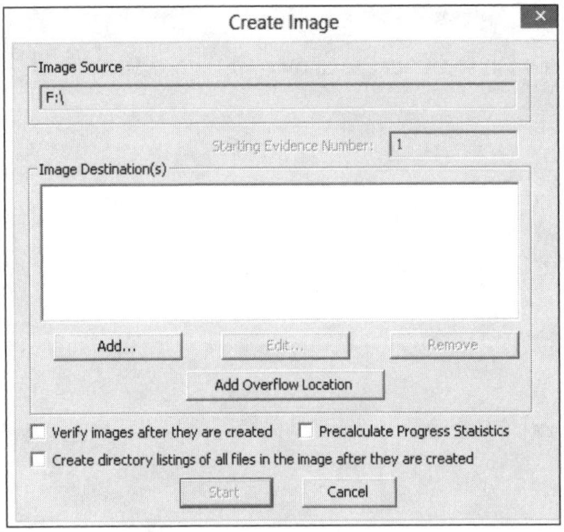

**FIGURE 14.5**   FTK Imager—Create Image.

The process for mounting an image is even easier. FTK Imager is well respected in the forensic community, easy to use, and free.

## Can You Ever Conduct Forensics on a Live Machine?

We have emphasized, and rightfully so, that whenever possible you should always create an image of the drive and perform the analysis only on that image. For a long time this was considered the only way to conduct computer forensics. However, the past few years have yielded some variation on that thinking. There are times when live forensics is possible or even desirable:

- When you find a machine running, you should conduct some analysis of running processes, memory, and so on before shutting it down.

- It may be necessary on clouds and clusters.

- When the machine has already been imaged, thus preserving evidence.

- When there is not a true forensic investigation, but rather asking a single question.

- Be careful shutting down; if the machine has drive encryption, then when you boot it back up you won't be able to retrieve data.

It is still important to keep in mind that imaging is the preferred method. The preceding list is just a list of suggested times when it may be possible to work with the live system. When doing live forensics, your report must explain why you did it, exactly what steps you did, and make sure the steps you take have the least impact on the system possible.

## Document Trail

Beyond not touching the actual drive, the next issue is documentation. If you have never worked in an investigative capacity, the level of documentation may seem onerous to you. But the rule is simple: *Document everything*.

When you first discover a computer crime, you must document exactly what events occurred. Who was present, and what were they doing? What devices were attached to the computer, and what connections did it have over the network/Internet? What hardware was being used, and what operating system?

Then when you begin your actual forensic investigation you must document every step. Start with documenting the process you use to make a forensic copy. Then document every tool you use, every test you perform. You must be able to show in your documentation everything that was done.

## Secure the Evidence

First and foremost, the computer must be taken offline to prevent further tampering. Now, there are some limited circumstances where a machine would be left online to trace down an active, ongoing attack. But the general rule is to take it offline immediately.

The next step is to limit access to the machine. No one who does not absolutely need access to the evidence should have it. Hard drives should be locked in a safe or secure cabinet. Analysis should be done in a room with limited access.

You must also be able to document who had access to the evidence, how they interacted with it, and where the evidence was stored. There must be no period of time that you cannot account for the evidence. This is called *chain of custody*.

## Chain of Custody

The concept of chain of custody is one of the cornerstones of forensic science, whether that is cyber forensics or some other forensic discipline. Chain of custody refers to detailed documentation showing the status of evidence at every point in time from the moment of seizure to the moment the evidence is presented in court. Any break in that chain of custody will likely render that evidence inadmissible at trial.

According to the Scientific Working Group on Digital Evidence Model Standard Operation Procedures for Computer Forensics:

> "The chain of custody must include a description of the evidence and a documented history of each evidence transfer"

This means that any time evidence is transferred from one location to another or from one person to another, that transfer must be documented. The first transfer is the seizure of evidence when the evidence is transferred to the investigator. Between that point in time and any trial, there may be any number of transfers.

Remember that it is almost impossible to over document. Detail what you do, what tools you use, who is present, who conducts what tests, and so on. I find it helpful to take frequent screenshots during my forensic analysis and to include those in my report.

## FBI Forensics Guidelines

Beyond the general guidelines we have just discussed, the FBI gives some specific guidelines. In most cases, they will overlap with what we have discussed, but it is still useful to cover the FBI recommendations.

If an incident occurs, the FBI recommends that the first responder preserve the state of the computer at the time of the incident by making a backup copy of any logs, damaged or altered files, and of course any files left by the intruder. This last part is critical. Hackers frequently use various tools and may leave traces of their presence. Furthermore, the FBI warns that if the incident is in progress, activate any auditing or recording software you might have available. Collect as much data about the incident as you can. In other words, this might be a case where you do not take the machine offline but rather analyze the attack in progress.

Another important step is to document the specific losses suffered due to the attack. Losses typically include the following:

- Labor cost spent in response and recovery. (Multiply the number of participating staff by their hourly rates.)

- The cost of the equipment, if equipment was damaged.

- The value of the data if any was lost or stolen. How much did it cost to obtain that data, and how much will it cost to reconstruct it?

- Any lost revenue, including losses due to downtime, having to give customers credit due to inconvenience, or any other way in which revenue was lost.

Documenting the exact damages due to the attack is just as important as documenting the attack itself.

The FBI computer forensic guidelines stress the importance of securing evidence. The FBI also stresses that you should not limit your concept of *computer evidence* to PCs and laptops. *Computer evidence* can include the following:

- Logs (system, router, chat room, IDS, firewall)
- Portable storage devices (USB drives, external drives)
- Emails
- Devices capable of storing data, such as iPod, iPad, and tablets
- Cell phones

The FBI guidelines also stress making a forensic copy of the suspect drive/partition to work with and creating a hash of that drive.

## U.S. Secret Service Forensics Guidelines

The United States Secret Service is another federal agency tasked with combating cybercrime and with computer forensics. It has a website devoted to computer forensics[2] that includes forensics courses. These courses are usually for law enforcement personnel.

The Secret Service also has released a guide for first responders to computer crime. It has listed its "golden rules" to begin the investigation:

- Secure the scene and make it safe.
- If you reasonably believe that the computer is involved in the crime you are investigating, take immediate steps to preserve the evidence.
- Determine whether you have a legal basis to seize this computer (plain view, search warrant, consent, and so on).
- Avoid accessing computer files. If the computer is off, leave it off.
- If the computer is on, do not start searching through it. If the computer is on, go to the appropriate sections in this guide on how to properly shut down the computer and prepare it for transportation as evidence.
- If you reasonably believe that the computer is destroying evidence, immediately shut down the computer by pulling the power cord from the back of the computer.

---

2. Secret Service Computer Forensics: www.ncfi.usss.gov/

- If a camera is available and the computer is on, take pictures of the computer screen. If the computer is off, take pictures of the computer, the location of the computer, and any electronic media attached.

- Determine whether special legal considerations apply (doctor, attorney, clergy, psychiatrist, newspapers, publishers, and so on).

These are all important first steps to both preserving the chain of custody and ensuring the integrity of the investigation.

## EU Evidence Gathering

The Council of Europe Convention on Cybercrime, also called Budapest Convention on Cybercrime or simply Budapest Convention, refers to electronic evidence as evidence that can be collected in electronic form of a criminal offence.

The Electronic evidence guide is a basic guide for police officers, prosecutors, and judges.

The EU also has five principles that establish a basis for all dealings with electronic evidence:

- **Principle 1: Data Integrity:** You must ensure that the data is valid and has not been corrupted.

- **Principle 2: Audit Trail:** Similar to the concept of chain of custody, you must be able to fully account for the evidence. That includes its location as well as what was done with it.

- **Principle 3: Specialist Support:** As needed, utilize specialists. For example, if you are a skilled forensic examiner but have limited experience with a Macintosh computer, get a Mac specialist should you need to examine a Mac.

- **Principle 4: Appropriate Training:** All forensic examiners and analysts should be fully trained and always expanding their knowledge base.

- **Principle 5: Legality:** Make certain all evidence is collected and handled in a manner consistent with all applicable laws.

Even if you don't work within the European Union, these guidelines, can be quite useful. Yes, they are rather broad, but they do provide guidance as to how to properly conduct a forensic examination.

## Scientific Working Group on Digital Evidence

Scientific Working Group on Digital Evidence, or SWGDE (www.swgde.org), creates a number of standards for digital forensics. According to SWGDE Model Standard Operation Procedures for Computer Forensics, there are four steps of examination:

1. **Visual Inspection:** The purpose of this inspection is just to verify the type of evidence, its condition, and relevant information to conduct the examination. This is often done in the initial evidence seizure. For example, if a computer is being seized, you would want to document whether the machine is running, what its condition is, and what the general environment is like.

2. **Forensic Duplication:** This is the process of duplicating the media before examination. It is always preferred to work with a forensic copy and not the original.

3. **Media Examination:** This is the actual forensic testing of the application. By *media*, we mean hard drive, RAM, SIM card—some item that can contain digital data.

4. **Evidence Return:** Exhibit(s) are returned to the appropriate location—usually some locked or secured facility.

These particular steps provide an overview of how a cyber forensic examination should proceed. SWGDE has a number of useful documents on its website that you should consult to delve deeper into the nuances of a proper cyber forensics examination.

## Locard's Principle of Transference

Dr. Edmond Locard was a forensic scientist who formulated what has become known as Locard's exchange principle or Locard's principle of transference.[3] This principle was first applied to physical forensics, and it essentially states that you cannot interact in any environment without leaving something behind. For example, someone cannot break into a house and not leave something. That something could be a fingerprint, a hair, a foot print, and more. Now, a careful criminal will cover up some of this, such as by using gloves to keep from leaving fingerprints. But something will be left behind.

This applies to computer evidence as well and is one reason we prefer to work with a copy. Take Windows for an example. Anytime you log in, open a file, or do anything at all, you have changed registry settings, perhaps left temporary files, and left some traces. For a forensic examination, this is in fact critical. But it also means the investigator has to be careful not to leave traces behind.

## Tools

We have previously discussed imaging a drive with either Linux commands or FTK disk imager. There are a variety of tools available for conducting forensic analysis and examination. In this section I will review a few of these for you. There are certainly other tools, but the ones listed here are very widely used.

### FTK

We mentioned FTK previously, a brief description is also given here. The company AccessData is the creator of the Forensic Toolkit, better known as simply FTK. This is a robust computer forensics tool that allows you to recover deleted files, examine registry settings, and perform a variety of forensic examination tasks. The software itself can be cost-prohibitive but is quite popular with law enforcement.

AccessData has added additional features such as Known File Filtering for finding certain types of files. FTK can also search and detect files involved in child pornography. AccessData makes a phone forensics tool as well. You can learn more at http://accessdata.com/.

---

3. http://www.forensichandbook.com/locards-exchange-principle/

## EnCase

This tool, made by Guidance Software, is quite popular with law enforcement and is a direct competitor with FTK. It allows you to image drives, recover deleted files, examine the registry, and other common tasks. It can also be cost-prohibitive for some organizations. You can learn more at https://www2.guidancesoftware.com/products/Pages/encase-forensic/overview.aspx.

## OSForensics

This is a newer tool, but one that has been well received in the forensic community. It is very low cost and easy to use. It is full featured, allowing you to recover deleted files, examine the registry, and search the drive. You can find out more and even download a fully working trial version at www.osforensics.com/.

## Sleuth Kit

This is actually a suite of open source tools. The full suite of tools is full featured but more difficult to use. Each tool can require you to learn a set of command line (or shell) commands to execute. You can find out more at www.sleuthkit.org/.

## Oxygen

This tool is specifically for phone forensics. It does a very good job of analyzing iPhones and a reasonably good job of analyzing modern Android. It is not (at least currently) as effective with older Androids or Windows phones. You can learn more at www.oxygen-forensic.com/en/.

## Cellebrite

This is perhaps one of the most popular phone forensics tools, at least with law enforcement. It is very effective with a number of different phones. The only downside is that it is one of the most expensive phone forensics tools available. You can find out more at www.cellebrite.com/.

# Finding Evidence on the PC

Once you have secured the evidence and made a forensic copy, it is time to start looking for evidence. That evidence can come in many forms. The tools mentioned in the preceding section can be used to extricate this evidence for you. However, in this section I will show you what it is these tools search for. It is important not to simply regurgitate what some automated tool tells you, but rather to understand what it is the tool is doing.

## Finding Evidence in the Browser

The browser can be a source of both direct evidence and circumstantial or supporting evidence. Obviously in cases of child pornography, the browser might contain direct evidence of the specific crime.

You may also find direct evidence in the case of cyber stalking. However, if you suspect someone of creating a virus that infected a network, you would probably only find indirect evidence such as the person having searched virus creation/programming-related topics.

Even if the person erases his history, it is still possible to retrieve it. Windows stores a lot of information in a file called index.dat (information such as web addresses, search queries, and recently opened files).

# Finding Evidence in System Logs

Regardless of what operating system you are using, the operating system has logs. Those logs can be critical in any forensic investigation, and you should retrieve them.

## Windows Logs

Let's start with Windows 7/8/10. With all of these versions of Windows, you find the logs by clicking on the Start button in the lower-left corner of the desktop and then clicking the Control Panel. You then click on Administrative Tools and the Event Viewer. Here are the logs you would check for. (Note that not all appear in every version of Windows.)

Note: With all of these, you have to turn the logging on; otherwise, there will be nothing in these logs.

- **Security log:** This is probably the most important log from a forensics point of view. It has both successful and unsuccessful login events.

- **Application log:** This log contains various events logged by applications or programs. Many applications will record their errors here in the application log.

- **System log:** The System log contains events logged by Windows system components. This includes events like driver failures. This particular log is not as interesting from a forensics perspective as the other logs are.

- **ForwardedEvents log:** The ForwardedEvents log is used to store events collected from remote computers. This will only have data in it if event forwarding has been configured.

- **Applications and Services logs:** This log is used to store events from a single application or component rather than events that might have systemwide impact.

Windows servers will have similar logs. However, with Windows systems, you have an additional possible concern. It is possible that the attacker cleared the logs before leaving the system. There are tools that will allow one to wipe out a log. It is also possible to simply turn off logging before an attack and turn it back on when you are done. One such tool is auditpol.exe. `auditpol \\ipaddress /disable` turns off logging. Then when the criminal exits, she can use `auditpol \\ipaddress /enable` to turn it back on. There are also tools, like WinZapper, that allow you to selectively remove certain items from event logs in Windows.

## Linux Logs

Obviously, Linux also has logs you can check. Depending on your Linux distribution and what services you have running on it (like MySQL), some of these logs may not be present on a particular machine:

- **/var/log/faillog:** This log file contains failed user logins. This can be very important when tracking attempts to crack into the system.

- **/var/log/kern.log:** This log file is used for messages from the operating system's kernel. This is not likely to be pertinent to most computer crime investigations.

- **/var/log/lpr.log:** This is the printer log and can give you a record of any items that have been printed from this machine. That can be useful in corporate espionage cases.

- **/var/log/mail.*:** This is the mail server log and can be very useful in any computer crime investigation. Emails can be a component in any computer crime and even in some noncomputer crimes such as fraud.

- **/var/log/mysql.*:** This log records activities related to the MySQL database server and will usually be of less interest to a computer crime investigation.

- **/var/log/apache2/*:** If this machine is running the Apache web server, then this log will show related activity. This can be very useful in tracking attempts to hack into the web server.

- **/var/log/lighttpd/*:** If this machine is running the Lighttpd web server, then this log will show related activity. This can be very useful in tracking attempts to hack into the web server.

- **/var/log/apport.log:** This records application crashes. Sometimes these can reveal attempts to compromise the system or the presence of a virus or spyware.

- **/var/log/user.log:** These contain user activity logs and can be very important to a criminal investigation.

# Getting Back Deleted Files

It is a fact that criminals frequently attempt to destroy evidence. This is also true with computer crimes. The criminals may delete files. However, there are a variety of tools you can use to recover such files, particularly in Windows. DiskDigger is a free tool that can be used to recover Windows files. This is a very easy-to-use tool. There are more robust tools, but the fact that this is free and easy to use makes it perfect for students learning forensics. Let's walk through its basic operation. It should be noted that all the aforementioned forensics tools will recover deleted files for you. It must also be noted that there are many file recovery tools available on the Internet. DiskDigger is simply shown as an example of what is available.

On the first screen, shown in Figure 14.6, you select the drive/partition you wish to recover files from.

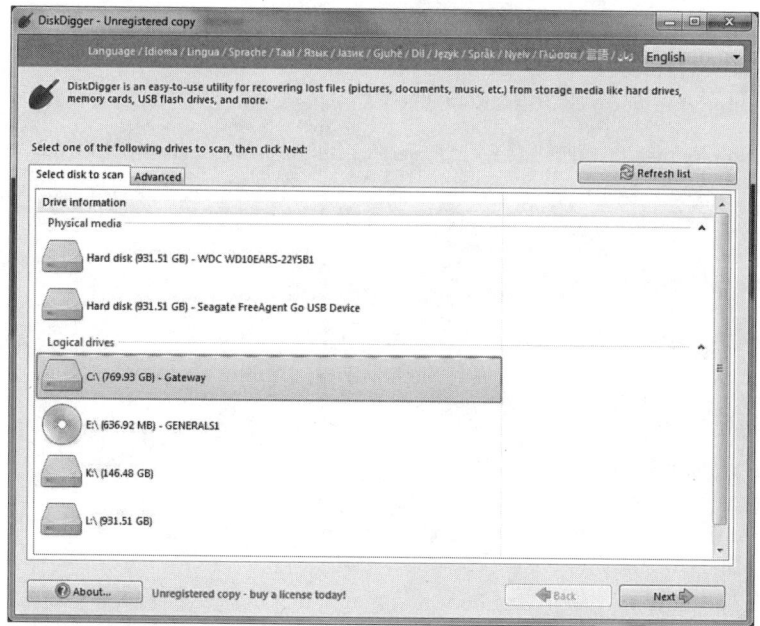

**FIGURE 14.6    Add a new scan.**

On the next screen, you select the level of scan you want to do. This is shown in Figure 14.7. Obviously, the deeper the scan, the longer it can take.

Then you will get a list of the files that were recovered. You can see this in Figure 14.8.

You can see the file and the file header. You can also choose to recover the file if you wish. Obviously, it is possible that DiskDigger will only recover a file fragment. But that can be enough for forensics.

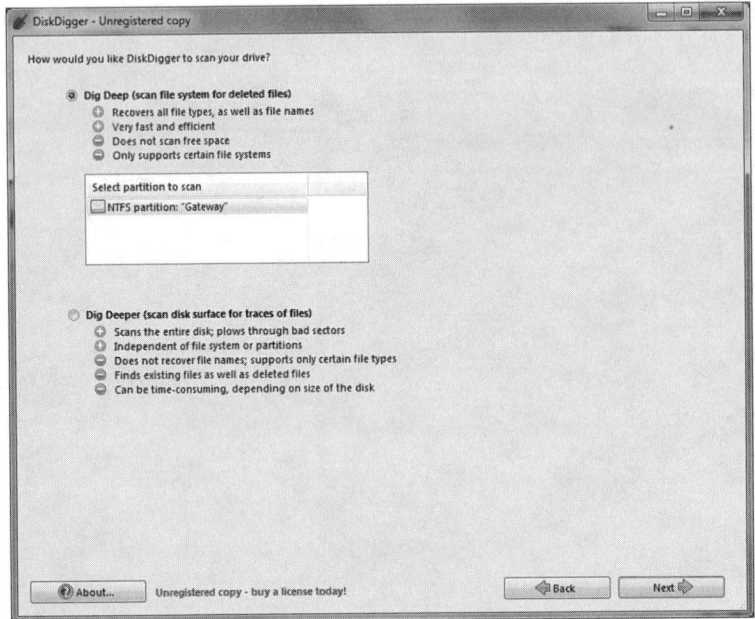

**FIGURE 14.7**    Select depth of scan.

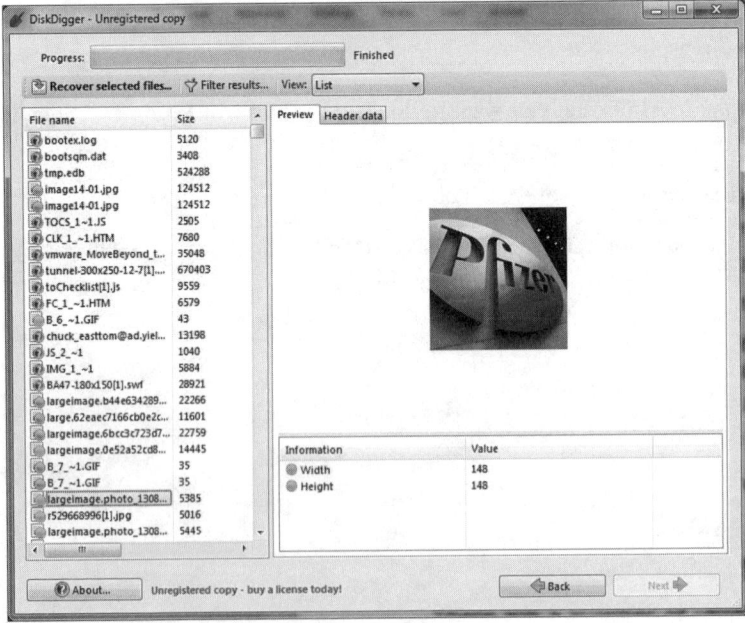

**FIGURE 14.8**    Recovered files.

> **NOTE**
>
> In addition to deleted files, it is important to check slack space. When a file is saved, the entire cluster is allocated whether it is needed or not. Consider this example: You have a computer with a cluster size of 10 sectors. You save a file that takes only up 3 sectors. As far as the operating system and file system are concerned, all 10 sectors are in use. That leaves 7 sectors unaccounted for. This space is slack space. It is possible to hide data in slack space.

# Operating System Utilities

There are a number of utilities built in to the operating system that can be useful in gathering some forensic data. Given that Windows is the most commonly used operating system, we will focus on those utilities that work from the Windows command line. However, one of the key issues in conducting forensics work is to be very familiar with the target operating system. You should also note that many of these commands are most useful on a live running system to catch attacks in progress.

## Net Sessions

This command lists any active sessions connected to the computer you run it on. This can be very important if you think an attack is live and ongoing. If there are no active sessions, the utility will report that, as shown in Figure 14.9.

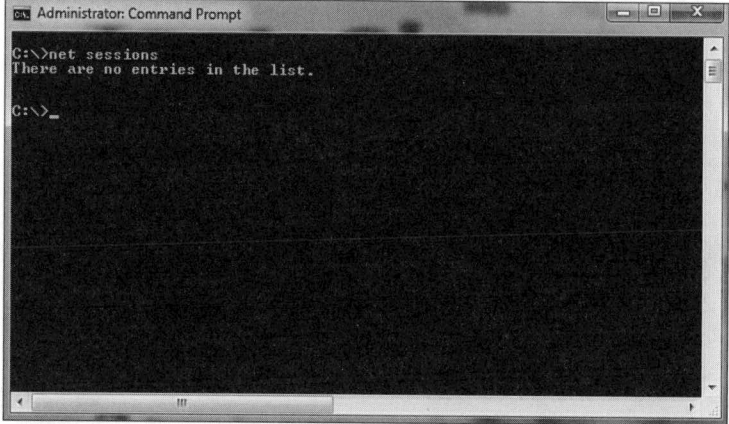

**FIGURE 14.9**  Net sessions.

## Openfiles

This is another command useful for finding live attacks ongoing. This command will list any shared files that are currently open. You can see this utility in Figure 14.10.

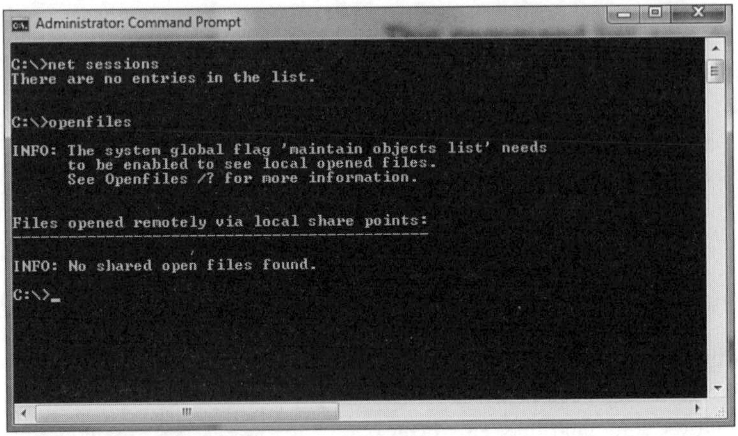

**FIGURE 14.10**    Openfiles.

# Fc

Fc is a command you can use with a forensic copy of a machine. It compares two files and shows the differences. If you think a configuration file has been altered, you can compare it to a known good backup. You can see this utility in Figure 14.11.

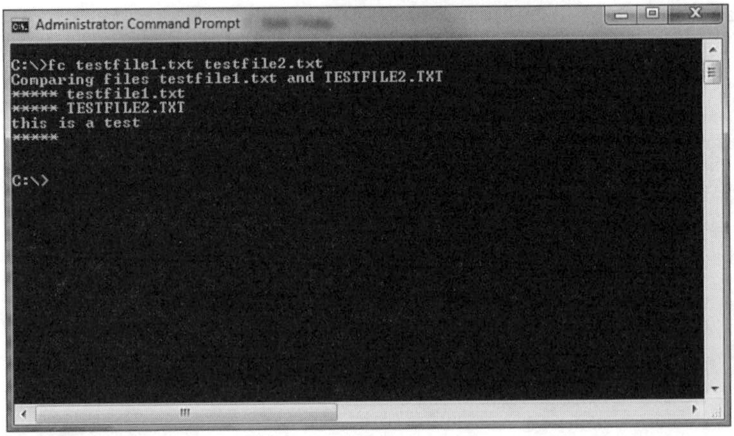

**FIGURE 14.11**    Fc.

# Netstat

This command is also used to detect ongoing attacks. It lists all current network connections—not just inbound, but outbound as well. You can see this utility in Figure 14.12.

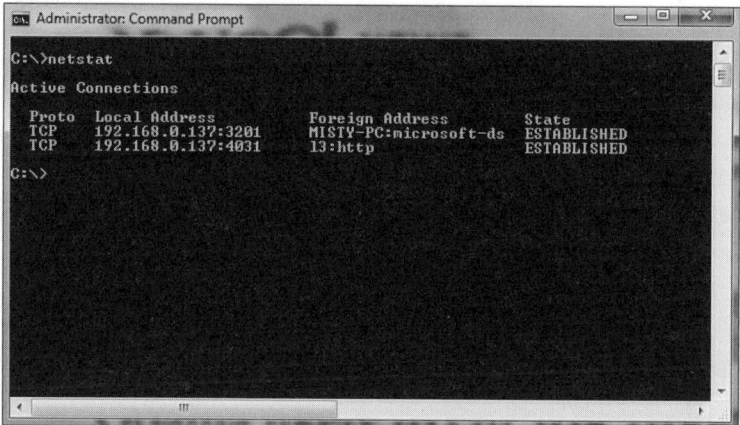

**FIGURE 14.12**   Netstat.

# The Windows Registry

The Windows Registry is an incredible repository of potential valuable forensics information. It is the heart of the Windows machine. There are a number of interesting pieces of data you can find here. It is beyond the scope of this chapter to make you an expert in the Windows Registry, but it is hoped that you will continue on and learn more. Microsoft describes the Registry as follows:

> "A central hierarchical database used in the Microsoft Windows family of Operating Systems to store information necessary to configure the system for one or more users, applications and hardware devices.

> The registry contains information that Windows continually references during operation, such as profiles for each user, the applications installed on the computer and the types of documents that each can create, property sheet settings for folders and application icons, what hardware exists on the system and the ports that are being used."[4]

The Registry is organized into five sections referred to as *hives*. Each of these sections contains specific information that can be useful to you. The five hives are described here:

1. **HKEY_CLASSES_ROOT (HKCR):** This hive stores information about drag and drop rules, program shortcuts, the user interface, and related items.

2. **HKEY_CURRENT_USER (HKCU):** This will be very important to any forensic investigation. It stores information about the currently logged-on user, including desktop settings and user folders.

3. **HKEY_LOCAL_MACHINE (HKLM):** This can also be important to a forensic investigation. It contains those settings common to the entire machine, regardless of the individual user.

---

4. Microsoft Computer Dictionary, Fifth Edition

4. **HKEY_USERS (HKU):** This hive is very critical to forensics investigations. It has profiles for all the users, including their settings.

5. **HKEY_CURRENT_CONFIG (HCU):** This hive contains the current system configuration. This might also prove useful in your forensic examinations.

You can see the Registry and these five hives in Figure 14.13.

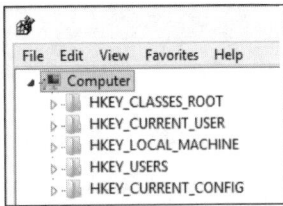

**FIGURE 14.13**   Windows registry.

Most people use the regedit tool to interact with the Registry. In Windows 7 and Server 2008, you select Start, Run and then type in `regedit`. In Windows 8 and 10, you will have to go to the applications list, select All Apps, and then find Regedit or use the Windows+R key and type in `regedit`. Most forensics tools provide a means for examining the Registry as well.

All Registry keys contain a value associated with them called LastWriteTime. This value indicates when this registry value was last changed. Rather than be a standard date/time, this value is stored as a FILETIME structure. A FILETIME structure represents the number of 100-nanosecond intervals since January 1, 1601. Clearly, this is important forensically.

It is also interesting to note that Microsoft rarely uses strong encryption to hide items in the Registry. If an item is encrypted, it is likely encrypted with some simple algorithm such as ROT 13.

Most internal text strings are stored and processed as 16-bit Unicode characters. Unicode is an international character set standard that defines unique 2-byte values (maximum 65,536 characters) for most of the world's known character sets.

You can export a specific key from the command line with

```
reg export HKEY_LOCAL_MACHINE\System\ControlSet\Enum\UBSTOR
```

or within regedit, you can right-click on a key and select Export.

## Specific Entries

Now that you have a basic working knowledge of the Registry, it is important to look at some specific Registry information you may find.

## USB Information

One of the first things most forensic analysts learn about the Windows Registry is that they can find out what USB devices have been connected to the suspect machine. The Registry key HKEY_LOCAL_ MACHINE\System\ControlSet\Enum\USBSTOR lists USB devices that have been connected to the machine. It is often the case that a criminal will move evidence to an external device and take it with him. This could indicate to you that there are devices you need to find and examine. This registry setting will tell you about the external drives that have been connected to this system. You can see this in Figure 14.14.

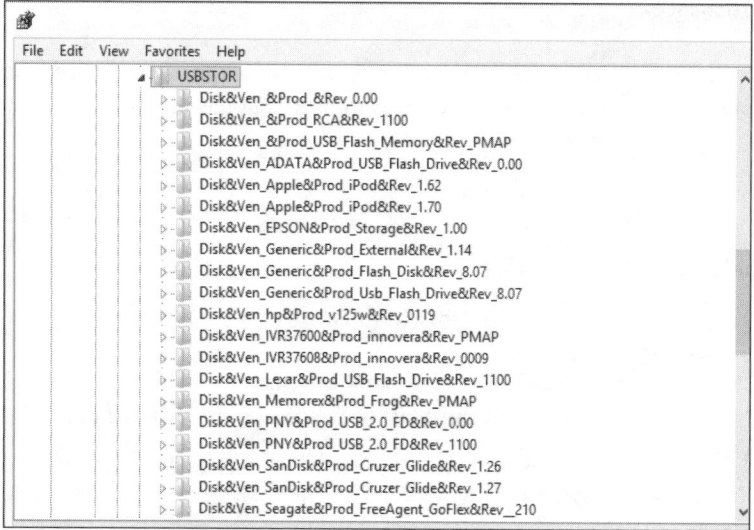

**FIGURE 14.14**   Windows Registry—USBSTOR.

However, this does not give the complete picture. Some related keys are quite useful:

SYSTEM\MountedDevices allows investigators to match the serial number to a given drive letter or volume that was mounted when the USB device was inserted. Incidentally, this particular Registry key is not limited to USB devices.

What user was using the USB device can be found here:

\Software\Microsoft\Windows\CurrentVersion\Explorer\MountPoints2

The vendor and product ID can be found here:

SYSTEM\CurrentControlSet\Enum\USB

All of these related USB Registry keys should be examined in order to get a complete and accurate picture of what happened regarding specific USB devices.

## Autostart Locations

This key is frequently used by malware to remain persistent on the target system. It shows those programs that are configured to start automatically when Windows starts.

Example: `HKEY_CURRENT_USER\Software\Microsoft\Windows\CurrentVersion\Run`

Obviously, you should expect to see legitimate programs in this Registry key. However, if there is anything you cannot account for, it could indicate malware.

## Last Visited

`HKCU\Software\Microsoft\Windows\CurrentVersion\Explorer\ComDlg32\LastVisitedMRU`

This key will show recent sites that have been visited. The data is in hex format, but you can see the text translation when using regedit, and you will probably be able to make out the site visited just by looking at regedit.

## Recent Documents

Recent documents can be found at the following key:

`HKCU\Software\Microsoft\Windows\CurrentVersion\Explorer\RecentDocs`

This can be quite forensically important, particularly in cases involving financial data or intellectual property. This key allows you to determine what documents have been accessed on that computer.

As you can see, this key is first divided into document types, Then, once you select the type, you can see the recent documents of that type that have been accessed.

## Uninstalled Software

`HKLM\SOFTWARE\Microsoft\Windows\CurrentVersion\Uninstall`

This is a very important registry key for any forensic examination. An intruder who breaks into a computer might install software on that computer for various purposes such as recovering deleted files or creating a backdoor. He will then, most likely, delete the software he used. It is also possible that an employee who is stealing data might install steganography software so he can hide the data. He will subsequently uninstall that software. This key lets you see all the software that has been uninstalled from this machine.

There are certainly other keys of interest. And the aforementioned forensics tools will pull this information (and more) for you. If you are going to be working with forensics, particularly with Windows machines, it is critical that you learn the Windows Registry.

# Mobile Forensics: Cell Phone Concepts

There are some basic devices and terminology you will need to know before we delve into cell phones. Some of these, such as SIM, are probably at least somewhat familiar to you.

## Cell Concepts Module

The following sections are the parts of a phone.

### Subscriber Identity Module

A subscriber identity module, or SIM, is the heart of the phone. It is a circuit, usually a removable chip. The SIM is how you identify a phone. It stores the international mobile subscriber identity (IMSI). The IMSI, which we will discuss in detail in just a moment, uniquely identifies a phone. So if you change the SIM, you effectively change the IMSI and thus change the phone's identity. This SIM will also usually have network information, services the user has access to, and two passwords. Those passwords are the personal identification number (PIN) and the personal unblocking code (PUK). The PUK is a code used to reset a forgotten PIN. However, using the code wipes the phone and resets it to its factory state, thus destroying any forensic evidence. If the code is entered incorrectly 10 times in a row, the device becomes permanently blocked and unrecoverable.

### International Mobile Subscriber Identity

The international mobile subscriber identity (IMSI) is usually a 15-digit number but can be shorter in some cases. (Some countries use a shorter number.) It is used to uniquely identify a phone. The first three digits are a mobile country code (MCC), and the next digits represent the mobile network code. In North America that is three digits; in Europe it is two digits. The remaining digits are the mobile subscription identifier number (MSIN) that identifies the phone within a given network. To prevent tracking and cloning, the IMSI is only sent rarely. Instead, a temporary value or TMSI is generated and sent.

### Integrated Circuit Card Identification

While the integrated circuit card identification (IMSI) is used to identify the phone, the SIM chip itself is identified by the ICCID. The ICCID is engraved on the SIM during manufacturing, so it cannot be removed. The first seven digits identify the country and issuer, and are called the Issuer Identification Number (IIN). After that is a variable length number that identifies this chip/SIM, then a check digit.

### International Mobile Equipment Identity

The International Mobile Equipment Identity (IMEI) number is a unique identifier used to identify GSM, UMTS, LTE, and satellite phones. It is printed on the phone, often inside the battery compartment. You can display it on most phones by entering #06# on the dial pad. Using this number, a phone can be blacklisted or prevented from connecting to a network. This works even if the user changes the SIM card.

# Cellular Networks

In addition to understanding the cell phones themselves, it is necessary to understand the networks. All cell phone networks are based on radio towers. The strength of that radio signal is purposefully regulated to limit its range. Each cell tower base station consists of an antenna and radio equipment. Following is a brief description of the different types of networks.

### Global System for Mobile Communications

Global System for Mobile Communications (GSM) is an older technology, what is commonly called 2G. This is a standard developed by the European Telecommunications Standards Institute (ETSI). Originally, GSM was developed just for digital voice, but it was expanded to include data. GSM operates at many different frequencies, but the most common are 900MHz and 1800MHz. In Europe, most 3G networks use the 2100MHz frequency.

### Enhanced Data Rates for GSM Evolution

Many consider Enhanced Data Rates for GSM Evolution (EDGE) a level between 2G and 3G. It is technically considered pre-3G but was an improvement on GSM (2G). It was specifically designed to deliver media such as television over the cellular network.

### Universal Mobile Telecommunications Systems

The Universal Mobile Telecommunications Systems (UMTS) is 3G and is essentially an upgrade to GSM (2G). It provides text, voice, video, and multimedia at data rates up to and possibly higher than 2 megabits per second.

### Long Term Evolution

Long Term Evolution (LTE) is what is commonly called 4G. It provides broadband Internet, multimedia, and voice. LTE is based on the GSM/EDGE technology. It can theoretically support speeds of 300 Megabits per second (Mbps). Unlike GSM and GSM-based networks, LTE is based in IP just like a typical computer network.

### Integrated Digitally Enhanced Network

Integrated Digitally Enhanced Network (iDEN) is a GSM-based architecture that combines cell phone, two-way radio, pager, and modem into a single network. It operates on 800MHz, 900MHz, or 1.5GHz frequencies and was devised by Motorola.

Understanding the networks that cell phones work on is important to understanding cell phone forensics. Today you are most likely encountering LTE, though 3G networks/phones still exist.

Remember that a modern cell phone or tablet is actually a computer. A few short years ago, this was not the case. However, modern mobile devices are, in every respect, full-fledged computers. This means they have hardware, operating systems, and applications (often called *apps*). It is important to have at least a working knowledge of the operating systems used on mobile devices in order to successfully perform forensic analysis.

## iOS

Apple's iPhone, iPod, and iPad are very common, and all run on the same operating system, iOS. The iOS operating system was originally released for the iPhone and iPod in 2007 and later expanded to include the iPad. It is based on a touch interface, wherein the user will perform gestures such as swiping, dragging, pinching, and tapping on the screen. The iOS is based on the OS X for Macintosh but is heavily modified.

The iOS is divided into four layers. The first is the Core OS layer, which is the heart of the operating system. This is a layer that users and applications don't directly interact with. Instead, applications interact with the Core Services layer, the second layer. The third layer, or Media layer, is responsible for music, video, and more. Finally, there is the Cocoa Touch layer, which responds to user gestures.

The iOS uses the HFS+ file system. HFS+ was created by Apple as a replacement for the Hierarchical File System (HFS) and is used in both iOS and OSX. iOS can use FAT32 when communicating with Windows machines (such as when synchronizing an iPhone with a Windows PC).

The iOS divides its data partition as follows:

- Calendar entries
- Contact entries
- Note entries
- iPod_control directory (this directory is hidden)
- iTunes configuration
- iTunes music

Clearly, the calendar and contact entries can be of interest in any forensic investigation. However, some of the data hidden in the iPod_control directory is also very important. Of particular interest to forensics investigation is the folder iPod_control\device\sysinfo. This folder contains two very important pieces of information:

- iPod model number
- ipod Serial number

## Android

The Android is the single largest alternative to iOS. It is based on Linux—in fact, it is a modified Linux distribution, and it is open source. That means that if you have the programming and operating system knowledge to follow it, you can download and read the Android source code for yourself at http://source.android.com/. It should be noted that proprietary Android phones often make their own modifications or additions to the open source Android source code.

The Android OS was first released in 2003 and is the creation of Rich Miner, Andy Rubin, and Nick Sears; however, Google acquired Android in 2005. The versions of Android have been named after deserts/sweets:

- Version 1.5 Cupcake released April 2009

- Version 1.6 Donut released September 2009

- Version 2.0–2.1 Éclair released October 2009

- Version 2.2 Froyo released May 2010

- Version 2.3 Gingerbread released December 2010

- Version 3.1–3.2 Honeycomb released February 2011

- Version 4.0 Ice Cream Sandwich released October 2011

- Version 4.1–4.2 Jelly Bean released June 2012

- Version 4.4 KitKat released September 2013

- Version 5.0 Lollipop released November 2014

- Version 6.0 Marshmallow released October 2015

The differences from version to version usually involve adding new features, not a radical change to the operating system. They are all Linux-based, and the core functionality, even from Cupcake to KitKat, is remarkably similar. This means that if you are comfortable with any version of Android, you should be able to perform a forensic analysis with all versions of Android.

## Windows

Microsoft has produced several variations of Windows aimed at the mobile market. The company's first foray into the mobile operating system market was Windows CE. That operating system was also released as the Pocket PC 2000, which was based on Windows CE version 3. In 2008, Windows Phone was released. It had a major drawback in that it was not compatible with many of the previous Windows Mobile apps. In 2010, Microsoft released Windows Phone 7.

With the advent of Windows 8, Microsoft is moving all of its devices to the same operating system. This means that PCs, phones, and tablets will use the same Windows—namely, Windows 8. This simplifies forensic analysis. Windows 10 follows the same process of having the same operating system on the phone, tablet, and PC.

## What You Should Look For

What are general principles that help you determine what to look for in a cell phone or other mobile device? Items you should attempt to recover from a mobile device include the following:

- Details of the phone itself

- Call history

- Photos and video

- GPS information

- Network information

Information about the phone should be one of the first things you document in your investigation. Just as you would document the specifics of a PC (model, operating system, and so on) you were examining, you should also document the phone or tablet specifics. This will include model number, serial number of the SIM card, operating system, and more. The more descriptive information you can document, the better.

The call history will let you know who the user has spoken to and for how long. Obviously, call records by themselves are not sufficient to prove most crimes. With the exception of stalking or breaking a restraining order, just showing that one person called another is not enough to prove a crime. However, it can begin to build a circumstantial case.

Photos and video can provide direct evidence of a crime. In the case of child pornography, the relevance is obvious. However, it may surprise you to know that it is not uncommon for some criminals to actually photograph or videotape themselves committing serious crimes. This is particularly true of young criminals conducting unplanned crimes or conducting crimes under the influence of drugs or alcohol. There are numerous cases of perpetrators filming or photographing themselves performing crimes ranging from vandalism to burglary and rape.

GPS information has become increasingly important in a variety of cases. So many individuals have devices with GPS enabled that it would seem negligent for a forensic analyst to not retrieve this information. GPS cannot confirm that a suspect committed a crime, but it can show that the suspect was at a location where a crime was committed. Of course, GPS can also help to exonerate someone. If a person is suspected of committing a crime but his vehicle and cell phone GPS are shown to be many miles away at the time of the crime, this can help establish an alibi.

Network information is also important. What Wi-Fi networks does the phone recognize? This might indicate where the phone has been. If a phone has connected to a coffee shop that is near the scene of a crime, it at least shows the perpetrator was in the area. It is also possible that traditional computer crimes, such as denial of service (DoS) and SQL injection, might trace back to a public Wi-Fi point, and the perpetrator was clever enough to mask his computer's identity. If you can show his cell phone GPS was connected to that Wi-Fi, it will help establish he had the opportunity to commit the crime.

# The Need for Forensic Certification

Why certifications? This question has been bandied about the information technology field for years. Various pundits come down upon one extreme or the other. Some claim certifications are invaluable, and others claim they are worthless. Also, some subindustries within IT have different attitudes about certifications. In the Cisco world, certifications are king. In the Linux community, certifications have negligible value. So what is the worth of certifications in forensics?

First, you must examine the purpose of certifications. What does it mean to be certified? Frequently, people who have a dim view of certifications have that view because they have encountered someone with a certification who was not very competent. This denotes a misunderstanding of what any certification is. Certification is supposed to indicate that the holder of that certification has met a minimum standard. It does not mean that the person in question is the master of that topic, but rather she is competent. Similarly, a medical degree does not guarantee the person is a great doctor, merely that she has obtained a minimum competency in medicine.

However, it is possible to pass a certification and not be very good at the topic. But the same is true of any field and any educational endeavor. There are certainly some medical doctors (thankfully few) who are incompetent. But if you suddenly have chest pains, I bet you would prefer someone call you a medical doctor rather than a plumber. The odds of a medical doctor having the requisite skill are much higher than that of a plumber. The same is true for IT certifications. While it is certainly possible that someone could be certified and not be competent, the odds that a certified person is competent are much higher. That is why employers frequently require or prefer certifications. It makes the job of filtering through applicants much easier.

Any IT certification can be one valuable indicator of a job applicant's skill. It is not the only indicator and certainly should not be the only thing considered, but it is one factor. This brings us to forensic certifications. Is there a need for another one? First look at what cyber forensics certifications are currently available. All forensics certifications come in one of two types. The first type is vendor certifications. These usually are focused only on the product (or products) that vendor sells. The second type is conceptual certifications. These tests are not about a specific tool, but rather forensic concepts.

AccessData, the creators of the Forensic Toolkit, has multiple certifications for its product. So does Guidance Software, the creators of EnCase. Both of those vendor certifications are quite good. However, they are both vendor certifications. The emphasis is on the particular proprietary suite of tools rather than a general coverage of cyber forensics. If you are going to work with either tool, it is a very good idea to get the appropriate vendor certification, but that is not the same thing as a broad-based cyber forensics course/test.

The EC-Council has its Certified Hacking Forensics Investigator test, and it has been somewhat popular. However, as the name suggests, it has an emphasis on hacking and counter hacking. The EC-Council's primary focus has always been hacking.

This brings us to the topic of ISC2's Certified Cyber Forensics Investigator. Is this certification test worth taking? The first thing to realize is that ISC2 has a long history of well-respected certification courses/tests, starting with the CISSP, which is the oldest and most well-known computer security certification. This means the CCFP is backed by a strong support organizations. The content of the course/test is also very good. The domains covered include forensic science, application forensics, investigatory procedures, law, and ethics. It is just the sort of broad coverage of cyber forensics that is needed.

The SANS Institute offers a number of certifications, including the Certified Forensics Analyst (GCFA) and Certified Forensics Examiner (GCFE). Both of these are well respected in the industry. The only issue with either one is the cost. SANS courses and their certification tests are among the most expensive in the industry.

# Expert Witnesses

At some point, any forensic examiner might be called to testify in court. Being an expert witness is very different from being a witness of fact. To begin with, an expert witness is allowed to testify about things he did not see or hear. Second, an expert witness is allowed to make inferences and formulate theories.

However, there are definite limits to and requirements for expert testimony. You cannot simply get on the stand and essentially state, "Well, I am an expert and this is true because I say so." There are some rules. The following sections give a brief overview of some of those rules.

## Federal Rule 702

Federal rule 702 defines what an expert witness is and the rules concerning when she can testify and what she can testify to. Essentially, rule 702 states the following[5]:

- A witness who is qualified as an expert by knowledge, skill, experience, training, or education may testify in the form of an opinion or otherwise if:

  a. the expert's scientific, technical, or other specialized knowledge will help the trier of fact to understand the evidence or to determine a fact in issue;

  b. the testimony is based on sufficient facts or data;

  c. the testimony is the product of reliable principles and methods; and

  d. the expert has reliably applied the principles and methods to the facts of the case.

What this means is that, first and foremost, the expert must be an expert in that specific topic or field. That person's testimony must be useful to the judge or jury in understanding technical or specialized facts in the case. But just as important, the expert must base her opinions on reliable scientific methods.

---

5. https://www.law.cornell.edu/rules/fre/rule_702

## Daubert

The Daubert standard is used in U.S. federal courts to determine whether or not an expert's scientific testimony is based on reasoning or methodology that is scientifically valid and can properly be applied to the facts at issue. Under this standard, the factors that may be considered in determining whether the methodology is valid are: (1) whether the theory or technique in question can be and has been tested; (2) whether it has been subjected to peer review and publication; (3) its known or potential error rate; (4) the existence and maintenance of standards controlling its operation; and (5) whether it has attracted widespread acceptance within a relevant scientific community. The Daubert standard is the test currently used in the federal courts and some state courts. This is very similar to Federal Rule 702.

# Additional Types of Forensics

Digital forensics is a growing field. Computer and phone forensics are the most widely encountered types of digital forensics, but not the only areas of digital forensics. In this section, you will see a brief overview of some other subdisciplines of digital forensics.

## Network Forensics

The first, must fundamental thing to learn about network forensics is packet analysis. Before we continue, you may wish to review the material from Chapter 2, "Networks and the Internet," and ensure you are comfortable with basic networking.

Essentially, network forensics involves capturing the network packets traversing the network and examining them for evidence. Many things can be determined from network forensics: where the packet came from, what protocol it is using, what port it is using, and if it is encrypted or not.

The following are some other popular tools for network analysis:

- **Wireshark:** See www.wireshark.org
- **CommView:** See www.tamos.com/products/commview/
- **Softperfect Network Protocol Analyzer:** See www.softperfect.com
- **HTTP Sniffer:** See www.effetech.com/sniffer/
- **ngrep:** See http://sourceforge.net/projects/ngrep/

Any of these tools can work for network analysis.

## Virtual Forensics

*Virtualization* is a broad term that encompasses many technologies. It is a way to provide various IT resources that are independent of the physical machinery of the user. The virtualization makes a logical IT resource that can operate independent of the end user's operating system as well as hardware. The most basic issue for forensics is the situation where a suspect machine has a virtual machine running on it. There are also issues with getting data from cloud servers.

## Virtual Machines

A virtual machine is an interesting concept and was the precursor of more broad-based virtual systems that we will discuss later in this chapter. A virtual machine essentially sets aside a certain portion of a computer's hard drive and RAM (when executing) to run in complete isolation from the rest of the operating system. It is much like you are running an entirely separate computer; it simply shares the resources of the host computer. It is, quite simply, a virtual computer—thus, the name virtual machine.

Each vendor stores data in a slightly different manner, but the next lists show the most interesting files (forensically interesting) for three of the most widely used virtual machine vendors.

- VMware Workstation:

  - **.log files:** This is simply a log of activity for a virtual machine.

  - **.vmdk:** This is the actual virtual hard drive for the virtual guest operating system. Virtual hard drives can be fixed or dynamic. Fixed virtual hard drives remain the same size. Dynamic virtual hard drives expand as needed.

  - **.vmem:** This is a backup of the virtual machine's paging file/swap file. This can be very important to a forensic investigation.

  - **.vmsn:** These are VMware snapshot files, named by the name of the snapshot. A VMSN file stores the state of the virtual machine when the snapshot was created.

  - **.vmsd:** A VMSD file contains the metadata about the snapshot.

- Oracle Virtual Box:

  - **.vdi:** These are VirtualBox disk images called virtual disk images.

  - **/.config/VirtualBox:** This is a hidden file that contains configuration data.

  - **.vbox:** This is the machine settings file extension. Prior to version 4.0, it was .xml.

- Virtual PC:

  - **.vhx:** These are the actual virtual hard disks. They are obviously quite important to a forensic examination.

  - **.bin files:** These contain the memory of the virtual machine, so these absolutely must be examined.

  - **.xml files:** These files contain the virtual machine configuration details. There is one of these for each virtual machine and for each snapshot of a virtual machine. These files are always named with the GUID used to internally identify the virtual machine in question.

## Cloud

A cloud has been defined as "a pool of virtualized computer resources."[6]

People often speak of the cloud as if there were only one cloud, or at least one type of cloud. This impression is inaccurate. There are multiple clouds and multiple types of clouds. Any organization with the appropriate resources can establish a cloud, and it may establish it for diverse reasons, leading to different types of clouds.

Public clouds are defined by the NIST as those clouds that offer their infrastructure or services to either the general public or at least a large industry group.

Private clouds are those used specifically by a single organization without offering the services to an outside party.[7] There are, of course, hybrid clouds that combine the elements of a private and public cloud. These are essentially private clouds that have some limited public access.

Community clouds are a midway point between private and public. These are systems wherein several organizations share a cloud for specific community needs. For example, several computer companies might join to create a cloud devoted to common security issues.

A cloud system depends on several parts. Each of these could be a location for evidence.

- **Virtual storage:** The virtual servers are hosted on one or more actual/physical servers. The hard drive space and RAM of those physical servers is partitioned for the various virtual servers' usage.

- **Audit monitor:** There is usually an audit monitor that monitors usage of the resource pool. This monitor will also ensure that one virtual server does not/cannot access data of another virtual server.

- **Hypervisor:** The hypervisor mechanism is the process that provides the virtual servers with access to resources.

- **Logical network perimeter:** Since the cloud consists of virtual servers, not physical ones, there is a need for a logical network and a logical network perimeter. This perimeter isolates resource pools from each other.

Individual cloud implementations might have additional utilities, such as administration consoles that allow a network administrator to monitor, configure, and administer the cloud.

There are two issues with cloud forensics. The first is jurisdictional. Often cloud data is replicated across servers in different countries, each with its own laws. Then there is the technical issue of getting the data. It is very unlikely that you would be able to image the entire cloud in question. So you will probably have to perform a logical copy of the data in question or even a live analysis.

---

6. http://www.ijcit.com/archives/volume1/issue2/Paper010225.pdf
7. http://www.ijarcsse.com/docs/papers/Volume_3/3_March2013/V3I3-0320.pdf

# Summary

In this chapter, you have seen the basics of computer forensics. The most important things you have learned are to make a forensics copy to work with and to document everything. You simply cannot over document. You have also learned how to retrieve browser information and recover deleted files, and you have learned some commands that may be useful forensically. You have explored the forensic value of the Windows Registry and even cloud forensics.

## Test Your Skills

### MULTIPLE CHOICE QUESTIONS

1. In a computer forensics investigation, what describes the route that evidence takes from the time you find it until the case is closed or goes to court?

    A. Rules of evidence

    B. Law of probability

    C. Chain of custody

    D. Policy of separation

2. Where does Linux store email server logs?

    A. /var/log/mail.*

    B. /etc/log/mail.*

    C. /mail/log/mail.*

    D. /server/log/mail.*

3. Why should you note all cable connections for a computer you want to seize as evidence?

    A. To know what outside connections existed

    B. In case other devices were connected

    C. To know what peripheral devices exist

    D. To know what hardware existed

4. What is in the Index.dat file?

    A. Internet Explorer information

    B. General Internet history, file browsing history, and so on for a Windows machine

    C. All web history for Firefox

    D. General Internet history, file browsing history, and so on for a Linux machine

5. What is the name of the Standard Linux command that is also available as a Windows application that can be used to create bitstream images and make a forensic copy?

   A. `mcopy`

   B. `image`

   C. `MD5`

   D. `dd`

6. When cataloging digital evidence, the primary goal is to do what?

   A. Make bitstream images of all hard drives.

   B. Preserve evidence integrity.

   C. Avoid removing the evidence from the scene.

   D. Prohibit the computer from being turned off.

7. The command `Openfiles` shows what?

   A. Any files that are opened

   B. Any shared files that are opened

   C. Any system files that are opened

   D. Any files open with ADS

8. "Interesting data" is what?

   A. Data relevant to your investigation

   B. Pornography

   C. Documents, spreadsheets, and databases

   D. Schematics or other economic-based information

9. Which of the following are important to the investigator regarding logging?

   A. The logging methods

   B. Log retention

   C. Location of stored logs

   D. All of the above

## EXERCISES

### EXERCISE 14.1: DiskDigger

Download DiskDigger and search your computer for deleted files. Attempt to recover one file of your choice.

### EXERCISE 14.2: Making a Forensic Copy

This exercise requires two computers. You must also download either Backtrack or Knoppix. (Both are free.) Then attempt to make a forensic copy of computer A by sending its data to computer B.

# Appendix A

# Glossary

This section contains terms from both hackers and security professionals. To truly understand computer security, you must be familiar with both worlds. General networking terms are also included in this Glossary.

**admin:** Short for system administrator.

**adware:** Software that is used to display advertisements.

**AES:** Advanced Encryption Standard. A symmetric cipher that uses 128-, 192-, or 256-bit keys.

**APT:** Advanced persistent threat. An attack that takes place over a long period of time using multiple, advanced techniques.

**audit:** A check of a system's security. This check usually includes a review of documents, procedures, and system configurations.

**authentication:** The process of proving that someone is who he claims to be.

**backdoor:** A hole in the security system deliberately left by the creator of the system.

**bid shielding:** Hiding an item from other bidders by putting a fake but very high bid on it to discourage other bidders.

**bid siphoning:** Attempting to lure bidders from a legitimate site to a site that may be used for malicious purposes such as phishing.

**black hat hacker:** Someone who uses hacking skills for malicious and illegal purposes.

**BlowFish:** A well-known symmetric key encryption algorithm that uses a variable-length key and was invented by Bruce Schneier.

**braindump:** The act of telling someone everything one knows.

**breach:** To successfully break into a system, to breach the security.

**brute force:** To try to crack a password by simply trying every possible combination.

**bug:** A flaw in a system.

**Caesar cipher:** One of the oldest encryption algorithms. It uses a basic mono-alphabetic cipher.

**CHAP:** Challenge Handshake Authentication Protocol, a commonly used authentication protocol.

**CIA triangle:** A common security acronym: confidentiality-integrity-accessibility.

**cipher:** Synonym for cryptographic algorithm.

**cipher text:** Encrypted text.

**code:** The source code for a program; or the act of programming, as in "to code an algorithm."

**codegrinder:** An unflattering reference to one who works in an uncreative corporate programming environment.

**cookie:** A small bit of data, often in plain text, that is stored by web browsers.

**cracker:** One who breaks into a system in order to do something malicious, illegal, or harmful. Synonymous with black hat hacker.

**cracking:** Breaking into a system or code.

**crash:** A sudden and unintended failure, as in "My computer crashed."

**cryptography:** The study of encryption and decryption.

**cyber fraud:** Using the Internet to defraud someone.

**cyber stalking:** Using the Internet to harass someone.

**demigod:** A hacker with years of experience who has a national or international reputation.

**DDoS:** Distributed denial of service attacks are denial of service attacks launched from multiple source locations.

**DES:** Data Encryption Standard, a block cipher that was developed in the 1970s. It uses a 56-bit key on 64-bit blocks. It is no longer considered secure enough.

**Diffie-Hellman:** An asymmetric protocol used for key exchange.

**DoS:** A denial of service attack is one that prevents legitimate users from accessing a resource. This is usually done by overloading the target system with more workload than it can handle.

**Encrypting File System:** Also known as EFS, this is Microsoft's file system that allows users to encrypt individual files. It was introduced in Windows 2000.

**elliptic curve:** A class of algorithms that provide asymmetric encryption.

**encryption:** The act of encrypting a message. Encryption usually involves altering a message so that it cannot be read without the key and the decryption algorithm.

**espionage:** Illicitly gathering information, usually from a government or corporate source.

**ethical hacker:** One who hacks into systems to accomplish some goal that he feels is ethically valid. Often called a penetration tester.

**firewall:** A device or software that provides a barrier between your machine or network and the rest of the world.

**gray hat hacker:** A hacker who usually obeys the law but in some instances will cross the line into black hat hacking.

**hacker:** One who tries to learn about a system by examining it in detail by reverse-engineering.

**hash:** An algorithm that takes variable length input and produces fixed-length output and is not reversible.

**honey pot:** A system or server designed to be very appealing to hackers, when in fact it is a trap to catch them.

**hub:** A device for connecting computers.

**IKE:** A method for managing the exchange of encryption keys.

**information warfare:** Attempts to influence political or military outcomes via information manipulation.

**intrusion detection system (IDS):** A system for detecting attempted intrusions.

**IP:** Internet Protocol, one of the primary protocols used in networking.

**IPsec:** Internet Protocol Security, a method used to secure VPNs.

**IP spoofing:** Making packets seem to come from a different IP address than they really originated from.

**key logger:** Software that logs keystrokes on a computer.

**MAC address:** The physical address of a network card. It is a 6-byte hexadecimal number. The first 3 bytes define the vendor.

**malware:** Any software that has a malicious purpose, such as a virus or a Trojan horse.

**MD5:** Message Digest 5: A cryptographic hashing algorithm.

**MS-CHAP:** A Microsoft extension to CHAP.

**multi-alphabet substitutions:** Encryption methods that use more than one substitution alphabet.

**NIC:** Network interface card.

**packet filter firewall:** A firewall that scans incoming packets and either allows them to pass or rejects them. It only examines the header, not the data, and does not consider the context of the data communication.

**penetration testing:** Assessing the security of a system by attempting to break into the system. Penetration testing is the activity of most penetration testers.

**phreaker:** Someone who hacks into phone systems.

**port scan:** Sequentially pinging ports to see which ones are active.

**PPP:** Point-to-Point Protocol, a somewhat older connection protocol.

**PPTP:** Point-to-Point Tunneling Protocol, an extension to PPP for VPNs.

**proxy server:** A device that hides your internal IP addresses and presents a single IP address to the outside world.

**router:** A device that connects two networks.

**RSA:** A public key encryption method developed in 1977 by three mathematicians: Ron Rivest, Adi Shamir, and Leonard Adleman. The name *RSA* is derived from the first letter of each mathematician's last name.

**RST cookie:** A simple method for alleviating the danger of certain types of DoS attacks.

**script kiddy:** A slang term for an unskilled person who purports to be a skilled hacker.

**SHA:** Secure Hashing Algorithm. A cryptographic hash that has several versions: SHA1, SHA2 (with variations), and SHA3.

**smurf:** A specific type of distributed denial of service attack.

**sneaker:** Someone who is attempting to compromise a system in order to assess its vulnerability. This is an old term; most people use the term penetration tester today.

**sniffer:** A program that captures data as it travels across a network. Also called a packet sniffer.

**snort:** A widely used, open source, intrusion detection system.

**social engineering:** The use of persuasion on human users in order to gain information required to access a system.

**SPAP:** Shiva Password Authentication Protocol. SPAP is a proprietary version of PAP. This protocol basically adds encryption to PAP.

**spoofing:** Pretending to be something else, as when a packet might spoof another return IP address (as in the smurf attack) or when a website is spoofing a well known e-commerce site.

**spyware:** Software that monitors computer use.

**stack tweaking:** A complex method for protecting a system against DoS attacks. This method involves reconfiguring the operating system to handle connections differently.

**stateful packet inspection:** A type of firewall that not only examines packets but knows the context within which the packet was sent.

**symmetric key system:** An encryption method where the same key is used to encrypt and decrypt the message.

**SYN cookie:** A method for ameliorating the dangers of SYN floods.

**SYN flood:** Sending a stream of SYN packets (requests for connection) and then never responding, thus leaving the connection half open.

**tribal flood network:** A tool used to execute DDoS attacks.

**Trin00:** A tool used to execute DDoS attacks.

**Trojan horse:** Software that appears to have a valid and benign purpose but really has another, nefarious purpose.

**virus:** Software that is self-replicating and spreads like a biological virus.

**war-dialing:** Dialing phones waiting for a computer to pick up. War-dialing is usually done via some automated system.

**war-driving:** Driving and scanning for wireless networks that can be compromised.

**white hat hacker:** A hacker who does not break the law, often synonymous with ethical hacker.

**worm:** A virus that can spread without human intervention.

# Appendix B

# Resources

Note: Links are valid as of March 2016.

## General Computer Crime and Cyber Terrorism

Cyber crime: www.justice.gov/criminal-ccips /

Computer security: www.cert.org

Symantec's antivirus site: www.symantec.com/security_response/

FBI Cyber Crime: www.fbi.gov/about-us/investigate/cyber

## General Knowledge

Hellbound Hackers: www.hellboundhackers.org/

Dark Reading: www.darkreading.com/

## Cyber Stalking

http://us.norton.com/cyberstalking/article/

www.cyber-stalking.net/

## Identity Theft

www.consumer.ftc.gov/features/feature-0014-identity-theft

www.idtheftcenter.org/

# Port Scanners and Sniffers

NMap: www.nmap.org

SecTools: http://sectools.org/tag/port-scanners/

# Password Crackers

Ophcrack: http://ophcrack.org/

Password crackers: http://resources.infosecinstitute.com/10-popular-password-cracking-tools/

# Countermeasures

Various security and hacking tools: insecure.org

Snort, an open source IDS system: www.snort.org/

The SANS Institute IDS FAQ: www.sans.org/resources/idfaq/

The Association of Computing Machinery IDS page: http://xrds.acm.org/

# Cyber Investigation Tools

WhoIs tool: http://whois.domaintools.com/

Various search tools: www.virtualgumshoe.com/

Viewing previous versions of websites: www.Archive.org

# General Tools

http://maxwells-alley.com/?reqp=1&reqr=

www.all-internet-security.com/security_scanners.html

Scanning tool: www.rawlogic.com/netbrute/

# Virus Research

CNET Virus Center: www.cnet.com/topics/security/

F-Secure: www.fsecure.com

Symantec virus encyclopedia: www.symantec.com/security_response/

vxHeaven: vxheaven.org/

# Appendix C

# Answers to the Multiple Choice Questions

## Chapter 1

1. C
2. B
3. B
4. B
5. A
6. C
7. D
8. A
9. C
10. A
11. C
12. A
13. A
14. A
15. B
16. B
17. B
18. B
19. C
20. C

## Chapter 2

1. D
2. D
3. A
4. C
5. A
6. B
7. B
8. B
9. A
10. C
11. A
12. B
13. C
14. B
15. C
16. C
17. B
18. A
19. A
20. C
21. A
22. B
23. A

| | | | | |
|---|---|---|---|---|
| 24. | A | | 10. | D |
| 25. | B | | 11. | C |
| | | | 12. | A |
| | | | 13. | A |

## Chapter 3

| | | | | |
|---|---|---|---|---|
| 1. | A | | 14. | D |
| 2. | B | | 15. | A |
| 3. | C | | 16. | D |
| 4. | A | | 17. | D |
| 5. | A | | 18. | A |
| 6. | B | | 19. | D |
| 7. | C | | 20. | A |
| 8. | B | | | |

## Chapter 5

| | | | | |
|---|---|---|---|---|
| 9. | A | | 1. | D |
| 10. | C | | 2. | A |
| 11. | B | | 3. | B |
| 12. | B | | 4. | C |
| 13. | D | | 5. | B, C |
| 14. | B | | 6. | A |
| 15. | C | | 7. | C |
| 16. | A | | 8. | A |
| 17. | C | | 9. | B |
| 18. | B | | 10. | D |
| 19. | A | | 11. | A |
| 20. | B | | 12. | B |
| 21. | A | | 13. | A |
| 22. | D | | 14. | D |
| 23. | C | | 15. | C |
| 24. | A | | 16. | B |
| | | | 17. | D |

## Chapter 4

| | | | | |
|---|---|---|---|---|
| 1. | A | | 18. | D |
| 2. | C | | 19. | A |
| 3. | D | | 20. | D |
| 4. | C | | | |

## Chapter 6

| | | | | |
|---|---|---|---|---|
| 5. | B | | 1. | B |
| 6. | D | | 2. | D |
| 7. | A | | 3. | A |
| 8. | A | | 4. | B |
| 9. | C | | | |

5. A
6. D
7. D
8. B
9. D
10. C
11. A
12. B
13. D
14. A
15. C

# Chapter 7

1. D
2. A
3. C
4. D
5. C
6. A
7. A
8. B
9. A
10. A
11. B
12. A
13. A
14. B
15. D

# Chapter 8

1. A
2. C
3. D
4. B
5. C
6. A
7. B
8. A

9. D
10. B
11. A
12. C
13. B
14. A
15. D
16. C
17. D
18. A

# Chapter 9

1. A
2. C
3. D
4. B
5. C
6. A
7. B
8. A
9. D
10. A
11. A
12. A
13. A
14. A
15. B

# Chapter 10

1. C
2. C
3. C
4. B
5. A
6. B
7. A
8. B
9. A

10.  B
11.  B
12.  D
13.  B
14.  C
15.  B

# Chapter 11

1.  B
2.  A
3.  A
4.  C
5.  B
6.  A
7.  D
8.  C
9.  A
10.  B
11.  C
12.  D
13.  D
14.  B
15.  A
16.  B
17.  C
18.  C
19.  A
20.  D

# Chapter 12

1.  C
2.  C
3.  C
4.  D
5.  B
6.  A
7.  B

8.  A
9.  A
10.  C
11.  B
12.  B
13.  D
14.  C
15.  D

# Chapter 13

1.  A
2.  B
3.  B
4.  D
5.  D
6.  B
7.  B
8.  C
9.  A
10.  D
11.  C
12.  B
13.  A
14.  D
15.  A

# Chapter 14

1.  C
2.  A
3.  B
4.  B
5.  D
6.  B
7.  B
8.  A
9.  D

# Index

# B

## S

# Z

# REGISTER YOUR PRODUCT at PearsonITcertification.com/register
## Access Additional Benefits and SAVE 35% on Your Next Purchase

- Download available product updates.
- Access bonus material when applicable.
- Receive exclusive offers on new editions and related products.
  (Just check the box to hear from us when setting up your account.)
- Get a coupon for 35% for your next purchase, valid for 30 days. Your code will
  be available in your PITC cart. (You will also find it in the Manage Codes
  section of your account page.)

Registration benefits vary by product. Benefits will be listed on your account page
under Registered Products.

---

PearsonITcertification.com—Learning Solutions for Self-Paced Study, Enterprise, and the Classroom
Pearson is the official publisher of Cisco Press, IBM Press, VMware Press, Microsoft Press,
and is a Platinum CompTIA Publishing Partner—CompTIA's highest partnership accreditation.
At **PearsonITcertification.com** you can

- Shop our books, eBooks, software, and video training.
- Take advantage of our special offers and promotions (pearsonitcertifcation.com/promotions)
- Sign up for special offers and content newsletters (pearsonitcertifcation.com/newsletters).
- Read free articles, exam profiles, and blogs by information technology experts.
- Access thousands of free chapters and video lessons.

**Connect with PITC – Visit PearsonITcertifcation.com/community**
Learn about PITC community events and programs.

# PEARSON IT CERTIFICATION

Addison-Wesley • Cisco Press • IBM Press • Microsoft Press • Pearson IT Certification • Prentice Hall • Que • Sams • VMware Press

ALWAYS LEARNING                                                                    PEARS